SIX SECONDS IN DALLAS

by the same author

THE LONELY LABYRINTH:

Kierkegaard's Pseudonymous Works

*by*
JOSIAH THOMPSON

# SIX SECONDS IN DALLAS

A Micro-Study of the Kennedy Assassination

*Published by*
*BERNARD GEIS ASSOCIATES*
*Distributed by Random House*

*This Book Designed by Arthur Hawkins*

Library of Congress Catalog Card Number: 67-23577

This book is for Nancy.

# WHY ANOTHER BOOK?

In the four years that have passed since the assassination of President Kennedy, forty-six books have been published in attempts to explain the mystery of the events in Dallas. Six were lurid and groundless speculations, twenty-seven comprised the government's Warren *Report* and its twenty-six volumes of supporting documents, eight were outright attacks on the *Report,* four were written in support of it, and one was a novel. In view of all this, the question immediately arises, "Why another book?"

The answer is simple: In spite of the proliferation of books, there is much evidence that has either been overlooked or improperly interpreted; and despite the extensive investigations, the public mind is filled with doubt. This book takes up where the others leave off. In essence, it is neither a critique of the Warren *Report* nor an attack on its critics. It finds its own way, by original use of the evidence (some of it introduced here for the first time), toward a new conclusion. As such it is the first of what might be called a "third generation" of assassination studies.

The first generation—Thomas Buchanan's *Who Killed Kennedy?* and Joachim Joesten's *Oswald: As-*

*sassin or Fall Guy?*—appeared in print before the
Warren *Report* itself was published in September,
1964. Forced to rely almost solely on press reports,
these authors built their speculations around questions already puzzling the general public. The Commission was aware of these books and dealt with the
questions they raised in the "Speculations and Rumors" section of the *Report*. Few problems from this
earliest generation of studies remain unsettled today.

But with publication of the *Report* and its twenty-
six volumes of testimony and exhibits, serious study
of the assassination could finally begin. One of the
first persons to purchase a complete set of these
volumes was Vincent Salandria, a Philadelphia attorney. Digging into the evidence in a systematic
manner, Salandria discovered that the Commission's
account of the assassination was fraught with misrep-
resentation and contradiction. In two articles for
*Liberation* magazine (January and March, 1965),
Salandria laid out the essential points that have constituted the backbone of responsible criticism of the
*Report* ever since. A year later Salandria published
in *The Minority of One* the startling revelation that
the FBI Summary Report of December 9, 1963 disclosed the bullet which wounded the President had
not exited. Soon afterward Edward Epstein published
the FBI Supplemental Report of January 13, 1964,
which reiterated the same conclusion. Epstein's book
*Inquest,* which paralleled the substance of Salandria's
earlier analysis of the evidence, became an overnight
bestseller. Epstein's book, together with Mark Lane's
*Rush to Judgment,* Harold Weisberg's *Whitewash* series, Richard Popkin's *The Second Oswald,* Léo Sauvage's *The Oswald Affair,* and Raymond Marcus' *The
Bastard Bullet,* constituted the "second generation" of
assassination studies. Each of these works offered
something different: Popkin developed with patient
care the thesis that a second man resembling Oswald
had been involved in the assassination; Marcus scruti-
nized the evidence surrounding Commission Exhibit
399; Sauvage examined the Warren *Report's* case from
the point of view of a reporter on the scene; Weisberg

displayed a number of acute analyses in a book flawed by its lack of editing and its consistent shrillness; Lane made known the results of a far-ranging investigation in Dallas in a book accurately advertised as a brief for the defense of Oswald; finally, Epstein provided a revealing glimpse into the inner workings of the Commission. Yet in spite of all their differences, these books displayed two common threads: (1) a deep debt to Salandria's pioneering and largely unsung research, and (2) a critical and negative stance vis à vis the Warren *Report*. They were all (in spite of superficial differences) attacks on the *Report*.

Since the appearance of these works, two "defenses" of the *Report* have been published—Charles Roberts' *The Truth about the Assassination,* and Lewis and Schiller's *The Scavengers and Critics of the Warren Report*. Hastily written for quick distribution, these books took advantage of the public interest stimulated by the Lane and Epstein books. By ignoring or glossing over the essential points of criticism, by judiciously selecting evidence and testimony, they sought to extricate the *Report* from its difficulties. When this strategy failed they used personal invective and invidious epithets, calling the critics "scavengers" or "devious" and implying that their labors were motivated solely by desire for fame and profit. Neither of these two works is a serious contribution to an understanding of the assassination.

Attacks on the Warren *Report* have stimulated attacks on the attackers. Charges have prompted countercharges. Reasoned argument has given way to personal invective and character assassination. The second generation of assassination studies has ended in public confusion and frustration. A first step of a radically different sort is now required.

This book attempts to take that step. Whereas the books of the first generation advanced frantic and irresponsible hypotheses and those of the second generation labored at point-by-point refutations of the *Report,* the purpose of this book is to synthesize the evidence (new and old) and point the way to an emerging conclusion. The critics have shown that the assassination could not have happened as the Commission said it happened. How, then, *did* it happen? Up to now critics of the *Report* have gotten by with simply discovering the errors of the Commission and displaying them. It is the responsibility of future works to address themselves to the question asked above, to begin drawing *all* the evidence together and to attempt to make sense of it.

JOSIAH THOMPSON

Haverford, Pennsylvania
*August, 1967*

# ACKNOWLEDGMENTS

I SHOULD like to express my deep thanks to all those who helped in the preparation of this book.

Vincent Salandria was unstinting in his assistance at every turn. In the summer of 1966 he spared no effort in acquainting me with the latest work in the field, pointing out at the same time the areas where new research would prove most fruitful. Both the initial impetus for the study and many of its essential findings owe a great deal to Salandria.

John Berendt, associate editor of *Esquire* magazine, counseled me during the preparation of the manuscript and offered extensive criticism. He has my gratitude not only for his efforts at freeing my prose from the strictures of the academy, but for a multitude of really first-rate ideas which have substantially improved the argument of the book.

David Butterworth's contribution to this book also was substantial. For nine months he worked as my research assistant, carrying out the hard research that shows in the references and citations which buttress the essential arguments. Almost single-handedly he put together the chart and master list of witnesses which form Appendix A.

Sylvia Meagher, author of the *Subject Index to the Warren Report and the Hearings and Exhibits* and of the book, *Accessories After the Fact: The Warren Commission, the Authorities, and the Report,* was kind enough to check the manuscript for factual errors. She has my thanks for this and also for preparing the index for this book—an onerous and time-consuming labor.

My association with *Life* magazine as a consultant on the assassination was an extremely fruitful one. From Ed Kern and Dick Billings I learned a healthy respect for the difficulties of the journalist's craft. While I was in Dallas, the *Life* subbureau rendered critical assistance in setting up interviews and providing information: I am grateful to Patsy Swank, Holland McCombs, and Shelley Katz for their help and patience.

Marion Johnson of the National Archives staff went out of his way to facilitate my researches, as did John Simmons and Bob Loftus.

Ted Hetzel, Carl Grunfeld, and Chris Kane offered valuable advice and professional assistance with the photographs. The clarity of many of the prints in this book can be ascribed to the professional expertise of Robert Swartz.

A great number of people helped in many ways—some large, some small: Richard Bernstein, Gerald Bowen, Carleton Dallery, Thomas D'Andrea, William Davidon, Faiza Estrup, Irving Finger, Rachel Gallagher, Daniel Gillis, Louis Green, Andrew Hacker, Jones Harris, William Hoffman, Charles Holbrow, Andrew and Carol Kner, Ariel Loewy, Norman Marsh, Vivianne Nachmias, Sidney and Judy Perloe, James and Jerilynn Ransom, Jane Rice, Melvin and Ursula Santer, Ben Schotz, Bruce Secrest, John Silber, Richard Sprague, Paul and Barbara Violich, Elizabeth Wright, and Jean Zinni.

Many of the arguments in this book are presented visually, and it is to the designer Arthur Hawkins that much of the credit goes for combining the complexities of text and illustration into a readable, cogent whole. Philip Johnson drew the medical illustrations, and Bernard Reder drafted the charts and diagrams.

No list of acknowledgments would be complete without a word concerning the contribution of Don Preston, Executive Editor of Bernard Geis Associates. He believed in this book from the very beginning and saw it through the most difficult of circumstances. If there is any single person who deserves the credit for the transition of this book from an idea to a finished work, it is Don Preston, editor and friend.

Finally, Bernard Geis. On many occasions during the past year he demonstrated to me that publication of this book was not dictated by commercial considerations. It is not unfitting, then, that these acknowledgments end with an excerpt from his first letter to me, written September 26, 1966:

> *I've decided that the motto that sold you on giving us your book—that our resolution was to publish the facts and let the chips fall where they may—just isn't erudite enough for a literary house such as ours.*
>
> *I therefore submit, in its place, the following:*
>
> Fiat justitia ruat cælum
>
> *I think well enough of this sentiment to recommend your using it, without translation, on the title-page of your book.*

# A NOTE FROM
# THE PUBLISHER

IN A publishing house that normally has as many
different opinions as there are executives, there is
one thing we would have agreed on in September of
1966 with unanimity and alacrity: The world in
general and we in particular did not want or need
another book on the Kennedy assassination or the
Warren Commission. We were aware that the conduct
of that body had left much to be desired and that its
*Report* richly deserved some of the attacks that had
been leveled against it. But the big guns had been
fired and the target had been riddled; unless new
evidence or a radically new approach were developed
there was no point in adding to the barrage.

Then our executive editor met a young philosophy
professor from Haverford and concluded that he deserved a hearing. We spent most of a day listening
to Professor Josiah Thompson's plan of action, reading his preliminary draft and looking over some of
the evidence he had collected. We ended the session
completely convinced that a new approach had indeed been found and new evidence, much of it unknown to the Commission, had in fact come to light.
We agreed on the spot to throw our resources behind his efforts, and Professor Thompson returned to

Frame No. 207 from Zapruder film of assassination.

Philadelphia and the mountainous task of assembling and constructing the actual book.

Then, on October 7, *Life* magazine ran a column by Loudon Wainwright calling for re-examination of the evidence and a reopening of the investigation. Since that was precisely the goal toward which Professor Thompson's book was aimed, we arranged a meeting between Wainwright, two members of the *Life* editorial staff who were conducting an investigation for the magazine, Professor Thompson and our own editorial staff. Thompson talked, outlining new evidence and radical new approaches to existing evidence; the *Life* people listened, questioned, and became at last so convinced of the validity of Thompson's approach that they invited him to help direct their assassination investigation at the same time that he gathered material for his own book.

This association made Thompson a virtual commuter between Dallas, the National Archives in Washington, the New York offices of *Life,* and his

Artist's rendering of scene shown in film.

home base in Philadelphia as he participated in the search for new evidence and the re-evaluation of existing evidence. However, the most important benefit from Thompson's point of view was that he now had access, for the first time, to *Life's* own first copy of the Zapruder assassination film, that remarkable amateur movie which has proved of such historical importance. Endless hours were spent in running this film, examining it frame by frame, and performing meticulous measurements and tests on it. The incredible results of these labors will be detailed in the following pages, and their vital importance to an understanding of this major historical event will be made clear.

After publishing one article, *Life* decided to suspend its work temporarily, and Thompson returned to his book. As it neared completion, he made a routine request for reproduction rights to those Zapruder frames on which he had labored so long and on which so much of his argument rested. To our amazement and chagrin, his request was denied, and all future efforts, through personal meetings, telephone pleadings, letters and intermediaries (including at last our offer to donate the entire profit on the book to *Life* in exchange for these few frames of the film) failed to alter *Life's* decision.

It seems clear to us that this crucial historical document should not be sequestered from the eye of responsible enquiry through an accident of private ownership, and our feelings have been echoed by others in the communications media; still, by law, the film belongs to *Life* and we cannot make use of it without their consent. We have therefore been forced to content ourselves with an artist's rendering of the events depicted on the Zapruder film, since the events themselves are John Kennedy's tragic legacy to us all. These charcoal sketches, a sample of which is shown on the preceding page alongside one of the few Zapruder frames available to the public, have been checked rigorously against the original sources and every attempt has been made to assure that their representation of the events is scrupulously exact. You are asked to make your own comparison of the two pictures and to accept our word that all of the other sketches have been executed with the same care and fidelity.

Still, the sketches are *not* the Zapruder film. The startling conclusions you will be led to in the pages that follow are of great historic importance, so much so that we were perfectly willing, as mentioned, to forego all profit for the sake of presenting to the people the primary evidence on which those conclusions are based. Surely it is now time for *Life* to release this unique body of evidence into the custody of its proper owners, the American people.

The people must have all the evidence and all the facts about an event of such great historical moment: it is to that end that this book is directed. It is the author's hope and ours that the task begun here will be continued, that the investigation will be reopened, and that the record will at long last be set straight.

BERNARD GEIS

# CONTENTS

SIX SECONDS IN DALLAS

# I

## THE VIEW FROM THE THIRTIETH FLOOR

As Abraham Zapruder left his home on the morning of November 22, 1963, the skies were overcast and threatening. He knew the President of the United States would be passing his office later that morning, but the day seemed poor for picture-taking, and anyway, as he was to tell his secretary, Lillian Rogers, later that morning, "I wouldn't have a chance even to see the President" (7H570).* And so Zapruder climbed into his car and headed for downtown Dallas, leaving his 8-millimeter movie camera at home.

Toward midmorning—just before the President was due to land at Love Field—the overcast lifted

* This and all succeeding references of the same form refer to the 26-volume *Hearings Before the President's Commission on the Assassination of President Kennedy*. This note refers to Vol. VII, p. 570, the testimony of Abraham Zapruder.

Two other abbreviated references are used in the text. (R97) refers to *Report of the President's Commission on the Assassination of President John F. Kennedy* (Washington: Government Printing Office, 1964), p. 97, while (*Archives, CD 80*) refers to the vast store of unpublished documents in the National Archives, Commission Document File No. 80.

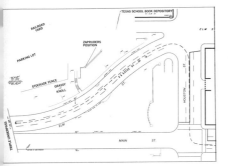

Abraham Zapruder's position during President Kennedy's motorcade.

Zapruder and his receptionist, Marilyn Sitzman (arrow at top), appear in a photograph taken by Philip Willis as the first shot struck the President (lower arrow).

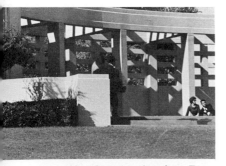

Seconds after the shooting, Zapruder and Sitzman leave their pedestal.

and the sun appeared. It had turned into a beautiful November day, full of light and color, the air freshened by occasional gusts of a northwest wind. With some urging from Mrs. Rogers, Zapruder returned home to get his camera.

The 14-mile round trip took Zapruder longer than usual. Roadblocks had been thrown up along the way and crowds were already beginning to clog the thoroughfares. Both curbs of Houston Street were packed by the time he returned, and he decided first to take pictures from his office window at 501 Elm Street. But Zapruder soon found the camera angle from this point too narrow, and he hurriedly left the office to search out a better vantage point in the Plaza below. The motorcade was late, which gave him time to try out several locations before finally stepping up onto a 4-foot pedestal of concrete on a slope overlooking Elm Street. To his left, 200 feet away, stood the Texas School Book Depository Building. To his right there was a triple underpass, a grassy incline at the top of which stood a stockade fence, and over his right shoulder a parking lot and railroad yard. The President would pass directly in front of him. It was a superb spot, affording a clear view of the motorcade as it would turn left on Elm Street and sweep down under the triple underpass.

Zapruder wound the camera, set the speed control on "Run,"[1] the lens on "Telephoto," and tested the mechanism by photographing a group of office workers sitting on the cement steps to his left. Looking through the viewfinder, he began to lose his balance, and so asked one of the group—his receptionist, Marilyn Sitzman—to join him on the pedestal and steady him as he photographed the motorcade. In other pictures taken that day we can see the two of them standing on the pedestal—Zapruder in a dark business suit, his eyes fixed on the viewfinder, and Marilyn Sitzman in a light tan suit, somewhat taller than Zapruder, looking down at the scene over his left shoulder.

From their vantage point on the concrete block they could see the motorcade emerge from the crowd

What Abraham Zapruder saw.

on Houston Street, Zapruder pressed the shutter release, and for the next 22 seconds the film that wound through his camera recorded for once not a home movie but one of the most macabre scenes in American history. First the lead car, then the motorcycle escort, and finally the long, black presidential limousine came into view. Smoothly the President's car turned left on Elm Street, Mr. Kennedy and Governor Connally smiling and waving to the crowds on their right. For a second the car disappeared behind a highway sign, and when it reappeared something had happened. "There was nothing unusual until the first sound, which I thought was a firecracker, mainly because of the reaction of President Kennedy," Marilyn Sitzman later told me. "He put his hands up as to guard his face and leaned toward the left, and the motorcade proceeded down the hill."[2] A split second later Governor Connally grabbed his chest and fell backward into his wife's lap. Both Zapruder and Marilyn Sitzman at first thought the President and

Z183                    SKETCH

Z225                    SKETCH

Z230                    SKETCH

Governor Connally were joking—that they too had heard the firecracker noise and were pantomiming "Oh, he got me!" But then the violence of the final shot made itself felt. The right front side of the President's head exploded in a burst of pink, snapping his body backward and to the left into his wife's arms. Zapruder kept his camera running as the car sped beneath the underpass and then swung it immediately to his right toward the stockade fence. Trembling from shock, Zapruder released his finger, lowered the camera, and stumbled away from the scene, screaming, "They killed him! They killed him!" His voice was drowned under a wail of sirens.

For Abraham Zapruder the consequences of bringing his camera to this spot were staggering. He had unwittingly become a prime source of history, and it would be largely through his camera that the world would come to know about the assassination in all its horror. Within hours *Life* magazine would pay him $25,000 for his film,[3] and over the succeeding weeks and months the specter of what he had seen would return to haunt his dreams. "I have seen it so many times," Zapruder told Warren Commission Counsel Wesley Liebeler. "I used to have nightmares. The thing would come every night" (7H575).

If the consequences for Zapruder were traumatic, his film's importance to the subsequent and continuing inquiry into the assassination has been momentous. Abraham Zapruder's movie served as a major piece of evidence for the Warren Commission, and it has become a crucial historical document for independent researchers ever since. To an untrained eye it appears to be only a silent, hurried, somewhat blurry view of the President's limousine. Yet if it is studied with the utmost care and under optimum conditions, it can yield answers to enormous questions. Where did the shots come from, and when were they fired? Limited in scope though it is, the Zapruder film is capable of answering these questions.

Nearly three years to the day after Zapruder stood on the low wall in Dealey Plaza, his film was

Z238                 SKETCH

Z313                 SKETCH

Z323                 SKETCH

screened on the thirtieth floor of the Time-Life Building in New York. Present at this screening, which I attended, were Dr. Cyril Wecht, Director of the Institute of Forensic Sciences, Duquesne University, Pittsburgh; U.S. Representative Theodore Kupferman of New York; Sylvia Meagher, researcher and critic of the Warren *Report*; and Edward Kern, Associate Editor of *Life*. As *Life*'s special consultant on the assassination, I had made several trips to Dallas with Kern. Together we had interviewed the principal witnesses, checked firing angles in Dealey Plaza, and visited the Depository. In company with another *Life* representative, Patsy Swank, I had interviewed doctors and nurses at Parkland Memorial Hospital and had reenacted the finding of the bullet (Commission Exhibit 399) in a hospital corridor. Kern and I had spent several days together examining physical evidence in the National Archives, and, on a subsequent trip to Washington, we would interview one of the autopsy surgeons. Although we had visited dozens of key figures, taken measurements and photographs in scores of places, and viewed innumerable video tapes, still photos, and movies, we always kept coming back to New York to study the Zapruder film—the single most important piece of evidence.

Quite obviously, the Zapruder footage contained the nearest thing to "absolute truth" about the sequence of events in Dealey Plaza. But even to the practiced eye the complete picture could not be fully comprehended in a single viewing or even in several. William Manchester reportedly watched it seventy-five times while writing *The Death of a President,* and even this did not prevent him from making several important errors.[4] Commission Counsel Liebeler saw it so often he lost track of the number of times. I had seen it countless times myself; in fact, I had spent a considerable time viewing the copy in the National Archives just a few days before. The crucial nuances and details in this film are easily overlooked, and one could never really be sure one had spotted them all or interpreted them correctly. This was the reason for yet another screening in *Life*'s offices. Sylvia

The Zapruder copies. The difference in clarity between the film the Commission studied and the one owned by *Life* is apparent in a comparison of copies of frame 207. A copy acquired from *Life* is above; a copy acquired from the Archives is below. Even disregarding the splice which runs through the middle of the Commission copy (arrow), it is much less clear than the *Life* copy.

Meagher had indexed the entire twenty-six volumes of Warren Commission *Hearings,* Theodore Kupferman had made known his dissatisfaction with the *Report* on the floor of Congress, and Cyril Wecht had written an article on the Kennedy autopsy for a professional journal. We hoped their experienced eyes might pick up something Edward Kern and I might have missed.

After an exchange of introductions the group sat down before the screen and the familiar images began again their now familiar sequence. Once again the motorcyclists appeared around the corner of Houston Street, and once again the dark blue Lincoln began its fatal glide down Elm Street. The President was hit, then the Governor, and finally the President again. I knew each movement in detail—yet this time there was something about the image on the screen that amazed and astounded me. I was certain the picture was infinitely brighter and clearer than the one I had seen only days before in the National Archives in Washington.

I knew that neither the lens of the Archives' projector nor its bulb could have accounted for the weaker image because I had checked them both; it was simply not as good a copy as the one we were watching now at *Life*. I turned and mentioned this to Kern, who then voiced an opinion that, when I later checked the record, turned out to be the case: While the film we were watching at *Life* was a copy made directly from the original (which was kept in a vault), the FBI's working copy was made not from the original but from a *copy* of it, which made their "official" version a copy of a copy, or a copy once removed.* And

* In a memorandum dated Jan. 28, 1964, Assistant Commission Counsel David Belin notes that "the FBI film of the assassination is a copy of a Secret Service copy of the original colored film taken by Zapruder. . . . FBI Special Agent Shaneyfelt . . . felt that with a more clear film print it could give a more precise determination of the data we are endeavoring to obtain" (*Archives,* Administrative Records). It seems, however, that Shaneyfelt never managed to acquire his clear print. Testifying four months later, on June 4, 1964, he pointed out that "the Secret Service loaned a copy to us long enough for us to make a copy for our use,

it was the Washington copy of the Zapruder film, inferior by comparison, with which the FBI had undertaken photoanalysis for the Commission.

My curiosity aroused, I got up and walked over to a lightbox to take a look at *Life*'s 4 by 5-inch color enlargements of each frame. I looked at several of them, and again they were unmistakably clearer than the smaller slides that the Commission had used and that I had seen at the Archives.[5] As I inspected the frames, one by one, the full impact of the Commission's oversight was brought home to me. Governor Connally had been hit, according to the Commission, at the same time as Kennedy. This was a central matter in proving that there had been only one assassin. The President and the Governor, said the Commission, had both been hit by the same bullet while the car was hidden behind the highway sign (Z210–225). But on the *Life* blowups, I saw for the first time enough evidence to prove that Connally had not been hit until at least thirteen frames (or three-quarters of a second) later—too late for it to have been the same bullet, too soon for it to have been a second bullet from the same rifle. The collapse of the Governor's shoulder, the air forced into his cheeks, the disarrayed lock of his hair—all of this was clearly visible and a simple matter to interpret in the *Life* copy, and it flatly contradicted the Commission's interpretation. As Connally himself had said, it was "inconceivable" to him that he had been hit by the same bullet that struck the President (4H135). But the Commission had chosen to disregard his testimony, prompted by their desire to believe that there had been only one assassin and aided, unknowingly perhaps, by the inferior quality of the film they had used for reference.

I turned my attention from the enlargements once again to the *Life* film, which was being run backward and forward. It was Sylvia Meagher who pointed out that, when the film was projected backward, the change in the Governor's facial expression was even

which we did, and this copy is the one I have been examining" (5H138). On Feb. 25, 1964, a representative of *Life* projected the original film for Shaneyfelt (5H138).

more noticeable, easier to pinpoint as to time, and that this seemed to corroborate a later hit than the Commission had cited.

This discrepancy would bear looking into further, but for the moment I wanted to hear Dr. Wecht's opinion about another interesting phenomenon in the film, one that had also been visible in the Commission's copy but that, even so, had not been mentioned in the *Report*. It was Kennedy's physical reaction to the last shot, the head shot. If, as the Commission had said, the shot came from the rear, then the force of the blow could be expected to jolt Kennedy forward, not *backward* as clearly appeared in the film. Wecht expressed surprise and said that it was most unlikely that a neuromuscular reaction could have countered the force of the bullet and accounted for Kennedy's backward thrust. The President's movements, he agreed, were indicative rather of an impact from the *front*.

Eyewitnesses Marilyn Sitzman and William and Gayle Newman (who were standing only 15 feet from the President at the time of the head shot) had told me when I spoke to them in Dallas that they had seen an impact on the right *front* side of the President's head. In the case of the Newmans, what they had seen made them question the Commission's findings. Their remarks had sent me searching through early press and radio reports for descriptions of the President's head wound. I had found that only an hour and a half after the assassination, NBC reported from Dallas that "the President was struck in the right temple by the bullet." Half an hour later the same network had reported that "a bullet struck him in front as he faced the assailant." The next day *The New York Times* had reported that "Mr. Kennedy also had a massive gaping wound in the back and one on the right side of the head." These early reports accorded much more closely with what the witnesses had seen, what the Zapruder film had revealed, and what Dr. Wecht had just expressed.

In all fairness, it must be said that all of us in that screening room had entered it with some doubts

Standing fifteen feet from the President, William and Gayle Newman (lower arrows) both saw an impact on the right front of the President's head. Behind them, Marilyn Sitzman (arrow at top) saw a hit "above the ear and to the front."

about the accuracy of the Warren *Report*. But even the most objective man in the world could not fail to have been impressed by the things we noticed that day. And perhaps the most shocking of all was the revelation that the Commission had not availed itself of the best evidence.

But Abraham Zapruder had not been the only man with a camera in Dealey Plaza that day. If the Commission could have been so incredibly inept in handling the Zapruder film, could they also have treated much of the other photographic evidence in the same way? I began to review the other photos in my mind.

There had, in fact, been no fewer than twenty-two people taking pictures in Dealey Plaza on November 22. Several were professional newsmen, but the majority were amateurs, snapping everything from Polaroids to 35-millimeter slides. They met with varying degrees of success. Mrs. Elsie Dorman, for instance, stood at a fourth-floor window of the Depository and photographed the parade with her new movie camera. Her view would have been the closest to that of an assassin from the sixth-floor window. Unfortunately, she took her eye away from the viewfinder at the crucial moment and missed the assassination. The *Report*, understandably, says nothing about Mrs. Dorman's movie, but neither does it mention nine perfectly clear color photographs taken by Miss Wilma Bond, who was standing in the middle of Dealey Plaza. Four of her pictures have revelance to the case, and they are reproduced and explained in this book.

The color movie taken by Robert Hughes, who stood at the corner of Main and Houston streets, is of even greater importance, yet scant mention is made of it in the 26 volumes. Hughes stopped taking pictures just seconds before the first shot, but even so the Commission's lack of interest is difficult to understand, since Hughes's camera range included the windows on the sixth floor of the Depository —right up until the time the limousine turned the last corner. The FBI apparently studied one

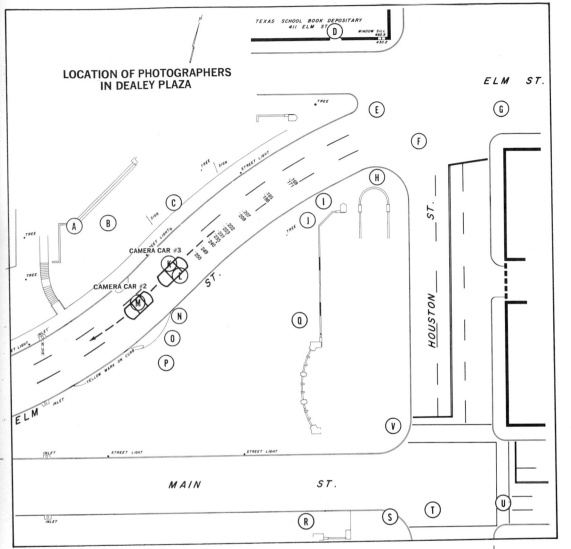

# LOCATION OF PHOTOGRAPHERS
## IN DEALEY PLAZA

TEXAS SCHOOL BOOK DEPOSITARY
411 ELM ST.

ELM ST.

HOUSTON ST.

ELM

MAIN ST.

The twenty-two photographers in Dealey Plaza and where they stood.

**A**
Zapruder (color movie)

**B**
Cancellare (black & white still)

**C**
Cablack (black & white still)

**D**
Dorman (color movie)

**E**
Weigman (black & white movie)

**F**
Dillard (black & white still)

**G**
Powell (color still)

**H**
Martin (color movie)

**I**
Willis (color still)

**J**
Betzner (color still)

**K**
Underwood (black & white movie)

**L**
Couch (black & white movie)

**M**
Rickerby (black & white still)

**N**
Moorman (black and white Polaroid)

**O**
Altgens (black & white still)

**P**
Bothun (black & white still)

**Q**
Muchmore (color movie)

**R**
Nix (color movie)

**S**
Bell (color movie)

**T**
Hughes (color movie)

**U**
Weaver (black & white Polaro

**V**
Bond (color still)

frame from the film and decided it could not make out the shape in the corner window. There is no record that anybody on the Commission itself ever looked at it, that anybody ever compared this frame and later frames to see if the shape moved, or that much attention was paid to a rather curious configuration in the window *next* to the one at the corner. This film will also be examined in later chapters.

A Polaroid photograph, snapped by Mrs. Mary Moorman from the grass in the middle of Dealey Plaza, has been reproduced often but never in sufficient detail to explain for sure what certain spots in it represent. The interesting thing about her one grainy picture is that it was taken from the opposite side of the street from Zapruder's position, and consequently the background is composed of the infamous grassy knoll. It was the opinion of many present in Dealey Plaza that day that the shots came from behind the stockade fence at the top of the knoll. In view of this, the Commission (which never mentioned the photograph in its *Report*) might have looked a little more closely at a dark shape, the size of a head, seemingly peering over the fence. It cannot be identified with any certainty, but as we shall see later, it is positioned precisely where the crucial witnesses said the shots originated. When I showed the photograph to one of these witnesses, he pointed right to the spot and said, "Well, do you know, I think you're looking right down the barrel of that gun!" The photograph bears looking into, but there is no indication that the Commission ever examined it.

One could hardly fault the Commission if its blunderings stemmed from lack of evidence. If, for example, a crucial source of information had remained undiscovered, then mistakes would have been forgivable. But most of the photographs taken that day were known to and available to the Commission. That the Commission was hasty in evaluating them is the Commission's fault and no one else's. For instance, a combination of the Zapruder film (which the Commission had), a picture taken by Philip Willis (which it also had), and statements made to the Commission by witnesses on the scene prove beyond a doubt that the first shot fired was the one that hit. The Commission, however, without bothering to piece together the available evidence, stoutly maintained that the first shot might have missed.

It seemed clear, then, that the Commission had either neglected or only hastily examined the photographic record of the assassination. It seemed equally clear that this record might constitute a primitive level of data on which a positive reconstruction could be built. The present study seeks to make proper use of the photographs inasmuch as they constitute the only inviolable form of evidence. Whereas witness reports can be in error (and witnesses can and have changed their stories) and pieces of physical evidence can be tampered with (the laundering of Governor Connally's clothes is a good example), photographic evidence is reliable. This new study, which uses photographs as a base and superimposes upon them the corroborated witness reports and the physical evidence, takes up where the Commission left off.

There are, of course, obstacles in the way of such a project. First is the Zapruder film itself. As *Life*'s special consultant on the assassination, I have had unlimited access to the film and have spent literally hundreds of hours examining it. But publishing the results of that examination is something else entirely. Although it might be argued that such a piece of evidence ought not to be the property of any private party,* *Life* owns it and has exercised its legal right

---

* At the close of a recently televised documentary on the Warren *Report,* Walter Cronkite offered a spirited appeal for the immediate release of the Zapruder film:

There is one further piece of evidence which we feel must now be made available to the entire public: Abraham Zapruder's film of the actual assassination. The original is now the private property of *Life* Magazine. A *Life* executive refused CBS News permission to show you that film at any price, on the ground that it is "an invaluable asset of Time, Inc." And that, even though these broadcasts have demonstrated that the film may contain vital undiscovered clues to the assassination.

*Life's* decision means you cannot see the Zapruder film

not to permit its publication by anyone else. Except for six inconsequential frames released by *Life* as a "public service," I have relied here on an artist's precise rendering of the events shown on the Zapruder film, checking each sketch carefully against the original sources for accuracy of detail.

The other prime obstacle is not as simple to cope with; in fact, it remains as much an obstacle today as it has been in the past, impervious to such influential bodies as *Life* and the Warren Commission: the inaccessibility of the autopsy photographs. It was never my intention, nor anyone else's for that matter, to publish them; but inasmuch as I wanted to base my study as much as possible on photographic evidence, I was hopeful that a qualified group of individuals would be permitted to see the pictures and discuss their contents. Although William Manchester, in his book *The Death of a President*, claimed that "three men [possessing] special professional qualifications"[6] examined them and found corroboration for the Commission's findings, it should be noted that Manchester refused to identify these individuals, and that none of them is known to either Dr. Milton Helpern (Chief Medical Examiner of the City of New York) or to Dr. Cyril Wecht. As Manchester admitted to Richard Goodwin, permission to view the films personally had been denied him, but he was reluctant to say so in his book.[7] After the viewing of the Zapruder film at *Life,* the five of us discussed the possibility of some independent forensic expert's gaining access to the autopsy X-rays and photos. Congressman Kupferman offered to ask the Archives to permit him, Dr. Wecht, and Dr. Helpern to see them. Unfortunately, and inexplicably, in January, 1967, his request was refused.[8] Until the autopsy photos are made available, researchers can only speculate on what they

in its proper form, as motion picture film. We believe that the Zapruder film is an invaluable asset, not of Time, Inc. —but of the people of the United States. (CBS News Inquiry, *The Warren Report,* June 28, 1967.)

Some rather important "undiscovered clues to the assassination" have been discovered and are presented for the first time in this book.

show. But for the present there is enough visual material in the public domain to reconstruct the assassination. And the reconstruction that follows does not square with any that have preceded it.


## NOTES

1. A lot of needless controversy has arisen with respect to the speed of Zapruder's camera.

In December, 1966, Harold Weisberg published in *Whitewash II: The FBI-Secret Service Coverup* (Hyattstown, Md.: Harold Weisberg, 1966) an FBI report that stated that "the camera was set to take normal speed movie film or 24 frames per second" (p. 184). If this report were true then the speed of the assassination would have to be boosted by 30 percent; the total time would be reduced to 4.3 seconds, considerably less than the minimum firing time of Oswald's rifle for three shots. Weisberg made quite a lot of this report, and his discovery was picked up by *The New York Times*. Unfortunately, he made no effort to check whether Zapruder's camera could have been set on 24 frames per second. It couldn't. On December 8 we learned from Mr. Jones, Bell & Howell's public relations director, that Zapruder's camera had four settings: (1) "Single Frame," (2) "Stop," (3) "Run"—set at the factory at 18 frames per second—and (4) "Slow Motion"—48 frames per second. Mr. Jones also told us that the Bell & Howell Company checked the speed of the camera and found it to run within .1 second of the FBI-determined 18.3 frames per second. See also 5H160 where FBI agent Shaneyfelt testifies concerning how the speed of the Zapruder camera was clocked at 18.3 frames per second.

2. Taped interview with Marilyn Sitzman, Nov. 29, 1966.

3. Paid by *Life,* this sum was later given away by Zapruder to the Dallas Fireman's and Policeman's Benevolence Association (7H576). Since that time additional sums have been paid to Zapruder by *Life*.

4. The few pages of Manchester's book dealing with the actual assassination are crowded with errors. Many are slips of detail—confusing the Criminal Courts Building with the Records Building (p. 153), misplacing the order of motorcyclists in the motorcade (p. 159), misspelling the names of witnesses and giving them mistaken locations (pp. 150, 154, 155)—but one error is substantial and especially difficult to understand in light of Manchester's claim in *Look* (Apr. 4, 1967) that he had watched the Zapruder film "until I had memorized every movement and found some that the Commission's investigators had missed." His book reaches its apex in describing the very moment of the President's death: "Now, in a gesture of infinite grace, he raised his right hand, as though to brush back his tousled chestnut hair. But the motion faltered. The hand fell back

limply. He had been reaching for the top of his head. But it wasn't there anymore" (p. 158). We know from the Zapruder film that no such gesture ever occurred.

5. Having studied the stills of the Zapruder film both at *Life* and at the Archives, there is no doubt in my mind that *Life*'s transparencies are the better of the two sets. The testimony of FBI expert Lyndal Shaneyfelt implies, however, that both sets of transparencies were made from the original film. If this is indeed the case, then the only explanation for the difference in quality must be that the copying job done by *Life* for the Commission was a poor one in comparison with the one done by *Life* for *Life*. In her book *Accessories After the Fact,* Sylvia Meagher points out how unclear she found the Archives' 35-millimeter slides of the Zapruder film to be. Yet it was this set of slides that was used by both the FBI and the Commission. See Sylvia Meagher, *Accessories After the Fact* (New York: The Bobbs-Merrill Company, Inc., 1967), p. 27.

6. William Manchester, *The Death of a President* (New York: Harper & Row, Publishers, 1967), pp. 156–57.

7. Edward Epstein, "Manchester Unexpurgated," *Commentary,* July, 1967, p. 30.

8. A lawsuit seems to be the only recourse left open at this point. A private individual (in this case the Kennedy family) can legally make an agreement with the Archives limiting access to material turned over to the Archives. But the private individual has to first own the material he turns over. The autopsy photos and X-rays were enclosures to an official government document. They were taken by a Navy photographer on government film at government expense. They were in government hands until August, 1965. The Kennedy family's claim to ownership of this material is (to put it mildly) quite dubious; that claim should, and probably will, be tested in the courts.

# II

## THE WITNESSES

J UST before noon, Ronald Fischer's boss in the Dallas County Records Building told him he could take a little extra time off for lunch. "Just go on down the street and watch the parade," Mr. Lynn had said (6H192). Thus, a half hour later, Ronald Fischer became one of the more than four hundred people to witness the assassination of President John F. Kennedy.

Most of the bystanders were present in Dealey Plaza, on the edge of downtown Dallas, primarily because they worked in buildings nearby. Many of them, like Fischer, were given time to view the motorcade; otherwise they might not have gone. Others, like Phil Willis, who took his children out of school so they could see the President, had carefully selected Dealey Plaza over all the other places because they thought it afforded the best view of the President and a good spot to take pictures. There are tall buildings on the eastern side of the Plaza, but the rest is open, and to the west, beyond a triple underpass, there are highways and the Trinity River. Crowds here would be predictably lighter than a few blocks up on Main Street, and bystanders wouldn't have to crane their necks. Furthermore, there were open spaces and grassy slopes, so an unobstructed view was virtually assured.

The unwitting witnesses began filtering into the Plaza around eleven o'clock. Mrs. Jean Hill, who accompanied Mary Moorman, told the Commission, "We had been there for about an hour and a half and had been walking up and down and back and forth" (6H206). Mrs. Moorman had brought along her Polaroid camera, and since she knew she would only be able to get one picture of the President, she and Mrs. Hill were looking for the best spot to stand. At noon Howard L. Brennan, a steam fitter who was working behind the Depository, walked over to a cafeteria on the corner of Main and Record streets and ate lunch (3H141). At 12:18 exactly, he thought he might still have time to watch the parade, so he went out and walked down Main Street to Dealey Plaza. In about 4 minutes he had seated himself on the retaining wall at the corner of Houston and Elm, directly across from the Depository. During the next 10 minutes, Brennan watched the people in the crowd, including a man who had an epileptic seizure down the street. After an ambulance carried the man away, Brennan casually resumed scanning the buildings that surrounded the plaza. He looked up at the Depository. "I observed quite a few people in different windows," he said. "In particular I saw this one man on the sixth floor which left the window to my knowledge a couple of times" (3H143). The next time he was to look up at the man he would see him holding a rifle and "aiming for his last shot" (3H144).

In the moments that preceded the assassination, the individuals in the crowd made their last moves to see better, to get closer, to have a longer look. Associated Press photographer James Altgens, having been denied permission to stand on the overpass, readied his camera at the intersection of Houston and Main. Danny Arce stepped off the sidewalk onto the grass in front of the Depository. Billy Lovelady, who had been sitting on the building's front steps eating his lunch, rose to his feet. And Ruby Goldstein, a local pawnbroker, circled the block in his gaudily painted station wagon.

Those who rode in the motorcade had been placed according to protocol in one of a number of limousines and cars or in the press bus. In the President's car, Secret Service agents sat in the front, Governor and Mrs. Connally on the jump seats, and the Kennedys in the rear. As the limousine turned onto Elm Street, Mrs. Kennedy glanced ahead at the overpass and thought "it would be so cool under that tunnel" (5H179). At the same time, Mrs. Connally turned to the President and remarked, "You can't say Dallas doesn't love you" (4H147). As if on cue, the shooting began.

It is from those gathered by chance in Dealey Plaza, and from the others in the motorcade, that much of the important information about the assassination has come. Admittedly, the photographic evidence (when *all* of it is considered) is extensive, and most of the President's ride is recorded in detail on film, as are relevant portions of the Plaza and surrounding buildings. But none of the pictures can by itself determine the number of shots, their timing, and their direction, and there was no sound equipment operating in Dealey Plaza. For this reason, the eyewitnesses are tremendously important.

But their testimony taken alone, makes for exceedingly vulnerable evidence. Memories fade or become *too* vivid, and inevitably stories conflict. Law professors like to prove this point by staging impromptu incidents in the middle of class, then asking the students to put in writing what happened. Dozens of variations are always offered, for the simple reason that nobody really has time to focus his attention fully on the incident. Obviously, this is precisely what happened to many of the bystanders during the assassination. George Rackley and James Romack, for instance, were standing together in the truck yards well behind the Depository at the time of the shooting, and Rackley says he heard nothing, while Romack says he heard three shots (6H275, 280). Clearly one of them is mistaken (the sixty-year-old "Pop" Rackley being the more likely). Still, with all of the pitfalls and inaccuracies considered, eyewitness testimony can be of some value if objectively and cautiously studied.

The greater part of the crowd in Dealey Plaza was dispersed along Houston Street; only a few scattered spectators dotted the sidewalk and grass on either side of Elm Street. Thus, when the gunfire broke out, only a few people were in close proximity to the presidential limousine. It is their testimony that provides, with graphic, chilling immediacy, the most detailed accounts of those six seconds.

Linda Kay Willis accompanied her parents and younger sister to Dealey Plaza that Friday. She stood next to her father, across Elm Street from Abraham Zapruder. Linda Kay was watching the President when the first shot rang out:

> *I heard one [shot]. Then there was a little bit of time, and then there were two real fast bullets together. When the first one hit, well, the President turned from waving to the people, and he grabbed his throat, and he kind of slumped forward, and then I couldn't tell where the second shot went . . . and then the third one, and that was the last one that hit him in the head (7H498).*

But Mrs. John B. Connally, sitting next to her husband in the left jump seat of the presidential car, did see where the second shot went. Questioned later by Assistant Commission Counsel Arlen Specter, she described the assassination in these words:

*Mrs. Connally: I heard a noise, and not being an expert rifleman, I was not aware that it was a rifle. It was just a frightening noise, and it came from the right.*

*I turned over my right shoulder and looked back, and saw the President as he had both hands at his neck.*

*Specter: And you are indicating with your own hands, two hands crossing over gripping your own neck?*

*Mrs. Connally: Yes; and it seemed to me there was —he made no utterance, no cry. I saw no blood, no anything. It was just sort of nothing, the expression on his face, and he just sort of slumped down.*

*Then very soon there was the second shot that hit John. As the first shot was hit, and I turned to look at the same time, I recall John saying, "Oh no, no, no." Then there was a second shot, and it hit John, and he recoiled to the right, just crumpled like a wounded animal to the right . . .*

*The third shot that I heard I felt, it felt like spent buckshot falling all over us, and then, of course, I could see that it was the matter, brain tissue, or whatever, just human matter all over the car and both of us . . . (4H147).*

Presidential Assistant Dave Powers was riding directly behind the President in the Secret Service follow-up car. His sworn affidavit reads as follows:

*We then turned off of Main Street onto Houston and made the sharp swing to the left up Elm Street . . . Shortly thereafter the first shot went off and it sounded to me as if it were a firecracker. I noticed then that the President moved quite far to his left after the shot from the extreme right hand side where he had been sitting. There was a second shot and Governor Connally disappeared from sight and then there was a third shot which took off the top of the President's head and had the sickening sound of a grapefruit splattering against the side of a wall. The total time between the first and third shots was about 5 or 6 seconds. My first impression was that the shots came from the right*

*and overhead, but I also had a fleeting im-*
*pression that the noise appeared to come*
*from the front in the area of the triple over-*
*pass (7H473).*

Although most witnesses to the assassination were
not in positions to observe what happened with the
clarity of those in the immediate vicinity, a canvass
of witnesses (undertaken here, surprisingly for the
first time) gives us an indication of the number and
timing of the shots.

Most of the witnesses agreed that three shots were
fired, as reflected in the overall survey of witness reports. Of those witnesses who expressed an opinion
as to the number of shots, and whose affidavit or
testimony is found in the Archives or in the twenty-
six volumes of hearings and exhibits, 83.4 percent
reported hearing three shots.* Some witnesses (Tom
Dillard of the *Dallas Morning News,* Senator Ralph
Yarborough, Steve Wilson, and Secret Service Agent
Forrest Sorrels) were so confident of the number of
shots that they were able to declare "three shots—no
more, no less."[1] Of the Secret Service agents who reported their opinions as to the number of shots, 87
percent declared they heard three.

Various estimates of the total time from first to
last shot were given, and these ranged all the way
from "a few seconds" to "five minutes." But 69 percent of the witnesses who expressed an opinion
gauged the total time to be between 4 to 6 seconds.
All the Secret Service agents who hazarded an opinion put the time factor in the 4- to 6-second range.

When we turn to other variables such as sound

---

* See Appendix A for a chart listing the names, references,
and observations of the 190 witnesses on whose testimony,
statement, or affidavit these statistics rest. A chart giving
the location of each witness forms a part of this Appendix.

Some witnesses reported hearing "two or three" or "three
or four" shots. Including all these reports under "three shots"
yields a figure of 88 percent; excluding them all yields a
figure of 79 percent. We split the difference to arrive at our
figure of 83.4 percent.

direction and sound spacing, we do not find general agreement among the witnesses. Dave Powers remarked that his "first impression was that the shots came from the right and overhead," but he also admitted to a "fleeting impression that the noise appeared to come from the front in the area of the triple overpass." Likewise, Paul Landis (a Secret Service agent riding in the same car) recalled that the first shot appeared to come "from behind me, over my right shoulder" while the last "shot came from somewhere towards the front, right-hand side of the road" (18H754–755). Their ambiguity in regard to sound direction is reflected in the total profile of witness reports. Only one-third of the witnesses answered this question; yet, of these, 52 percent thought the sound came from the area of the grassy knoll to the right front of the presidential limousine, while 39 percent thought the sound came from the direction of the Depository. A small number of witnesses believed the shots came from the east side of Houston Street, while slightly over 6 percent of those reporting thought the shots came from two directions.

It is difficult to know what weight to give these conflicting reports. Defenders of the Warren Commission have claimed that Dealey Plaza is an "echo chamber" and that shots fired from the Depository might sound as if they came from the knoll.[2] But actually, there is no evidence for such a judgment, since the Warren Commission neglected to make any studies of the acoustical properties of the Plaza. Theoretically, just the opposite effect would be the most likely: Since the knoll is covered with sound-absorbing foliage, one would expect shots fired from there to echo off the hard, flat surfaces of surrounding buildings, rather than the reverse, so that reports of sound coming from the Depository might actually have been echoes from a shot originating on the grassy knoll. This sharp disagreement over sound direction may be ascribed either to echo effects or to the generally untrustworthy character of earwitness testimony with respect to sound direction. Yet it may also accurately reflect the true state of affairs, namely,

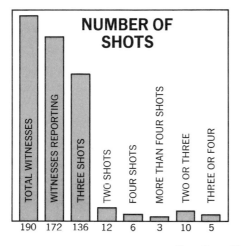

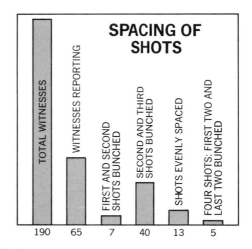

Overall profile of witness reports.

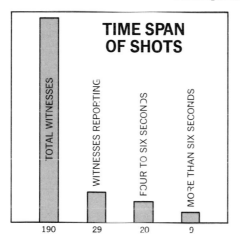

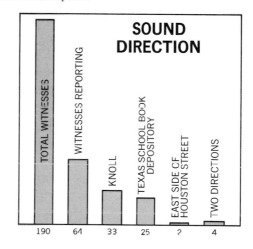

that shots really were fired from more than one location.

Witness testimony with regard to sound spacing is flawed by a similar conflict. Presidential Assistant Kenneth O'Donnell reported that "the first two . . . came one right after the other, there was a slight hesitation, then the third one" (7H448), while Linda Kay Willis recalled hearing one shot: "Then there was a little bit of time, and then there were two real fast bullets together" (7H498). This conflict is reflected in the overall profile of witness reports with respect to sound spacing. Only about one-third of the witnesses (65 out of 190) mentioned the timing. Of these, 61.5 percent, although not all agreeing about the number of shots, thought the last two shots were bunched, 20 percent thought that the shots they heard were evenly spaced, 11 percent thought the first two were bunched, while a smaller percentage, 7.7 percent, thought that there were two shots bunched at the beginning and two bunched at the end.

Once again the validity of witness reports is called into question. Some witnesses even gave different estimates of spacing at different times. In November, 1966, for example, Linda Kay Willis told me she thought the shots were evenly spaced, while earlier she had told the Warren Commission she thought the last two were bunched. Although Senator Ralph Yarborough was quoted in the press on November 23 as saying the first two shots were bunched, his later affidavit to the Commission insisted that the last two shots were bunched (7H440). Similarly, Barbara Rowland's November 22 affidavit indicated the shots were approximately evenly spaced (19H493), while her later testimony indicated the last two shots were closer together than the first two (6H184).

Probably the most sensible explanation of this conflict was given to me by another witness, F. M. Bell. Standing at the corner of Main and Houston streets, Mr. Bell heard two of the shots definitely bunched but could not honestly say which shots these were. "Anyone could be mistaken on the bunching of shots," he told me. "It happened within a few seconds and there was emotion, excitement, and fear involved."[3]

The 190 witnesses on record either testified before the Warren Commission or spoke with a law-enforcement officer whose report of the conversation found its way into the Commission files. There were, however, between four hundred and five hundred people in Dealey Plaza, so the number interviewed is less than half the total. We have no way of knowing whether the selection process produced a random or nonrandom sample. Since statistics as a science demands that the sample under analysis be known to be random, no statistical analysis can be performed on these figures. This does not mean, however, that an intelligent speculation cannot be based on them. Within limits, this overall study of witness reports does define a general profile of what happened in Dealey Plaza.

Over 90 percent of the 190 witnesses gave an opinion as to the number of shots. Of these 172 witnesses, over 90 percent again estimated that *at least three shots* were fired. Surely the virtual unanimity of witnesses on this point cannot be overlooked. Given this weight of testimony, it would seem difficult to argue that *fewer* than three shots were fired.

The same is true with respect to the total firing time. Although only twenty-nine witnesses gave an estimate of the total time factor, it surely is significant that twenty of these twenty-nine put the total time in the range of 4 to 6 seconds.

The conflicting testimony with regard to sound direction is probably without much significance. True, over half the witnesses reporting thought the sound came from the knoll, and photos taken seconds after the assassination show people reacting in this direction. But crowds are known to be highly suggestible, and without an acoustical study of Dealey Plaza no firm conclusion can be drawn.

The disparity of views on time between the shots is a different matter. For although there was considerable disagreement among witnesses over *which* shots were bunched, 80 percent of the witnesses reporting thought that *some* shots were bunched. This, as we shall see, is significant by itself.

The overall profile of the assassination which emerges from this survey of witness reports is a series of *at least* three shots, *not* evenly spaced, in a total interval of 4 to 6 seconds.

If we had to rely on witness reports alone, it would be impossible to refine this general pattern much further. At this point the critical importance of the photographic evidence becomes apparent. For using this evidence as a firm foundation for the witness testimony, the picture that emerges will be more detailed and logically much more convincing.

## NOTES

1. See 6H166, 7H440, 22H685, 7H345.

2. See Charles Roberts, *The Truth about the Assassination* (New York: Grosset & Dunlap, Inc., 1967), pp. 33–34; Richard Warren Lewis and Lawrence Schiller, *The Scavengers and Critics of the Warren Report* (New York: Dell Publishing Co., Inc., 1967), pp. 25–31.

3. Author's questionnaire completed by F. M. Bell, Feb. 26, 1967. Mr. Bell was never questioned by the federal or local agencies or by the Commission, even though he filmed parts of the assassination with an 8 millimeter movie camera. No part of his film was examined by any of the authorities, nor has any part of it been published. Selected frames appear for the first time in this book.

# III

## THE FIRST SHOT

*Two bullets probably caused all the wounds
suffered by President Kennedy and Governor
Connally. Since the preponderance of the
evidence indicated that three shots were fired,
the Commission concluded that one shot
probably missed the Presidential limousine
and its occupants.*
—*Warren Commission Report, p. 117.*

ON September 24, 1964, after ten months of intensive research, the Warren Commission turned in its conclusions about the bullets fired at President Kennedy: three shots, two hits, one miss. To this neat ballistic scenario the Commissioners added a disturbing footnote. They were not sure which shots caused which hits or which of the three shots missed.

The first hit, according to the Commission, pierced Kennedy's neck and went on to strike Governor Connally. The second hit struck President Kennedy in the head, and a third bullet went astray. The bullet that missed might have been the first shot (preceding the two hits), the second (coming between them), or the last.

Z183                                                    SKETCH

Z207                                                    SKETCH

The President's hand-waving continues naturally until he disappears behind the sign.

To some, this frank admission of doubt concerning the basic events of the assassination may appear as an admirable reticence to draw conclusions beyond the bounds of evidence. To others, it may seem a sly attempt to prop up the single-bullet, double-hit theory. The main thrust of the evidence, however, seems to be quite clear: None of the shots missed; all found their mark. The first shot struck the President in the back.

## PINPOINTING A FIRST-SHOT MISS

The firmest piece of working evidence is the 8-millimeter movie film of the assassination taken by Abraham Zapruder. The Commission used this film as a basis for all of its findings relating to the shooting, and thus it is more than appropriate to refer to it here in explaining just where the Commission went wrong.

In the early frames of the Zapruder film the President can be seen smiling and waving to the crowds on his right. This natural waving movement continues as the President disappears from view behind the Stemmons Freeway sign at Z207. On the film we see no evidence to suggest that a bullet has struck until the President begins to emerge from behind the sign at Z224. In this frame we see the President's hands rising to his face, a movement that becomes even more apparent in the frames that follow. By frame 230 the President's elbows are elevated and his clenched fists have reached the level of his chin and neck. His motions at this point leave no doubt that he has been hit and that he was just starting to react at frame 224. The question then arises: If there was a shot that missed before this, when could it have been fired?

Let us assume with the Commission that such a shot was fired from Oswald's rifle as the assassin lay hidden on the sixth floor of the Depository. If we know the minimum firing time of Oswald's rifle, we can determine the approximate time at which a previous shot could have been fired.

FBI firearms expert Robert Frazier tested Oswald's rifle to determine the minimum time required to work the bolt and pull the trigger. His fastest time for getting off three shots was 4.6 seconds. Such a speed, he testified, "is firing this weapon as fast as the bolt can be operated" (3H407). The Commission divided this figure in two and arrived at 2.3 seconds as the minimum firing time for Oswald's rifle (R97)—a figure that includes no time for aiming the rifle and

Z224                                        SKETCH

Z225                                        SKETCH

Z230                                        SKETCH
The President emerges from behind the sign obviously hit.

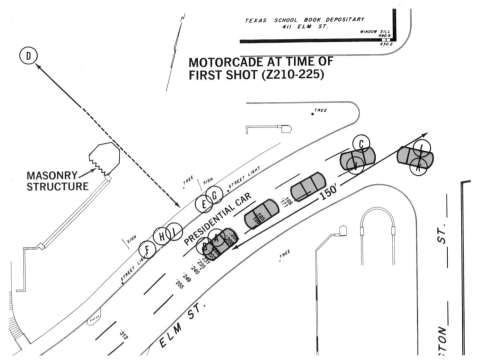

Witnesses pinpoint the time of the first shot.

**A. GOVERNOR CONNALLY:** "We had—we had gone, I guess, 150 feet, maybe 200 feet, I don't recall how far it was, heading down to get on the freeway . . . when I heard what I thought was a shot." (4H132)

**B. ROY H. KELLERMAN:** "As we turned off Houston onto Elm and made the short little dip to the left going down grade, as I said, we were away from buildings, and were—there was a sign on the side of the road which I don't recall what it was or what it said, but we no more than passed that and you are out in the open, and there is a report like a firecracker, pop." (2H73)

**C. JERRY D. KIVETT:** "As the motorcade was approximately ⅓ of the way to the underpass, traveling between 10 and 15 miles per hour, I heard a loud noise." (18H778)

**D. LEE BOWERS:** "At the moment of the first shot, as close as my recollection serves, the car was out of sight behind this decorative masonry wall in the area." (6H288)

**E. MRS. BILLIE P. CLAY:** "Just a few seconds after the car in which President John F. Kennedy was riding passed the location where I was standing, I heard a shot." (22H641)

**F. JOHN ARTHUR CHISM:** "And just as he [the President] got just about in front of me, he turned and waived at the crowd on this side of the street, the right side; at this point I heard what sounded like one shot." (19H471)

**G. JEAN NEWMAN:** "The motorcade had just passed me when I heard something that I thought was a firecracker at first, and the President had just passed me, because after he had just passed there was a loud report, it just scared me." (19H489)

**H. KAREN WESTBROOK:** "The car he [the President] was in was almost directly in front of where I was standing when I heard the first explosion." (22H679)

**I. GLORIA CALVERY:** "The car he [the President] was in was almost directly in front of where I was standing when I heard the first shot." (22H638)

**J. JOE HENRY RICH:** "We turned off of Houston Street onto Elm Street and that was when I heard the first shot." (18H800)

**K. MRS. EARLE CABELL:** "We were making the turn . . . just on the turn, which put us at the top of the hill you see . . . I heard the shot, and without having to turn my head, I jerked my head up." (7H486)

**L. MAYOR EARLE CABELL:** "We were just rounding the corner of Market [sic] and Elm, making the left turn, when the first shot rang out." (7H478)

assumes that an expert rifleman is operating the bolt.* In 2.3 seconds Zapruder's camera would have rolled through forty-two frames. Thus, if we assume that the President was reacting to a hit when he emerged from behind the sign (Z224), then an earlier miss could not have been fired later than Z182 (224 minus 42). But we know that at this point a tree hid the President from the sixth-floor sniper's nest (R98). If the missed shot was fired at Z182, the gunman was firing blindly into a tree. In all likelihood, if the first shot missed, it was fired before the President disappeared behind the tree, which means before Z166. Is there any evidence for such an early missed shot?

Not one of the several hundred witnesses in Dealey Plaza that day reported hearing a shot that could have come as early as Z166. In fact, by taking a series of witness reports, we can triangulate the position of the car at the time of the first shot. Its position falls in the range of Zapruder frames 210–224.

It should be pointed out that the position of the presidential limousine established by triangulating these witness reports compares favorably with the position given in early government reports. *The Report of the Secret Service on the Assassination of President Kennedy* (December 18, 1963) notes that "when the President's car had proceeded approximately two hundred feet down Elm Street . . . there was a sharp report" (*Archives,* CD 3). This would have been at Zapruder frame 291. The FBI Summary Report of December 9 notes: "As the motorcade was

---

* If this appears to be a long interval between shots, it is accounted for by the awkward design of the Carcano. As Melvin M. Johnson, Jr., has pointed out in his book *Rifles and Machine Guns,* "The (Mannlicher) Carcano bolt handle is too far ahead of the trigger for efficient rapid-fire" (p. 66). Both CBS and the BBC obtained somewhat faster firing times by employing expert riflemen shooting weapons other than Oswald's. It is difficult to say what evidential value this has in light of the considerable differences between individual rifles. I have worked the action of Oswald's rifle in the National Archives; even for a Carcano, it is particularly sluggish. Frazier's test stands as our most accurate measure of the minimum firing time of Oswald's rifle.

Philip Willis' picture, snapped in the range of Zapruder 205 to 225, was taken (according to Willis) as the first shot was heard.

traveling through downtown Dallas on Elm Street about fifty yards west of the intersection [approximately frame 239] with Houston Street, three shots rang out" (*Archives,* CD 1). No evidence was adduced by the Commission to indicate a shot fired prior to Z210.

### FIRST SHOT, FIRST HIT

All these witness reports (and many more besides) place the position of the car at the time of the first shot in the range Z210–224. In addition, photographic evidence corroborates such a finding.

Philip Willis took a photograph of the presidential limousine at a time determined to be in the range Z205–225 (15H696–697). Willis testified before the Commission that this photo was taken simultaneously with the first shot. As Willis put it, "the shot caused me to squeeze the camera shutter, and I got a picture of the President as he was hit with the first shot" (7H493). As we saw in the Zapruder film itself, the President's sudden movement at Z224 and thereafter gives the first indication that a shot has been fired. In subsequent Zapruder frames we see Governor Connally turn sharply to his left, a movement he said he made just after the first shot. Officer B. J. Martin, riding the outboard cycle to the left rear of the presidential car, testified that he turned his head sharply to the right immediately following the first

Z222                                  SKETCH

Frames 222 and 230: Governor Connally turns to his left, a movement he said he made immediately after the first shot.

Z230                                  SKETCH

shot (6H291). At frame 230 he is still looking straight ahead. The evidence of both the Zapruder and Willis films points to a first shot fired in the range Z210–224 —a first shot that did not miss but struck the President in the back.

There is no evidence that a shot was fired prior to Z210. Yet for such a missed shot to have been fired from Oswald's rifle, it must have been fired no later than Z182 and, because of interference from the tree, probably before Z166. The conclusion follows that the shot to which the President is most visibly reacting at Z224 is the *first* shot. This is precisely what most witnesses believed at the time.[1]

The sound of the first shot led certain witnesses to believe that it had found its mark. Philip Willis gave the following description of the shooting to the FBI:

Z230                                    SKETCH

Policeman B. J. Martin (arrow) said he turned to his right after the first shot. At Z230 he is still looking straight ahead.

> *Willis advised that at just about the time that the limousine carrying President Kennedy was opposite the Stemmons Freeway road sign he heard a loud report and knew immediately it was a rifle shot and knew also the shot "had hit" . . . Willis says he knows from his war experience the sound a rifle shot makes when it finds its mark and he said he is sure all three shots fired found their mark* (Archives, *CD 1245*).

Garland Slack was standing on Houston Street several hundred feet from Willis when the shots were fired. He also concluded from their sound that they had found their mark:

> *I heard a report and I knew at once that it was a high-powered rifle shot. I am a big game hunter and am familiar with the sound of hi-powered rifles and I knew when I heard the retort* [sic] *that the shot had hit something (19H495; affidavit dated Nov. 22).*

This earwitness testimony is corroborated by the eyewitness reports of a host of different observers. Emmett Hudson "was looking directly at President Kennedy and saw his head slump to one side simultaneously with the loud report made by the first shot" (*Archives,* CD 5). Mary Moorman heard "three or four shots real close together" and noticed that "the first one hit him [the President]."[2] Mrs. Connally testified that she heard a shot, turned to her right, "and saw the President as he had both hands at his neck . . . then very soon there was the second shot that hit John" (4H147). Jean Newman recalled how the first shot had scared her as she stood at the Elm Street curb. She "noticed that the President jumped, he sort of ducked his head down . . . I saw him put his elbows like this, with his hands on his chest" (19H489). John Chism remembered that he "heard what sounded like one shot, and I saw him, 'The President,' sit back in his seat and lean his head to his left side" (19H471). Gayle Newman heard "a noise like a firecracker going off. President Kennedy kind of jumped like he was startled and covered his head with his hands and then raised up" (19H488). "He was leaning out waving," Kenneth O'Donnell testified. "He may have just been withdrawing his hand. And the shot hit him, and threw him to the left" (7H449). Sitting next to O'Donnell in the follow-up car, Dave Powers heard the first shot and "noticed then that the President moved quite far to his left after the shot from the extreme right hand side where he had been sitting" (7H473). Yet perhaps the most graphic description of the impact of the first shot was given to me by William Newman:

> *We were looking back up the street to see if the motorcade was coming and the first two shots were fired, and of course the first shot, boom, the President threw his arms up like that, spun around sort of . . . and then it looked like he was looking in the crowd, you know, like he was looking for something, just kind of a wild expression (Taped interview, Nov. 30, 1966).*

What all these witnesses seem to be describing is exactly what we see on film in Zapruder frames 224 ff. Kenneth O'Donnell saw the President waving just before he was hit; we see the President waving until he disappears behind the sign at Z207. O'Donnell and Powers saw the force of the shot move the President left from his sitting position on the extreme right-hand side of the seat; we see this movement occurring in Zapruder frames 230–270. Mrs. Connally and Jean Newman saw the President's hands and elbows raised after the first shot; we see this occurring in Zapruder frames 224–250. The first shot did not miss; it struck the President, and we observe him reacting to this wounding in Zapruder frames 224 ff. How much earlier than 224 the wounding should be placed must remain in some doubt.[3] The speed of the President's reaction seems to indicate that he was wounded not earlier than Z215. But the exact frame of impact must remain somewhat indefinite. The Commission stated the case fairly when it concluded that the President was hit for the first time between Z210 and Z225 (R105). Where it failed to state the case fairly was in neglecting the preponderance of evidence indicating that this was also the first shot fired.

## WHERE DID THE FIRST BULLET GO?

If we are persuaded that the first shot fired struck the President between Zapruder frames 210 and 224, then the obvious question arises: What happened to this bullet? Did it transit the President's body, as the Warren Commission claims, continuing on to wound the Governor, or did it lodge in the President's back? Upon the answer to this question hinges a crucial part of the Commission's case: the existence of a lone assassin. For if the Governor was hit by a separate bullet, the time factor involved necessitates a second gunman—the Governor was hit before the Carcano could have fired again. As Assistant Counsel Norman Redlich put it: "To say that they [Kennedy and Connally] were hit by separate bullets is synonymous with saying that there were two assassins."[4]

The President's reaction to his wounding (as we observe it in the Zapruder film) does not help us determine whether or not the bullet transited. Most accounts of this wounding describe the President as "clutching" his throat.[5] This has led to the speculation that in "clutching" his throat the President is reacting to a throat wound—to a laceration of his trachea. A close study of the Zapruder film, however, reveals that the President's fists are clenched and that the movement carries his hands up above his neck. Gayle Newman described how the President "covered his head with his hands" (19H488), and Marilyn Sitzman told me how "he put his hands up as to guard his face." These descriptions accurately characterize what we see on the Zapruder film: instead of clutching his throat, the President seems to be guarding his face with his clenched fist, his elbows elevated at either side. Such a movement seems as consistent with a shot lodged in his back as with a transiting shot: there is no science of the way a person reacts to a bullet hit.

The testimony of Secret Service Agent Roy Kellerman adds weight to the theory that the first bullet only lodged in the President's back. Seated in the right front seat of the presidential limousine, **Kellerman** heard Kennedy yell, "My God! I'm hit!" just after the first shot (2H73; 18H724). Since the projectile that caused the throat wound ripped his windpipe in passing, it seems unlikely that the President could have spoken *after* receiving the throat wound. Assistant Counsel Specter, aware of the threat Kellerman's testimony posed to his theory that a bullet pierced Kennedy's neck, pressed Kellerman on this point:

Special Agent Roy Kellerman with the President at Love Field, Dallas, November 22, 1963.

*Specter: With relationship to that first noise that you have described, when did you hear the voice?*
*Kellerman: His voice?*
*Specter: We will start with his voice.*
*Kellerman: OK. From the noise of which I was in the process of turning to determine where it was or what it was, it carried on right then. Why I am so positive, gentlemen, that it was his voice—there is only one man in that back seat that was from Boston, and the accents carried very clearly.*
*Specter: Well, had you become familiar with the President's voice prior to that day?*
*Kellerman: Yes; very much so.*
*Specter: And what was the basis for your becoming familiar with his voice prior to that day?*
*Kellerman: I had been with him for 3 years.*
*Specter: And had you talked with him on a very*

*frequent basis during the course of that as-*
*sociation?*

*Kellerman: He was a very free man to talk to; yes.*
*He knew most all the men, most everybody*
*who worked in the White House as well as*
*everywhere, and he would call you.*

*Specter: And from your experience would you say*
*that you could recognize the voice?*

*Kellerman: Very much, sir; I would (2H74-75).*

Despite Kellerman's certainty on this point, we must take into account that none of the passengers in the rear of the limousine heard the President's cry (4H134, 147; 5H180). In the absence of corroboration from other witnesses, Kellerman's testimony can be taken as significant but not as determinative.

## THE AUTOPSY

Most relevant to deciding a question of this sort is the medical evidence—in particular, the autopsy report on the President's body. The principal forensic reason for conducting such an autopsy was to establish the location and character of the victim's wounds. It was to obviate any such question as to whether or not a bullet transited that the autopsy was performed in the first place. It is ironic, then, that instead of answering this question the autopsy has made it the focus of sharp controversy.

On the morning of November 23 the Dallas FBI field office received a wire communicating the results of the autopsy performed at Bethesda Naval Hospital the night before. A document recently discovered in the National Archives reveals what those results were:

### RESULTS OF AUTOPSY ON
### JOHN F. KENNEDY

*On November 23, 1963 an autopsy was per-*
*formed on the body of former President John*
*F. Kennedy at the National Naval Medical*
*Center, Bethesda, Maryland. A total body*

*X-ray and autopsy revealed one bullet hole located just below shoulders to right of spinal column and hand-probing indicated trajectory at angle of 45-60 degrees downward and hole of short depth with no point of exit. No bullet located in body.*

*         *         *

*With respect to the bullet hole located in the back, pathologist at National Naval Medical Center was of the opinion this bullet worked its way out of the victim's back during cardiac massage performed at Dallas hospital prior to transportation of the body to Washington (Archives, CD 5).*

It seemed that the results of the autopsy were clear and that the issue had been decided: The President had been struck in the back by a bullet that penetrated only a short distance before it fell out during cardiac massage. The first shot, which struck the President at Z210–224, did not transit his body.

Yet the results of the autopsy did not remain clear for long. For at about the same time that the message reached the Dallas field office, the pathologist named in the message called the doctors at Parkland Memorial Hospital in Dallas. During the autopsy he had observed a surgical incision in the President's throat.

Dr. Malcolm Perry, who performed a tracheotomy on the President at Parkland Memorial Hospital in Dallas.

*I had the impression from seeing the wound [Commander James J. Humes later told the Commission] that it represented a surgical tracheotomy wound, a wound frequently made by surgeons when people are in respiratory distress to give them a free airway. To ascertain that point, I called on the telephone Dr. Malcolm Perry and discussed with him the situation of the President's neck when he first examined the President (2H361).*

What Dr. Perry told the Navy pathologist threw all the medical findings into turmoil. Unknown to the

Bethesda doctors, Perry had made his tracheotomy incision through an already existing throat wound. Perry told me in Dallas that when Humes heard about the wound he seemed taken aback for a moment and then exclaimed, "So that's it!"[6] What "that" was, was a new conclusion concerning the back wound that would be urged on the basis of a re-thinking of all the autopsy data. Thus it was that some forty-eight hours after the "Results of Autopsy on John F. Kennedy" were flashed over the FBI wire, results diametrically opposed were delivered to the White House physician, Admiral George C. Burkley. These results reflected a new inference on the part of the Bethesda doctors that the missile that had entered the President's back had exited through his throat.* On the basis of this revised autopsy report it seems that the bullet that struck the President's back at Z210–224 transited his body.

## THE BACK WOUND

This autopsy has become the center of intense controversy. Certain new facts concerning it have recently come to light and will be discussed in later chapters. But what concerns us here even more than the President's autopsy is the central question whether

---

* Humes's assistant, Commander J. Thornton Boswell, testified that the official autopsy report was "the culmination of our examination *and our subsequent conference*" (2H377; emphasis added). Assistant Counsel Specter pointed out in a *U.S. News & World Report* interview: "In fact, Dr. Humes had formulated a different conclusion, tentative as it might have been, when he had a chance to talk to Dr. Perry by telephone in Dallas. That was when he found that there had been a bullet hole on the front of the neck, before the tracheotomy was performed" (*U.S. News & World Report,* Oct. 10, 1966, p. 49). Boswell's and Specter's remarks accorded with what an FBI spokesman told Fletcher Knebel of *Look,* namely, that the FBI's "initial reports did not reflect *the doctor's decision*" (*Look,* July 12, 1966, p. 71; emphasis added). Nevertheless, the Warren *Report* falsely asserts that the change resulted from "further exploration *during the autopsy*" (R88, emphasis added).

or not his body was transited by a bullet. Of direct relevance are the character and the location of the President's back wound.

In addition to the medical personnel attending the President's body, representatives of the Secret Service and FBI were also present. They were there to observe the autopsy from a forensic standpoint, to receive any bullet that might be recovered, and to report to their respective agencies on the conclusions reached. The two FBI agents, James F. Sibert and Francis X. O'Neill, submitted a five-page, single-spaced report on their evening at Bethesda. In this document—a document that would constitute an essential element in the investigation already under way—Sibert and O'Neill wrote:

### AUTOPSY OF BODY OF PRESIDENT JOHN FITZGERALD KENNEDY

*During the latter stages of this autopsy, Dr. Humes located an opening which appeared to be a bullet hole which was below the shoulders and two inches to the right of the middle line of the spinal column.*

*This opening was probed by Dr. Humes with the finger, at which time it was determined that the trajectory of the missile entering at this point had entered at a downward position of 45 to 60 degrees. Further probing determined that the distance traveled by this missile was a short distance inasmuch as the end of the opening could be felt with the finger* (Archives, *CD 7*).

I asked Commander Humes's assistant, Commander J. Thornton Boswell, about Humes's inserting his finger in the President's back wound and feeling its end. Boswell told me that this was correct and that, in fact, all three doctors had probed this wound with their fingers up to the first or second knuckle—a penetration of 1 to 2 inches.[7] Boswell also indicated that the back wound had been examined with a metal probe—a thin piece of stiff wire some 8 inches long with a knob on the end.[8] Secret Service Agent Roy Kellerman gave this description of the doctors' exploration of the wound with such a metal probe:

> *There were three gentlemen who were performing the autopsy. A Colonel Finck—during the examination of the President, from the hole that was in his shoulder, and with a probe, and we were standing right alongside of him, he is probing inside the shoulder with his instrument and I said, "Colonel, where did it go?" He said, "There are no lanes for an outlet of this entry in this man's shoulder"* (2H93).*

Kellerman's partner, Special Agent William Greer, was also in the autopsy room, and was later asked by Assistant Counsel Specter: "Was anything said about any channel being present in the body for the bullet to have gone on through the back?" Greer replied: "No, sir; I haven't heard anything like that, any trace of it going on through" (2H127). Sibert and O'Neill further reported that, since no bullet had been found in the back, "the individuals performing the autopsy were at a loss to explain why they could find no bullets" (*Archives,* CD 7).

During the autopsy news reached Bethesda that a 6.5-millimeter bullet had been found on a stretcher in Parkland Hospital.

---

* Recently, I asked Dr. Cyril Wecht whether a probe of this size might be expected to fall along the course of a bullet. He told me: "Generally with a bullet of that size, it's been my experience that a very narrow caliber probe can follow through along the course of the bullet. With a bullet of this size it would seem to me that the probe should have been able to go through the track.

"The bigger the bullet the more discernible the track. Sometimes a little .22 caliber can be a real pain in the neck. But this was a 6.5 mm.—¼ of an inch—that is a pretty good-sized bullet" (Wecht interview, May 26, 1967).

Commission Exhibit 399: The bullet found on the stretcher
at Parkland Hospital.

*Immediately following receipt of this infor-*
*mation [Sibert and O'Neill continued], this*
*was made available to Dr. Humes who ad-*
*vised that in his opinion this accounted for*
*no bullet being located which had entered*
*the back region and that since external car-*
*diac massage had been performed at Park-*
*land Hospital, it was entirely possible that*
*through such movement the bullet had*
*worked its way back out of the point of entry*
*and had fallen on the stretcher* (Archives,
*CD 7*).\*

\* Confronted with a discrepancy between the official autopsy
report and the report of FBI agents Sibert and O'Neill,
Assistant Counsel Specter questioned the two agents on
March 12, 1964. Not only did they stick by their account of
the autopsy, but even reinforced it, pointing out that it was
the opinion of both Commander Humes and Lieutenant
Colonel Pierre Finck that the bullet might have been
forced out. The following citation is from Specter's account
of that meeting, only recently discovered in the Archives.
"On March 12, 1964, I interviewed Special Agents
Francis X. O'Neill and James W. Sibert in my office from
approximately 10:00 a.m. to 10:45 a.m.
"SA O'Neill and SA Sibert advised that the autopsy surgeons made substantial efforts to determine if there was a
missile in President Kennedy's body to explain what happened to the bullet which apparently entered the back of
his body. They stated that the opinion was expressed by
both Commander Humes and Lt. Col. Finck that the bullet
might have been forced out of the back of the President's
body upon application of external heart massage. They
stated that this theory was advanced after SA Sibert called
the FBI laboratory and talked to SA Killion who advised
that a bullet had been found on a stretcher in Parkland
Hospital. SA Sibert relayed that information to the doctors
(*Archives*, Presidential Commission Administrative Records,
J. Lee Rankin: December, 1963–March 1964).

Commander Humes apparently expressed such confidence in this explanation that Sibert and O'Neill
could couch the autopsy conclusions in these words:

> *Dr. Humes stated that the pattern was clear,*
> *that the one bullet had entered the Presi-*
> *dent's back and worked its way out of the*
> *body during external cardiac massage and*
> *that a second high velocity bullet had entered*
> *the rear of the skull and had fragmentized*
> *prior to exit through the top of the skull. He*
> *further pointed out that X-rays had disclosed*
> *numerous fractures in the cranial area which*
> *he attributed to the force generated by the*
> *impact of the bullet in its passage through the*
> *brain area. He attributed the death of the*
> *President to a gunshot wound of the head*
> (Archives, *CD 7*).

With respect to this back wound the official autopsy report notes that "the missile path through the
fascia and musculature cannot be easily probed"
(16H981). The evidence adduced above indicates
that this admission is something less than the truth—
that in fact the wound could not be probed at all!

Various explanations have been offered to account
for the failure of the doctors' probing efforts. The *Report* itself suggests that "the bullet had passed between two large strap muscles and bruised them without leaving any channel, since the bullet merely
passed between them" (R88). Jacob Cohen, speaking in defense of the *Report,* has advanced a more
ingenious explanation.[9] Since (argues Cohen) the
Zapruder film shows Kennedy waving when he was
hit, and since he was examined in a relaxed, supine
position, it is quite possible that the relaxation of the
shoulder muscles closed off the missile channel.

However, neither the official explanation nor the
Cohen addendum accounts for the essential fact that
emerged during the autopsy: that a missile channel
*was* discovered in the back, that it penetrated 1 to
2 inches, and that "the end of the opening could be

felt with the finger." Cohen's relaxation hypothesis cannot explain why the muscles immediately under the skin to a depth of 1 to 2 inches did not relax, while deeper muscles did. Nor does the relaxation hypothesis make sense on other grounds. Dr. Milton Helpern has indicated that "it is a *sine qua non* of forensic pathology that if a bullet passes through a body, it must leave a discernible path."[10] The idea that a relaxation of muscles would hide such a path is preposterous: this, at least, is the judgment of Dr. Cyril Wecht, who told me that the Cohen hypothesis is "medical nonsense."[11] Equally nonsensical is the idea that a bullet would make a channel for 1 to 2 inches and then "pass between two large strap muscles . . . without leaving any channel." In discussing this case Dr. Helpern remarked, "There is no such thing as a rifle bullet's passing through a neck without leaving a path."[12] He estimated that a 6.5-millimeter bullet would leave a track 1/4 inch in diameter.[13] The evidence cited above indicates that no such track was ever found.

If the *character* of the President's back wound suggests that the bullet did not transit, its *location* is also relevant. Secret Service Agent Glen Bennett was riding behind the President in the follow-up car. In a handwritten report jotted down on Air Force One as the presidential party flew back to Washington, Bennett noted: "I saw a shot hit the Boss about 4 inches down from the right shoulder" (24H542). Sibert and O'Neill, we recall, placed the back wound "below the shoulders and two inches to the right of the middle line of the spinal column." Greer and Kellerman placed it respectively "in the soft part of the shoulder" (Greer: 2H127) and just below "that large muscle between the shoulder and the neck" (Kellerman: 2H81). When the autopsy had been completed, Kellerman summoned another Secret Service agent, Clint Hill, to view the President's wounds. Hill later testified that he "observed a wound about six inches down from the neckline on the back just to the right of the spinal column" (18H744; 2H143). All these descriptions of the back wound's location match

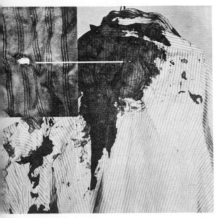

Bullet holes in the back of the President's clothing are consistent with testimony given by Secret Service and FBI agents present at autopsy.

perfectly with bullet holes discovered in the President's clothing.* According to measurements performed by the FBI's Robert Frazier, the hole through the President's jacket was found to lie 5⅜ inches (shirt: 5¾ inches) below the top of the collar and 1¾ inches (shirt: 1⅞ inches) to the right of the midline (5H59–60).

The curious thing about all these descriptions of the back wound is that they specify a location on the back actually *below* the supposed exit wound in the front of the throat. If one connects the two points they yield an upward trajectory from back to front. Yet a bullet fired from the sixth-floor window of the Depository in the interval Z210–224 would have entered the President's back on a *downward* trajectory of 17 degrees (5H160; 18H89–90).

The relationship of the two wounds becomes apparent if we consult the autopsy face sheet prepared by Commander Boswell while the autopsy was in progress. On this sheet are outlined front and back views of a human body. In the lower third of the throat we see sketched a 6.5-millimeter surgical incision. On the back we find a round hole sketched in at the same location defined both by witness reports and by the holes in the President's clothing. The hole in the President's back appears appreciably *lower* than the incision in the throat.

When the press first pointed this fact out to Commander Boswell, he replied that the sketch was only meant to mark a rough location and that he had mistakenly placed the back wound too low. The doctor's answer may prove to be the correct explanation; the release of the autopsy pictures may show

---

* Defenders of the *Report* have tried to rebut the very strong evidence of the clothing holes by suggesting that the President's coat and shirt may have been bunched at the moment of impact, thus causing the appearance of a lower hit than was in fact the case. A close study of Willis Slide 5 (supposedly taken simultaneously with the first shot) disproves this hypothesis; the President's clothing is most assuredly *not* bunched at the time of the first shot.

For a fuller discussion of this point together with the relevant photo evidence, see Chap. X.

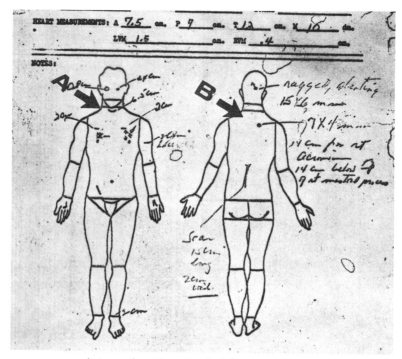

Autopsy face sheet marked by Commander Boswell during autopsy. Hole in back (arrow B) appears lower than the alleged exit in throat (arrow A).

FBI agents reenact assassination. According to the Warren *Report*, "The back of the stand-in for the President was marked with chalk at the point where the bullet entered. The Governor's model had on the same coat worn by Governor Connally when he was shot with the hole in the back circled in chalk" (R97).

this. But at this time two points should be made: (1) If the doctor made a mistake in mislocating the back wound, then this is the *only* mistake on the diagram —all the other wounds are placed in their proper positions. (2) It is curious that the doctor's "mislocation" of the back wound lines up perfectly with the spot defined by the holes in the President's clothing and by the observations of every other person who saw the body. It is a coincidence of the strangest sort that Commander Boswell should misplace only this wound, and that his mistake should align perfectly with the location defined by all the other evidence.

What are we to make of all this evidence concerning the location and character of the President's back wound?

The exact location of the wound cannot now be conclusively determined. If it turns out to be located where Commander Boswell placed it on the face

sheet, the throat wound will be ruled out as a consequence of the first shot. But even if the autopsy
photos show a location somewhat higher, the issue
will not yet be decided in the Commission's favor.
For wherever the wound is finally located we know
now that it was the military physicians' judgment on
the night of the assassination that the bullet did not
transit. They made this judgment on the basis of a
physical examination of the wound itself: "the end
of the opening could be felt with the finger." Hence
it is the character of the wound and not its location
that remains the crucial factor.

It might be argued that the character of this wound
is not fully known. It was explored with fingers and
metal probes, but it was not dissected. Here is an essential problem that no number of autopsy photos
and X-rays can clear up. Among forensic specialists
it is known that the only ultimately conclusive way
to trace the course of a bullet is to dissect the tissue
along its path.[14] Probes may go askew and fingers
misfeel, but dissection of the area involved will reveal to the naked eye the course of the bullet. Such
dissection is laborious and painstaking; it takes time.
And time, it seems, was not what the autopsy surgeons
had in abundance on November 22. Yet without such
dissection, the character of the President's back wound
must remain forever in doubt. The photos and X-rays
now sequestered in the National Archives cannot
help us much—bullet paths through flesh do not show
up on X-rays. And decomposition has already made
exhumation impractical. We are left with the evidence
now at hand, however unsatisfactory it may be.

The path of the bullet from back to front was *inferred,* not *observed.* It was inferred after the fact,
and its significance was to extricate the military doctors from the embarrassment of having to admit that
the President's body had passed through their hands
without their ever having recognized one of his
wounds as a bullet wound. Three years after the
event one fact emerges from the evidence: No single
physician ever knowingly examined *all* of the President's wounds—the Parkland doctors because they

never realized the back wound existed, the Bethesda doctors because they never recognized the tracheotomy incision as a bullet wound. The doctors' inference was drawn out of logical necessity—the throat wound existed; it had to be accounted for. On November 23 and 24 only partial information was available to the autopsy surgeons. Since that time additional facts have come to light that validate an alternative explanation of the throat wound.

## THE THROAT WOUND

Various descriptions of the small hole in the President's throat were given at Parkland Hospital by the doctors who saw it before a tracheotomy incision erased its outline. While some described its periphery as smooth and regular (6H3, 9, 54; 3H372) and others remembered it as jagged (6H32, 48, 65, 141), all seemed to agree on the size of the hole. It was small—so small, in fact, that one doctor believed it was too small to be even the *entry* hole of a high velocity bullet (6H56). Dr. Perry described it over the phone to Commander Humes as between 3 and 5 millimeters in diameter (17H29). This is half the diameter of an ordinary pencil, much too small to be the exit wound of a transiting bullet.*

That a transiting bullet could not have caused such an extremely small wound is further attested to by an experiment performed for the Commission by Dr. Alfred G. Olivier of the Army's Edgewood Arsenal. In order to simulate the passage of a bullet

Notes made by Commander Humes at Bethesda Hospital during telephone conversation with Dr. Malcolm Perry in Dallas. Size of throat wound given as "3 to 5 millimeters."

---

* I recently asked Dr. Wecht whether a hole of this diameter could be the possible exit hole of a 6.5-millimeter projectile. He replied: "Again very, very unlikely. There are atypical entrance and exit wounds. But again with this kind of bullet, and with the kind of entrance described and the course of the bullet postulated and then subsequently adopted in the Commission *Report,* I find a 3–5 mm. wound in the neck as described by surgeons at Parkland Hospital, I find that very, very hard to buy as an exit wound for a bullet which would have entered in the back. Very hard. Again something which I would not buy were I doing an autopsy" (Wecht interview, May 26, 1967).

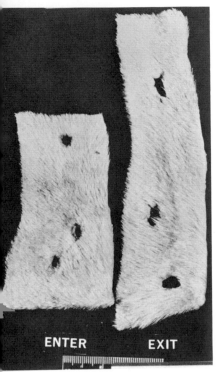

ENTER   EXIT

Commission Exhibit 850: Goat-skins used in ballistic test to simulate President's neck wounds. Note exit holes are at least twice the size of entry holes.

FBI Exhibit 60: Slit in the front of President's shirt and nick in tie showed no evidence of metallic traces.

through the President's neck, Dr. Olivier clipped 14 centimeters of goat meat between two goat skins, pinned shirt and jacket cloth over one side of the package, and then fired three 6.5-millimeter bullets through it (5H77–78). Although the entry holes are the same size as the entry wound in the President's back, the exit holes are at least twice the size of the President's throat wound. While the long diameter of the President's throat wound was given by Dr. Perry as "3 to 5 mm," the smallest exit hole obtained in Dr. Olivier's experiment was 10 millimeters (see illustration). If the experiment proves anything, it is that the autopsy explanation of Kennedy's throat wound is invalid. Apparently, the hole was too small to have been the exit wound of a whole bullet. And there is further evidence suggesting that the wound may not even have been caused by any part of a bullet.

Special Agent Robert Frazier examined the President's shirt at the FBI laboratory. In the upper back he found a small hole, ¼ inch in diameter, the fibers pushed inward around the periphery, and on these fibers traces of copper (5H60, 62). But on the shirt front, just under the collar button, he found a ½-inch vertical slit without any metallic residue whatsoever (5H59–60). Nor could Frazier find any metallic residue on a small nick in the President's tie. Frazier was very guarded in his testimony about this (5H62): "I could not actually determine from the characteristics of the hole whether or not it was caused by a bullet. However, I can say that it was caused by a projectile of some type which exited from the shirt at this point" (5H61). Earlier he had cautioned the Commission: "It is an irregular slit . . . that is not specifically characteristic of a bullet hole to the extent that you could say it was to the exclusion of being a piece of bone or some other type of projectile" (5H61).

Frazier's suggestion that the throat wound might have been caused by a fragment (possibly bone) had already been made by one of the Parkland doctors who helped Perry make his tracheotomy inci-

Damage to the President's throat as described by Parkland doctors

**A.** *Dr. Malcolm Perry:* "I noticed a small ragged laceration of the trachea on the anterior lateral right side" (3H370).

**B.** *Dr. Malcolm Perry:* "In the lower part of the neck below the Adam's apple was a small, roughly circular wound of perhaps 5 mm. in diameter from which blood was exuding slowly" (3H368).

**C.** *Dr. Charles F. Baxter:* "There was considerable contusion of the muscles of the anterior neck and a moderate amount of bleeding around the trachea" (6H42).

*Dr. Robert N. McClelland:* "That damage consisted mainly of a large amount of contusion and hematoma formation in the tissue lateral to the right side of the trachea and the swelling and bleeding around the site was to such an extent that the trachea was somewhat deviated to the left side" (6H33).

**D.** *Dr. Don T. Curtis:* "The President's head was extended or hyperextended and I noticed that in the suprasternal notch there was a mass that looked like a hematoma to me, or a blood clot in the tissues...I think it was 5 cm. in size" (6H60).

**E.** *Dr. Charles J. Carrico:* "In inserting the endotracheal tube, a larynzo scope was inserted and it was noted that there was some discoloration at the lateral edge of the larynx and there appeared to be some swelling and hematoma" (6H6).

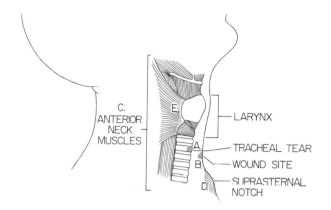

sion. Only three hours after the assassination, Dr. Robert N. McClelland had written an "admission note" in which he had remarked: "The President was at this time comatose from a massive gunshot wound of the head with a fragment wound of the trachea" (R526). As another Parkland doctor pointed out in his testimony, the idea of such a fragment driven downward and out the throat by the head impact had been discussed at Parkland Hospital on that Friday afternoon (6H5).

When we consider the testimony of the Parkland doctors we can come to understand why such an explanation seems plausible.* All of them agreed on the nature of the damage to the President's neck. None of them believed it to be an exit wound from a whole bullet. Without exception, their testimony described a vertical channel of contusion (bruise), laceration, and hematoma (swelling filled with blood) stretching above and below the tiny exit hole. The

---

* This same hypothesis was put forward by various government spokesmen in December, 1963. Citing governmental sources, *Newsweek* (Dec. 30, 1963), *Time* (Dec. 27, 1963), and the Washington *Post* (Dec. 18, 1963) all carried stories asserting that the autopsy had produced evidence that a fragment from the second bullet (the head shot) had been deflected downward and had passed out through the throat. *The Journal of the American Medical Association* (Jan. 4, 1964) reported that "a small fragment of this bullet [the head shot] angled down and passed out through Kennedy's throat."

hole itself was located an inch and a half below the larynx (Adam's apple) (3H370; 6H42). Immediately behind the hole was a ragged tear of the right front windpipe (3H370; 6H42). Both above and below this tear was a region of contusion and hematoma stretching from the larynx to below the suprasternal notch (6H11, 33, 42, 60). This channel stretched at least 4 to 6 inches up and down the President's neck. Such a channel, of course, lies at right angles to the trajectory of a bullet passing horizontally through the neck. It is consistent not with the first shot to Kennedy's back but with the later head shot, as we shall see presently.

None of the medical testimony from Parkland Hospital was available to the autopsy surgeons when they decided that the throat wound had been caused by the exit of a whole bullet traveling horizontally. One can search the official autopsy report in vain for any mention of what Dr. James Carrico had described in Dallas as "some contusions and hematoma to the right of the larynx, with a minimal deviation of the larynx to the left" (3H360). A reading of the official report makes it quite apparent that almost all the information concerning the throat injury was gleaned from the phone conversation with Dr. Perry (16H979, 981). As far as the throat wound is concerned, autopsy surgeon Humes testified that he "had the impression from seeing the wound that it represented a surgical tracheotomy" (2H361). Thus the neck area was never fully dissected and the fact that it might have been a bone or bullet fragment wound went unconsidered. Yet in addition to this neck injury, there was other damage discovered by the autopsy surgeons themselves that lent credence to the idea of a fragment exit in the throat. Unfortunately, this damage was discovered by them only *after* they had submitted their official report.

During the autopsy, the President's brain was removed and placed in a formalin solution for later examination. Long after the official autopsy report had been delivered to Admiral Burkley, an examination of the brain turned up one rather startling fact.

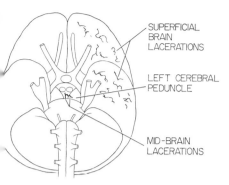

SUPERFICIAL BRAIN LACERATIONS

LEFT CEREBRAL PEDUNCLE

MID-BRAIN LACERATIONS

BASILAR ASPECT OF BRAIN

The location of two lacerations deep and low in the President's brain suggest a possible downward trajectory of a fragment or fragments.

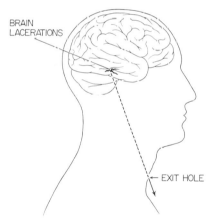

BRAIN LACERATIONS

← EXIT HOLE

Possible path of fragments from head impact out throat.

Deep in the brain at the level of the midbrain and the left cerebral peduncle were found two rather sizable, communicating lacerations (see diagram).[15] It is possible to pass a line through these lacerations from a point on the right rear of the skull that will also pass through and out of the lower throat (see diagram). If we suppose that a bullet (or more likely a bone) fragment was driven downward on a slight right-to-left trajectory through the midbrain, we have a hypothesis that accords with all the known facts surrounding the throat wound. Such a hypothesis postulates the downward passage of a fragment through the midbrain, contusing the larynx before tearing the windpipe, and exiting the body through a vertical slit in the shirt. Other fragments could have continued parallel to the windpipe, bruising the strap muscles of the throat and contusing the superior mediastinum and the apex of the right pleura. Such a hypothesis would explain the total pattern of neck and thoracic injuries we know about. The sharp, downward trajectory would explain why the slit in the shirt is twice the length of the skin wound, and the slight right-to-left course would explain the cut on the right front side of the windpipe and the nick on the left side of the tie knot. The absence of copper traces on the shirt fibers would indicate that bone (not metal) fragments did the major work of disruption.

If the throat wound can thus be attributed to the "head shot," then it is quite easy to see that the first bullet is not required to do all the Commission said it did. It need only have struck the President in the back, penetrating less than 2 inches and falling out during cardiac massage. This is what the autopsy surgeons had originally determined. It was the discovery of the throat wound that prompted them to rethink the problem and come up with the back-to-front transit. But once the facts about the throat wound are known, the necessity for the transiting bullet disappears. True, a well-defined path downward through the brain has not been found, but neither, it should be pointed out, was the Commission able to find a back-to-front path through President Kennedy's neck. Both are inferred paths. Yet the one developed above deals more adequately with *all* the facts now known to surround the President's throat wound: its small size, the 4- to 6-inch vertical injury immediately behind it, the right *front* placement of the tracheal tear, the slit in the shirt and the nick on the tie (both lacking metal traces), the lacerations in the midbrain. The hypothesis sketched above more adequately explains this total fabric of evidence. It would be interesting to know whether, on the basis of these new considerations, Commander Humes and his colleagues might be willing to rethink their conclusions—once again.

## THE FIRST SHOT AND THE EVIDENCE

All of the Warren Commission's difficulty with the first shot stems from its prejudice in favor of the "single-bullet" theory. This is the only reckoning that permits a lone assassin, but it places arduous demands on the sequence of events in Dealey Plaza. One of the bullets had to pass through Kennedy and go on to hit Connally, and another had to miss the car completely. The Commission felt it might have been the first shot that missed. But as we have seen, the combined evidence of film, eyewitness testimony, and the minimum firing time of the murder rifle makes clear that if any shot missed, it could not have been the first. As for this bullet passing through Kennedy's neck, there is autopsy evidence to the contrary that the Commission ignored, and a variant hypothesis, offered above, that makes plausible a different explanation of the wound in Kennedy's throat.

The first shot, then, was the first hit. And the bullet, according to the best evidence available, lodged in the President's back. If this interpretation of the first shot is to be accepted, then, in contradiction to the Warren *Report,* it is automatically proved that neither of the other shots missed: one had to strike Connally and the other cause the President's head wound. Indeed, we shall find that this is the most reasonable explanation of what happened.

## NOTES

1. Of several hundred witnesses present in Dealey Plaza just two gave evidence indicating that the first shot missed.

Mrs. Donald Sam Baker (née Virgie Rackley) was standing on the pavement in front of the Depository. She later told a Commission lawyer that she heard a "firecracker" noise and saw something hit the pavement behind the presidential auto (7H509–510). She also remarked that when this first shot was fired the car had gone down Elm Street partially out of sight and was "near the signs" (7H509). This places it in the range Z210–224. Moreover, Mrs. Baker's deposition before Counsel Liebeler did not agree with what she had told the FBI earlier. A March 19 statement she gave the FBI contains no mention of something hitting the pavement (22H635–636), while an earlier interrogation report notes that she saw something hit the pavement *in front of* the presidential car (*Archives,* CD 5).

The report of Secret Service agent Glen Bennett seems to have more substance to it. Bennett stated: "the President's auto moved down a slight grade and the crowd was very sparse. At this point I heard a noise that immediately reminded me of a firecracker. I immediately, upon hearing the supposed firecracker, looked at the Boss's car. At this exact time I saw a shot that hit the Boss about 4 inches down from the right shoulder" (24H542).

In discussing Agent Bennett's report the Commission notes that "it is possible, of course, that Bennett did not observe the hole in the President's back, which might have been there immediately after the first noise" (R111). This is a plausible explanation, especially in light of other evidence that indicates that Governor Connally was hit by a second shot about a second after the first hit the President: Bennett might have confused the President's reaction with the second shot. Still, his testimony is troubling. It validates the dictum that in this case unanimity among witnesses is a very rare commodity.

2. WFAA-TV video tape for the afternoon of Nov. 22; Tape PKT-24, at 21 minutes, 8 seconds into the tape.

3. Professor Alexander Bickel of the Yale Law School has advanced the interesting thesis that the President was wounded by a shot through a small hole in the foliage at Z186.

The Commission itself explored this idea and rejected it, I believe, with sound reason. The following considerations militate against this thesis:

(1) No witness recalled a shot that early; many, many witnesses placed the first shot in the interval Z210–224.

(2) Many witnesses recalled a virtually instantaneous reaction of the President to being hit by the first shot. This thesis requires that the President continued smiling and waving to the crowds for at least twenty-one Zapruder frames after he was shot.

View of the President from the sixth-floor window was blocked during the 2.4 second interval from Zapruder frames 166 to 210. At one point (Z186) a small hole in the tree permitted a view of the car for one-sixth of a second.

Frame 166: view through rifle scope.

Frame 186: view through rifle scope.

Frame 210: view through rifle scope.

(3) The size of the tree opening (see illustration) gave the gunman no time to aim at his moving target. As the Commission concluded: "It is doubtful that even the most proficient marksman would have hit him [the President] through the oak tree (R105).

(4) There seems to be no motivation for such a shot. To quote the Commission: "It is unlikely that the assassin would deliberately have shot at him with a view obstructed by the oak tree when he was about to have a clear opportunity" (R98).

4. Told to Edward Jay Epstein and cited in his book *Inquest* (New York: The Viking Press, Inc., 1966), p. 43.

5. A recent issue of *Life,* for example, captions Zapruder frame 230: "Kennedy clutches his throat. Connally says he still felt nothing" (*Life,* Nov. 25, 1966, p. 45).

6. Perry interview, Nov. 3, 1966.

7. Boswell interview, Jan. 11, 1967.

8. *Ibid.*

9. Cohen advanced this hypothesis on a WNEW-TV (New York) program screened on Nov. 12, 1966. His remarks concerning it can be found on p. 106 of the transcript of that broadcast disseminated by WNEW-TV.

10. Cited by Epstein, *op cit.,* p. 58.

11. Conference with Dr. Wecht at *Life* magazine, December, 1966.

12. Epstein, *op. cit.,* p. 58.

13. *Ibid.*

14. Conference with Dr. Wecht at *Life* magazine, December, 1966.

15. "When viewed from the basilar aspect the disruption of the right cortex is again obvious. There is a longitudinal laceration of the mid-brain through the floor of the left ventricle just behind the optic chiasm and the mammillary bodies. This laceration partially communicates with an oblique 1.5 cm tear through the left cerebral peduncle" (16H987).

# IV

## THE SECOND SHOT

*Mr. Howlett [Secret Service Agent J. J. Howlett] stated that Secret Service agents, using the 8 mm film [the Zapruder film] had been unable to ascertain the exact location where Governor John B. Connally was struck.*

*S.A. Howlett advised that it had been ascertained from the movies that President Kennedy was struck with the first and third shots fired by the assassin, while Governor Connally was struck with the second shot.*
*—FBI report dated Nov. 29, 1963, emphasis added; Archives, CD 5.*

IF Assistant Counsel Arlen Specter is right (and the FBI report quoted above wrong), President Kennedy and Governor Connally were hit at the same instant by a bullet traveling at twice the speed of sound. According to Specter, this bullet—one of three fired that day—passed through the President's neck, continuing on to strike the Governor in the back.

The validity of this "single-bullet" theory depends on all three of its major contingencies: that one of the shots missed, that a bullet transited Kennedy's neck, and that Kennedy and Connally were hit almost simultaneously by the same bullet. The first two of these contingencies were called into question in the previous chapter. As we saw, a survey of photographic evidence and eyewitness reports indicates that the first shot did not miss but hit Kennedy in the back. Second, FBI autopsy reports (ignored by the Commission), together with new interpretations of the medical evidence, strongly suggest that the first shot did not go all the way through, and that the wound in the throat was caused by a fragment from a later shot.

Given the conclusion that the first shot hit but did not pass through Kennedy, the third contingency—that he and Connally were struck by the same bullet—becomes logically impossible. There is, however, evidence in addition to that contained in the previous chapter proving that it was the *second* shot that hit Connally. This evidence, much of it either ignored or glossed over by the Commission, includes firsthand reports of eyewitnesses, press reports, secret official documents, photographs, and statements by Connally and his doctors.

## THE EYEWITNESSES

In late November, 1966, Edward Kern and I interviewed S. M. Holland, whose position on the railroad overpass provided a bird's-eye view of the shooting on Elm Street. I particularly wanted to learn whether he felt any shots had missed the car, or if none had, which shots had hit the President and which the Governor:

*Thompson: I'd like to ask your opinion as to whether either . . . any of these bullets, any of these three or four shots missed, and if so, which one; and if not, well, which bullets hit whom?*
*Holland: The first shot, as I said, the first report that I heard, the President slumped over, similar to that, and his hands went up to his neck.*

Witness S. M. Holland (arrow) on bridge shortly after shooting.

Holland's view. Photographed by S. M. Holland on the morning of November 23.

*Thompson: So you correlate the President's movement with the first shot?*

*Holland: And the Governor turned this . . . to his right, similar to this; then he turned like that, and that's when the Governor was shot. . . . And I made the statement immediately after the assassination to the Warren Commission that he did turn to his right and his left and he was shot and hit by the second bullet. He definitely was not hit by the first shot.*

*Thompson: So you believe the Governor was hit by the second shot?*

*Holland: I* know *the Governor was hit by the second shot.*

*Kern: You saw the Governor hit by the second shot?*

*Holland: I'm positive of that (Taped interview, Nov. 30, 1966).*

What Holland saw was echoed in the statements of many other witnesses in Dealey Plaza. Not one of these several hundred witnesses saw the assassination as the Warren Commission believed it happened; not one believed that a single bullet wounded both the President and the Governor, or even that they were hit at the same time by different bullets. Nor did any of these witnesses believe the second shot missed.* Yet it is clear that if the second shot did not miss, since the President was hit by the first shot and no bullet impacts were found in the car, the second shot must have hit the Governor. This is precisely what the witnesses on the scene thought had happened.

Jean Hill believed the second shot hit the Governor. She was standing with her friend Mary Moorman

* This statement needs qualification only by calling attention to the affidavit of Royce G. Skelton. Standing on the overpass, he "heard something which I thought was fireworks," and then "saw something hit the pavement at the left rear of the car" (19H496). From Skelton's remarks it is unclear whether this "something" hit the pavement after the first or the second shot. Furthermore, it should be pointed out that no one else on the overpass saw what Skelton claimed to have seen, and the Warren *Report* disclosed that examination of the area showed no indication of a bullet strike (R116).

on the grass to the south of Elm Street and had an unobstructed view of the presidential car as it swept past her. She heard some shots, saw the President move, and then saw Governor Connally fall. In March, 1964, she was questioned by Assistant Counsel Specter:

*Specter: And when in point of time did you see him [Governor Connally] fall?*

*Mrs. Hill: After the President was shot, but I wouldn't —it wasn't with the first shot. To me he wasn't hit when the first shot hit.*

*Specter: And what is the basis for your saying that, Mrs. Hill?*

*Mrs. Hill: Well, I just think he was hit after Kennedy was hit because, well just the way that it looked, I would say that he was hit later.*

*Specter: Now, do you associate the time that Governor Connally appeared to have been hit with any specific shot that you heard?*

*Mrs. Hill: The second.*

*Specter: And what specifically did you observe at the time of the second shot?*

*Mrs. Hill: Well, that's what I thought had happened —that they had hit someone in the front part of the car (6H209).*

What Jean Hill "thought had happened" was precisely what the Governor's wife was very certain had happened. She later told the Commission:

> I heard a noise, and not being an expert rifleman, I was not aware that it was a rifle. It was just a frightening noise, and it came from the right.
>
> I turned over my right shoulder and looked back and saw, and saw the President as he had both hands at his neck . . .
>
> Then very soon there was the second shot that hit John. As the first shot was hit, and I turned to look at the same time, I recall John saying, "Oh, no, no, no." Then there was a second shot and it hit John, and as he re-

Jean Hill (right) and Mary Moorman (left) during the assassination.

*coiled to the right, just crumpled like a wounded animal to the right, he said, "My God, they are going to kill us all" (4H147).*

Dave Powers could not see the Governor clearly from his position in the back seat of the presidential follow-up car and he did not see Connally struck. Nevertheless, he did recall that "there was a second shot and Governor Connally disappeared from sight" (7H473). Linda Kay Willis likewise saw the first and third shots hit the President but "couldn't tell where the second shot went" (7H498). When in November, 1966, I asked Linda Kay where the second shot went, she told me that she and her whole family (all present in Dealey Plaza that day) had believed from November 22 on that Governor Connally had been wounded by the second shot.[1] What they saw was essentially what Gayle Newman reported in her affidavit of November 22: "After I heard the first shot, another shot sounded and Governor Connally kind of grabbed his chest and lay back on the seat of the car" (19H488).*

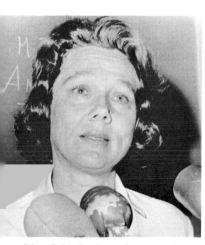

Mrs. John B. Connally at Parkland Hospital after the assassination.

The witnesses' unanimity on this point was expressed both in newspaper accounts and official reports. On November 24 *The New York Times* reported that after President Kennedy was hit by the first bullet, "the Governor turned to see what had happened when he was struck in the back by another bullet." This remained the orthodox account in the press right up to the time the Warren *Report* with its controversial "single-bullet theory" made its debut. That the Warren *Report* and the press should be at variance on this point is not necessarily disturbing, but for the Warren *Report* to be contradicted by key *official* documents is upsetting indeed. In the first Secret Service report, mentioned nowhere in the Warren *Report* or its volumes, we find the following:

---

* There is also earwitness testimony indicating the second shot hit. Garland Slack reported: "Within a few seconds I heard another report [after the first] and knew it also had hit something" (19H495). Phil Willis told the FBI: "About two seconds later [after the first shot], he heard another rifle shot which also hit as did the third shot which came approximately two seconds later" (*Archives*, CD 1245).

PRELIMINARY SPECIAL DALLAS
REPORT NO. 1, ASSASSINATION OF
THE PRESIDENT

*At the foot of Elm Street, at a point approxi-
mately 200 feet east of the Houston Street
Triple Underpass, on the approach to the
Stemmons Freeway, President Kennedy, who
was seated on the right rear seat, was shot.
Immediately thereafter Governor Connally,
seated in the right jump seat, was shot once.
The President was then shot the second time*
(Archives, *CD 87, dated Nov. 28*).

The Secret Service was not the only investigative
agency to share with press and public the orthodox
view that Governor Connally had been wounded by
the second bullet. The FBI compiled a five-volume
report on the assassination, which it turned over to
the Commission on December 9, 1963. In this report
we read:

INVESTIGATION OF ASSASSINATION
OF PRESIDENT JOHN F. KENNEDY
NOVEMBER 22, 1963

*As the motorcade was traveling through
downtown Dallas on Elm Street about fifty
yards west of the intersection with Houston
Street (Exhibit 1), three shots rang out. Two
bullets struck President Kennedy, and one
wounded Governor Connally. The President,
who slumped forward in the car, was rushed
to Parkland Memorial Hospital, where he
was pronounced dead at 1:00 pm* (Archives,
*CD 1*).

The agreement of witness reports, press dispatches,
and official statements on this point is suggestive, but
not conclusive. More is needed: witnesses may prove
(even unanimously) to be in error; press dispatches
and official statements are not infallible. Evidence of
a more substantial sort is required if we are to reach
a conclusive finding. In (1) the testimony of Governor Connally, (2) the pictorial evidence of the Za-

pruder film, and (3) medical findings concerning the Governor's back wound we have such evidence.

## CONNALLY'S TESTIMONY

Since the time of the assassination, Governor Connally's statements on this point have shown remarkable consistency. On November 22 he was in no condition to talk with anyone, but several days later he had recovered enough to discuss the circumstances of his wounding with one of his physicians, Dr. Tom Shires. Dr. Shires later gave the Commission this account of their conversation:

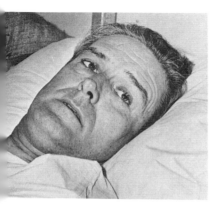

Governor John Connally at Parkland Hospital.

> *He remembered hearing a shot—he remembers turning to the right, he remembered being struck by a bullet, and his next thought as he fell over toward his wife was "They're going to kill all of us," and that's the last really clear memory that he expressed to me until he remembers vaguely being in the emergency room (6II108, see also Dr. Shaw's testimony, 6H92).*

A few days later Connally gave an interview to newsman Martin Agronsky in which he repeated essentially the same story:

> *We heard a shot. I turned to my left. I was sitting in the jump seat. I turned to my left in the back seat. The President had slumped. He had said nothing.*
>
> *Almost simultaneously, as I turned, I was hit, and I knew I'd been hit badly, and I said —I knew the President had been hit—and I said, "My God, they're not going to kill us all"* (The New York Times, *Nov. 28, 1963*).

Of all the witnesses present in Dealey Plaza that Friday noon, Connally, as a victim, is best qualified to decide which bullet struck him. And his testimony on this point is detailed and consistent. In light of these early reports it seems impossible to argue that his account is a product of a fertile imagination active at a later time.[2] In fact, as the record shows, his later testimony before the Commission agrees in almost every detail with these early statements.

Connally's appearance before the Commission on Tuesday, April 21, 1964, drew an extraordinarily large audience to the hearing room at 200 Maryland Avenue, Washington, D.C. Not only were six of the seven Commissioners in attendance (an event exceptional in itself), but also present were two of Connally's doctors, the attorney general of Texas, two observers, and no fewer than six Commission counsel. Connally took his place in the witness chair and, after some preliminaries, Assistant Counsel Arlen Specter asked him to describe what happened after the car had turned left on Elm Street. The Governor gave this account:

*Gov. Connally: . . . We had just made the turn, well, when I heard what I thought was a shot. I heard this noise which I immediately took to be a rifle shot. I instinctively turned to my right because the sound appeared to come from over my right shoulder, and I saw nothing unusual except just people in the crowd, but I did not catch the President in the corner of my eye, and I was interested because once I heard the shot in my own mind I identified it as a rifle shot, and I immediately— the only thought that crossed my mind was that this is an assassination attempt.*

*So I looked, failing to see him, I was turning to look back over my left shoulder into the back seat, but I never got that far in my turn. I got about in the position I am in now facing you, looking a little bit to the left of center, and then I felt like someone hit me in the back.*

*Specter: What is the best estimate that you have as to the time span between the sound of the first shot and the feeling of someone hitting you in the back which you have just described?*

*Gov. Connally: A very, very brief span of time. Again my trend of thought just happened to be, I suppose along this line, I immediately thought that this—that I had been shot. I knew it when I just looked down and I was covered with blood, and the thought immediately passed through my mind that there were either two or three people involved or more in this or someone was shooting with an automatic rifle. These were just thoughts that went through my mind because of the rapidity of these two, of the first plus the blow that I took, and I knew I had been hit, and I immediately assumed because of the amount of blood, and, in fact, that it had obviously passed through my chest, that I had probably been fatally hit.*

*So I merely doubled up, and then turned to my right again and began to—I just sat there, and Mrs. Connally pulled me over to her lap. She was sitting, of course, on the jump seat, so I reclined with my head in her lap, conscious all the time, and with my eyes open; and then, of course, the third shot sounded, and I heard the shot very clearly. I heard it hit him. I heard the shot hit something, and I assumed again—it never entered my mind that it ever hit anybody but the President. I heard it hit (4H132–133).*

A bit later Assistant Counsel Specter pursued the critical question of which bullet struck the Governor:

*Specter: In your view, which bullet caused the injury to your chest, Governor Connally?*
*Gov. Connally: The second one.*
*Specter: And what is your reason for that conclusion, sir?*
*Gov. Connally: Well, in my judgment, it just couldn't conceivably have been the first one because I heard the sound of the shot. In the first*

*place, I don't know anything about the veloc-
ity of this particular bullet [test bullets from
Oswald's rifle were clocked at an average
speed of nearly 1,300 mph], but any rifle has
a velocity that exceeds the speed of sound,
and when I heard the sound of that first shot,
that bullet had already reached where I was,
or it had reached that far, and after I heard
that shot, I had the time to turn to my right,
and start to turn to my left before I felt anything.*

*It is not conceivable to me that I could
have been hit by the first bullet, and then I
felt the blow from something which was obviously a bullet, which I assumed was a bullet,
and I never heard the second shot, didn't
hear it. I didn't hear but two shots. I think I
heard the first shot and the third shot.*

*Specter: Do you have any idea as to why you did not
hear the second shot?*

*Gov. Connally: Well, first, again I assume the bullet
was traveling faster than the sound. I was hit
by the bullet prior to the time the sound
reached me, and I was either in a state of
shock or the impact was such that the sound
didn't even register on me, but I was never
conscious of hearing the second shot at all.*

*Obviously, at least the major wound that
I took in the shoulder through the chest
couldn't have been anything but the second
shot. Obviously, it couldn't have been the
third, because when the third shot was fired I
was in a reclining position, and heard it, saw
it and the effects of it, rather I didn't see it,
I saw the effects of it—so it obviously could
not have been the third, and couldn't have
been the first, in my judgment (4H135–136).*

It is hard to imagine testimony more unequivocal
than this. Governor and Mrs. Connally are both certain that their memories of what happened that day
are both total and accurate. "I'll bet," the Governor

Z230                    SKETCH

Z231        SKETCH

Z232        SKETCH

234        SKETCH

235        SKETCH

challenges friends who even today question whether his recall could be so perfect, "that you can recall every detail of the circumstances under which you heard of the assassination—or Pearl Harbor Day or the death of F.D.R. And that's why I know every split second of what happened in that car until I lost consciousness. When I heard that first shot, and was starting to turn to my right to see what had happened, Nellie [Mrs. Connally] saw the President's hands reaching for his throat. I started to look around over my left shoulder, and somewhere in that revolution I was hit. My recollection of that time gap, the distinct separation between the shot that hit the President and the impact of the one that hit me, is as clear today as it was then."[3]

When Assistant Counsel Specter's single-bullet theory is presented, the Governor shakes his head and says: "They talk about the 'one bullet' or 'two bullet theory,' but as far as I'm concerned, there is no 'theory.' There is my absolute knowledge, and Nellie's too, that one bullet caused the President's first wound, and that an entirely separate shot struck me."

"No one will ever convince me otherwise," adds Mrs. Connally.

"It's a certainty," concludes the Governor. "I'll never change my mind."[4]

## CONNALLY AND THE ZAPRUDER FILM

Although the Governor will never change his mind, the Commission chose to disregard his account of the events of November 22. Recognizing that to believe the Governor's account meant also to believe in the existence of a second assassin, the Commission put forth its "delayed reaction" theory. "There was conceivably," the *Report* suggests, "a delayed reaction between the time the bullet struck him and the time he realized that he was hit, despite the fact that the bullet struck a glancing blow to a rib and penetrated his wrist bone" (R112). On the surface this is a plausible theory; many men are hit in combat and do not

Z236                    SKETCH

Z237                    SKETCH

Z238                    SKETCH

Z239                    SKETCH

realize it until later. The Zapruder film, however, lays this "delayed reaction" theory to rest.

As the quotation at the beginning of this chapter indicates, the Secret Service viewed the Zapruder film in late November, 1963, and concluded that "Governor Connally was struck with the second shot" (*Archives,* CD 5). Although Agent Howlett was unable to specify the exact frame of impact, many other persons tried. Governor Connally himself saw the film briefly before testifying on that Tuesday in April, 1964, and concluded that he was hit in the interval Z231–234 (4H145). Two and one-half years later he was given an opportunity to study 4-x-5-inch transparencies made by *Life* from the original print. After several hours of intense scrutiny, he decided that the bullet struck him in frame 234. Mrs. Connally also studied the film in Washington and told the Commission she thought her husband was hit in the interval Z229–233 (4H149). Connally's chest surgeon, Dr. Robert Shaw, picked the impact point as "236, give or take 1 or 2 frames" (4H114), while Dr. Charles Gregory, the wrist surgeon, permitted himself to say only that in frames 234 through 236 the Governor was in the proper position to have incurred the wounds he suffered (4H128). With the exception of Assistant Counsel Specter and the autopsy surgeons (chief proponents of the "single-bullet" theory), no one known to me has seen the Zapruder film and placed the Governor's wounding prior to Z230.

When we ourselves turn to the Zapruder film we see not only why this is so, but also why the "delayed reaction" theory is unacceptable.

At frame 230 Kennedy has obviously been hit; his hands and elbows are raised, he grimaces. Connally has now turned left so that he is facing straight ahead, his hand holding his Stetson. According to the Commission, he also has been hit. Arlen Specter told *Life* he sees Connally "wincing" in this frame.[5] When Governor Connally was shown this and the immediately preceding frames he told *Life:* "You can see the grimace in the President's face. You cannot see it in

Z240                    SKETCH

241                    SKETCH

242                    SKETCH

243                    SKETCH

mine. There is no question about it. I haven't been hit yet."[6] In succeeding frames the Governor seems to begin turning to his right. At Z232 he appears to alter slightly the position of his right hand as it holds the brim of his hat. At Z235–236 his mouth opens—perhaps in the cry, "Oh, no, no, no!" that he remembers making just before being hit. Finally, in frame 238 we see a very definite change indicating the impact of a bullet: his right shoulder collapses,[7] his cheeks and face puff, and his hair is disarranged.

The disarrangement of a lock of the Governor's hair in Z238 is the least important of the signs of impact. But it is a sign. We see the Governor's hair in earlier frames (230 and 236 especially), and it appears quite normal. But in 238 ff. (especially 239) a lock of hair on the right side has been quite clearly displaced. What this means is open to interpretation. It becomes significant only when combined with the remaining two (much more important) indications of a hit.

In frames up to 236 the Governor's mouth is closed. In Z236–237 his mouth opens in what appears to be an exclamation. Then, suddenly, in Z238 his cheeks puff and, in succeeding frames, his mouth opens wide—he gives the appearance of someone who has just had the wind knocked out of him. Dr. Gregory told me in Dallas that a necessary consequence of the shot through Connally's chest would be a compression of the chest wall and an involuntary opening of the epiglottis, followed by escaping air forcing open his mouth.[8] Dr. Gregory estimated the interval between impact and mouth opening to be on the order of ¼ to ½ second.[9] Thus the surge of air to the cheeks in Z238 and the subsequent mouth opening indicate the impact of a bullet only the barest fraction of a second earlier. More important, the fact that the Governor's mouth remains closed for so long lends further support to the view that he was struck later than the President. Had both victims been hit by the same bullet, we would expect Connally to be manifesting the signs of impact at least sixteen frames earlier.

Impact on the Governor is apparent through these frames by (1) collapse

Z239 SKETCH

right shoulder, (2) puffing of his cheeks, and (3) disarrangement of his hair.

Z240 SKETCH

Yet the clearest indication of the impact of a bullet is the sudden collapse of the Governor's shoulder. Connally gave the Commission this description of what it felt like to be wounded in the shoulder:

> *I would say it is as if someone doubled his fist and came up behind you and just with a 12 inch blow hit you right in the back right below the shoulder blade (4H144).*

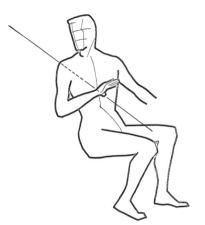

Sharp downward trajectory through the Governor as measured by the Commission. A bullet striking in this manner would easily have caused the instantaneous collapse of the shoulder seen in the Zapruder frames.

Since the path of the bullet through Connally was later measured as taking a downward course of 27 degrees (4H138), the effect of such a blow to his right shoulder would be to drive it sharply down. Connally is seen making a normal turning motion to his right. Suddenly, at Z238, his right shoulder buckles.

This shoulder collapse can be seen quite readily by comparing the slope of the Governor's shoulder against some relatively constant line—such as the top of the car door. When we do this we find that the slope steepens dramatically at Z238 by some 20 degrees, and remains steep through successive frames. Although the change is obvious to the naked eye, the following graph gives more precise measurements:

What is so important about all these changes apparent in Z238 is that they are not voluntary but *involuntary* responses. They depend not upon the victim's recognizing what is happening to him, but only upon the momentum transfer of the striking bullet. Connally did not decide to disarrange his hair, or puff his cheeks, or collapse his right shoulder, nor were these nervous reflex actions. They were direct effects of the striking bullet: the impact disarrayed his hair, the compression of the chest wall forced air into his cheeks and opened his mouth, the striking momentum of the bullet drove down his shoulder. We confront here not the effects of nerve physiology and reaction time, but the physical effect of a bullet transferring its momentum to a human body. The Commission's lame excuse that "there was, conceivably, a delayed reaction between the time the bullet

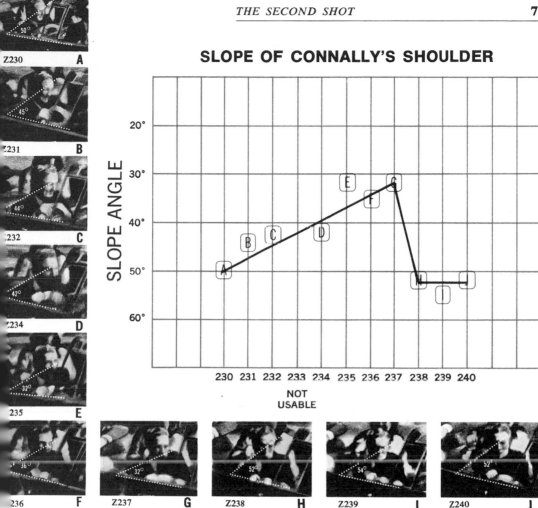

Z230 **A**

Z231 **B**

Z232 **C**

Z234 **D**

235 **E**

236 **F**       Z237 **G**       Z238 **H**       Z239 **I**       Z240 **J**

lope of Governor Connally's
houlder gets shallower as he turns
ntil frame 238, when it suddenly
eepens by 20°.

struck him and the time he realized that he was hit"
is quite beside the point. What we see at Z238 is not
the effect of his *realizing* he was hit (this will show
up later in the film), but simply the physical consequences of a bullet striking his body. This indisputable photographic evidence shatters both the "single-
bullet" theory and its offspring, the "delayed reaction" theory.

Governor Connally picked 234 as the actual frame
of impact. He may be correct, but he is stretching the
limits of precision allowed him by science. Surely the
impact must be before Z238, but how much before
cannot be exactly established. The driving down of
the right shoulder and forcing of air into the mouth
should occur almost simultaneously with impact; four

Zapruder frames (4/18 second) would seem to be a maximum value. One could not be faulted for locating the impact in the interval Z234–238 with the emphasis on the last two frames. If we locate the first hit on the President in the interval Z210–224, the Governor was hit by the second shot anywhere from ½ to 1½ seconds later.

This timing accords well with statements from S. M. Holland and William Newman that the first and second shots were "about a second apart."[10] It also accords with the Governor's judgment at the time that "there were either two or three people involved or more in this or someone was shooting with an automatic rifle"* (4H133).

## CONNALLY'S BACK WOUND

There is one final piece of information suggesting that the Governor was hit by a later bullet than the one that struck the President. On that Tuesday in April, 1964, when the Governor testified before the Commission, the surgeon who had operated on his chest was also questioned by Assistant Counsel Specter. Dr. Robert Shaw was asked whether, after viewing the Zapruder film, he had "any opinion as to what, in fact, did happen?" Dr. Shaw replied:

> *Yes. From the pictures, from the conversation with Governor Connally and Mrs. Connally, it seems that the first bullet hit the President in the shoulder and perforated the neck, but this was not the bullet that Governor Connally feels hit him; and in the sequence of films I think it is hard to say that the first bullet hit both of these men (4H114).*

* Cecil Ault, observing the motorcade from the Criminal Courts Building, also thought the first two shots were so rapid that they might have come from an automatic rifle. He later told the FBI: "He noted that the first and second shots sounded to him to be close together and the third shot was spaced more after the second shot, the first two shots sounding close enough to be from an automatic rifle" (24H534).

Constrained by the straitjacket of Specter's line of questioning, Dr. Shaw did not give his chief reason for resisting the "single-bullet" theory. I learned of it only much later, in November, 1966, from Dr. Shaw's colleague, Dr. Charles F. Gregory.

At one point in our interview, Dr. Gregory indicated that both he and Dr. Shaw thought it highly unlikely that the President and the Governor had been hit by the same bullet. Their reasoning, it soon became apparent, concerned the character of the Governor's back wound. This was a small wound, 1.5 centimeters in its largest diameter, elliptical in shape, with rather clean-cut edges (4H104). What impressed both Drs. Gregory and Shaw was that no fibers from the Governor's clothes had been carried into this wound. Dr. Gregory contrasted it with the wound in the Governor's wrist, which contained a great number of wool suit threads. The absence of any cloth fibers in the back wound, together with its clean-cut edges, suggested to both physicians that it had been caused by a pristine bullet, one that had not already passed through a human body. Dr. Gregory went on to relate how he and Dr. Shaw were so impressed by the character of the back wound that both were convinced that the President and the Governor had been hit by different bullets.[11]

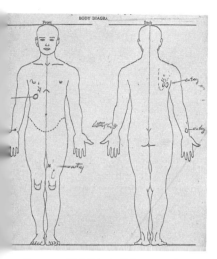

Gregory Exhibit 1. Diagram showing location of Governor Connally's wounds.

Shortly after *Life* magazine published its interview with Governor Connally in November, 1966, the Governor called a news conference. Surely two paragraphs in the Governor's prepared statement should be recorded for posterity:

> *I am convinced, beyond any doubt, that I was not struck by the first bullet. I know that I heard the first shot, that I turned to see what happened and that I was struck by a second shot. The third shot struck the President and not me.*
>
> *As I said earlier, this testimony was presented to the Warren Commission. They*

*chose to disagree, which is their privilege. I maintain my original view, always shall. I want to make it very clear, however, that simply because I disagree with the Warren Commission on this one detail does not mean that I disagree with the substance of their overall findings* (The New York Times, *Nov. 24, 1966*).

The Governor chooses to disagree with the Commission on "one detail" (namely, that he and the President were hit by the same bullet), yet does not mean to "disagree with the substance of their overall findings." Yet the Governor's "one detail" has awesome implications. Commission Counsel Redlich did not speak idly when he remarked that if the men were hit by separate bullets it would mean there were two assassins.[12] Oswald's rifle could not have been fired twice in less than 2.3 seconds. President Kennedy could not have been hit earlier than Z210, for the tree shielded him in earlier frames. Experts testified that Governor Connally had turned so that his wounds could not have been caused by a bullet from the sixth-floor sniper's perch after Z240 (5H158, 170). Subtract 210 from 240 and we get thirty Zapruder frames or 1.6 seconds. This was not enough time to get off another shot. Although the Governor could not know it at the time, the thought that rushed through his mind as the car swept down Elm Street would later be verified by the facts of the case: ". . . and the thought immediately passed through my mind that there were either two or three or more people involved . . ." (4H133).

The Zapruder film indicates that the President and the Governor were struck no more than 1.6 secs. apart. Such a shooting schedule would place impossible demands on a rifleman operating Oswald's Carcano, as illustrated.

| ZAPRUDER FRAME NO. | TIME FROM 1st SHOT | COMMENT | REENACTMENT FRAME | ZAPRUDER FRAME |
|---|---|---|---|---|
| 210 | 0.0 secs. | FIRST SHOT POSSIBLE | | |
| 222 | 0.656 secs. | CONNALLY TURNING LEFT | | |
| 225 | 0.830 secs. | KENNEDY REACTING | | |
| 230 | 1.093 secs. | KENNEDY HIT, CONNALLY UNINJURED | | |
| 238 | 1.530 secs. | CONNALLY HIT | | |
| 244 | 1.858 secs. | CONNALLY OBVIOUSLY HURT | | |
| 252 | 2.295 secs. | SECOND SHOT POSSIBLE | | |

## NOTES

1. Interview of Willis family, Nov. 29, 1966:

*Thompson: Is it your opinion now that the President was hit with the first shot, the Governor with the second, and the President with the third?*

*Mrs. Willis: Yes. That's right.*

*Thompson: And tell me something offhand. Has this been something you've all been pretty persuaded of ever since the . . .*

*Mr. Philip Willis: Oh yes, from the very first thing.*

*Thompson: I mean look. I wasn't there. Was it pretty darn clear that this is what happened?*

*Linda Kay Willis: Absolutely.*

*Mr. Willis: That's right. The Warren Commission didn't seek us out and finally Linda and I were interviewed a long time later. But at home we all agreed. We stayed home there for a week just glued to the television. And we agreed all along as to how and what happened.*

*Thompson: And it was your conviction all along, I take it, that the President was hit with the first, the Governor with the second?*

*Linda Kay Willis: We've had these opinions ever since the night . . .*

*Mrs. Willis (interrupting): The night that it happened.*

*Thompson: If I walked in that night as the official representative of the U.S. Government and said: "Phil Willis and family—the President and the Governor were hit by the same bullet." What would you have said?*

*Linda Kay Willis: We would have said that's wrong.*

2. Yet this *was* precisely the excuse offered by Assistant Counsel Arlen Specter when he was interviewed by *Life* in November, 1966.

3. *Life* interview with Connally, Oct. 30, 1966.

4. All the above remarks were made during the same *Life* interview with Governor and Mrs. Connally, Oct. 30, 1966.

The recent CBS News documentary, "The Warren Report," gave many viewers the impression that Governor Connally had changed his mind on this crucial point. The transcript of his CBS interview, however, shows that he still maintains his original view:

*Eddie Barker: Do you believe, Governor Connally, that the first bullet could have missed, the second one hit both of you, and the third one hit President Kennedy?*

*Gov. Connally: That's possible. That's possible. Now, the best witness I know doesn't believe that.*

*Eddie Barker: Who is the best witness you know?*

*Gov. Connally: Nellie was there, and she saw it. She believes the first bullet hit him, because she saw him after*

*he was hit. She thinks the second bullet hit me,*
*and the third bullet hit him.*

5. *Life* interview with Specter, Nov. 10, 1966.

6. *Life* interview with Connally, Oct. 30, 1966.

7. Raymond Marcus of Los Angeles first discovered this shoulder collapse in the spring of 1965.

8. Interview with Dr. Charles F. Gregory, Nov. 2, 1966.

9. *Ibid.*

10. Taped interviews with S. M. Holland (Nov. 30, 1966) and William Newman (Nov. 29, 1966).

11. An effort was made to get confirmation of this report from Dr. Shaw himself. Unfortunately, in the fall of 1966 he was on the S.S. Hope, and in the spring of 1967 he was in Afghanistan.

12. Edward Jay Epstein, *Inquest* (New York: The Viking Press, Inc., 1966), p. 43.

# V

## THE HEAD SHOTS

*It [the head shot] was right, but I cannot say for sure that it was rear, because when I mounted the car it was—it had a different sound, first of all, than the first sound that I heard . . . [it] had almost a double sound.*
*—Secret Service Agent Clinton J. Hill (2H144).*

I N November, 1966, there was an autumn chill in the air as Edward Kern and I drove our rented car out of Dallas on our way to Irving, Texas, to interview S. M. Holland, signal supervisor for the Union Terminal Railroad and critically important witness of the assassination. What had so impressed us about Holland's testimony as we read it in the *Hearings* was the way his eye seemed to have picked out details other witnesses had missed. Basically his testimony agreed with his November 22 affidavit, yet it revealed a wealth of detail (much of it corroborated by other witnesses) of critical importance to the case. The most outstanding detail was his statement that simul-

S. M. Holland on overpass points toward stockade fence where he saw a puff of smoke on November 22.

Holland standing behind stockade fence where he found footprints and cigarette butts moments after the assassination.

taneous with the impact of the last shot on the President's head he had noticed a puff of smoke in front of the stockade fence to the north of Elm Street. From November 22 on, Holland had steadfastly maintained that one of the shots had come from behind that fence. We wanted to meet Holland and try to determine whether his insistence on this point was founded firmly in fact or was simply the result of innate stubbornness. Then too, Holland had told several individuals that the Warren Commission had not transcribed his testimony as he had given it. For all these reasons it seemed important that we get Holland's story from him directly.

Holland met us at the door of his home on Lucille Street and ushered us into the living room. He carefully inspected our identification and told us he had done some checking on us with his old friend, Dallas County Sheriff Bill Decker. He knew that we were from *Life* magazine and that we were the individuals we claimed to be (Mark Lane had earlier used the alias "Blake" with Holland). But he wanted to know just what our angle was, just what we wanted to prove. We told him that we only wanted to find the truth. At first he did not believe us, and with good reason. For the government, too, had told him that it wanted to find the truth, and he had talked twenty to thirty times with its investigators. Yet finally the government had chosen not to believe him and had failed even to print his testimony as he had given it.[1] And private investigators were no better—they had lied to him about the use to which his words would be put and had badgered him unceasingly, trying to prove first one point and then another. Thus the first part of the evening was spent in salving the wounds Holland had suffered in earlier interviews. Finally, he was able to see from our questions that we wished to plead no special case, and he opened up.

He told us of the shooting, of the motorcade sweeping toward him as he stood on the railroad overpass, of the sound of shots. Holland had heard *four* shots, not three, and the third and fourth were fired so close together that they sounded almost like a double shot.

*Thompson: Could you contrast the sounds of the reports? You mentioned that shots one, two, and four had a certain similar sound, and that three was rather different. Could you work on the contrast between three and the rest?*

*Holland: Well, it would be about like I was telling you awhile ago. It would be like you're firing a .38 pistol right beside a shotgun, or a .45 right beside a shotgun.*

*Thompson: I'm not very experienced in firearms. Is one sharper than the other?*

*Holland: One is not near as loud as the other.*

*Kern: And the third shot was not so loud?*

*Holland: Oh no, the third shot was not so loud; it was like it came from a .38 pistol, compared with a high-powered rifle.*

*Thompson: And this shot . . . you heard the report of this curious sounding . . .*

*Holland: That's what drawed my attention.*

*Thompson: I see.*

*Holland: The report of the third shot wasn't nearly as loud as the first and second shot or the fourth shot.*

*Thompson: And there was a definite sound direction to it?*

*Holland: There was definitely a sound of direction where it was coming . . .*

*Thompson: Could you tell me . . . you know we speak of simultaneous and almost simultaneous . . . were the third and fourth reports, were they "bloo-oom"? [Thompson indicating two sounds almost together.] Were they like that? Or were they "boom, boom"?*

*Holland: Well, like "boom-boom" [Holland makes two distinct but very close together sounds].*

*Thompson: Pretty fast together.*

*Holland: Pretty fast together. They weren't simultaneous, as we say. They were "boom-boom."*

*Thompson: So in other words, if rifles were fired from rather different locations, one rather close to you and one rather distant from you, the difference in the reports might be due to the distance from you as sound travels to you?*

*Holland: That's right. The sounds . . .*

*Thompson: In other words, the bullets might have been fired at the same time?*

*Holland: The bullets travel faster than sound, but the report that I heard of the third one—I heard that before I heard the fourth one, the fourth shot.*

*Thompson: And the fourth resembled the first two.*

*Holland: The fourth resembled the first two.*

*Thompson: Did it seem to come from . . . where did the fourth one seem to come from?*

*Holland: The upper end of the street . . . the north end of Houston Street.*

*Thompson: North end of Elm Street?*

*Holland: I could tell what direction they were being fired from, but I didn't know whether they were from a building, or whether it was from a street corner or the middle of the street. From where I was I couldn't tell because I was . . . the trees hid that part of . . . hid from me.*

*Thompson: Let me ask you, having seen this from this cockpit view, which bullet hit whom, and how . . . I mean, you heard the first bullet?*

*Holland: Well, the third and the fourth bullets hit the President.*

*Thompson: You think both bullets hit the President?*

*Holland: Well, I say this; the President fell over when the third and fourth shots were fired. Now whether he was caught in a crossfire or whether both of them hit him, I can't say.*

*Thompson: Did you see any dust fly up from the pavement, or anything which would indicate that one of those two missed?*

*Holland: I didn't, and I was observing very close because that's what I was up there for.*

*Thompson: Is it your opinion then . . . What is your opinion? That the third and fourth did hit the President?*

*Holland: My opinion is that the third and the fourth
        did, did hit the President.*
*Thompson: In the head?*
*Holland: In the head (Taped interview, Nov. 30,
        1966).*

Holland's testimony had held up; we found no flaw
in its details. I was convinced that his persistence
was not stubbornness but a rare kind of courage.
Even more important, Holland's story fitted the last
piece into a jigsaw puzzle that long had lain incomplete. It was a puzzle whose shape I had first per-
ceived some five months earlier in the July heat of
Washington.

## THE DOUBLE MOVEMENT

I had gone to the National Archives to test the
validity of a new way of viewing the Zapruder film.
Developed by Philadelphia attorney Vincent Salandria, this technique consisted of using two slide projectors placed side by side and superimposing their
images on the screen. By inserting 35-millimeter
slides of sequential Zapruder frames in alternate
projectors, it was possible to isolate the movement
of people in the presidential car. For by matching up
fixed points on the car, and then by switching from
one projector to the other, one could see with the
naked eye any movement occurring between frames.
This came to be of great importance in studying the
movement of the President's body at Z313—the instant when the head shot impacts. By applying this
technique to Z313 and successive frames, Salandria
had determined that the President's head was driven
backward and to the left under impact.* Since the

* On a recent radio broadcast Assistant Counsel Wesley J.
Liebeler admitted that the Commission never paid much attention to the President's head movement. "It's only since the
critics have raised this point," Liebeler conceded, "that anybody has ever looked at it closely " (Stan Lomax Program,
KTTV [Los Angeles], February, 1967).

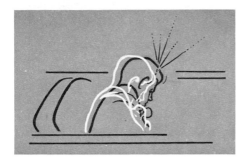

Superimposition of Zapruder frames 312 (white outline) and 313 (black outline) shows a sharp forward movement (in 1/18 sec.) before the left, backward snap.

When Zapruder frames 313 (black outline) and 316 (white outline) are superimposed, it is clear that the President was forced left and backward under impact of the fatal shot.

momentum of an impacting bullet is transferred in a direction along its line of flight, this movement appeared to suggest a shot from the right front. I had gone to Washington to study the Zapruder film and to verify for myself Salandria's findings.

The screen and the two projectors were set up. Frames 313 and 314 were focused on the same screen and I switched back and forth—the President's head appeared to move slightly to the rear. I tried 313 and 315—now the movement became quite apparent. Between 313 and 316 there appeared to be a tremendous snap of the head backward and to the left. This was exactly the same movement I had seen earlier on the 8-millimeter movie film—a tremendous wrench of the head and shoulders backward and to the left.

Since frame 313 was somewhat indistinct, I decided to try 312 as a control frame. I switched between 312 and 313 and found something puzzling: The President's head seemed to move *forward,* not backward. I tried 312 and 314—hardly any change, but perhaps a slight forward movement. When 312 and 316 were viewed, the head could be seen to move quite obviously backward. Again and again I switched between 312 and 313; it was quite apparent that there was a definite forward movement of several

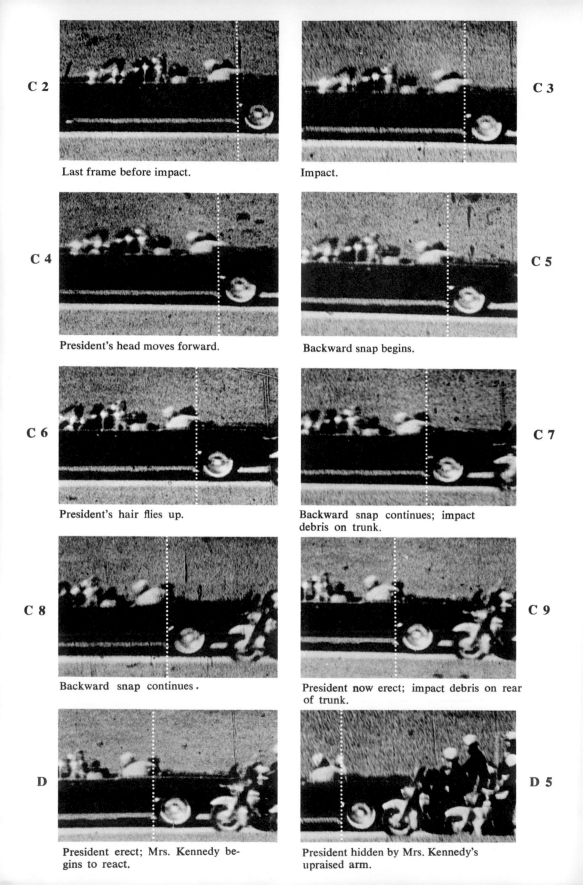

C 2
Last frame before impact.

C 3
Impact.

C 4
President's head moves forward.

C 5
Backward snap begins.

C 6
President's hair flies up.

C 7
Backward snap continues; impact debris on trunk.

C 8
Backward snap continues.

C 9
President now erect; impact debris on rear of trunk.

D
President erect; Mrs. Kennedy begins to react.

D 5
President hidden by Mrs. Kennedy's upraised arm.

inches between these two frame numbers. And it was just as apparent that there was an immediate sharp backward movement in the frames that followed. What I had discovered was a double movement of the President's head separated by only 1/18 second.[2] What could possibly cause such a movement? A nerve/muscle reflex to the first hit from behind? A sudden braking or acceleration of the car? An almost simultaneous impact of two bullets? Before speculating further I knew I needed a very accurate measure of the magnitude of both movements.

The obvious way to quantify such a movement was to take two fixed points a known distance apart on the car and measure the distance between them and the President's head through a series of frame numbers. This I did many times, first using the indistinct Zapruder copies in Volume XVIII of the *Hearings,** then later returning to the Archives to focus the slides on large sheets of white drawing paper. Although the results bore out the witness of the naked eye (the President's head did appear to move forward and then backward), the copies were so poor that measurement error proved excessive. It was not until later, when I was able to study 8-x-10-inch enlargements in the offices of *Life*, that the measurements could be made with sufficient precision. With the help of Bill Hoffman, a bright young physicist, and the use of a dissecting microscope, I was able to measure with great accuracy the movement of the

Sequential frames from the film shot by Orville Nix show the double movement of President Kennedy's head under the impact of the fatal bullets.

* As Director J. Edgar Hoover of the FBI has admitted in a letter dated Dec. 14, 1965, frames 314 and 315 of the Zapruder film were switched in being printed in Volume XVIII. Curiously, this is the only switch in the printing of 163 Zapruder frames. The effect of this mistake is to make a *backward* movement look like a *forward* movement.

President's head. After holding steady for some twelve frames, it is suddenly driven forward between frames 312 and 313. Amazingly, in the very next frame, 314, it is already moving backward, a movement it continues in succeeding frames until the President's shoulders strike the seat cushion at Z321. The graphs on the following page suggest the magnitude of this movement.

Its magnitude is substantial. Measured parallel to the axis of the car the President's head has been given a forward acceleration of 69.6 feet per second per second between frames 312 and 313. One-eighteenth second later, this movement has been reversed and the head has been given an acceleration backward and to the left of 100.3 feet per second per second.[3] These accelerations are quite large* (a falling body at the earth's surface, for example, accelerates at a rate of 32 feet per second per second), and what is even more striking is the brevity of the interval in which the movement is reversed. What could cause such a reversal? How could this violent double movement be explained?

Several alternatives present themselves:

*(1) The President's head perhaps struck some fixed surface in the car, thus reversing its direction of travel.* The Zapruder film shows that no fixed surface is in such proximity to the President's head as to cause such a change in direction. At Z313 his head is approximately 2½ feet from the jump seat directly forward.

---

\* Large though they may be, they are only *minimum* values. We have every reason to believe that the true acceleration values are perhaps 20 times larger.

Our measured values of acceleration are average accelerations for the 56 milliseconds between frames. Since a projectile would pass through the head in 2 or 3 milliseconds (transferring its momentum and accelerating the head in that time interval), our measured values are much too small. Had Zapruder been using a high-speed camera which ran, say, at 1,000 frames per second, we would have been able to arrive at more accurate values. But for purposes of analysis the minimum values are sufficiently large to make the point.

## PLOT OF DISTANCE OF PRESIDENT'S
## HEAD FROM REAR HANDHOLD

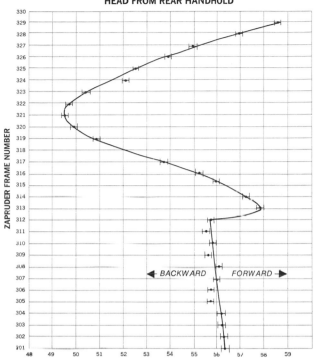

## PLOT OF DISTANCE OF PRESIDENT'S
## HEAD FROM TOP OF BACK SEAT

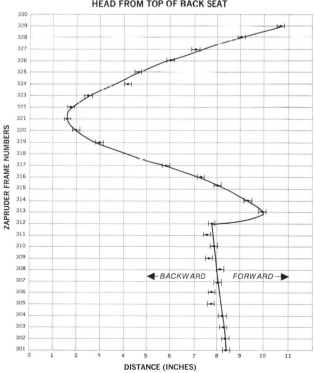

*(2) Mrs. Kennedy pulled the President into her arms after the impact, thus accounting for the left/ backward snap.* The force of the impact drove the President's body between Mrs. Kennedy and the rear seat. No movement on her part to grab the President is apparent in the films, and as her testimony shows, her failure to seize him and pull him down between the first and the third shots was a source of great torment to her (5H180).

*(3) The car suddenly accelerated or decelerated during this time, thus throwing the President either forward or backward.* This possibility can be ruled out by referring both to witness testimony and to the Zapruder film. Both Governor and Mrs. Connally indicated that the car did not accelerate until after the head shot (R50). Clint Hill, the Secret Service agent who jumped on the back of the President's car, testified that the car accelerated just after he reached it. "The initial surge was quite violent," Hill remarked, "because it almost jerked me off the left rear stepboard" (2H141). FBI photo expert Lyndal Shaneyfelt testified that "Special Agent Hill placed one foot on the bumper of the car at frame 368, which is approximately three seconds after frame 313" (15H699). The combined testimony of all these witnesses indicates that the car did not accelerate until some 3 seconds after the President was struck in the head. And the Zapruder film shows conclusively that no acceleration or deceleration occurred in this critical period. Any quick acceleration or deceleration would have thrown the other occupants of the car off balance, yet the film shows no such movement—Mrs. Kennedy, the Governor, and Mrs. Connally all remain still relative to the car during this crucial interval. Furthermore, using background objects as control points, we can actually measure the velocity of the car from frame to frame. These measurements indicate that during the interval in question the car maintained a fairly constant speed of approximately 10 miles per hour (see Appendix C for graph).

*(4) There was some neuromuscular reaction to the shot from behind that arched the President's body in the opposite direction.* The extremely small time factor combined with the relatively large mass of the President's head would tend to rule out such an explanation. The fastest reflex action known to science —the startle response—takes place over an interval of 40 to 200 milliseconds. Beginning with an eyeblink in 40 milliseconds, the response wave moves the head forward in 83 milliseconds, and then continues downward reaching the knees in 200 milliseconds.[4] The change in direction we observe occurs in 56 milliseconds (1/18 second), and involves not the negligible mass of an eyelid but the considerable mass of a human head moving forward under an acceleration of several g's. Still other factors indicate that we are dealing with the results of a physical impact and not a neuromuscular phenomenon. The graph shown at left exhibits the familiar profile of a collision. One billiard ball strikes another and almost instantaneously transfers its momentum to the second; after a brief instant of high acceleration, the velocity of the second ball remains constant. Similarly, we find the President's head undergoing a violent acceleration at Z313 after which its velocity remains nearly constant. Were a neuromuscular phenomenon involved, we would expect the muscles of the neck to keep accelerating the head; its velocity would not show the constancy it does after Z314. But since the motor strip (pre-central gyrus) was blown out by the entering bullet, the likelihood of any muscular reaction at all is considerably diminished. Even if this area did excite some nerve impulse before it was torn from the brain, the resultant movement would be general and random; it would not throw the President's body in any particular direction. As a neurologist explained it to me, the expected neurological effect of such a shot to the head would be for the victim's body to go limp.

*(5) There is some physical principle or law of nature that explains the double movement.* The physics

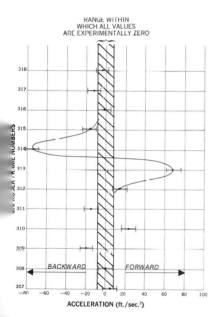

RANGE WITHIN
WHICH ALL VALUES
ARE EXPERIMENTALLY ZERO

ZAPRUDER FRAME NUMBERS

BACKWARD    FORWARD

ACCELERATION (ft./sec.²)

Plot of acceleration (ft/sec²) versus Zapruder frame number $\bar{Z}$, where $\bar{Z}=(Z, Z-2)$ is the interval over which the acceleration values were averaged

The marked acceleration of President Kennedy's head (first forward and then backward) indicates the possibility of a double hit.

of impacting bodies is quite clear. As Dr. A. J.
Riddle, member of the Brain Research Institute and
Assistant Professor of Physics at the University of
California at Los Angeles, has pointed out in an unpublished study of the Kennedy assassination, the effects of such impacts are governed by Newton's second law of motion:

> *Newton's second law of motion [namely, that
> the rate of change of momentum is propor-
> tional to the impressed force, and* is in the
> direction in which the force acts] *has re-
> mained inviolate for three centuries. Not
> even the advent of relativity and quantum
> mechanics has disturbed its validity. No
> physical phenomenon is known that fails to
> obey it. One of the most immediate conse-
> quences is the conservation of momentum;
> basically the law says that an object hit by a
> projectile will be given a motion that has the
> same direction as that of the projectile. At a
> shooting gallery, for instance, the ducks fall
> away from the marksman, not toward him.
> Thus, if someone is shot, and the shot strikes
> bone, the general direction of recoil will be
> away from—not toward—the marksman.*[5]

Applying Newton's second law to the case in question and supposing that a bullet fired from the rear
struck the President's head, we would expect to see
his head and body driven forward, the force of the
impact perhaps forcing him out of the rear seat onto
the floor. We see the beginning of such a movement
at Z312–313. But then it is suddenly interrupted and
replaced by a movement in the opposite direction.
If we account for the sudden forward movement as
the consequence of a bullet's impact, only a similar
hypothesis could account for the equally sudden
backward movement. What we see on the Zapruder
film are the effects of a double transfer of momentum
—one forward, the other backward.* At Z313 we

* Dr. Cyril Wecht had an opportunity to study closely *Life's*
copy of the Zapruder film. Sometime later I asked him

witness the effect of a virtually simultaneous double impact on the President's head. One shot was fired from the rear, and the other from the right front.

This is, of course, just what S. M. Holland saw from his vantage point on the railroad viaduct ("the third and fourth bullets hit the President . . . in the head"). He had seen with his own eyes what I had only deduced with the help of photographs, microscopes, and complicated mathematical equations. The fact that he had seen the assassination just the way I believed it must have happened buoyed my confidence and gave my inquiry a new foundation.

The next stage was clear. If what Holland saw (and what my measurements indicated) was really what happened—that the President had been caught in a crossfire and that his head had been driven backward by one shot a fraction of an instant after being driven forward by another—then further clues should be buried in the evidence. A thorough search ought to turn them up. I returned to the witness testimony.

## EARWITNESS REPORTS

Unlike the photographic evidence, the eye- and

---

whether this double movement could be explained as the result of a shot from behind. He told me:

"It certainly doesn't seem consistent with what we would expect in a penetrating injury of this kind considering where it is alleged to have been fired from and the force of the impact that such a high-speed rifle would have had. It seems quite inconsistent with all this. It doesn't seem to fit; there is no question about it. And you recall that we looked at these films hours, backwards and forwards, slow motion, fast motion. It just doesn't seem to fit.

"Again let me say that I think there is a very distinct possibility that a bullet, or another bullet striking the head virtually simultaneously, could have been fired from off to the side or from a slightly forward angle, coming in from the front of the car. To put it another way, the Zapruder film certainly doesn't allow one to arrive at the unequivocal conclusion that a bullet entered the President's head having been fired from behind and at a point upward. On the contrary, it raises the distinct possibility that the bullet may have been fired from elsewhere" (Wecht interview, May 26, 1967).

earwitness reports have to be accepted with certain reservations. As discussed in depth in Chapter II, they are the least reliable sources of information. But, when the subject warrants, a cautious look at the firsthand accounts is justifiable.

Like S. M. Holland, a number of other witnesses reported hearing nearly simultaneous shots. Jean Hill, who was standing on the grass along the south curb of Elm Street (6H206), recalled two distinct flurries of shots (6H207) as the car approached. The first shots, she said, "were fired as though one person were firing . . . they were rather rapidly fired but there was some small interval between them" (6H207). Then there was "a distinct pause" followed by more shots (6H207). These later shots, Mrs. Hill remembered, "were different—I thought the sequence was different . . . quicker, more automatic" (6H207). A bit later in her testimony Jean Hill recalled her immediate impression that more than one person had been firing on the motorcade:

*Mrs. Hill: . . . I did think there was more than one
        person shooting.*
*Specter: You did think there was more than one
        person shooting?*
*Mrs. Hill: Yes sir.*
*Specter: What made you think that?*
*Mrs. Hill: The way the gun reports sounded and the
        difference in the way they were fired—the
        timing.*
*Specter: What was your impression as to the source
        of the second group of shots . . . ?*
*Mrs. Hill: Well, nothing, except that I thought that
        they were fired by someone else.*
*Specter: And did you have any idea where they were
        coming from?*
*Mrs. Hill: No; as I said, I thought they were coming
        from the general direction of that knoll
        (6H213).*

A number of the Secret Service agents described the last two shots as sounding extremely close together. George Hickey, riding in the back seat of the Secret Service follow-up car, recalled:

> *At the moment he [Kennedy] was almost sitting erect I heard two reports which I thought were shots and that appeared to me completely different in sound than the first report and were in such rapid succession, that there seemed to be practically no time element between them. It looked to me as if the President was struck in the right upper rear of his head (18H762).*

Secret Service agents Hill, Kellerman, and Greer after testifying before the Warren Commission.

The testimony that is most striking in this regard comes from the agents who were closest to the President at the time he was shot. William Greer, the driver of the presidential limousine, recalled that "the last two shots seemed to be just simultaneously, one behind the other" (2H118). Sitting next to Greer, Roy Kellerman could only describe the final shots as a "flurry." Specter pressed him on this point:

*Specter: Now in your prior testimony you described a flurry of shells into the car. How many shots did you hear after the first noise which you described as sounding like a firecracker?*
*Kellerman: Mr. Specter, these shells came in all together.*
*Specter: Are you able to say how many you heard?*
*Kellerman: I am going to say two, and it was like a double bang—bang, bang (2H76).*

U.S. Representative Gerald Ford asked Kellerman to describe even more precisely the sound of the final "flurry," and Kellerman offered this description:

> *Let me give you an illustration, sir, before I can give you an answer. You have heard the sound barrier, of a plane breaking the sound barrier, bang, bang? (2H76).*

Yet of all the descriptions given of the sound of the final shots, the most vivid came from Clint Hill, Mrs. Kennedy's personal bodyguard. After hearing the first shot, Hill leaped from his position on the follow-up car's running board and ran to the presidential limousine. Before he could reach it, the President's head exploded in a pink halo. "I jumped from the follow-up car and ran toward the presidential automobile," Hill recalled in a statement dated November 30. "I heard a second firecracker noise* but it had a different sound—like the sound of shooting a revolver into something hard" (18H742). Several months later he was asked by Assistant Counsel Specter about the direction of origin of this "different sound":

> *It was right, but I cannot say for sure that it was rear, because when I mounted the car it was—it had a different sound, first of all, than the first sound that I heard . . . [It] had almost a double sound—as though you were standing against something metal and firing into it, and you have both the sound of the gun going off and the sound of the cartridge hitting the metal place, which could have been caused probably by the hard surface of the head. But I am not sure that that is what caused it (2H144).*

Unfortunately, Clint Hill was never asked what else in his opinion might have caused this curious "double sound." Did he perhaps suspect that the "double sound" in fact came from two weapons firing simultaneously from different locations? His testimony gives no clue.

## IMPACT DEBRIS

At one point in his testimony Roy Kellerman described the finely shredded material blown into the front seat at the time of the head shot. "This is a rather poor comparison," he remarked, "but let's say

* Apparently, in the excitement of running to the presidential limousine Hill failed to hear the shot that struck the Governor.

Frames from the Nix film showing a white mass (arrow) moving rearward over the trunk of the limousine. According to witness testimony, this may be impact debris from the President's head.

Charles Brehm (arrow), who saw what appeared to be "a portion of the President's skull . . . flying slightly to the rear of the President's car and directly to its left."

you take a little handful of matter—I am going to use sawdust for want of a better item—and just throw it" (2H78). Both Governor and Mrs. Connally likewise testified that after the head shot they were covered with small particles of brain tissue—Mrs. Connally described it as "like spent buckshot falling all over us" (4H147) and the Governor recalled how on his trousers he had discovered "one chunk of brain tissue as big as almost my thumbnail" (4H133). These reports describe a first umbrella of impact debris dispersed forward over the occupants of the limousine in a pattern that would be the natural outcome of a shot fired from the rear.

But there is another pattern of debris, greater in magnitude, that distributed itself over the left rear of the car and over the two motorcyclists riding behind and to the left. James Altgens observed the head shot from a position on the south curb of Elm Street and gave this description of debris: "There was flesh particles that flew out of the side of his head in my direction from where I was standing, so much so that it indicated to me that the shot came out the left side of his head" (7H518).

Altgens' description was echoed in the remarks of Charles Brehm, who, with his young son, was standing on the same side of Elm Street, somewhat closer to the limousine. "I very definitely saw the effect of the second bullet that struck the President," Brehm later pointed out. "That which appeared to be a portion of the President's skull went flying slightly to the rear of the President's car and directly to its left. It did fly over toward the curb to the left and to the rear." [6] Mrs. Kennedy's actions would tend to confirm Brehm's report. Although she has no recollection of climbing out on the trunk of the limousine (5H180), Clint Hall recalled that "[she] was, it appeared to me, reaching for something" (2H138). Hill went on to say that, although he could not be sure, "I thought I saw something come off the back, too . . . I do know the next day we found the portion of the President's head . . . in the street" (2H140).

Officers Hargis and Martin testified that they were spattered with debris from the head impact. They were to the left rear of the President.

After the shooting, Hargis (arrow in both photos) stopped, got off his motorcycle, and led the chase up the grassy knoll. Later, he told the Commission that he thought a shot had come from that direction.

The main thrust of the impact debris was directed over the rear of the car onto the two motorcyclists riding in convoy to the left.[7] Clint Hill went on to point out how there "was blood and bits of brain all over the entire rear portion of the car. Mrs. Kennedy was completely covered with blood" (2H141). Officer B. J. Martin, riding the outboard cycle some 5 feet to the left and 6 to 8 feet to the rear of the presidential car, later noticed "blood stains on the left of my helmet . . . [and] other material that looked like pieces of flesh" (6H290). He told the Commission also how there was blood and other material on his uniform and on the windshield and motor of his cycle (6H292).

Officer Martin's partner, riding the inboard cycle, was even more splattered. "It seemed like his head exploded," testified Officer Bobby W. Hargis, "and I was splattered with blood and brain, and kind of bloody water" (6H294). This debris hit Officer Hargis with such force that he told reporters the next day, "I thought at first I might have been hit."[8] The splash of this debris established in his mind the idea that the shot came from the right front.

> *At the time [he told the Commission], there was something in my mind that said they probably could have been coming from the railroad overpass, because I thought since I had got splattered with blood—I was just a little back to the left of Mrs. Kennedy (6H294–295).*

Later that afternoon Deputy Sheriff Seymour Weitzman found a sizable piece of skull, which fortunately had missed Officer Hargis. It was found some 8 to 12 inches from the south curb of Elm Street—a location some 10 to 15 feet to the *left* of the car's path (7H107).

This was probably what both Charles Brehm and Clint Hill saw driven back over the left rear of the presidential car. It would be revealing to know exactly where Weitzman found this skull fragment.[9] If it was found in front of where the limousine was at

Z313, this would tend to confirm the Commission's version. If it was found much behind this location, this would further strengthen the view that the President was shot from the right front. It would also be helpful to know just where in the skull this bone originated. If it came from one of the frontal bones this would strengthen the Commission's case. However, if it came from the occipital bone at the rear of the skull this would be evidence for the front-shot view. Sadly, neither of these questions can be answered, since Weitzman was never asked to point out where along the curb he found the bone, nor were the characteristics of the bone ever identified.

With respect to another piece of bone found along Elm Street, we have additional and very important information. Late in the afternoon of November 23 Billy Harper, a student at Texas Christian University, was taking photographs of the assassination site when he found a piece of bone in the grass on the south side of Elm Street (*Archives,* CD 5). The exact location where Harper found the bone is somewhat ambiguous: the FBI report notes only that it was found "approximately 25 feet south of the spot where President Kennedy was shot" (*Archives,* CD 5). Harper took the bone to his uncle, Dr. Jack C. Harper, who identified it as human skull bone and then took it to Methodist Hospital where it was photographed and examined by the chief pathologist. On November 26 it was turned over to the FBI, and the following day was delivered to Admiral Burkley at the White House (*Archives,* CD 5).

The crucial fact may be found in the report of the pathologist who examined it. Dr. A. B. Cairns, chief pathologist at Methodist Hospital, told the FBI his examination disclosed that "the bone specimen looked like it came from the occipital [rear] region of the skull" (*Archives,* CD 5). It is difficult to understand how a shot from the rear could drive a piece of the occipital bone 25 feet to the left of the vehicle's path. It is not so difficult to understand how a shot from the right front exploding through the rear of the skull could produce precisely that effect.

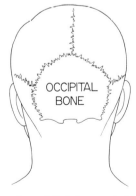

Location of occipital bone at the rear of the skull. It was a piece from this bone that was found twenty-five feet to the left of the car's path.

## HEAD WOUND CHARACTERISTICS

Z313                         SKETCH

The impact on the President's head at Zapruder frame 313. Note skull fragment (arrow) which has been driven down and *rearwards* by the impact.

One of the most troubling features of the Zapruder film has always been the actual appearance of the President's head under impact. In frame 313 we see a red halo and several fragments flying off in various directions. One of these fragments appears to be actually flying toward the *rear,* while they all seem to originate at a point midway between the President's ear and right temple. The epicenter of the explosion (there is no other word for it) would seem to lie at this point. This manifestly appears to be the impact of a bullet in the right parietal-frontal region. This is precisely what the two best witnesses to the head shot actually saw.

Marilyn Sitzman was only some 75 feet away looking down into the car when the President's head exploded.

*Miss Sitzman: And the next thing that I remembered clearly was the shot that hit directly in front of us, or almost directly in front of us, that hit him on the side of his face.*

*Thompson: Where on the side of the head did that shot appear to hit?*

*Miss Sitzman: I would say it'd be above the ear and to the front.*

*Thompson: In other words, if one drew a line vertically upward from the tip of the ear, it would be forward of that line?*

*Miss Sitzman: Yes.*

*Thompson: It would then be back of the temple, but on the side of the head?*

*Miss Sitzman: Between the eye and the ear. And we could see his brains come out, you know, his head opening; it must have been a terrible shot because it exploded his head more or less (Taped interview, Nov. 29, 1966).*

Officer James Chaney, shown above looking directly at Kennedy, saw "the President struck in the face" by the final bullet.

Officer Chaney at Parkland Hospital.

Much closer to the President was Officer James Chaney of the Dallas Police. Riding motorcycle escort at the right rear of the presidential limousine, he looked left into the passenger compartment immediately after the first shot. The President was leaning to his left, Chaney told a TV interviewer on the afternoon of November 22, and he then saw "the President struck in the face" by the final bullet.[10]

The impressions of Marilyn Sitzman and James Chaney were corroborated by William and Gayle Newman. Standing on the north curb of Elm Street, they were only 15 feet from the President at the time of the head shot:

William and Gayle Newman saw the President hit in the side of the head (above) and, believing the last shot to have come from directly behind them, they threw themselves on the ground (below).

*Thompson: Now could you tell me about the impact on the President's head, what you saw? There's a diagram you drew for me where you put it right at the ear.*

*Wm. Newman: That's what I saw. The way he was hit, it looked like he had just been hit with a baseball pitch; just like a block of wood fell over his . . .*

*Thompson: You just bobbed your head backwards and over towards the left. The location that you drew is right about the ear.*

*Wm. Newman: In my opinion the ear went.*

*Thompson: Now could I ask you a little more about this, try to get your immediate response? I take it, it was your immediate response—in your affidavit of the 22nd—that the shots were somehow right back of you?*

*Wm. Newman: That's right. Well, of course the President's being shot in the side of the head, by the third shot—I thought the shot was fired from directly above and behind where we were standing. And that's what scared us, because I thought we were right in the direct path of gunfire. And . . .*

*Thompson: By the President's head, you mean the actual appearance of the impact on the side of his head here and the way his head flipped back over this . . .*

*Wm. Newman: Right, right. My thoughts were that the shot entered there and apparently the thoughts of the Warren Commission were that the shot came out that side.*

*Thompson: But it's your feeling that the shots were coming from over your . . . right behind you, based on (1) the sound of the shots, (2) the impact on the President's head, and (3) the movement of the President's head after impact. Would that be a fair statement?*

*Wm. Newman: Right. Well I think everybody thought the shots were from where I'm saying—behind us—because everybody went in that direction. Must have.*

*Thompson: Everyone* did *run in that direction; I've seen the films. This is probably pushing your own recollections too far, but I'll try it anyway. When you say in back of you, do you have any feeling . . . say, if I stand here, and I say "in back of me," do you have any feeling if it was back of me in this direction or back of me in this direction? Did it appear to be in back of you towards the Texas School Book Depository or towards the general area of the stockade fence and railroad? Do you have any recollection at all?*

*Wm. Newman: Well, this is going to sound peculiar, but I was thinking more just the opposite of the building . . . actually the thought never entered my mind that the shots were coming from the building.*

*Thompson: Is that right?*

*Wm. Newman: But, of course I've talked to people and they say, at that height, it echoes.*

*Thompson: But I take it, it was your first impression that the shots were coming a little bit from the right front of the vehicle?*

*Wm. Newman: The thought never entered my mind that it was coming from the rear (Taped interview, Nov. 29, 1966).*

At the end of the interview I asked William and Gayle Newman if there was anything that they thought I ought to pursue. Mr. Newman replied: "No. Except exactly where the bullet went in and where the bullet went out. That would be of great interest to me."

As he explained it, he was still greatly troubled by the Commission's conclusion that the bullet had exited in front when his own eyes told him a different story.

S. M. Holland, we recall, saw the President's body as it passed under his vantage point on the overpass. And we recall too his statement that the "whole right side" of the President's head "including part of his face" had been blown off. Hurchel Jacks, driver of the Vice-Presidential car, saw the President's body at Parkland Hospital. "Before the President's body was covered," Jacks related in a statement filed November 28, "it appeared that the bullet had struck him above the right ear or near the temple" (18II801). Seth Kantor, a Scripps-Howard reporter, jotted down in his notebook at Parkland Hospital the phrase "intered [*sic*] right temple" (20H353), apparently in reference to the President's wounds.

> We drove to the emergency entrance of Parkland Memorial Hospital. The President's car was stopped in the ambulance parking place. At that time I saw that the Vice President, Mrs. Johnson and Senator Yarbrough was out of my car and safely in the hospital. I went back to the President's car to see if I might assist. At that time the Secret Service Agents were removing Governor Connally from the jump seat. I could see that Governor Connally had been hit just below the right shoulder blade in the back. They removed Governor Connally, then picked Mrs. Kennedy from over the President's body. At that time one of the Secret Service Agents said he has been hit, put your coat over him. One of the Agents removed his suit coat and spread it over the President's body from his chest up.
>
> Before the President's body was covered it appeared that the bullet had struck him above the right ear or near the temple. They removed his body at that time Reporters began to arrive. We were assigned by the Secret Service to prevent any pictures of any nature to be taken of the President's car or the inside.
>
> Thomas J. Kelly                                    Hurchel Jacks
> Witness                                            Hurchel Jacks

Hurchel Jacks, Texas State Trooper and driver of the vice-presidential car, noted in a deposition that the President had been struck above the right ear near the temple.

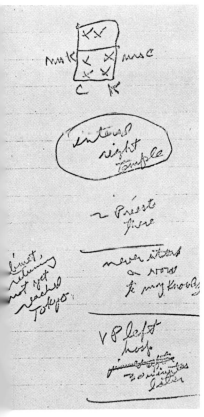

Newsman Seth Kantor took notes at Parkland Hospital and recorded that a shot entered the right temple.

The report that the President had been struck in the temple was the first description of his head wound to be broadcast by NBC. Only an hour and a half after the assassination this network reported that "the President was struck in the right temple by the bullet"; half an hour later it amplified: "The President was wounded in the back of the head and on the right side of the head: there was a loss of blood and brain tissue. A bullet struck him in front as he faced the assailant." *The New York Times* reported the next day that "Mr. Kennedy also had a massive gaping

wound in the back and one on the right side of the
head. However, the doctors said it was impossible to
determine immediately whether the wounds had been
caused by one bullet or two." The *Times* went on to
quote Dr. Kemp Clark, the attending neurosurgeon
in Dallas, as saying, "A missile had gone in and out
of the back of his head causing external lacerations
and loss of brain tissue."

Dr. Clark, the only neurosurgeon ever to see the
President's head injury, declared that he felt it was a
"tangential" wound and not an "exit" wound. Questioned by the Commission, Dr. Clark was asked about
his participation in a press conference held November
22 in which he described the President's head wound
as "tangential":

*Specter: What, if anything, did you say in the course
of that press conference?*

*Dr. Clark: I described the President's wound in his
head in very much the same way as I have
described it here. I was asked if this wound
was an entrance wound, an exit wound, or
what, and I said it could be an exit wound
but I felt it was a tangential wound (6H21).*

Dr. Clark was asked to describe the difference between "tangential" and other types of wound, and
he did. But Specter never asked him to indicate why
he thought the President's wound was tangential, nor,
indeed, even to describe with precision the characteristics of that wound. Yet if we combine Dr. Clark's
earlier cited statement that "a missile had gone in
and out the back of his [the President's] head" with
his judgment that the wound was "tangential," a pattern begins to emerge. What apparently is being described is a shot tangentially striking the right side
of the President's head blowing out the right rear
octant. Such a pattern would accord well with the
remaining descriptions of the head wound we get
from Parkland Hospital.

Dr. Ronald Coy Jones described "what appeared to be an exit wound in the posterior portion of the skull" (6H56). Dr. Malcolm Perry noted "a large avulsive [exploded] injury of the right occipitoparietal area" (6H11), while Dr. Charles Baxter recalled "a large gaping wound in the back of the skull . . . literally the right side of his head had been blown off" (6H40–41). Dr. Gene Akin observed how the "back of the right occipitalparietal portion of his head was shattered, with brain substance protruding" (6H65). Yet certainly our most detailed description of the Kennedy head wound appears in the testimony of Parkland Physician Dr. Robert N. McClelland:

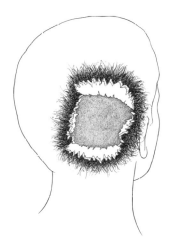

A pictorial representation of President Kennedy's head wound as described by Dr. Robert N. McClelland of Parkland Hospital.

*As I took the position at the head of the table . . . I was in such a position that I could very closely examine the head wound, and I noted that the right posterior portion of the skull had been blasted. It had been shattered, apparently, by the force of the shot so that the parietal bone was protruded up through the scalp and seemed to be fractured almost along its posterior half, as well as some of the occipital bone being fractured in its lateral half, and this sprung open the bones that I mentioned in such a way that you could actually look down into the skull cavity itself and see that probably a third or so, at least, of the brain tissue, posterior cerebral tissue and some of the cerebellar tissue had been blasted out (6H33).*

This is the clearest description we have of the Kennedy head wound.[11] In reading it we can understand quite readily why neurosurgeon Clark called the wound "tangential." For Dr. McClelland is quite clearly describing an impact on the right side of the head that blasted backward, springing open the parietal and occipital bones [see diagram] and driving out a mass of brain tissue. The precise character of the brain tissue is also important, for only a deep-ranging shot could have blown out cerebellar tissue, which is located very low in the brain. Dr. Marion Jenkins of Parkland remembers how "there was herniation and laceration of great areas of the brain, even to the extent that the cerebellum had protruded from the wound" (17H15; cf. 6H48), and Dr. James Carrico speaks of how the head wound "had avulsed [exploded] the calvarium [skull]" (17H4). A nurse, Pat Hutton, later recalled how "a doctor asked me to place a pressure dressing on the head wound. This was of no use, however, because of the massive opening on the back of the head" (21H216).

What all those reports seem to describe is a massive impact that exploded outward through the back of the skull driving bone and brain tissue with it.* We know where this mass of bone and tissue went. It splattered motorcycle officers Martin and Hargis, the biggest piece of skull continuing on a left and downward course until it came to rest only inches from the south (or left) curb of Elm Street. A smaller piece of skull broken off the occipital bone at the rear of the skull was thrown even farther to the left onto the grass verge where it was found the following day by Billy Harper.

Given such a wound, how could the Bethesda autopsy fail to reveal its true character?

Dr. Milton Helpern has stated that, if permitted to see the Kennedy autopsy X-rays, he would look for traces of metal indicating the presence of another head wound.[12] Although he is not particularly sanguine about the possibility of finding such traces,

---

* The Sibert-O'Neill autopsy report notes that the Bethesda doctors found two discernible fragments in the President's head. The largest fragment was found in a frontal sinus just behind the right eye; this fragment was subsequently found to weigh 1.65 grains (5H73) and is mentioned in the official autopsy report. "The next largest fragment," according to Sibert and O'Neill, "appeared to be at the rear of the skull at the juncture of the skull bone" (*Archives,* CD 7). No mention of this "next largest fragment" is made in the official autopsy report or in the testimony of the autopsy surgeons. Its location would be more consistent with a front-entering shot blowing out the right rear octant of the President's skull than with a rear-entering bullet.

he does not rule out the possibility that the Bethesda pathologists may have overlooked another entrance wound:

> *Often, quite often, wounds of entrance in the head are completely overlooked because they are covered naturally by the hair. The wound may barely bleed at all. If you don't take a comb and go over the entire scalp inch by inch, separating the hair carefully and meticulously, it's easy to miss a head wound entirely. There is no evidence that this type of examination was made.*[13]

Nor should the possibility be ruled out that the explosive impact of two bullets on the President's skull blew out all traces of the right front entry. What the Bethesda doctors found was an enormous wound in the President's head (Commander Boswell told me that the President's brain was quite easily removed without recourse to surgery) with a small entry hole in the right occiput. They observed a long, back-to-front laceration parallel to the midline of the brain, and examined a bone fragment that showed the beveled curve of an exit opening. On the basis of these three pieces of information the Bethesda doctors concluded that the bullet that entered the back of the President's skull blew out the right top of his head. Let us examine each of these bits of information in turn.

A half-moon-shaped fragment of bone is sketched on the back of the autopsy face sheet prepared by Commander Boswell (see illustration). This particular fragment was presented to the doctors in the course of their autopsy. One of its edges matched up with an edge of skull in place so that it was possible to locate this bone fragment at the very crown of the President's head on the midline.[14] Since the characteristic beveling of an exiting projectile was apparent in one corner of this fragment, they assumed that a large bullet fragment had exited through this hole.

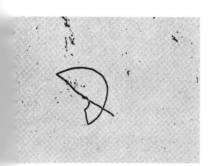

Commission Exhibit 397: Half-moon-shaped fragment of bone sketched on the back of the autopsy face sheet by Commander Boswell.

Commission Exhibits 386 and 397 are in apparent disagreement regarding the direction of the head entry wound. The diagram drawn by Commander Boswell during the autopsy ( right) shows entry canted to the left, though a later artistic rendering presented to the Commission in lieu of the photographs ( left ) shows an entry wound canted to the right.

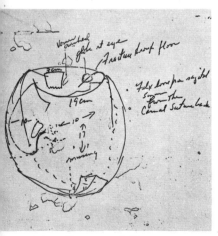

The diagram of Kennedy's skull drawn by Boswell shows a good deal of information never recorded in the official autopsy report. For example, area of fracture in left temple region, crushed vomer bone, and fracture in the globe of the right eye socket.

Now if we suppose that two bullets struck the President's head, it is impossible to tell which projectile or fragment exited through this hole. The physical characteristics of the bone fragment (its beveling) accord equally well with a shot from the front or the rear; in itself it is indeterminative as to direction of impact.

The small bullet hole in the rear of the President's head, however, causes considerable difficulty for the official theory. Although the axis of this wound is drawn on Commission Exhibit 386 as pointing to the right, on the original autopsy face sheet we find an arrow pointing from this wound, *not to the right* (where the bullet would have had to go in order to exit from the right top), *but rather to the left—toward the midtemple region* (see illustration).

On the back of the autopsy face sheet we find further information to corroborate the leftward-pointing arrow. Here we find a diagram of the skull drawn once again by Commander Boswell. Although unmentioned in the official report, this sketch shows clearly an area of fracture in the left midtemple region marked "3 cm." in width. Other notations on the same sketch indicate that the vomer bone (located slightly above and behind the nose) is crushed, and that there is a fracture through the floor of the skull at the right eye. Commander Boswell confirmed to me that there was indeed this large area of skull damage in the mid- and low-temple region although none of these fractures had broken the skin.[15] Combining this information with the long front-to-back laceration discovered in the brain, a coherent pattern begins to emerge. The main thrust of the rear shot apparently drove forward through the brain toward the midtemple region. One fragment deposited itself behind the right eye. Another fragment drove down through the midbrain fracturing the skull floor and penetrating the President's throat. Still other fragments exploded forward toward the car's windshield.[16]

Such a pattern of damage would match perfectly our expectations for a shot fired from the sixth-floor

Depository window entering the President's occiput at Z313. As both the reenactment photo and Z312 indicate, such a shot would not blow out the right side of the President's head but would drive forward into the low- and midtemple region. This is precisely what the autopsy face sheet and the brain examination indicate happened.

The autopsy doctors' own report and working papers vitiate their conclusion that the rear-entering bullet blew out the right side of the President's head. What these papers and reports do show is the moderate damage caused by a bullet that entered the President's skull from the rear and drove forward to the temple.

The pattern that emerges from this study of medical evidence is a dual one. From the Parkland doctors we get the picture of a bullet that struck the right front of the President's head on a tangent, ranged backward causing massive damage to the right brain hemisphere, sprung open the occipital and parietal bones, and exploded out over the rear of the limousine. From the Bethesda surgeons we get the picture of a bullet entering the rear of the President's head and driving forward to the midtemple region. Putting the two pictures together, we discern the outlines of the double impact. First, a bullet from behind exploding forward, and in that same split second another bullet driving into the exploding mass, forcing tissue and skull in the opposite direction. This is not a pretty picture, but it reconciles the evidence of the Zapruder film, eye- and earwitness reports, and the curious double dispersion of impact debris. A coincidence[17] certainly, but a coincidence whose reality is confirmed by the overwhelming weight of evidence.

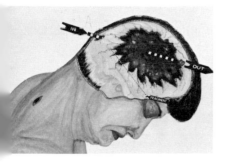

In order to make plausible a shot entering the occipital region and exiting the right top of the head, a Navy medical artist had to distort the position of the President's head under the impact of the fatal bullet. Zapruder frame 312 (below) shows its actual position at the instant of impact.

312                    SKETCH

## NOTES

1. Holland told us that the testimony printed in the *Hearings* does not accord with his recollection of what he told Assistant Counsel Samuel Stern. Some weeks after he testified, Holland returned with his lawyer and together they corrected the transcript. "We red marked . . . red pencilled that statement from beginning to end," Holland told us, "because there was a lot of errors in it. I don't know whether it was made with people attacking it or whether the girl that took the testimony made mistakes. But there were a lot of mistakes in it and we corrected it with a red pencil." Holland went on to tell us that apparently his corrections were lost somewhere along the line because "the statement that I made, as well as I remember, isn't in context with the Warren Commission [*Hearings*]."

2. This double movement was discovered independently by researcher Raymond Marcus of Los Angeles. Harold Weisberg apparently made a similar discovery in the autumn of 1966. In his second book, *Whitewash II* (Hyattstown: Harold Weisberg, 1966), he notes: "Prior to Frame 313, the 'fatal' shot, his body makes a short, sharp lurch. His head and shoulders alone seem to be involved. Although the *Report* insists the President was hit only from behind, his head goes both ways. The motions are discontinuous, violent and unmistakable" (p. 221).

3. In arriving at this figure an angle of 45 degrees is assumed; see Appendix B. Since acceleration measures the rate of change of velocity, and since velocity is measured in units of distance/time, the units of acceleration are (distance/time)/time = distance/(time)$^2$—in this case feet per second per second or feet/(second)$^2$.

4. Robert S. Woodworth and Harold Schlosberg, *Experimental Psychology* (New York: Henry Holt & Co., 1956), p. 184. The startle response is particularly fast. The familiar "hot stove" reflex, for example, occurs in an interval of 268–888 milliseconds (p. 18).

5. Unpublished study of the Zapruder film done for *Ramparts* magazine; see *Ramparts,* January, 1967, p. 89.

6. Tape-recorded interview with Brehm conducted by Mark Lane on Mar. 28, 1966, cited in Mark Lane, *Rush to Judgment* (New York: Holt, Rinehart & Winston, Inc., 1966), p. 56.

7. Another motorcyclist was riding to the rear and to the right of the presidential automobile. Officer James Chaney can be seen in the Altgens photo looking directly at President Kennedy. Given a shot from the rear, blowing out the right side of the President's head, we would expect Chaney (not the *left* rear motorcyclists) to have been splattered. Was he splattered? I made an attempt to talk with Chaney in Dallas and was rebuffed by the Dallas Police. Although he was in a unique position to observe the shooting he was never questioned by the Commission. The testimony of another motor-

cyclist perhaps indicates why. Officer Marrion Baker told the Commission he talked with Chaney on the afternoon of November 22 and that Chaney told him two bullets hit the President and still a third struck the Governor (3H266). If it turns out that Chaney was not splattered with impact debris, then the Commission had a double reason for not calling him to testify.

8. New York *Daily News,* Nov. 24, 1963.

9. In the fall of 1966 and the spring of 1967 I made an effort to find Weitzman in order to ask him where he found the skull fragment. My inquiries disclosed that he left Dallas in early 1964 and that his present whereabouts were unknown. Billy Harper (mentioned in a similar connection in the next paragraph) also has left Dallas.

10. WFAA-TV, Video Tape PKT-24, at 21 minutes, 8 seconds into the tape.

11. The official autopsy description is unhelpfully vague, noting only that "there is a large irregular defect of the scalp and skull on the right involving chiefly the parietal bone but extending somewhat into the temporal and occipital regions" (16H980). This vagueness is not dissipated by Commander Humes's testimony, where the wound is described as "a huge defect over the right side of the skull . . . approximately 13 centimeters in greatest diameter" (2H351).

12. Marshall Houts, *Where Death Delights* (New York: Coward-McCann, 1967), p. 61.

13. *Ibid.,* pp. 61–62.

14. Boswell interview, Jan. 11, 1967.

15. *Ibid.*

16. The Commission's *Report* mentions two points of damage to the front of the limousine: a dent in the chrome just above the rearview mirror, and a radial pattern of cracks in the windshield (R77). The Commission notes that "there is some uncertainty whether the dent in the chrome on the windshield was present prior to the assassination" (R77). Yet it had in its files a letter from Secret Service Chief James J. Rowley which indicated unambiguously that the dent had not been caused at the time of the assassination. Rowley's Jan. 6, 1964, letter states: "In a photograph attached and labeled Exhibit 2, taken by the FBI, there is a dent in the chrome topping of the windshield, just above the attachment of the rear-view mirror to the top of the windshield frame. SA Gies, who was responsible for the care and maintenance of this vehicle, believes that this damage was on this car prior to November 22, 1963, and it is his recollection that the damage was done in New York at the. Empire Garage (Lincoln-Mercury Dealer) on November 1, 1961. Gies thinks the damage was done while he and employees of the Empire Garage were removing the 'header' on the leatherette top to make repairs to the crank which

Photograph of a dent in the chrome windshield trim of the President's limousine.

Photo of cracks in windshield.

Photo taken by James Altgens just *before* the last shot (note undamaged windshield). Another photograph taken seconds *after* the final shot shows the cracks in the windshield.

secures the convertible top in place on this vehicle" (*Archives,* CD 80).

On the other hand, the pattern of cracks in the windshield was caused during the assassination by a fragment from the head shot. Robert Frazier of the FBI testified that lead residue found on the inside surface of the glass showed conclusively that it had been struck from the rear (5H69). Frazier went on to point out that, although the cracks could not have been caused by a bullet traveling at full velocity, they could have been caused by a bullet fragment traveling at "fairly high velocity" (5H70). Two fragments, ballistically matched to Oswald's rifle, were found in the front seat of the limousine on the evening of November 22. Although the Commission did not venture to say which shot caused the windshield crack, there is photographic evidence proving indisputably that the windshield cracks were caused by a fragment from the Z313 head shot. In a picture taken by James Altgens after the first two shots, no cracks are apparent in the windshield, while in a later shot by the same photographer (taken just after the Z313 head shot) the telltale cracks have appeared.

17. Actually, given the hypothesis of three gunmen firing on the motorcade in an interval of less than 6 seconds, it is not so improbable that two shots would be virtually simultaneous.

# VI

## TRAJECTORIES AND
## FIRING POINTS

*Well, now you have something here ... I
didn't see this man before. [About 20 seconds
pass, then Holland says:] Well, do you know,
I think that you're looking right down at the
barrel of that gun right now!*
*—S. M. Holland, taped interview, Nov. 30,
1966.*

### THE STOCKADE FENCE

A wooden stockade fence 5 feet high at the top
of a grassy slope partially bounds the north side of
Elm Street and then angles sharply back from the
street. The evenly cropped branches of a hedgerow
in front of the fence leave a gap some 18 inches high
between the serrated fence top and their spreading
foliage. Behind the fence a small parking lot for railroad employees gives way to the railroad yards beyond. Dominating the yards and controlling their
maze of switches, tracks, and signal lights is the North
Tower of the Union Terminal Railroad.

On November 22, 1963, Lee Bowers worked the

Lee Bowers' view of parking lot and stockade fence.

7:00 A.M. to 3:00 P.M. shift as "tower man" in the North Tower. From his perch 14 feet above the ground Bowers controlled eleven tracks in the Union Station and two additional freight sidings. He also had a grandstand seat for observing some unusual happenings in the area of the stockade fence and the parking lot behind.

Traffic into the parking area was cut off at 10:00 A.M. (6H285). The lot was already jammed with the cars of people who had come to downtown Dallas to watch the presidential motorcade. Bowers recalled that nothing unusual happened until shortly before noon. His affidavit filed on November 22 tells the story:

> At about 11:55 am I saw a dirty 1959 Oldsmobile station wagon come down the street toward my building. This street dead ends in the railroad. This car had out of state license plates with white background and black numbers, no letters. It also had a Goldwater for "64" sticker in the rear window. This car just drove around slowly and left the area. It was occupied by a middle-aged white man partly grey hair. At about 12:15 pm another car came in the area with a white man about 25 to 35 years old driving. This car was a 1957 Ford, Black, 2 doors with Texas license. This man appeared to have a mike or telephone in the car. Just a few minutes after this car left at 12:20 pm another car pulled in. This car was a 1961 Chevrolet, Impala, 4 door, am not sure that this was a 4 door, color white and dirty up to the windows. This car also had a Goldwater for "64" sticker. This car was driven by a white male about 25 to 35 years old with long blond hair. He stayed in the area longer than the others. This car also had the same type license plates as the 1959 Oldsmobile.[1] He left the area about 12:25 pm. About 8 or 10 minutes after he left I heard at least 3 shots very close together. Just after the shots

*the area became crowded with people com-*
*ing from Elm Street and the slope just north*
*of Elm (24H201).*

Four months later Bowers was asked by the
Commission how he knew the man in the black Ford
was operating a radio. He replied:

*He was holding something up to his mouth*
*with one hand and he was driving with the*
*other and gave that appearance. He was very*
*close to the tower. I could see him as he pro-*
*ceeded around the area (6H286).*

Apparently Lee Bowers was not the only person
watching the parking lot and stockade fence to the
north of Elm Street. About half a minute before the
motorcade passed the corner of Elm and Houston
Streets, Bob Edwards and Ronald Fischer noticed a
young man standing at a sixth-floor, southeast-corner
window of the Depository looking in the same direction. Fischer testified:

*Bob punched me and said, "Look at that*
*guy there in that window." And he made*
*some remark—said, "He looks like he's un-*
*comfortable"—or something.*
*    And I looked up and watched the man*
*for, oh, I'd say, 10 or 15 seconds . . . This*
*man held my attention for 10 or 15 seconds,*
*because he appeared uncomfortable for one,*
*and secondly, he wasn't watching—uh—he*
*didn't look like he was watching for the*
*parade. He looked like he was looking down*
*toward the Trinity River and the triple under-*
*pass down at the end—toward the end of*
*Elm Street. And—uh—all the time I watched*
*him, he never moved his head, he never*
*moved anything. Just was there transfixed*
*(6H193).*

It is, of course, impossible to know for certain why
the sniper on the sixth floor of the Depository was
more interested in the area to the north of Elm

Street than in the motorcade approaching him. A possible clue is furnished by Lee Bowers.

Bowers had worked in the North Tower for over ten years and hence knew by sight the railroad employees who worked in the yards. On that Friday morning he noticed two men he had never seen before standing behind the stockade fence. "They were standing within 10 or 15 feet of each other," Bowers told the Commission, "and gave no appearance of being together, as far as I knew. They were facing and looking towards Main and Houston, and following the caravan as it came down" (6H287). Bowers watched the motorcade turn right on Houston Street. Then it disappeared, to emerge a moment later on Elm Street. Just as the presidential car disappeared behind the concrete colonnade to the north of Elm Street, the shots rang out. At precisely this instant Bowers noted some "commotion" near the stockade fence (6H288). Asked by Commission Counsel Joseph A. Ball to be more explicit about what attracted his attention, he replied:

> *I just am unable to describe rather than it was something out of the ordinary, a sort of milling around, but something occurred in this particular spot which was out of the ordinary, which attracted my eye for some reason, which I could not identify (6H288).*

Much later Bowers was asked by Mark Lane to amplify his answer. In a tape-recorded interview Bowers remarked:

> *At the time of the shooting, in the vicinity of where the two men I have described were, there was a flash of light or, as far as I am concerned, something I could not identify, but there was something which occurred which caught my eye in this immediate area on the embankment. Now, what this was, I could not state at that time and at the time I could not identify it, other than there was some unusual occurrence—a flash of light or smoke or something which caused me to feel like something out of the ordinary had occurred there.[2]*

Bystanders rush to the grassy knoll moments after the shooting. Several said they thought shots came from the knoll.

This "unusual occurrence—a flash of light or smoke or something" was observed by other witnesses who reported it to law-enforcement officers on the scene. Deputy Sheriffs L. C. Smith, Seymour Weitzman, A. D. McCurley, and J. L. Oxford all later spoke of witnesses who called their attention to the stockade fence. Smith reported that as he ran toward the knoll "I heard a woman unknown to me say the President was shot in the head and the shots came from the fence on the north side of Elm Street" (19H516). Weitzman recalled that:

> As he came to the fence at the top of the grassy slope, some bystander mentioned that the firecracker or shot had come from the other side of the fence, and he requested a bystander to bend over and he used the bystander's back as a step and vaulted over the fence (Archives, CD 5).

McCurley and Oxford independently reported being told by a witness or witnesses that smoke had been seen near the corner of the stockade fence. McCurley recalled:

> I ran over and jumped a fence and a railroad worker stated to me that he believed the smoke from the bullets came from the vicinity of a stockade fence which surrounds the park area (19H514).

Oxford gave a similar account:

> We jumped the picket fence which was

*along Elm Street and ran over into the rail-
road yards. When we got there, there was a
man who told us that he had seen smoke up
in the corner of the fence (19H530).*

The "railroad worker" mentioned by McCurley and
the "man" noted by Oxford may in fact be the same
person. And this might possibly be S. M. Holland,
who, only hours after the shooting, signed an affidavit which reads in part:

*The President's car was coming down Elm
Street and when they got just about to the
Arcade I heard what I thought for the moment was a firecracker and he slumped over
and I looked over towards the arcade and
trees and saw a puff of smoke come from
the trees and I heard three more shots after
the first shot but that was the only puff of
smoke I saw . . . the puff of smoke I saw
definitely came from behind the arcade
through the trees (20H163).*

Four and one-half months later Holland reiterated
his contention concerning the puff of smoke to Assistant Counsel Stern:

*There was a shot, a report . . . and a puff of
smoke came out about 6 or 8 feet above the
ground right out from under those trees. And
at just about this location from where I was
standing you could see that puff of smoke,
like someone had thrown a firecracker, or
something out, and that is just about the way
it sounded. It wasn't as loud as the previous
reports or shots (6H244).*

Counsel Stern pressed Holland on whether he had
indeed heard four shots. Holland replied:

*I have no doubt about it. I have no doubt
about seeing that puff of smoke come out
from under those trees either (6H244).*

When we interviewed Holland in Dallas we asked
him to point out on a photograph exactly where he
had seen the puff of smoke. He told us:

*Right under these trees, right at that exact spot, about ten or fifteen feet from this corner, the corner of the fence here, back this way, right under this clump of trees, right under this tree, particular tree. It's that exact spot, right there ... That's where it was ... just like somebody had thrown a firecracker and left a little puff of smoke there; it was just laying there. It was a white smoke; it wasn't a black smoke or like a black powder. It was like a puff of a cigarette, but it was about nine feet off the ground. It would be just about in line with, or maybe just a little bit higher than that fence, but by the time it got out underneath the tree, well, it would be about eight or nine feet ... [the ground slopes off sharply in front of the fence] (Taped interview, Nov. 30, 1966).*

"Right under these trees . . . it was just like somebody had thrown a firecracker and left a little puff of smoke there." S. M. Holland.

Holland was not the only witness to see the puff of smoke. Richard Dodd, who had stood next to Holland on the overpass, later reported that "the shot . . . the smoke came from behind the hedge on the north side of the Plaza."[3] Austin Miller swore out an affidavit on November 22 in which he declared: "I saw something which I thought was smoke or steam coming from a group of trees north of Elm off the railroad tracks" (24H217). When interviewed by the FBI in March, 1964, James Simmons reported seeing "fumes of smoke near the embankment in front of the TSBD [Depository]" (22H833), while Clemon Johnson stated that "white smoke was observed near the pavilion" (22H836).[4] In addition, both Walter Winborn and Thomas Murphy told an independent investigator that they had observed smoke in the trees along the knoll.[5] In all, at least seven people standing on the overpass saw smoke in the area of the parking lot and the stockade fence.

Dodd, Simmons, and Holland were so sure a shot had come from the corner of the fence that (as soon as the President's car disappeared beneath them) they ran to their left off the overpass and into the

Holland retraces his steps from the overpass around to the back of the stockade fence.

Area behind stockade fence.

parking lot adjoining the fence. They had to leap a steam pipe and then make their way across the tangle of cars in the lot. Jumping over bumpers and crawling over hoods, they arrived near the corner of the fence a minute or two later. Dodd recalled that "there were tracks and cigarette butts laying where someone had been standing on the bumper looking over the fence."[6] Seymour Weitzman joined the railroad workers at about this time and later reported noticing "numerous kinds of footprints that did not make sense because they were going different directions" (7H107). Holland gave a similar description of these strange footprints to the Warren Commission (6H245–246). During our interview we asked Holland about these footprints and he told us:

> *And I got over to the spot where I saw the smoke come from and heard the shot; I was looking for empty shells or some indication that there was a rifleman or someone over there. Well, you know it'd been raining that morning and behind the station wagon from one end of the bumper to the other, I expect you could've counted four or five-hundred footprints down there. And on the bumper, oh about twelve or eighteen inches apart, it looked like someone had raked their shoes off; there were muddy spots up there, like someone had been standing up there (Taped interview, Nov. 30, 1966).*

Later on in the interview Holland told us that the marks were men's footprints and that he was puzzled by their narrow grouping. "That was the mystery to me," Holland exclaimed, "that they didn't extend further than from one end of the bumper to the other. That's as far as they would go. It looked like a lion pacing a cage."

It is possible that these footprints bear some relation to the sixth-floor sniper's interest in this area. It is also possible that the prints belonged to one of the two strangers spotted behind the fence by Lee

Bowers. But if we suppose that someone was standing here (some 10 to 15 feet down from the fence corner) at the time of the shooting, then what happened to this individual? How did he disappear in that 1- or 2-minute interval between the last shot and when Dodd, Simmons, Holland, and Weitzman arrived on the scene?

Holland himself has provided a plausible suggestion:

> *Just to the west of the station wagon [Holland told us], there were two sets of footprints that left . . . I noticed these two footprints leaving; now they could have stepped out between the second and third cars on the gravel or they could've got in the trunk compartment of this car and pulled the lid down, which would have been very, very easy (Taped interview, Nov. 30, 1966).*

On this theory, so Holland suggests, since the trunk compartments of cars in the lot were not searched, a confederate may have returned to the area sometime later and driven away the car in question.

If the person did not secrete himself in a car trunk, then, since crowds were soon entering the lot from east and south, he must have made good his escape to the northwest. It is possible J. C. Price saw such a person escaping the area. Price was watching the motorcade from the roof of the Terminal Annex Building across Dealey Plaza from the knoll. In an affidavit filed on the afternoon of November 22, Price noted:

> *I saw one man run towards the passenger cars on the railroad siding after the volley of shots. This man had a white dress shirt, no tie, and khaki colored trousers. His hair appeared to be long and dark and his agility running could be about 25 years of age. He had something in his hand. I couldn't be sure but it may have been a head piece (19H492).*

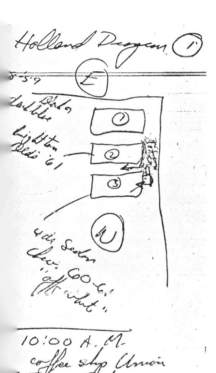

S. M. Holland's diagram of footprints behind the stockade fence. Prints are indicated by black marks to the right of car No. 2.

Just what the man was carrying in his hand must remain an open question. Sometime later Price told Mark Lane that the man "was carrying something in his right hand" that "could have been a gun."[7] "He was bareheaded," Price continued, "which gave me the suspicion that he was doing the shooting, but I could be mistaken."[8]

There is one final solution to the mystery of what happened to the man behind the fence. He could have stayed right where he was, perhaps mingling with the crowd as it filled the parking lot. The strange adventure of Dallas Patrolman Joe Marshall Smith lends credence to such an idea. Smith was directing traffic at the corner of Elm and Houston Streets when the shooting occurred. Immediately afterward, a woman rushed up to Smith and yelled, "They are shooting the President from the bushes" (7H535). Smith ran down Elm Street and entered the parking lot behind the stockade fence (7H535). An FBI report from December 9 tells part of the story of what he found there:

Stunned spectators swarm through parking lot shortly after the assassination. Several thought the shots had come from that direction.

> *He [Patrolman Smith] stated he did smell what he thought was gunpowder[9] but stated that this smell was in the parking lot near the TSBD and not by the underpass. He advised he never at any time went to the underpass and could not advise if there was the smell of gunpowder in the underpass [The U.S. Attorney had forwarded a report to the FBI saying Smith had "definitely distinguished the aroma of gunpowder near the underpass."] (Archives, CD 205).*

When Smith was questioned by the Commission six months later, he was never asked about smelling gunpowder. However, the questioning of Assistant Counsel Liebeler did bring to light an equally suspicious event:

*Liebeler: You proceeded up to an area immediately behind the concrete structure here that is described by Elm Street and the street that runs immediately in front of the TSBD, is that right?*

*Smith: I was checking all the bushes and I checked all the cars in the parking lot.*

*Liebeler: There is a parking lot in behind the grassy area back from Elm Street toward the railroad tracks, and you went down to the parking lot and looked around?*

*Smith: Yes, sir: I checked all the cars, I looked into all the cars and checked around the bushes. Of course, I wasn't alone. There was some deputy sheriff[10] with me, and I believe one Secret Service man when I got there.*

*I got to make this statement, too. I felt awfully silly, but after the shot and this, I pulled my pistol from my holster, and I thought, this is silly, I don't know who I am looking for, and I put it back. Just as I did, he showed me that he was a Secret Service agent.*

*Liebeler: Did you accost this man?*

*Smith: Well, he saw me coming with my pistol and right away he showed me who he was.*

*Liebeler: Do you remember who it was?*

*Smith: No, sir, I don't . . . (7H535).*

Encountering a Secret Service agent at the scene of the assassination would not seem to be a strange or suspicious event. It becomes so only when we learn by checking the individual reports of the agents who accompanied the motorcade that *none* of them remained at Dealey Plaza, but that *all* went with the motorcade to Parkland Hospital (18H722–799).[11] The man Patrolman Smith surprised with drawn revolver behind the fence could not have been a Secret Service agent, although he showed what appeared to be Secret Service credentials. Who was he? To this day no one knows.

From films of the assassination we can see that the witnesses closest to the corner of the stockade fence threw themselves to the ground immediately after the final shot. William and Gayle Newman dropped to the ground and tried to shield their two children with their own bodies. Bill Newman told me why:

> *I thought the shots were coming from right off the tops of our heads . . . When we turned around, I think . . . well, several people hit the ground.*
>
> *Well, of course, the President's being shot in the side of the head by the third shot—I thought the shot was fired from directly behind where we were standing. And that's what scared us, because I thought we were right in the direct path of gunfire (Taped interview, Nov. 29, 1966).*

The Newmans were the last spectators standing along the sidewalk on the north side of Elm Street. However, somewhat behind and to their right stood three men on the steps leading up to the monument area. The identity of two of these men is unknown, but the third, Emmett Hudson, filled out an affidavit on November 22 and was later questioned by the FBI and the Commission. In his affidavit Hudson declared that "the shots that I heard definitely came from behind and above me" (19H481). On November 26 he was questioned by the FBI and was even more explicit about the location of the shots:

> *Hudson said the shots sounded as if they were fired over his head and from some position to the left of where he was standing. In other words, the shots sounded as if they were fired by someone at a position which was behind him, which was above him, and which was to his left (Archives, CD 5).*

Emmett Hudson said the shots had come from behind, above, and to his left.

Emmett Hudson can be located in the Polaroid photo taken by Mary Moorman. "Behind him, above him, and to his left" is the corner of the stockade fence. Such a firing location would coincide with the other witness reports adduced earlier in this chapter.

A photograph taken by Mary Moorman reveals two curious marks at the top of the stockade fence. By comparing this with a photograph taken at a later date, it can be seen that the one on the right (arrow) is a signal tower and that the one on the left (circle) is no longer there.

The signal tower.

The Moorman photo now becomes of crucial significance. On the afternoon of November 22 Mrs. Moorman remarked on television that after the President's head exploded she threw herself to the ground. "I was fifteen feet from the car," she pointed out, "and evidently I was in the line of fire."[12] If a shot had been fired from near the corner of the stockade fence, then her immediate impression was correct. Correlation of her picture with the Zapruder film shows that it was taken simultaneously with Z314–315. She took her picture no more than 1/5 second after the President was struck in the head. At this time (as her picture shows) the President is directly between her and the corner of the stockade fence. Thus the supposed gunman must at this time have had a line of sight to the President's head. Yet if he had such a line of sight, Mary Moorman must have had a line of sight to him—he should show up in her picture. If the hypothesis of a shot from the stockade fence is correct, then it should be validated by the Moorman picture. Is it so validated? Does the gunman appear in her picture?

The evidence indicates he does, and moreover he appears in the precise location predicted by the testimony of Hudson, Newman, Holland, Simmons, Dodd, Weitzman, *et al.* Along the fence line in the Moorman photo there are two anomalous shapes to the west of the corner. By comparing a photo taken from Mrs. Moorman's position sometime later, it is possible to see that the more elongated of these shapes is actually a railroad signal tower in the background. But with respect to a round shape some 14 feet down from the corner, no such explanation is possible—nothing in the background aligns with this shape. When we took Holland to the assassination site and asked him to stand in the position where he found the curious footprints and saw the smoke, his head appeared in the exact position defined by this shape. Earlier, we had shown him the Moorman photo in a particularly clear print. He looked at the photo for a long time, and then announced:

*Well, now you have something here . . . I didn't see this man before. [About twenty seconds pass, then Holland continues:] Well do you know I think that you're looking right down at the barrel of that gun right now! (Taped interview, Nov. 30, 1966).*

S. M. Holland stands where he saw the puff of smoke and where, coincidentally, the shape appears on the Moorman photograph.

## RECORDS BUILDING
## CRIMINAL COURTS BUILDING
## DAL-TEX BUILDING

"The thought immediately passed through my mind," Governor Connally testified, "that there were either two or three people involved or more in this or someone was shooting with an automatic rifle" (4H133). As we saw in Chapter IV, there is reason to believe that the Governor's first impression was correct—the Zapruder film establishes that the *maximum* time interval between the hits on the Governor and the President is less than the *minimum* firing time for Oswald's Mannlicher-Carcano. The conclusion inescapably follows that either (1) Oswald's rifle *and* another weapon were used ("there were two or three people involved in this") or (2) a weapon *other* than Oswald's was used ("someone was shooting with an automatic rifle").

It is fairly obvious from the weight of available evidence that Oswald's Mannlicher-Carcano did at least some of the shooting that day. If not, then we must assume that somehow his rifle was planted on the sixth floor of the Depository, together with three spent shells, and that two ballistically matched bullet fragments and one whole bullet were placed by conspirators in the presidential limousine and on a stretcher at Parkland Hospital respectively. We submit that this is beyond the ability of any conspirator, no matter how deft. Clearly, Oswald's rifle was used. Whether it was fired by Oswald himself is still open to question, but the contention that it was the *only* weapon fired at the President becomes increasingly unacceptable as the facts accumulate.

DAL-TEX BLDG.

RECORDS BLDG.

T
S
B
D

A shot at Governor Connally occurring at Zapruder frame 236 would, because of his position, have to have come from one of the buildings along Houston Street. Dotted line simulates a 27° trajectory from the roof of the County Records Building. Measurements later showed that a bullet passed through Governor Connally's body at a downward angle of 27°.

We know where Abraham Zapruder stood on that Friday afternoon, and from his film we can determine the position of Governor Connally during the interval Z234–238. Although the Governor is turning to his right during this interval, its midpoint (Z236) finds him directly facing Zapruder's camera. In the presence of the Commission, Drs. Shaw and Gregory measured the trajectory of the bullet through the Governor's body; it had a declination of 27 degrees (4H138).[13] Further measurements on the Governor's jacket by the FBI indicated the bullet transited his body on a right-to-left trajectory of 20 degrees (Archives, CD 827). Putting all this information together, it is possible to infer the trajectory of the bullet that struck the Governor. As the diagram indicates, the most probable point of origin for such a bullet would be the roof of the Dallas County Records Building.

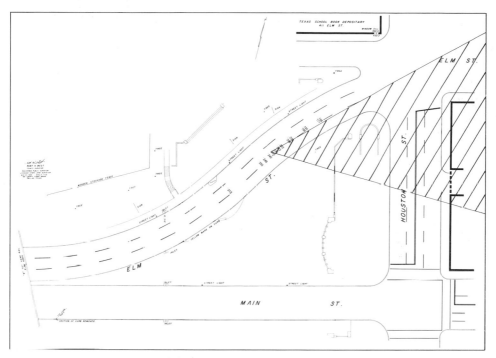

The shot which hit Governor Connally could have come from anywhere within the cross-hatched spectrum. Again, the 27° trajectory would indicate a rooftop firing point.

We must be careful not to strain our powers of analysis too far. We do not know that the Governor was struck at exactly Z236—this is only the midpoint of the interval during which he could have been struck. The 27-degree angle of declination was measured by Drs. Shaw and Gregory on Governor Connally's body, but should not be taken as more accurate than plus or minus 2 degrees. Likewise the Commission's 20-degree deflection angle was only a rough estimate made from a jacket that had already been dry-cleaned.[14] A more judicious conclusion from the available data would affirm that the shot originated somewhere in the region described by the diagram. This region would include the Records Building as well as parts of the Dal-Tex and Criminal Courts buildings.*

* One physical feature would tend to rule out the Criminal Courts Building roof as the source of this shot. A brick parapet 15 feet high and less than 2 feet wide borders the Houston Street roof line, making a shot from there almost

A possible sniper's view of Elm Street from the Records Building...

... and from the Dal-Tex Building.

Is there any independent evidence that a shot originated in this general area?

F. Lee Mudd later reported that he thought one or more of the shots came from the direction of the Dal-Tex Building. Standing at the north curb of Elm Street, he dropped to the ground when the shots were fired and looked toward the Elm/Houston corner.

*He looked around him [the FBI report relates], and he recalled that in looking toward the building nearby, he noted several broken windows on the fourth floor of the Dal-Tex Building, and the thought occurred to him that possibly the shots had been fired through these broken windows . . . [He] stated that when the shots were fired, they sounded as if they came from the direction of the Dal-Tex Building (24H538).*

It should be pointed out that within minutes of the assassination a young man was arrested by police in the Dal-Tex Building.[15] The police report states only that the suspect "had been up in the building across the street from the book depository without a good excuse" and that he had been taken to the Sheriff's Office (20H499). Curiously enough, the Sheriff's Office interrogation reports show no record of this man or what alibi he gave (19H526–527). He apparently arrived at the Sheriff's Office and then disappeared in the confusion of the moment.

Eyewitness Charles Brehm told the FBI that "it seemed quite apparent to him that the shots came from one of two buildings back at the corner of Elm and Houston Streets" (22H837).[16] Assistant District Attorney Sam Paternostro told the same agency that he recalled hearing a shot that "came from the TSBD building or the Criminal Courts Building or the triple

---

impossible. The roof lines of the other two buildings, however, are traced by low walls that would both hide a potential assassin from the crowds below and provide a convenient gun rest.

overpass" (24H536). Other witnesses pointed more directly to the Records and Criminal Courts buildings.

Elsie Dorman watched the motorcade from an open fourth-floor window of the Depository. Two days after the assassination she told the FBI "she felt that these shots were coming from the area of the Records Building" (*Archives,* CD 5).

Otis N. Williams watched the motorcade from the steps of the Depository. Just after the presidential limousine had passed the building and dipped out of sight down Elm Street, Williams "heard three loud blasts" (*Archives,* CD 5). The FBI report goes on to say that Williams "thought these blasts came from the location of the court house" (*Archives,* CD 5). Both the Dallas County Records Building and the Criminal Courts Building would lie between Williams and the "court house." [17]

Such witness reports establish only the possibility that one or more shots may have come from the east boundary of Dealey Plaza. What turns this possibility into a probability is the web of evidence and logic that necessitates another gun besides Oswald's firing on the motorcade from behind. For even if Oswald's rifle was used on November 22, the shot that hit the Governor must have come from another weapon. The Governor's own testimony together with the pictorial evidence of the Zapruder film indicates he was hit in the interval Z234–238. Yet if he was hit during this interval, we know from his position and from the angle of trajectory that the shot must have come from the east side of Dealey Plaza. Height and isolation may have prevented the early detection of this gunman. But the logic of the case necessitates his existence.

## THE DEPOSITORY

The paucity of information concerning the Kennedy back wound makes it impossible for us to establish the trajectory of the first shot from medical evidence alone. Most of the trustworthy information about this wound comes from the Sibert-O'Neill report, namely, that the wound was below the shoulders and 2 inches to the right of the spinal column, and that the bullet penetrated less than a finger's length on a downward trajectory of 45–60 degrees.[18] Such a wound incurred at Z210–224 requires a trajectory from a point above and behind the President. It is consistent with a shot from an upper story of the Depository, but it does not require such a location to the exclusion of all others. Fortunately, however, other evidence can establish the location of the gunman who fired the first shot.

James Altgens' photograph, taken simultaneously with Z255, shows Secret Service Agents John Ready and Paul Landis in the follow-up car reacting to the sound of the first shot by turning strenuously to their right rear. Both of these agents were later to state that the first shot came from that direction (18H749, 754), Landis recalling that he "heard what sounded like the report of a high-powered rifle from behind me, over my right shoulder" (18H754). Their judgment that the first shot came from the right rear was supported by the statements of Agents Greer (18H723), Hickey (18H762), Hill (18H742), Kellerman (18H724), Kivett (18H778), and Taylor (18H782).[19]

Immediately after the first shot, Secret Service agents Ready and Landis turn toward the Depository.

> We were making the turn [testified Mrs. Earle Cabell, riding four cars behind the President], I heard the shot and jerked my head up [towards the Depository] in the direction from which the shot came . . . I saw a projection out of one of those windows (7H486).

Two photographers, Robert Jackson and Malcolm Couch, riding in an open press car on Houston Street, looked up at the Depository just after the third shot and saw a rifle barrel being withdrawn from the corner window of the sixth floor (2H159, 6H157). At least four other witnesses declared in sworn affidavit or testimony that they also saw a rifle being fired from the Depository.[20] Of these witnesses How-

Howard Brennan (arrow) looks up at the Depository window where minutes before he had seen an assassin take his last shot.

ard L. Brennan gave the most detailed description of the shots fired from the Depository. Sitting on a retaining wall at the corner of Elm and Houston streets, Brennan had an unobstructed view of the motorcade and the Depository towering behind it:

> *After the President had passed my position . . . I heard this crack that I positively thought was a backfire . . . Well, then something, just right after this explosion, made me think that it was a firecracker being thrown from the Texas Book Store. And I glanced up. And this man that I saw previous was aiming for his last shot . . . (3H143–144).*

Brennan is one of the Commission's star witnesses. Yet on one critical point his story diverges from the Commission's. "The first shot and the last shot is my only positive recollection of two shots," Brennan continued. "The first shot was positive and clear and the last shot was positive and clear, with no echo on my part" (3H154).[21] While the Commission claims that *three* shots were fired from the Depository, Brennan reports only *two*. He heard a noise, looked up, and saw the gunman aiming for his last shot. He saw the gunman fire and then watched as he slowly withdrew the rifle to his side. Brennan's recollection would agree perfectly with the hypothesis that only the first and third (Brennan would have heard this shot as the "last") shots came from the Depository.*

An 8-millimeter movie film, never published be-

* Brennan's observation that only two shots came from the Depository is further buttressed by a curious pattern that shows up in a collation of witness testimony. With no exceptions all those witnesses who were deep inside the Depository (either at work or in hallways) report hearing fewer than three shots. See 22H637, 24H206, 24H521.

In this regard Bonnie Ray Williams' testimony is of interest. He was watching the parade from the window immediately below the sixth-floor sniper's nest. Although he later revised his estimate of the number of shots, on November 22 he swore out an affidavit that reads in part: "We saw the President coming around the corner on Houston from Main Street. I heard 2 shots it sounded like they came from just

The sixth-floor window of the Depository is visible in this movie frame taken by Robert Hughes moments before the shooting started. Frames from four seconds of the movie show that the shape changes in width and gets narrower (arrow). It may be the gunman Brennan saw turning to his right to get into firing position.

fore, shows the sixth-floor sniper's nest only seconds before the first shot. Taken by Robert Hughes from the corner of Main and Houston streets, it shows the presidential limousine making its fatal turn onto Elm Street. Looming above the motorcade is the Depository and its sixth-floor, southeast-corner window. The FBI examined the film and decided that "there are no images in any of the exposures . . . that can be interpreted as the form of an individual. The forms recorded in this window can be interpreted as in the same general shapes of boxes, found at and just behind the window in question" (*Archives,* CD 205). But the FBI never bothered to compare individual frames of the movie series against each other. Had they performed this elementary comparison they would have recognized that the boxlike shape in the window changed in width—getting narrower as time went on. Although the form cannot be distinguished as a human figure, it must be animate since it changes in time. It is almost certainly the gunman Brennan saw, slowly turning to his right (thus presenting a profile to Bob Hughes's camera) as he moves into firing position.

The "last" shot fired by Brennan's gunman struck the President's head at Z312/313. From his perch in the Depository the declination angle to the President's head was 12 degrees;[22] the right-to-left deflection angle was 6 degrees. Such a trajectory would accord perfectly with the observed channel of laceration down the midline of the President's brain and with the fractures in the mid- and left-temple regions. The impact of a bullet fired on such a trajectory would also produce just that kind of forward jerk we observe at Z312/313. Such a trajectory to the President's head at Z313 would align almost perfectly with the impact point of a bullet fragment on the

above us" (24H229). An FBI report of an interview with Williams the following day (November 23) has him reiterating the observation that *two* shots came from over his head: "While they were watching this car pass, Williams heard two shots which sounded like they came from right over his head" (*Archives,* CD 5).

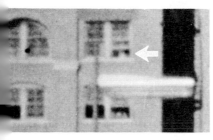

Main Street curb. Such a trajectory would also account for the fragment impact inside the front windshield and for the fragments found in the front seat, fragments that were ballistically identified as having come from the rifle found on the sixth floor of the Depository. Finally, it should be reiterated that the entry holes of two of the President's wounds (4 by 7 millimeters in the back, and 6 by 15 millimeters in the occipital region of the skull) would be consistent with projectiles fired from the rifle found on the sixth floor of the Depository.

Combining all of the findings so far, we arrive at the following picture: Three assassins fired four shots from three different locations. The first and third shots were fired from the Depository—most likely from the sixth-floor, southeast-corner window later identified by the Warren Commission as the sniper's nest. The second shot, wounding the Governor, was fired from the east side of Dealey Plaza—most likely from a building rooftop. The fourth and final shot was fired from a point near the corner of the stockade fence to the north of Elm Street. Although the first and third shots came from a small (probably 6.5-millimeter) weapon, the second and fourth shots exhibit patterns of damage consistent with much more powerful weapons.

The following table summarizes the details of our conclusions with respect to trajectories:

| Shot number | Firing point | Distance to victim from firing point | Zapruder frame number | Declination angle from firing point to victim | Angle from car's axis to firing point |
|---|---|---|---|---|---|
| One | Depository, sixth-floor corner window | 177–191 ft. | 210–224 | 18.5–17° | 163–167° |
| Two | East side of Dealey Plaza | 225–275 ft. | 234–238 | 22–28° | 190–250° |
| Three | Depository, sixth-floor corner window | 265 ft. | 312–313 | 12° | 174° |
| Four | Corner, stockade fence | 115 ft. | 312–314 | 6.5° | 50° |

## NOTES

1. States whose 1963 license plates matched Bowers' description are Rhode Island, Tennessee, and Virginia.

2. Tape-recorded interview with Mark Lane, Mar. 31, 1966; cited by Lane, *Rush to Judgment* (New York: Holt, Rinehart & Winston, 1966), p. 32.

3. Taped interview with Mark Lane, Mar. 24, 1966; played by Lane on TV program *The Warren Commission: A Minority Report*, WNEW-TV (Nov. 12, 1966). See WNEW-TV transcript, p. 42.

4. Johnson went on to suggest to the FBI the possibility that the smoke "came from a motorcycle abandoned near the spot by a Dallas policeman" (22H836). Such an explanation is not plausible since the Hughes, Bell, and Willis photos show clearly that the motorcycle was abandoned on Elm Street some 60 feet from where the smoke was seen. When I asked Holland about this explanation of the smoke, he replied that it didn't make sense since (as he put it) "I saw the smoke before the motorcyclist left the street to go up there" (Taped interview; Nov. 30, 1966).

An alternative explanation sometimes proffered by governmental sources—namely, that the smoke was really escaping steam from a steam line in the vicinity—makes even less sense. At the time Holland and the other railroad workers saw the smoke, they were standing not a foot from the steam line in question. This line parallels the railroad tracks and at no time is anywhere near the corner of the stockade fence.

5. Taped interviews of Winborn (May 5, 1966) and Murphy (May 6, 1966) by Stewart Galanor; cited in Lane, *op. cit.,* p. 40.

6. Taped interview with Mark Lane, Mar. 24, 1966; WNEW-TV transcript, p. 42. On Mar. 28, 1966, Simmons told Mark Lane that he saw "footprints in the mud around the fence, and there were footprints on the wooden two-by-four railing on the fence." Like Dodd and Holland, Simmons also noted mud footprints "on a car bumper there, as if someone had stood up there looking over the fence" (Lane, *op. cit.,* p. 34).

7. Taped interview of Price by Mark Lane, Mar. 27, 1966; cited by Lane, *op. cit.,* p.. 33.

8. *Ibid.*

9. Patrolman Smith had earlier told Ronnie Dugger of *The Texas Observer* that he had "caught the smell of gunpowder" behind the fence. "I could tell it was in the air," Smith had pointed out (*The Texas Observer,* Dec. 13, 1963).

10. The "deputy sheriff" mentioned here is most probably Seymour Weitzman. Weitzman mentions in his own testimony the presence of a "Secret Service" agent in the area behind the fence, thus providing corroboration for Smith's report (7H106–107).

11. In the *Report of the Secret Service on the Assassination of President Kennedy* submitted by Chief Rowley on Dec. 18, 1963, we find the following statement: *"All the Secret Service agents assigned to the motorcade stayed with the motorcade all the way to the Hospital. None remained at the scene of the shooting,* and none entered the School Book Depository Building at or immediately after the time of the shooting. (This was consistent with Secret Service procedure which requires that each agent stay with the President and Vice President and not be diverted by any distractions unless he must do so in order to protect the President and Vice President.)"*(Archives,* CD 3, Part I; emphasis added.) Sylvia Meagher was the first to discover this anomaly; see *Accessories After the Fact* (New York: Bobbs-Merrill Company, Inc., 1967), pp. 25-26.

12. WFAA-TV video tape; Tape PKT-24 at 21 minutes, 8 seconds into the tape.

13. FBI measurements of his jacket put the angle of declination at 35 degrees (*Archives,* CD 827).

14. The extraordinary adventures that befell the Governor's clothing before it reached the hands of competent authority will be related in the next chapter.

15. The Willis family described to me the arrest of this young man. Dressed in a black leather jacket and black gloves, he was led out of the building by two uniformed police officers. To the catcalls of the assembled crowd he was ushered into a waiting police car, which quickly drove off (Taped interview; Nov. 29, 1966).

16. Holland, we recall, indicated that some of the shots appeared to come "from the north end of Elm Street" (Taped interview; Nov. 29, 1966).

17. Williams is most likely referring to the "Old Court House," which lies directly across Main Street from the Criminal Courts Building. He gave this statement to the FBI on Nov. 24. When he was reinterviewed on Mar. 19, he gave a different story indicating that he thought "these blasts or shots came from the direction of the viaduct which crosses Elm Street" (22H683). The paucity of evidence concerning a shot from the east side of Dealey Plaza may partially spring from a tendency of many witnesses to make their recollections seem more "orthodox."

18. Sibert and O'Neill must have exaggerated somewhat the declination angle of this wound. There is no vantage point in any adjacent building that would produce such a sharp trajectory at Z220.

19. See also the testimony of Hurchel Jacks (18H801), Mrs. Lyndon B. Johnson (5H565), Kenneth O'Donnell (7H448), and Dave Powers (7H473).

20. Mrs. Carolyn Walther (24H522), James Richard Worrell (24H231), Amos Lee Euins (26H936, 2H204), Howard Leslie Brennan (3H143–154, 19H470).

21. Brennan's affidavit of Nov. 22 suggests even more

clearly that he was aware of only two shots fired from the Depository's sixth-floor window: "I heard what I thought was a backfire. It run in my mind that it might be someone throwing firecrackers out of the window of the red brick building and I looked up at the building. I then saw this man I have described in the window and he was taking aim with a high powered rifle. I could see all of the barrel of the gun. I do not know if it had a scope on it or not. I was looking at the man in this window at the time of the last explosion" (24H203). See additional statements made by Brennan to the FBI on Nov. 22 (*Archives,* CD 5) and Jan. 10 (24H406).

22. Since the President is inclined forward at this point, this angle may take a somewhat smaller value.

# VII

## PHYSICAL EVIDENCE

*My initial feeling was that if this was a simple assassination, as the Commission claimed, with one assassin firing three shots from one vantage point, the facts would come together very neatly. If there were more than one assassin the details would not fit.—Vincent J. Salandria,* The Greater Philadelphia Magazine, *August, 1966.*

### THE CARTRIDGE CASES

Three 6.5-millimeter cartridge cases were found on the sixth floor of the Depository shortly after the assassination. Since the evidence presented in the previous chapter indicates that only two shots were fired from this location, how do we account for the third, or extra, cartridge case?

On the face of it, the presence of one, two, or three cartridge cases does not establish that any particular number of shots was fired from a location. More shots could have been fired and some of the cases retrieved. Fewer shots could have been fired

The clip found in the rifle on the sixth floor holds six cartridges but held only four on November 22.

Commission Exhibit 139: Oswald's rifle, found on the sixth floor of the Depository.

Lt. J. C. Day of the Dallas Police Department, carrying the rifle from the Depository on the afternoon of the assassination.

and an extra case dropped. Moreover, when we consider the condition of the rifle and the cartridges when they were discovered, it becomes even harder to draw clear inferences from them.

Although the rifle clip can hold six rounds (and an extra in the chamber), only four bullet casings were found—a live round in the chamber and three cartridge cases on the floor. No fingerprints were found on any of the cases or on the rifle clip (4H253, 258–260). In fact, the only print on the rifle was found after disassembly on a portion of the barrel ordinarily covered by the front stock.[1] Whoever fired this rifle curiously loaded it with only four rounds when it would hold six or seven, and then was careful to remove all fingerprints from it and from the cases fired.

These considerations merely point up certain oddities about the condition in which the rifle and cases were found. It is only when we begin examining the three cases themselves that our suspicions are aroused. In this examination Lieutenant J. C. Day of the Dallas Police is a central figure.

### Two and One

On November 22, 1963, Lieutenant Day headed the crime scene search section of the Dallas Police. In company with his assistant, R. L. Studebaker, he arrived at the Depository about 1:12 P.M. and went immediately to the sixth floor (4H249). Learning that some cartridge cases had been found near a southeast-corner window, he instructed Studebaker to photograph them from various angles, and then he dusted them for fingerprints (4H250). Studebaker's photos show two cases lying next to the window wall and a third some 5 feet away to the northwest.

It would be interesting to know which of the three cartridges had been thrown so oddly distant from the other two. Lieutenant Day, however, scooped up all three cartridges and placed them in an envelope before they were marked with respect to their location of discovery (4H253, 7H162–163). So today, no one has any idea which of the three cases was the one lying 5 feet down the wall. This is unfortunate in light of certain disparities between one of the cases and the other two and particularly in view of what next happened to the envelope.

Detective Richard H. Sims helped Lieutenant Day pick up the cartridge cases. He then took the envelope containing the cases and turned it over to Captain Will Fritz at police headquarters (7H183). When Lieutenant Day was given the envelope later that evening, it contained only two cases—the third had been removed by Captain Fritz and was being held by him (4H254). Day now marked the two cases with his initials and forwarded them to the FBI lab with other evidence (4H254). These two cases were subsequently given FBI designations C7 and C38 and Commission Exhibit Numbers 544 and 545 (4H254–255).

Both of these cases had marks "identified as having been produced by the chamber of Oswald's rifle" (26H449–450). One of them had a "set of marks identified as having been produced by the magazine follower" [the spring-tensioned lever that presses up the last cartridge in the clip] of Oswald's rifle (26H450), while the other showed marks that could have come only from the bolt of Oswald's rifle (24H449). Both of these cases showed marks indicating that each had been loaded into a weapon (not necessarily Oswald's) at least twice (24H449–450).

The remaining cartridge case (designated C6 and CE 543) differed from the other two in a number of respects. It was kept by the Dallas Police until the FBI demanded it from Captain Fritz in the early morning hours of November 28 (7H404). Its most astonishing characteristic is a sharp dent in its lip of sufficient magnitude to prevent the fitting of a projectile in the opening. In its present condition it could not have been fired in any rifle on November 22.

The crucial question arises as to when this dent was incurred. Could it have happened after it was

Photo of sniper's nest in the Depository taken by the Dallas Police. Note two cases next to the wall and a third some distance away.

Commission Exhibit 543: This dented cartridge case found on the sixth floor of the Depository could not (in this condition) have held a projectile on November 22.

fired but before it was photographed and retrieved by Lieutenant Day? Perhaps it was dented in striking the wall or floor during the ejection process? This suggestion must be immediately ruled out—the case is made of rigid brass and would not dent under any such impact.* Could it have been stepped on? Two facts work against this possibility. First, the dent itself is sharply defined—it resembles what happens when an empty case is "dry loaded" in the breech and strikes some sharp metal projection. It does not have the gentler contours that would be the expected result of contact with a person's shoe. Second, it was discovered and guarded by Sheriff's Officer Luke Mooney, who tells of the care he took in moving in the area and his anxiety that no evidence be disturbed (3H284). If anyone stepped on the cartridge it would have had to have been Mooney, yet, in May, 1967, Mooney assured me in no uncertain terms that neither he nor anyone else stepped on any of the cases before they were picked up by the Dallas Police.[2]

Thus, it seems extremely unlikely that CE 543 was dented after being ejected from Oswald's rifle. But in its present condition it could not have been fired in any rifle—its lip will not receive a projectile. The possibility suggests itself that CE 543 was never fired on November 22 but was dropped by one of the assassins, either inadvertently or as a means of throwing the subsequent investigation off the track. Certain other features of CE 543 urge such a conclusion even more strongly.

Marks found on the dented case indicated that it had been loaded in and extracted from a weapon at least three times (26H449). In addition, it had "three sets of marks on the base" that were not found on the others or on any of the numerous test cartridges obtained from Oswald's rifle (26H449). A ballistics expert testified that these anomalous marks were possibly caused by a "dry firing" run—that is, by insert-

* I have thrown hundreds of similar cases against a wall and never succeeded in denting one.

ing the empty cartridge case in the breech while practicing with the rifle (3H510). Of all the various marks discovered on this case, only one set links it to Oswald's rifle, and this set was identified as having come from the magazine follower. Yet the magazine follower marks only the last cartridge in the clip, a position that must have been occupied on November 22 not by the dented case but by the live round subsequently found in the chamber. Thus, unlike the other two cases that bear marks from the chamber and bolt of Oswald's rifle, the only mark borne by the dented case, linking it to Oswald's rifle, could not have been incurred on November 22.[3]

All this excites our suspicion with respect to CE 543, the dented cartridge case. What is most surprising—perhaps conclusive—about this cartridge case is that it lacks a characteristic impression along the side exhibited in one form or other by all the other cartridges we know to have been seated in the chamber of Oswald's rifle. I first noticed this characteristic mark while supervising the photographing of the cartridges for *Life*. I observed on two of the cartridge cases (CE's 544, 545) an impression on the side in the same relative position on each. I examined the third and saw that no such impression was apparent. The anomaly did not excite my interest until I noticed that the live round found in the chamber of Oswald's rifle (CE 141) exhibited a similar impression in the same place. On the live round the mark was not as pronounced—perhaps due to the fact that it had not been fired. The pressure of firing would tend to accentuate any indentation caused by contact with the chamber. I now had three cartridge cases, all of which ostensibly were at one time or other in the chamber of Oswald's rifle and all of which evidenced a characteristic mark. If this mark was caused by a characteristic of the chamber of Oswald's rifle, then the lack of it on CE 543 might indicate that it had never been fired in Oswald's rifle. One way to test my hypothesis was to examine CE 577—two cartridge cases from test rounds fired in Oswald's rifle. Both of these cases displayed the

Three of the four cartridge cases bear chambering marks characteristic of Oswald's rifle. The fourth lacks a chambering mark and has a dented lip.

characteristic mark in the same spot.[4] Thus the cartridge case that had an extra dent in the lip seemed to lack a mark exhibited by every other case we know to have been in the breech of Oswald's rifle.

The combination of these factors—the peculiar treatment accorded CE 543 by the Dallas Police, its inexplicably dented lip, the three sets of marks on the base absent on the other cases while present on 543, and finally its lack of the characteristic chambering mark—suggests that although two of the cartridge cases may have been ejected from Oswald's rifle, the third, CE 543, is most likely an extra, unfired shell and possibly a deliberate fake. Such a conclusion would mate perfectly with the description of events earlier laid down, namely, that only two of the shots fired that day in Dealey Plaza came from the Depository.

Commission Exhibit 399: A portion was sliced from the tip of this bullet for FBI spectrographic comparison with other bullet fragments. The results of this test were never released.

## SUPERBULLET: COMMISSION EXHIBIT 399

Deep in the recesses of the National Archives, carefully packed in cotton and enclosed in a small plastic case marked Commission Exhibit Number 399, rests a copper-jacketed 6.5-millimeter bullet. Along its straight sides can be seen the spiral channels of rifling grooves. Although the bullet's tail is somewhat squeezed, its nose and midsection are perfectly preserved. Given such a perfect projectile, experts had no difficulty in matching it to Oswald's rifle to the exclusion of all other weapons (3H429, 499–500).

No piece of physical evidence has excited more controversy than CE 399. Basically, the controversy turns on the Commission's contention that "all the evidence indicated that the bullet found on the Governor's stretcher could have caused all his wounds" (R95). As succeeding pages will show, "all the evidence" indicates precisely the opposite; not only does it appear extremely unlikely that this bullet could have caused all the Governor's wounds, but subsequent investigation at Parkland Hospital has dis-

The hole in Governor Connally's shirt front suggests the large size of the exit wound in his chest.

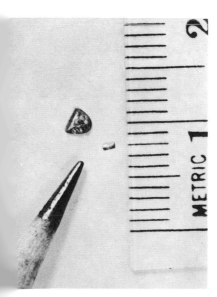

Commission Exhibit 842: Bullet fragments removed from the Governor's wrist.

closed that bullet 399 was most likely found on a stretcher unconnected with the care of either Governor Connally or President Kennedy.

## A Perfect Bullet

According to the Commission's "single-bullet" theory, the missile that wounded the Governor had first transited the President's neck. Following this transit, it entered the Governor's back, making a 1.5 centimeter hole before shattering his fifth rib and blowing out an exit hole 5 centimeters wide. The bullet continued on to smash Connally's forearm and wrist, splintering the radius bone at its largest point and leaving along its path a trail of bone and metal fragments. This bullet finally embedded itself in the Governor's thigh, leaving behind two small fragments before falling out on the stretcher. According to the Commission, the bullet that accomplished all this—that shattered two bones and caused seven separate wounds in two people—was Commission Exhibit 399 (R95).[5]

Critics of the *Report* have argued against this conclusion on two grounds. First, they point to the minuscule loss of CE 399's substance and to the conviction of two of the autopsy surgeons that 399 could not have caused the Governor's wounds for the simple reason that more metal was found in his wrist than was missing from 399. Second, they point to 399's undeformed state as evidence that it could not have caused the damage ascribed to it. The second argument is much stronger than the first.

FBI firearms expert Robert Frazier weighed CE 399 on the evening of November 22 and found it to weigh 158.6 grains (3H430). He weighed three other 6.5-millimeter bullets chosen at random and found them to weigh 160.85, 161.5, and 161.1 grains (3H430).[6] Asked by Assistant Counsel Specter if this meant that there was a weight loss to CE 399, he replied "there did not necessarily have to be any weight loss to the bullet" (3H430).

A number of metal fragments were left scattered

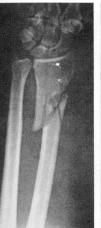 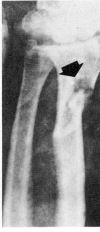

Pre-operative          Post-operative

Pre-operative and post-operative X-rays of Governor Connally's wrist show that two bullet fragments remain (arrow).

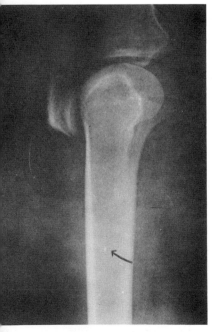

X-ray of Governor Connally's thigh shows a bullet fragment embedded in his femur.

through Connally's body. Two small fragments were removed from his wrist and are preserved as CE 842. Postoperative X-rays show additional fragments remaining in his wrist as well as a small fragment embedded in his thigh (see X-rays).[7] Dr. Charles Gregory mentions a small fragment removed from the thigh wound that apparently has been lost.[8] Finally, Dr. George T. Shires, Chief of Surgery at Parkland, said that postoperative chest X-rays showed "a small fragment remaining" (6H111).[9]

Given this distribution of bullet fragments through the Governor's body, the question arises whether more metal resided in his body than was missing from CE 399. In pursuing this question Assistant Counsel Specter asked Lieutenant Colonel Pierre Finck of the Army's wound ballistics section if CE 399 "could have been the bullet that inflicted the wound on Governor Connally's right wrist" (2H382). The Army doctor replied, "No, for the reason that there are too many fragments described in the wrist" (2H382). Earlier, Specter had addressed a similar question to another autopsy surgeon, Commander James J. Humes:

*Specter: And could that missile [CE 399] have made the wound on Governor Connally's right wrist?*

*Humes: I think that is most unlikely . . . Going to Exhibit 392, the report from Parkland Hospital, the following sentence referring to the examination of the wound in the wrist is found: "Some small bits of metal were encountered at various levels throughout the wound, and these were, wherever they could be identified and picked up, picked up and submitted to the pathology department for identification and examination." The reason I believe it is most unlikely that this missile could have inflicted either of these wounds [referring also to the President's head wound] is that this missile is basically intact; its jacket appears to me to be intact, and I do not understand how it could possibly have left fragments in either of these locations (2H374–375).*

Continuing his examination, Specter asked Commander Humes if CE 399 could have caused the Governor's thigh wound. Humes replied:

*I think that extremely unlikely. The report, again Exhibit 392 from Parkland tells of an entrance wound on the lower mid-thigh of the Governor, and X-rays taken there are described as showing metallic fragments in the bone,\* which apparently by this report were not removed and are still present in Governor Connally's thigh. I can't conceive of where they came from this missile. (2H376)*

Dr. Robert Shaw was just as positive in replying to a similar question by Assistant Counsel Specter:

*As far as the wounds of the chest are concerned, I feel that this bullet could have inflicted those wounds. But the examination of the wrist both by X-rays and at the time of surgery showed some fragments of metal that make it difficult to believe that the same missile could have caused these two wounds. There seems to be more than three grains of metal missing as far as the—I mean in the wrist. (4H113)*

---

\* The existence of a metal fragment embedded in the Governor's thigh casts further suspicion on the hypothesis that CE 399 lodged in his thigh. For how could a spent bullet with only sufficient velocity to break the skin throw off a fragment of such higher velocity that it penetrated several layers of fascia and muscle before embedding itself in the femur? Dr. George T. Shires, the Parkland surgeon who operated on Connally's thigh, was also puzzled by this (6H106). In a conversation on May 31, 1967, he confirmed to the author that the fragment was indeed *embedded* in the bone.

Dr. Shaw was then asked by Specter to state his opinion as to "whether bullet 399 could have inflicted all of the wounds on the Governor." His reply could well stand as a summary of medical testimony on CE 399: [10]

> *I feel that there would be some difficulty explaining all of the wounds as being inflicted by bullet Exhibit 399 without causing more in the way of loss of substance to the bullet or deformation of the bullet (4H114).*

This medical testimony is more imposing on first glance than after analysis. Drs. Finck, Hume, and Shaw felt confident that the weight of the fragments found in the Governor's body was too much for them to have come from CE 399. But what was the total weight of the metal scattered through the Governor's chest, wrist, and thigh?

Of the two fragments recovered from the Governor's wrist, the larger was found to weigh 0.5 grain (5H72). The smaller one plus the flakes of metal remaining in his wrist might account for a like weight. This gives us a total of about one grain for the wrist. What about the chest and thigh fragments? Dr. Shires, who noticed the chest fragment on X-ray, never estimated its weight, but he spoke of it as being the same general size as the fragment embedded in the femur. The weight of this fragment was estimated as "a fraction of a grain, maybe, a tenth of a grain" (6H106, 111). If we add to these two fragments the flake observed just under the skin in the thigh wound, we have a total weight of perhaps 0.5 grain in the thigh and chest. Adding this to the wrist fragments yields a total weight for all observed fragments of 1.5 grains. Clearly then, Dr. Shaw was mistaken when he testified that "there seems to be more than three grains of metal missing . . . in the wrist" (4H113). The upshot of all this medical testimony with respect to weight loss is inconclusive. About 1.5 grains of metal were found in Governor Connally's wounds.

An unfired projectile like 399 might be expected to weigh about 161 grains (3H430). Subtracting the weight of CE 399 (158.6 grains) from this figure yields a possible weight loss of up to 2.5 grains. Hence, simply from the point of view of total weight, the various fragments in Connally's body could have come from CE 399. The critics have been wrong in contending that weight loss alone precludes CE 399 from being the bullet that wounded Governor Connally.

What does preclude such a conclusion is the lack of "deformation of the bullet" alluded to by Dr. Shaw. Although absent from the published record, documents recently discovered in the Archives show that members of the Commission staff were aware of this as early as April, 1964. On April 14 a viewing of the Zapruder film was arranged for various staff members together with the autopsy surgeons and two experts from the Army's Wound Ballistics Branch at Edgewood Arsenal. Assistant Counsel Melvin Eisenberg wrote a "Memorandum for the Record" describing this meeting, and recorded the following conclusion:

> *Since the bullet recovered from the Governor's stretcher does not appear to have penetrated a wrist, if he was hit by this (the first) bullet, he was probably also hit by the second bullet.[11]*

Commission Exhibits:

399

856

853

857

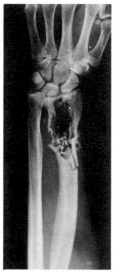

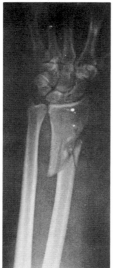

Commission Exhibit 856 and the cadaver's wrist through which it was fired. Commission Exhibit 399 and Governor Connally's wrist through which it was supposedly fired.

A similar meeting a week later ended with wound ballistics experts F. W. Light, Jr., and Joseph Dolce urging even more strongly the same conclusion:

> *Drs. Light and Dolce expressed themselves very strongly of the opinion that Connally had been hit by two different bullets, principally on the ground that the bullet recovered from Connally's stretcher could not have broken his radius without having suffered more distortion. Dr. Oliver [another wound ballistics specialist] withheld a conclusion until he has had the opportunity to make tests on animal tissue and bone with the actual rifle.[12]*

The results of Dr. Olivier's tests were to validate the conclusions of his two colleagues. Under his direction a slug from Oswald's rifle was fired through a cadaver's wrist to simulate the Connally wrist injury; the nose of the resulting bullet (CE 856; see illustration) was badly smashed. Another bullet was fired through an anesthetized goat to simulate 66 percent of the resistance encountered by a bullet transiting the Governor's chest; this projectile was badly squeezed along a longitudinal axis (CE 853; see illustration). Another bullet was fired into a skull; the resulting two pieces of bullet are scarcely recognizable (CE 857; see illustration). None of these test bullets looks

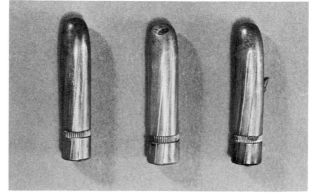

Two of the bullets above were fired into long tubes filled with cotton. The third, according to the Commission, was fired through two people, causing seven separate wounds, and shattering two large bones. (The bullet in the middle, CE 399, is the one purported to have done all the damage.)

anything like CE 399. Only the ballistic comparison rounds (CE 572; see illustration) resemble it, yet these rounds were carefully fired into long tubes of cotton waste to prevent any deformation.

The results of Dr. Olivier's experiments validated a principle long accepted in wound ballistics and forensic pathology, namely, that a high-velocity bullet striking bone is always grossly deformed. I discussed this point with Dr. Cyril Wecht. After studying X-rays of Connally's chest and wrist together with multiple close-up photos of CE 399, Dr. Wecht told me:

> *I do not think that it could have been possible for the bullet shown as CE 399 to have been a bullet that transversed the bodies of both President Kennedy and Governor Connally. I think that it's something which I could not accept, that this bullet which is not fragmented, not deformed or mutilated, with just a slight defect at the tail could have inflicted this amount of damage. Particularly the damage I'm talking about to the bony structures, the rib and the right radius (just above the junction of the wrist)—I doubt that this bullet could have done it. It just does not seem to fit with any of the cases I've seen of what happens to bullets after they have struck bone.[13]*

Dr. Wecht's opinion is echoed in the following observation by Dr. Milton Helpern, world-renowned forensic pathologist and Chief Medical Examiner of the City of New York:

> *This bullet wasn't distorted in any way. I cannot accept the premise that this bullet thrashed around in all that bony tissue and lost only 1.4 to 2.4 grains of its original weight. I cannot believe either that this bullet is going to emerge miraculously unscathed, without any deformity, and with its lands and grooves intact . . .[14]*

Asked whether he believed Governor Connally was struck by the second bullet, Dr. Helpern replied:

> *Yes, I definitely do. His testimony is most persuasive. I just can't buy this theory that this beautifully preserved first bullet is going to have power enough to pass all the way through the seven layers of skin of the two men, plus other soft tissue, plus rib and wrist bone, and end up losing no more than 2.4 grains of its weight. In my opinion, the second bullet that wounded Governor Connally is the one that is missing.*[15]

Thus Dr. Wecht and Dr. Helpern, as well as the Commission's own ballistics experts, rejected the hypothesis that CE 399 caused the wounds to Governor Connally. This same hypothesis was invalidated by the very experiments performed at the Commission's request in order to test it. In light of all this information, to continue to believe that CE 399 wounded Governor Connally is (in the words of David Lifton) "to defy the laws of probability, the laws of physics, and the laws of forensic pathology."[16]

Although the argument from weight loss fails, the more critical argument from deformation succeeds. The nearly pristine character of CE 399 precludes its being the bullet that injured the Governor. Still, there is one additional piece of evidence that should not be overlooked—where it was found.

### Which Stretcher?

An investigation at Parkland Hospital, including the reenactment of the bullet's discovery in the presence of the principal witnesses, has disclosed that 399 was actually found on a stretcher unrelated to the care of either Connally or Kennedy. The history of 399 is complex. Before attempting to offer a plausible account of how it came to be discovered on a stretcher in Parkland Hospital, it is imperative that we understand clearly what is known and unknown about both its discovery and subsequent transmission to Washington. The place to begin is at the FBI Crime Laboratory in Washington on the night of November 22.

We know that Robert Frazier of the FBI Crime Lab received 399 on the evening of November 22 from another FBI agent, Elmer Todd (3H428, 24H412). They both marked the bullet with their initials (24H412). Todd, in turn, had received it a few minutes earlier from Chief Rowley of the Secret Service, who had been given it by one of his agents, Richard Johnsen (24H412). When Johnsen turned the bullet over to Rowley he attached a short note of explanation which reads as follows:

These two photos show the location of the stretcher and the bullet in the elevator vestibule at Parkland Hospital.

> *The attached expended bullet was received by me about 5 minutes prior to Mrs. Kennedy's departure from the hospital. It was found on one of the stretchers located in the emergency ward of the hospital. Also on this same stretcher was rubber gloves, a stethescope and other doctors' paraphernalia. It could not be determined who had used this stretcher or if President Kennedy had occupied it. No further information was obtained. Name of person from whom I received this bullet*
>
>         *Mr. O. P. Wright*
>         *Personnel Director of Security*
>         *Dallas County Hospital District*
>
> *By*
>
>         *Richard E. Johnsen*
>         *Special Agent*
>         *7:30 p.m.*
>         *Nov. 22, 1963*     *(18H800)*

Since the presidential party departed from Parkland Hospital at approximately 2:00 P.M. (18H726, 744, 756–757), we infer that Agent Johnsen received the bullet from Mr. Wright at approximately 1:55 P.M. Wright first learned of its existence when hospital engineer Darrell Tomlinson came to him and told him of its discovery on a hospital stretcher. Together they went to a vestibule where the bullet was seen to lie on a stretcher blocking the corner entrance to the men's room. The bullet lay exposed between the stretcher mat and its rim. Wright examined it and then went to find a federal officer who would take custody of the bullet. After one refusal from an FBI agent, he found Agent Johnsen, who agreed to accept the bullet. From this information we can draw the very important conclusion that *Tomlinson found the bullet between 1:45 P.M. and 1:50 P.M. on November 22.* Much later Tomlinson and Wright were shown CE 399 and both declined to identify it as the bullet they each handled on November 22 (24H412).[17]

In a report dated November 30 Richard Johnsen reiterates what his note of November 22 had affirmed, namely, that Mr. Wright had told him that the stretcher on which the bullet was discovered also carried "rubber gloves, a stethoscope, and other doctors' paraphernalia" (18H799). Again in November, 1966, Mr. Wright told me that this was the case. He also verified that the stretcher on which the bullet rested was the one in the corner—the one blocking the men's room door. All these seemingly trivial details become important when we turn to the testimony of Darrell Tomlinson, the man who first discovered the bullet.

Tomlinson was interviewed by Assistant Counsel Specter on Mar. 20, 1964. To aid in his testimony, Tomlinson drew a small sketch of the vestibule area that is reproduced to the left. He had come to the vestibule shortly after 1:00 P.M. in answer to a call for someone to operate the elevator (6H129):

*Specter: Was there anything on the elevator at that time?*

*Tomlinson: There was one stretcher.*

*Specter: And describe the appearance of that stretcher, if you will, please.*

*Tomlinson: I believe that stretcher had sheets on it and had a white covering on the pad.*

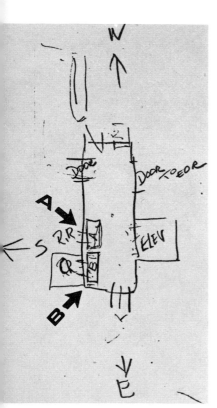

Sketch drawn by Darrell Tomlinson during his interview with Assistant Commission Counsel Specter. Note position of stretcher A (taken from the elevator) and stretcher B (found by Tomlinson in vestibule). Much to Specter's consternation, Tomlinson testified he found the bullet on stretcher B.

*Specter: What did you say about the covering on the pad, excuse me?*

*Tomlinson: I believe it was a white sheet that was on the pad.*

*Specter: And was there anything else on that?*

*Tomlinson: I don't believe there was on that one, I'm not sure, but I don't believe there was.*

*Specter: What, if anything, did you do with that stretcher?*

*Tomlinson: I took it off of the elevator and put it over against the south wall.*

\*     \*     \*

*Specter: Was there any other stretcher in that area at that time?*

*Tomlinson: There was a stretcher about 2 feet from the wall already there (6H129–130).*

Assistant Counsel Specter then asked Tomlinson: "Will you mark with a 'B' the stretcher which was present at the time you pushed stretcher 'A' off the elevator?" (6H130). Tomlinson complied and then went on to explain how he made several trips up and down on the elevator. Sometime later he noticed that stretcher "B"—the vestibule stretcher—had been pushed out from the wall by someone entering the men's room:

*Tomlinson: Well, he pushed the stretcher out from the wall to get in, and then when he came out he just walked off and didn't push the stretcher back up against the wall, so I pushed it out of the way where we would have a clear area in front of the elevator.*

*Specter: And where did you push it to?*

*Tomlinson: I pushed it back up against the wall.*

*Specter: What, if anything, happened then?*

*Tomlinson: I bumped the wall and a spent cartridge or bullet rolled out that apparently had been lodged under the edge of the mat.\**

---

\* Tomlinson's observation that the bullet "had been lodged under the edge of the mat" has fed attacks on the Commission's *Report*. For how, critics ask, could a bullet fall out of the Governor's thigh and manage to get "*under* the edge

*Specter: And that was from which stretcher?*

*Tomlinson: I believe it was "B".*

*Specter: And what was on "B" if you recall; if any-*
*thing?*

*Tomlinson: Well, at one end they had one or two*
*sheets rolled up; I didn't examine them. They*
*were bloody. They were rolled up on the east*
*end of it and there were a few surgical in-*
*struments on the opposite end and a sterile*
*pack or so (6H130–131).*

Could it have been President Kennedy's stretcher
on which Tomlinson found the bullet? Almost certainly not. The President was taken to Trauma Room
1, where he was pronounced dead at 1:00 P.M. His
body remained on this stretcher in Trauma Room 1
until the casket arrived at 1:40 P.M. (18H814). It
was then lifted up and placed in the casket while
the stretcher was stripped of sheets and rolled across
the hall into Trauma Room 2 (6H138, 142, 146).
There is every reason to believe that the President's
stretcher was still in Trauma Room 2 when the
presidential party departed at 2:00 P.M. But Tomlinson found the bullet at approximately 1:45 P.M.
Thus, the Kennedy stretcher could not have been
the one on which the bullet was found because (1)
it was stripped of linen while Tomlinson's stretcher
carried both sheets and equipment, and (2) its movements are accounted for until after the time the bullet
was found.

Could it have been Governor Connally's stretcher?
No again, and here we differ with the Commission.
When the presidential limousine arrived at Parkland

---

of the mat"? The record should be set straight on this detail.
At no time did Tomlinson see the bullet roll out from under
the mat. He told me that he pushed the stretcher against
the wall and then heard a clink of metal on metal. He walked
over and saw the bullet lying between the pad and the rim
of the stretcher. It could have been lying there all along,
and taken a roll only when he pushed the stretcher. Or it
could have rolled out from under the pad. Tomlinson agreed
that neither he nor anyone else will *ever* be able to judge
with certainty which one of these two possibilities was in
fact the case.

Hospital, two stretchers were brought out to accommodate the wounded men, one from Major Surgery, the other from OB/GYN (6H135). The President and the Governor were placed on these stretchers, which, after pausing at the Triage Desk, were taken into Trauma Rooms 1 and 2.

In Trauma Room 2 Governor Connally's clothes were removed,* a bandage was applied to his chest wound, and a drainage tube inserted (6H84, 116). Before the Governor's clothing had been completely removed, Dr. Shaw (the thoracic surgeon) arrived and said the Governor could be taken up to Surgery (6H84). His stretcher was wheeled out of Trauma Room 2 into the emergency elevator, and carried up to the second-floor operating suite (6H117).

When the elevator reached the second floor, the stretcher was wheeled into the operating suite to a point just outside Operating Room 5 (6H121). The Governor was then lifted up and placed on an operating room table (6H121, 126). Jane Wester, R.N., pushed the stretcher some 20 or 30 feet in the direction of the elevator, removed "several glassine packets of hypodermic needles . . . some alcohol sponges, and a roll of 1 inch tape," and then turned the stretcher over to Orderly R. J. Jimison (6H122).[18] Jimison rolled it the remaining distance into the elevator and closed the door (6H126). Since anesthesia was started on the Governor at 1:00 P.M. (*Archives,* CD 379), and since Jimison testified that the stretcher was put on the elevator "less than 10 minutes" after Governor Connally entered the Operating Room (6H127), we can conclude that the Governor's stretcher was put on the elevator in the interval 1:00–1:05 P.M.

---

* I talked to Rosa Majors, a nurse's aide at Parkland, who removed the Governor's trousers, shoes, and socks. She told me that after removing his trousers, she held them up and went through the pockets for valuables. Had a bullet fallen out of the Governor's thigh, it would have been trapped in his trousers. When Rosa Majors held them up, any such bullet should have fallen out and been discovered at that time. She told me she never saw any bullet while she was caring for Governor Connally. Much later she heard that a bullet was supposed to have been found on his stretcher. She can't conceive where such a bullet could have come from.

It was at just this time, we recall, that Darrell Tomlinson found stretcher "A" on the elevator and wheeled it off into the vestibule. According to Tomlinson, this stretcher had "a white sheet that was on the pad" (6H129). When asked by Specter if there was anything else on the stretcher, he replied: "I don't believe there was on that one" (6H129). Jimison last remembered the Connally stretcher as empty except for the sheets:

*Specter: What was on the stretcher at that time?*
*Jimison: I noticed nothing more than a little flat mattress and two sheets as usual.*
*Specter: And what was the position of the sheets?*
*Jimison: Of course, them sheets was, of course, as usual, flat out on the bed.*
*Specter: Had they been rolled up?*
*Jimison: More or less, not rolled, which, yes, usually they is, the mattress and sheets are all just throwed, one of them about halfway, it would be just throwed about halfway.*
*Specter: Were the sheets flat or just turned over?*
*Jimison: Well, just turned over (6H126).*

Jimison went on to testify that there were no other stretchers placed on the elevator from the second floor up until 3:00 P.M. (6H127). Subsequent inquiries at Parkland Hospital disclosed that in the interval 12:30–2:30 P.M. no patients besides Governor Connally were treated in Surgery (second floor) or in the Delivery Rooms (third floor). Since any stretcher found in the elevator must have come from one of these two floors,[19] it seems virtually a certainty that the stretcher found in the elevator by Tomlinson at approximately 1:00 o'clock belonged to Governor Connally. The description of the Governor's stretcher given by Jimison matches Tomlinson's description of the stretcher he found in the elevator.

Yet Tomlinson maintains that the bullet was not found on the elevator stretcher (stretcher "A") but on the vestibule stretcher (stretcher "B"). This stretcher, which he found already present in the vestibule at 1:00 P.M., carried two rolled-up bloody sheets, doctors' equipment, some gauze pads, and rubber gloves. It would seem that the stretcher on which the bullet was found was used neither in the care of Governor Connally nor President Kennedy, but in the treatment of some other patient unconnected with the assassination. But if so, which patient? And how did it get its bloody sheets (rolled up at one end) and its medical equipment?

### Ronald Fuller

In the Emergency Room Admission Records for November 22 we find Governor Connally admitted at 12:40 P.M.; his chief complaint was listed as "gunshot wound" and he was given admission number 24744 (21H156). The next admission number, 24745, was given to Ronald Fuller, age two and one-half, chief complaint: "fell" (21H156). Ronnie Fuller was admitted 14 minutes after the Governor at 12:54 P.M. (21H156). It is one of history's final ironies that Commission Exhibit 399—the bullet that supposedly struck both President Kennedy and Governor Connally—was very likely found on a stretcher used for a cut and bleeding two-and-one-half-year-old child.

Triage Orderly Joe Richards reported that he helped lift Governor Connally out of the presidential limousine. After pushing the Governor into Trauma Room 2, he helped some Secret Service men find telephones. Then:

> *Minutes later, a lady brought her child to the Registration Desk [Triage Desk] with a cut chin, and I carried him back, placed him on a carriage [stretcher] in the hallway near the Nurses' Station. After the mother calmed down enough to register the child in, I escorted her to where he was (21H226).*

The "hallway near the Nurses' Station" is in Major Surgery not far from Trauma Rooms 1 and 2 (see diagram). Aide Shirley Randall corroborates Richards' account:

Emergency room registration list, which suggests a possible origin for the stretcher in the hallway on which bullet 399 was found.

*Just as I got out there, a lady brought her little boy in who had been cut on the jaw. Blood was all over he [sic] and the child. She started to faint and the triage orderly [Richards] grabbed the child and I grabbed the mother and took her to the nearest chair. Miss Lozano watched her while I went right across from the desk to the Blood Bank and got some ammonia for the mother to smell; she got alright then. I led her to the Emergency Room and found a booth in [Major] Medicine for the doctor to suture the baby. That is when he told me and some more aides that the President was dead (21H218).*

The little boy with the bloody cut is undoubtedly Ronnie Fuller. But when did all this occur? The admissions list places his admission at 12:54 P.M.[20] Was he put on the stretcher and removed from it in time for Tomlinson to find it empty shortly after 1:00 P.M.? The statement of Aide Era Lumpkin furnishes some assistance:

*The doctors got ready to take Gov. Connally up to second floor to Surgery. I left out of trauma II and went back into Maj. Surg. near the nurses' station.*

*Someone brought in this baby that was all bloody. Mrs. Nelson said, "Rosa, you and Era take the baby and put him on a cart". We got the baby's clothes off, trying to determine from where the blood was coming. I spotted the cut on the cheek. I asked about the mother. No one knew where she was. I went out to the desk and was told the mother was on her way inside the Emergency Room.*

*When I got back into the Emergency Room, the mother had arrived. A doctor said, "Put the child in a booth." So we put the child in a booth. The child was crying so loud, someone asked us to carry the baby in major medicine and set up a booth for suturing (21H208–209).[21]*

## PARKLAND MEMORIAL HOSPITAL
## EMERGENCY AREA

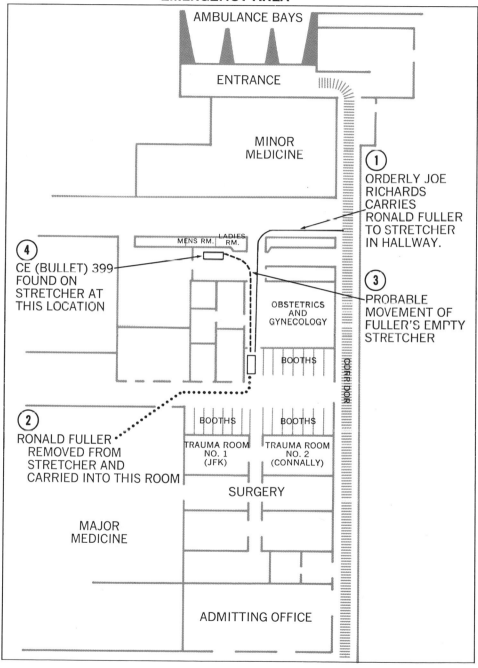

The known and possible movements of Ronald Fuller and his stretcher.

Ronnie Fuller arrived at Parkland Hospital shortly before the Governor was taken up to Surgery. Bleeding profusely, the little boy was placed on a stretcher "in the hallway near the Nurses' Station." He stayed there for only a brief time before being picked up and carried into Major Medicine. He left behind a stretcher whose sheets were soiled with blood. This is as far as we can trace Ronnie Fuller's stretcher. We cannot know for certain that it was then rolled some 30 feet into the elevator vestibule where, shortly after 1:00 P.M., it was seen by Tomlinson. Certain facts, however, indicate that this is what happened.

It was standard hospital procedure to shift used stretchers into the elevator vestibule. The bloody sheets clearly would label this stretcher as "used," and the crowded conditions in Major Surgery would necessitate its speedy removal. Then, too, there was the equipment found on the vestibule stretcher— gauze pads, rubber gloves, stethoscope, and "other doctors' paraphernalia." Rosa Majors told me that she and Era Lumpkin had used gauze pads to clean the child, that either she or Era had been wearing rubber gloves, and that Era had had a stethoscope.[22] She cannot remember what happened to this equipment—the events of that afternoon were so confusing. But it is possible that it was left behind on the stretcher when the two aides carried Ronnie Fuller into Major Medicine.

We do not know for certain that it was Ronnie Fuller's stretcher on which CE 399 subsequently was found. We know his stretcher was empty and 30 feet from the vestibule at approximately 1:00 P.M. We know that standard hospital procedure would require its movement into that vestibule. We know that it carried bloody sheets and that gauze pads, rubber gloves, and a stethoscope were used in the treatment of its last patient. All this only establishes the likelihood that Ronnie Fuller's stretcher was the one in question. As with most aspects of this case, final certainty again eludes us.

Yet if we cannot know with certainty the identity of the stretcher on which the bullet was found, we can know a far more important fact with something approaching certainty: Whatever stretcher the bullet was found on, it was *not* a stretcher used in the care of either President Kennedy or Governor Connally. On this one fact hangs a considerable mystery.

### Origin of the Stretcher Bullet

The Commission's claim with respect to bullet 399 fails on both counts. For not only does "all the evidence" indicate that bullet 399 could *not* have caused the Governor's wounds, but that same evidence (amplified by inquiries at Parkland Hospital) indicates even more conclusively that bullet 399 was not found on the Governor's stretcher. Yet CE 399 *does* exist; I have held it in my hand. And it *was* traced to Oswald's rifle. How can it be accounted for? Obviously it did not find its own way to the stretcher on which it was found. Someone must have placed it there. But who?

The elevator vestibule where it was discovered lay just outside the main perimeter of security guarded by Secret Service and hospital personnel. Only a few feet away two Secret Service agents knocked down an unidentified man claiming to be an FBI agent. Secret Service Agent Andrew Berger describes the incident:

> *At approximately 1:30 p.m., the Chief Supervising nurse, a Mrs. Nelson started to enter the emergency room with an unidentified male (WM, 45 yrs., 6'2", 185-190 lbs., grey hair). As the reporting agent and SA Johnsen started to ask his identity he shouted that he was FBI. Just as we began to ask for his credentials he abruptly attempted to enter the emergency room and had to be forcibly restrained by us. ASAIC Kellerman then appeared and asked this individual to go to the end of the hall (18H795).*

Berger also described "an unidentified CIA agent" who miraculously appeared in that same hospital corridor only minutes after the assassination (18H795).

Two other witnesses testified to having seen Jack
Ruby at Parkland Hospital at about the time the
President's death was announced (15H80; 25H216).
A number of people could have had access to that
hospital vestibule on November 22. It would have
been a task of no great difficulty to plant a bullet on
the stretcher where CE 399 was found. The recently
bloodied sheets would have suggested that here was
a stretcher used in the care of the President or the
Governor. As Professor Richard Popkin has pointed
out, such a plant would play a crucial role in impli-
cating Oswald:

> *Bullet 399 plays a most important role in
> the case since it firmly links Oswald's rifle
> with the assassination. At the time when the
> planting could have been done, it was not
> known if any other ballistics evidence sur-
> vived the shooting. But, certainly, the pris-
> tine bullet, definitely traceable to Oswald's
> Carcano, would have started a chase for and
> pursuit of Oswald if nothing else had, and
> would have made him a prime suspect.*[23]

Subsequent investigation may show the "plant"
theory to be the most satisfactory explanation of
the origin of CE 399; for many months I shared
Popkin's enthusiasm for it. Yet it appears to me now
that there is another explanation more plausible than
the Commission's version yet less sinister than the
"plant" theory. It is based on the following considerations:

(1) Bullet 399 is an *atypical projectile*. None of
the other bullets fired from Oswald's rifle at *standard
muzzle velocity* preserved their pristine state after
hitting anything. Even one of the two ballistics comparison rounds—projectiles fired into long tubes of
cotton waste—was twisted along a longitudinal axis.

When a bullet penetrates cloth, the weave of cloth
tends to etch fine lines on the bullet's tip. Ballistics
expert Joseph D. Nicol examined the tip of CE 399
and found that "although there were some fine stria-

tions, there was nothing of such a nature that it would suggest a pattern" (3H505). The possibility arises that these "fine striations" might have been caused by a projectile passing through cloth at a greatly reduced velocity.

(2) The wound in the President's back was an *atypical wound*. Dr. Boswell told me that its depth could be probed only up to the first or second knuckle of the little finger—a depth of 1 to 2 inches. According to the Sibert-O'Neill report, the bullet penetrated downward at an angle of 45 to 60 degrees—an angle inconsistent with any possible trajectory from a building in Dealey Plaza. Copper traces around the coat and shirt indicate the wounding projectile was copper-jacketed. The dimensions of this wound (4 by 7 millimeters) match exactly the dimensions of the tail-end of CE 399.

(3) The ammunition used in the rifle found on the sixth floor of the Depository was government surplus ammunition last manufactured in 1944.[24] A spokesman for the company that manufactured the ammunition declared that "the reliability of such ammunition would be questionable today."[25]

(4) At least fifty-two witnesses reported that the first shot sounded more like a "firecracker" or a "backfire" than a rifle shot. Taking the Secret Service agents as a group familiar with firearms, we find that agents Bennett (18H760), Hickey (18H765), Hill (18H742), Kellerman (18H724), Kivett (18H778), Ready (18H749), Taylor (18H782), and Young-blood (18H766) all took the first shot for a "firecracker," while Greer (18H723) thought it was a "backfire." Kellerman recalled the sound of the first shot as "a report like a firecracker, pop" (2H73), while Kivett remembered that "it sounded more like an extremely large firecracker, in that it did not seem to have the sharp report of a rifle" (18H778).

What Kellerman heard as "a report like a firecracker, pop" may have been the report of a "short charge"—that is, a cartridge whose explosive power was far less than standard. Such a supposition would explain many things in addition to its odd, firecracker-like sound. It would explain why the first shot (the shot we would normally expect to be most accurate) missed, and why it missed by falling nearly a foot low.* It would explain the copper traces on the President's jacket as well as the "fine striations" on the tip of 399. The very low muzzle velocity of such a projectile would explain the pristine character of the bullet as well as the otherwise inexplicable short penetration into muscle.

Commander Humes was perhaps correct in suggesting on November 22 that "the one bullet [that] had entered the President's back . . . had worked its way out of the body during external cardiac massage" (*Archives,* CD 7). But even if the bullet did work its way back out again, how did it get to the stretcher where Tomlinson found it? To answer this question we must appeal to an old, traditionally American institution—souvenir hunting.

Penn Jones, Jr., a Texas newspaper editor, was at Parkland Hospital shortly after the assassination. He reported that one of the hospital employees—in the general craze for souvenirs then reigning—actually had the nerve to ask Mrs. Kennedy if he might keep the President's undershirt.[26] Since the President wore no undershirt, the garment in question must have belonged to the Governor. Sometime later, an FBI representative admitted to Jones that the story was true, "but we got that back."[27] Since no mention or picture of the Governor's undershirt appears in the twenty-six volumes, it would seem that the FBI took some time to recover their loss.

In such a chaotic atmosphere as that which reigned at the hospital, is it beyond the realm of possibility that some hospital employee found bullet 399 on the floor, in the President's clothes, or on his stretcher, and momentarily snatched it as a souvenir,

---

* Assuming a downward trajectory of 17 degrees and a range of 186 feet, a drop of one foot would indicate a muzzle velocity of 760 feet per second—a velocity high enough to penetrate cloth and skin, but too low to do much damage.

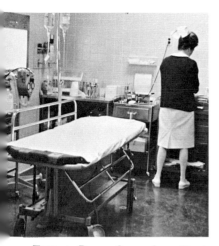

Trauma Room One, where President Kennedy was treated and pronounced dead and from which bullet 399 may have been taken.

only to recognize its importance and quickly secrete it on a stretcher where it might be found by someone else—no questions asked? At one time or another some twenty people were in Trauma Room 1. After the President died, his body was partially cleaned and some attempt made to wipe up the blood that drenched the floor of the room. It was only then that the hospital personnel were released and sent down to get coffee. As they filed out of the Emergency Room and made their way to the basement, they brushed past the stretcher in the vestibule, the stretcher on which CE 399 was soon afterward found.

Although we have no direct evidence that this is indeed what happened—no one has come forward to admit it—the main drift of evidence points to it as more plausible and less complicated than any other explanation that has so far been offered. If we reject it we are thrown back on the Popkin theory, a theory that demands not only a conspirator at the hospital soon after the assassination, but also an accounting for the lack of any bullet or bullet fragments in the President's back. For if bullet 399 is not the bullet that struck the President in the back, then where is that bullet? *

---

* Some recent remarks of Dr. Helpern have suggested a possible answer to this question. Asked what the autopsy X-rays might show to an experienced observer, Dr. Helpern replied:

> *Who knows? Probably absolutely nothing. I don't like to engage in rank, blind speculation; so I can only explain how I would approach them. My first interest would be to see whether there could be another bullet or fragment of bullet in the body which has not been accounted for.*
>
> *Remember that the Warren Commission concluded that the preponderance of the evidence indicated that three shots altogether were fired. Only one relatively intact bullet and the fragments of a second bullet were found. This leaves a missing third bullet. I definitely do not agree with the Commission's conclusion that only two bullets caused all the wounds suffered by both President Kennedy and Governor Connally; but we'll pass that for the moment.*
>
> *Since the X-rays of the President's body were*

Professor Popkin has suggested that "for those who do not accept the Commission's one-bullet hypothesis, there is a genuine problem of explaining where the bullets went."[28] I want to suggest that the discussion of the last few pages offers a solution to this problem.

CE 399 is the bullet that lodged in the President's back. A fragment from the explosive head shot caused the small throat wound. Fragments from this shot were found in the front seat and under the left jump seat in the passenger compartment. Thus the bullets that struck the President are all accounted for. Only the bullet or bullets that hit Governor Connally remain to be explained.

### The Governor's Bullets

The wounds to the Governor's chest and wrist were through-and-through injuries; the missile that caused them kept on going. The surgeon who treated the superficial thigh wound believed it to be caused by the tangential striking of a missile that ended up "elsewhere" (6H106, 111). Thus, from the condition of Connally's wounds we would not expect to find a bullet lodged in his body. The missile that wounded him would appear to be "elsewhere"—but *where?*

The missile could have escaped the car after smashing through his wrist. Some evidence for such

---

*not filed as exhibits, we must rely entirely upon the observations of the Navy doctors that they skillfully eliminated the possibility that a third bullet, or a fragment of some bullet, did not enter the body and somehow meander down to come to rest in some illogical, remote spot. Apparently, the doctors did not feel confident enough to rely on the X-rays during the autopsy when they went probing, or rather tried to go probing, for the bullet that was found on the stretcher in Parkland Hospital. They have now been quoted as saying that they did have the X-rays available to them that night. Bullets do have a funny habit of showing up in the most astonishing places in the body.*[29]

Should subsequent examination of the X-rays reveal the presence of a bullet in the President's body, then the Popkin theory (that CE 399 was a plant) would have been justified.

a hypothesis is furnished by an FBI report recently
discovered[30] in the Archives:

> *On September 29, 1964, Eugene P. Al-*
> *dredge, 9304 Lenel, Dallas, Texas, tele-*
> *phonically advised that he disagreed with the*
> *President's Commission report that Oswald*
> *did not have help in the assassination.*
>
> *Aldredge stated he saw a television pro-*
> *gram shortly after the assassination, believed*
> *to be on Channel 4, in which a mark on the*
> *sidewalk was pointed out.*
>
> *Approximately three months ago, he stated*
> *he viewed such mark, which he is sure was*
> *caused by a bullet, and that this mark is*
> *approximately six inches long. He described*
> *the location of this mark as being in the mid-*
> *dle of the sidewalk on the north side of Elm*
> *Street, which side is nearest the Texas School*
> *Book Depository Building and that the*
> *above-described mark is approximately*
> *eight feet east of the lamp post on the side-*
> *walk. He stated that a reporter for "The*
> *Dallas Morning News," Carl Freund, has*
> *also stated this is a bullet mark* (Archives,
> *CD 1546).*[31]

The interesting thing about this mark is that, if we
take Aldredge's description of its location as accurate,
it lines up perfectly with a trajectory through Governor Connally at Z234–238, assuming a firing point
on the east boundary of Dealey Plaza. If the missile
that tore through the Governor's chest and wrist
was deflected out of the car by the second impact,
then the tangential thigh wound may have been
caused by a fragment from the later Kennedy head
shot—at this time (Z313) the Governor is reclining
backward into his wife's arms, thus exposing his left
thigh to such a fragment.

There are difficulties with such an explanation. It
is by no means clear, for example, that the Governor's
wrist at Z234–238 is in such a position as to deflect
a missile out of the car. Yet even if the chest, wrist,
and thigh wounds all were incurred by the same mis-

sile, the subsequent handling of the Governor's clothes precludes any determination as to what happened to such a missile. Mrs. Connally was handed some of the Governor's clothes in a paper sack at Parkland Hospital while the rest were discovered sometime later in the Washington, D.C., office of U.S. Representative Henry Gonzales.[32] All the clothes were either washed or dry-cleaned before the FBI had a chance to examine them, thus precluding any determination concerning the kind of bullet that struck the Governor.[33] Given this kind of cavalier treatment it is quite possible that the complete missile or missile fragments were trapped in the Governor's clothing but lost before experts were given a chance to perform their examinations. As distinguished a forensic authority as Dr. Milton Helpern has suggested that this is precisely what happened to the missile which struck the Governor:

> *In my opinion, the second bullet that wounded Governor Connally is the one that is missing . . .*
>
> *It is not unusual at all for spent bullets that have passed through a human body to become lost. Most longtime homicide detectives can spin off several tales of cases of lost bullets. If I had to venture a guess as to what happened to the bullet that wounded Governor Connally, I would suggest that it fell out of his pants leg while he was being removed from the car and placed on the stretcher; or it could have fallen out at any stage of his hospital experience.*[34]

In light of all these factors, it is not incumbent on critics of the Commission's version to produce the bullet or bullets that did the damage ascribed to CE 399. The possible loss of the missile—either through carelessness or through deflection outside the limousine—makes such a demand illegitimate. Although the whereabouts of this missile must remain in doubt, the discussion of the last few pages offers a solution to Professor Popkin's problem: for the most part, we can explain now "where the bullets went."

## NOTES

1. 4H260–263. Sylvia Meagher describes the curious way in which this palm print was handled by the Dallas Police. See Sylvia Meagher, *Accessories After the Fact* (New York: The Bobbs-Merrill Company, Inc., 1967), pp. 120-127.

2. Author's interview with Luke Mooney, May 31, 1967.

3. This conclusion emerges from J. Edgar Hoover's June 2, 1964, letter to the Commission, a letter in which he recounts the results of FBI examinations on the cartridge cases (26H449–450). His letter conflicts with earlier testimony furnished by FBI firearms expert Robert Frazier (3H390–441). On Mar. 31 Frazier testified that microphotographs of the base of the cartridge cases showed up points of similarity with the bolt of Oswald's rifle. Frazier concluded from this similarity that all the cases at one time or another had been in contact with the bolt of Oswald's rifle (3H414–419). This conclusion is in direct conflict with Hoover's later letter. In it the Director of the FBI explicitly states that *only* one cartridge case, C7, had a set of marks "identified as having been produced by contact with the bolt of C14" (26H449–450).

My own opinion is that CE 543 was most likely "dry loaded" in Oswald's rifle at some earlier time. Such a "dry loading" would account for (1) the magazine follower marks noted in Hoover's letter (26H449), (2) the microscopic bolt similarities noted in Frazier's testimony (3H519), and (3) the sharp dent in the lip. If we suppose that the lip of CE 543 was dented in such a "dry loading" operation, this also accounts for the missing chambering mark—because 543 was lighter than a loaded cartridge, its lip struck the metal projection rather than the cartridge body, as was the case with the other exhibits. Another reason for believing in the existence of such a "dry loading" operation with respect to CE 543 is the conviction that a would-be assassin would take this minimal precaution with respect to evidence destined to be left at the scene of the crime.

4. Although quite obvious on one of the cases, the mark was more difficult to discern on the other. Since these two cases were selected from some thirty or more test firings (3H402, 426), the difference between the two marks may very well reflect a difference in firing order—the more pronounced mark suggesting a case early in the firing series, the less pronounced mark suggesting a case later in the series.

5. As pointed out in Chapter III, there are a multitude of reasons for believing that no bullet at all transited the President's neck. We restrict ourselves only to one part of the Commission's thesis, namely, that CE 399 caused all the Governor's wounds.

6. Frazier's description of the bullets leaves the impression that they never had been fired; that, unfired, they had been pulled from their cartridge cases and weighed. This

impression is further buttressed by a letter written to *Commentary* magazine (April, 1967, p. 14) by Assistant Counsel W. David Slawson. In this letter Slawson states that Frazier's weighings established the "normal pre-firing weight" of the projectiles in question.

Yet if the weights given by Frazier were obtained from *unfired* projectiles, they may be deceptive. For the passage of a bullet through the barrel of a rifle tends to shave off quantities of metal from the rifling grooves; a fired projectile usually weighs less than an unfired one.

This difference in weight becomes critical only when the unfired projectiles are compared with CE 399. A more enlightening comparison would be between the weights of CE 399 and the two ballistic comparison rounds fired into cotton (CE 572). To establish the weight of these projectiles, I carried a very sensitive Mettler balance all the way from Philadelphia to the Archives. Unfortunately, the Deputy Archivist denied permission for these bullets to be weighed. He said that if the FBI would recall them, the FBI lab could weigh them. However, the FBI's cooperation in this matter is not to be anticipated. Upon personal inquiry at the Bureau I was told by one of the Director's assistants, Special Agent C. Benjamin Fulton, that no FBI personnel would be able to provide any information with regard to the assassination. My inquiry was made as part of an effort to find Agents Sibert and O'Neill and to ask Robert Frazier which bullets he weighed.

7. During our November interview with Dr. Charles Gregory, I called his attention to one of the postoperative X-rays of the Governor's right wrist. In this X-ray (CE 692) several pieces of metal appear to be still embedded in the radius. Dr. Gregory examined the X-ray and concurred that indeed at least two fragments still appeared to be embedded in the Governor's wrist.

8. In testifying before the Commission Dr. Gregory was asked to describe the thigh wound. He remarked that "a fragment of metal . . . lies just beneath the skin, about a half inch on the medial aspect of the thigh" (4H125). I asked him about this fragment in November, 1966, and he reiterated that such a fragment had been discovered and subsequently removed. This fragment does not appear in any of the Commission exhibits. I presume it was lost after removal.

9. In a telephone interview on May 31, 1967, **Dr. Shires** confirmed that such a fragment was observed in the chest on postoperative X-rays.

10. In addition to these three doctors, Dr. Gregory also had doubts as to whether a single bullet had sufficient velocity to cause all of Connally's wounds, and he also held that the damage to the Governor's wrist—the fact that cloth fibers had been carried into the wound as well as the radial nerve and a tendon being cut—indicated the passage of a distorted missile with sharp edges (4H124, 127). All the

doctors asked by Specter whether CE 399 could have caused Governor Connally's wounds gave skeptical or negative replies. Specter's only support came from an Army veterinarian, Dr. Olivier. Asked by Specter, "Do you have an opinion as to whether, in fact, Bullet No. 399 did cause the wound on the Governor's wrist, assuming if you will that it was the missile found on the Governor's stretcher at Parkland Hospital?", Olivier replied, "I believe that it was. That is my feeling" (5H90)—an answer that seems to refer more to the bullet's location of discovery than to its activities. For an excellent discussion of the medical evaluation of CE 399, see Richard Popkin's letter to *The New York Review of Books,* Oct. 6, 1966, p. 33.

11. Presidential Commission Administrative Records, National Archives.

12. *Ibid.*

13. Author's interview with Cyril Wecht, M.D., on May 26, 1967.

14. Marshall Houts, *Where Death Delights* (New York: Coward-McCann, 1967), pp. 62-63.

15. *Ibid.,* p. 64.

16. David Lifton, "The Case for Three Assassins," *Ramparts,* January, 1967, p. 86.

17. In the report of the FBI agent who showed Tomlinson and Wright CE 399 we learn that although neither could positively identify 399 as the bullet they handled on November 22, nevertheless they thought it bore a general resemblance to 399. This makes all the more strange what Wright told me in November, 1966.

I asked him what the bullet looked like, and he replied that it had a pointed tip like the one I held in my hand (earlier he had procured a .30 caliber unfired projectile that we had placed on the stretcher cart in our reenactment). I then drew three bullet shapes: one pointed like the .30 caliber; another long with rounded tip—like 399; still another squat and rounded, like a .38 caliber. Wright picked the pointed tip as the one that most resembled the bullet found on the stretcher. I then showed him photographs of CE's 399, 572 (the two ballistics comparison rounds from Oswald's rifle), and 606 (revolver bullets), and he rejected all of these as resembling the bullet Tomlinson found on the stretcher. Half an hour later in the presence of two witnesses, he once again rejected the picture of 399 as resembling the bullet found on the stretcher. Sometime later he asked me if one of the pictures I had shown him was supposed to be the bullet found on the stretcher. I replied, "Yes," and he seemed quite prepared to stick by his story. As a professional law-enforcement officer, Wright has an educated eye for bullet shapes. Tomlinson's recollection of bullet shapes was not very clear, and he could say only that the bullet found resembled either CE 572 (the ballistics comparison rounds) or the pointed, .30 caliber bullet Wright had procured for us.

O. P. Wright believes that the stretcher bullet he examined on November 22 looked like the sharp-nosed bullet above. The Commission, however, insists it was blunt-nosed CE 399, below.

This is an appalling piece of information, for if Wright's recollection is accurate, then CE 399 must have been switched for the real bullet sometime later in the transmission chain. This could have been done only by some federal officer, since it was in government possession from that time on. If this is true, then the assassination conspiracy would have to have involved members of the federal government and been an "inside" job.

18. Miss Wester also mentioned that she believed she had rolled up the sheets on this stretcher, a detail that is in conflict with the testimony of Jimison (6H126) and Tomlinson (6H129). I asked her about this in May, 1967. She pointed out that she couldn't be certain she had rolled up the sheets since this was not standard hospital procedure—"sometimes you do, sometimes you don't." She continued in this vein: "You have to take into consideration the fact that the operating room at that time was not anywhere near the normal state that it usually is. And when you have something like 15 or 30 people standing very close trying to get into the OR and us trying to keep them out, you have a problem. It was mass confusion. So like I say, that is the best I can remember. I . . . maybe, I remembered wrong. I don't know."

19. On November 22 this elevator operated only from the basement to the third floor, with floors one through three being patient treatment areas.

20. Ronnie Fuller most likely arrived at the hospital Emergency Room some minutes before this. This time was recorded by a time clock after the admission slip was filled out. As Shirley Randall indicated, the mother fainted upon arrival in the Emergency Room. Since she had to be revived before the admission slip could be filled out, 12:54 gives a very late time for the child's arrival; 12:45 to 12:50 would be a more accurate estimate.

21. Due to a new hospital rule prohibiting interviews with Parkland personnel, I was unable to interview Shirley Randall, Joe Richards, or Era Lumpkin. Before this rule went into effect I had the good fortune to interview Rosa Majors, who cleared up two points of possible confusion in Era Lumpkin's statement: (1) Richards and Randall stated that Richards placed the child on a stretcher while Era Lumpkin leaves the impression that she and Rosa Majors did this. Rosa Majors told me that Richards took the child and placed him on a stretcher near the Nurses' Station in Major Surgery. (2) Era Lumpkin states that "someone asked us to carry the baby in major medicine." Does this mean "carry in the arms" or "carry on the stretcher"? I asked Rosa Majors this:

*Thompson: So you took the child in your arms?*
*Majors: We carried it and laid it in there on the carriage.*
*Thompson: Now where was the carriage?*
*Majors: It was in the Major Medicine area.*

22. It seemed strange to me that nurses' aides would be

equipped with stethoscopes. I was told that this was to enable them to monitor frequently the blood pressure of Emergency Room patients.

23. Richard H. Popkin, "The Second Oswald: The Case for a Conspiracy Theory," *The New York Review of Books,* Vol. VII, Number 1 (July 28, 1966), p. 14.

24. In *Rush to Judgment* (New York: Holt, Rinehart & Winston, Inc., 1966) Mark Lane reproduces photographically (p. 411) a letter from the Winchester-Western Division of Olin (the maker of the cartridges found on the sixth floor of the Depository) which states that the "previous production of this cartridge was made against government contracts completed back in 1944."

25. Letter from H. J. Gebelein to Sylvia Meagher, April 20, 1965; see Meagher, *op. cit.,* p. 113.

26. Penn Jones, Jr., *Forgive My Grief* (Midlothian: The Midlothian Mirror, 1966), I, 185–86.

27. *Ibid.,* p. 186.

28. Richard H. Popkin, letter to *The New York Review of Books,* Oct. 6, 1966, p. 33. If the solution offered above is rejected, only one other alternative remains—that a bullet still rests in the President's body.

29. Houts, *op. cit.,* p. 61.

30. This document was discovered in the fall of 1966 by Harold Weisberg.

31. The following day two FBI agents went down to Dealey Plaza to check Aldredge's report. Thirty-three feet from the second lamp post they found "an approximately four inches by one-half inch wide dug-out scar, which could possibly have been made by some blunt-end type instrument or projectile" (*Archives,* CD 1546). Their report went on to note that "this scar lies in such a direction that if it had been made by a bullet, it could not have come from the direction of the window . . . used by Lee Harvey Oswald when firing his assassination bullets at the late President" (*Archives,* CD 1546).

32. *Life,* Nov. 25, 1966, p. 48.

33. 5H63–66; *Archives,* CD 827.

34. Houts, *op. cit.,* p. 64.

# VIII

## A RECONSTRUCTION

THE Hertz sign atop the Depository flashed 12:00 noon. Inside, the floor-laying crew on the sixth floor had knocked off for lunch. The old flooring was to be ripped up, and, as a preparatory move, most of the book cartons had been shifted to the front (or southern) side of the building. This side was now a jumble of cartons, some piled five or six high, others scattered across the floor. Everything lay under a heavy covering of warehouse dust, illuminated here and there by a naked light bulb. Within the next half hour an assassin would make his way through the jumble

of cartons and take up his position at a corner window. Within the hour, every foot of this floor would be explored by police officers, sheriff's deputies, and reporters. But now, as the Hertz sign flashed noon and the crowds began to gather in the Plaza below, it was empty.

Empty too were the roofs of the adjacent buildings along Houston Street. To those who have watched motorcades for Presidents or foreign dignitaries in other cities, this may seem an unusually lax security arrangement. But at noon on Houston Street there were no guards on the Records or Dal-Tex buildings. The first housed Dallas County offices and the second furnished quarters for various textile firms. Architecturally, these buildings diagonally across the corner from the Depository were undistinguished, but from the point of view of a potential assassin they were outstanding. Their roofs were circuited by low stone parapets that, in addition to shielding a gunman from view, offered a firm gun rest. At 12:00 noon these roofs were empty. Yet in the next half hour, as one assassin was climbing toward the sixth floor of the Depository, an accomplice was making his way to a rooftop lair in one of these buildings. There was no one to stop him at any point along the way.

If the accomplice had reached his rooftop position shortly after noon, he could have looked across the Plaza and seen a blue and white 1959 Oldsmobile station wagon circling the parking lot behind the knoll (6H286). A little later he could have seen a 1957 black Ford doing the same thing, only this time the driver would be talking into a radio mike (6H286). We do not know, of course, that either of these cars had anything to do with the subsequent events in Dealey Plaza. Nor for that matter, do we know that the two strangers whom Lee Bowers saw behind the stockade fence at 12:25 (6H287–288) had anything to do with the assassination. What we do know, however, is that by 12:30 it would have been relatively easy for three assassins to have reached their firing locations: one in the sixth-floor

Trajectories of the four shots fired in Dealey Plaza.

window of the Depository, one on the roof of an adjacent building, and one behind the stockade fence.

Around noon the people who were soon to serve
as witnesses began their unwitting entrances.

Arnold Rowland and his wife reached Dealey
Plaza at around 12:05. They moved up and down
Houston Street trying to find a good vantage point,
and finally settled on a spot midway between Elm
and Main Streets. Some minutes later Rowland
looked up at the Depository and noticed in a south-
west-corner window of the sixth floor a young man
wearing "a very light-colored shirt . . . open at the
collar" (2H171) and cradling a rifle:

> *I noticed on the sixth floor of the building
> that there was a man back from the window,
> not hanging out the window. He was stand-
> ing and holding a rifle. This appeared to me
> to be a fairly high-powered rifle because of
> the scope and the relative proportion of the
> scope to the rifle, you can tell about what
> type of rifle it is (2H169).*

Rowland was asked what time he saw this man and
indicated that it was almost 12:15—he had noticed
the time on the Hertz clock (2H168–169). At about
this time Mrs. R. E. Arnold, a secretary at the Depository, noticed one of her co-workers standing in a
first-floor hallway. She tells about it in an FBI report
recently discovered in the Archives:

> *[She] left that office between 12:00 and
> 12:15 PM, to go downstairs and stand in
> front of the building, she stated she thought
> she caught a fleeting glimpse of Lee Harvey
> Oswald standing in the hallway between the
> front doors leading to the warehouse, located
> on the first floor. She could not be sure that
> this was Oswald, but said she felt it was and
> believed the time to be a few minutes before
> 12:15 (Archives, CD 5).*

During his later interrogation Oswald claimed to have gone to lunch on the first floor shortly after noon (R600, 605, 613, 4H468). When the President was shot, Oswald claimed he was eating lunch there on the first floor (R600, 605).

The motorcade was due to pass the corner of Main and Houston Streets at 12:25. But at that time, the procession was far up Main Street. Thus, it was nearly 12:30 when Robert Hughes heard the wave of shouting and applause ripple toward him down Main Street (**A**). As the pilot car driven by Police Chief Jesse Curry turned the corner, Hughes began taking movies with his 8-millimeter camera. As seen in his film, the high buildings along Main Street cast their shadows across the motorcade, and for a moment only the winking red lights of the escort motorcycles are visible (**B**). Then the presidential Lincoln sweeps smoothly into the sunlight of the corner. Jacqueline Kennedy's left hand rises to steady her pillbox hat (**C**) as the giant limousine begins its run up Houston Street (**D**).

Hughes's camera continued to grind as first the Records Building (**E**), then the Dal-Tex Building, and finally the Depository appeared in his viewfinder (**F**). As both the Kennedy limousine and the Secret Service follow-up car completed their turns onto Elm Street (**G**) he stopped his camera. "About five seconds after I quit taking pictures," he later recalled, "we heard the shots."[1] (**H**).

At a distance of a city block from the Depository, Hughes could not have made out a light-colored shape appearing at a corner sixth-floor window. It first appears on his film as the presidential limousine is heading down Houston Street. In early frames it appears quite wide, but as the car turns onto Elm Street it narrows strikingly. Apparently, the gunman at the sixth-floor window has turned and is now raising his rifle into firing position.

Thirty seconds before Hughes turned his camera in the direction of the Depository, Ronald Fischer and Bob Edwards saw this gunman. They were standing near the reflecting pool at the southwest

A   Motorcade on Main Street.

B   Motorcade on Main Street. Pilot car in foreground.

C Presidential limousine turns from Main onto Houston Street.

D Presidential limousine on Houston Street.

E Limousine and Secret Service follow-up car on Houston Street.

F Motorcade begins turn onto Elm Street under Texas School Book Depository building.

G The turn onto Elm Street.

H Just after turn onto Elm Street.

I  Elm Street, in front of the Depository.

J  The first shot.

K Limousine under fire.

L Impact on President's head.

M  Secret Service Agent Clint Hill runs to car.

N  Hill reaches car.

O Hill and Mrs. Kennedy on trunk.

P Limousine heads toward underpass.

corner of Elm and Houston streets. As they waited for the motorcade, Bob Edwards' eyes drifted upward to the Depository. In a corner sixth-floor window he saw a young man dressed in a "light colored sport shirt" (19H647). "There was a stack of boxes around him," Edwards later recalled, and there was something about this man that made Edwards call his friend Fischer's attention to him. "The man held my attention for 10 or 15 seconds," Fischer later told the Commission, "because he appeared uncomfortable for one, and secondly he wasn't watching—uh—he didn't look like he was watching for the parade. He looked like he was looking down towards the Trinity River and the triple underpass . . . And all the time I watched him, he never moved his head, he never—he never moved anything. Just was there transfixed" (6H193). Fischer looked away when the roar of the crowd up the street signaled the approach of the motorcade.

That roar also drew the attention of the gunman in the sixth-floor window. Looking down on the knoll, he may have been trying to catch a glimpse of his confederate. But the trees shielded the corner of the stockade fence from his view. A rustle in the crowd drew his attention back to Houston Street. An unmarked white Ford—the pilot car—had made its right turn and now was coming straight toward him. A phalanx of motorcycles followed and then the dark blue presidential Lincoln. Looking down he could see the President smiling at Mrs. Connally. His grip tightened on the rifle. This was the perfect shot—as the President approached the Depository. Had he been a lone assassin, this would have been the time to shoot; he would have fired while the car was still on Houston Street. But he was not alone, and must hold his fire until the guns of his two confederates could bear on the limousine. If he fired now (perfect though the shot might be for him), the Lincoln might stop, turn sharply, and escape the trap.

As Bill Greer eased the 4-ton limousine around the 120-degree turn onto Elm Street, the gunman above shifted into firing position. The victim had entered the trap.

View of stockade fence from sixth-floor Depository window.

The shot not fired . . . while the motorcade was still on Houston Street (re-enactment photo).

Ahead of him, Greer noticed a number of people on the overpass and wondered how he could veer at the last moment to pass under a vacant section of the viaduct if the need arose (2H117). To his right Kellerman was beginning to relax. The crowds were sparse now; only a few people on either side lined the pavement as Elm Street swung under the railroad tracks. Soon the motorcade would be over; already Lawson in the pilot car had signaled they were only 5 minutes from the Trade Mart. In the passenger compartment behind Kellerman and Greer, Mrs. Connally pointed out the underpass to Jacqueline Kennedy and said, "We're almost through; it's just beyond that."[2] The President's wife was thinking how nice it would be to get out of the glaring Texas sun (5H179) **(I)**.

The gunman on the sixth floor had sighted in on the agreed-upon spot just opposite the freeway sign. Hidden for a moment in the foliage of an oak tree, the limousine slowly emerged at a speed of 11 miles per hour. The gunman saw the President's back and shoulders appear in his scope and carefully aligned the cross hairs on the President's head. Rifle stock pressed close to his cheek, the barrel braced against a box, he squeezed the trigger **(J)**.

Jacqueline Kennedy heard the first shot as a backfire (5H180). Mrs. Connally heard it only as "a frightening noise" that came from the right (4H147). Turning, she caught a glimpse of the President, both hands to his neck, and heard her husband yell, "Oh, no, no, no!" just as a second shot crashed into his back.

As the first gunman pulled the trigger, the second was preparing his shot. From his perch on the roof of a Houston Street building he had a perfect view of the car as it moved down Elm Street. Following it in his sights, he waited until it approached the Stemmons Freeway sign, and then, the sound of the first shot ringing in his ears, he fired—wounding the Governor.

It was now little over a second since the first shot (**K**). The President's elbows were splayed upward from shoulder level, his face showing more surprise than pain, and the Governor, his right wrist dangling, was falling backward into his wife's arms.

Neither victim had been wounded fatally. As the first assassin worked the awkward bolt of the Carcano, he could see that his first shot had missed the President's head. Carefully he sighted the cross hairs again. Squeezing the trigger, he saw the President's head explode in a halo of red (**L**).

Behind the stockade fence, a third assassin had heard the first two shots and seen that the President was still sitting upright. His backup shot, fired perhaps from a long-barreled pistol at a range of less than 40 yards, would be the conspirators' insurance policy. It did not fail them. As the evidence adduced earlier shows, it drove into the right temporal region of the President's skull, snuffing out John Kennedy's life and covering his wife, car, and two motorcycle escorts with brain and flesh. As the wail of the follow-up car's siren absorbed the echoes of the final shots, the limousine slid toward the underpass (**M, N**). For a moment Jacqueline Kennedy and Clint Hill were silhouetted on the trunk of the Lincoln (**O**) and then the car disappeared under the bridge (**P**). As it emerged on the other side, Clint Hill could be seen pounding the trunk in rage and frustration.

Having watched the fatal head shot, the first gunman believed his second shot had done its job. "He drew the gun back from the window," Howard Brennan remembered, "as though he was drawing it back to his side and maybe paused for another second as though to assure himself that he hit the mark and then he disappeared" (3H144). The blast from his own gun had covered the sound of the fourth report, but he had heard the second shot. Ejecting his second cartridge, he threw down a third, wiped his fingerprints from the rifle, hid it behind some boxes, and quickly left the building.

Since apparently little suspicion had been cast on the buildings along Houston Street,* the second gunman would have had no difficulty in leaving the scene. The third assassin, however, was in a very precarious position, and only speed and expert planning could make possible his escape. His shot from the knoll had frightened the few people standing along the north curb of Elm Street. Mary Elizabeth Woodward, Bill and Gayle Newman, Emmett Hudson and his companions had all dropped to the ground after the third shot, as photos show. It was Motorcycle Officer Bobby Hargis, splattered with brain debris from a shot that he thought came from the right front, who first led the chase into the knoll. About a minute, however, intervened between the last shot and Hargis' chase. This would have been enough time for the third assassin to hide himself and his gun in the trunk of the four-door sedan noticed by S. M. Holland. His confederate could have slammed the trunk shut and then assumed the identity of a Secret Service agent. Sometime later, after he had flashed his fake creden-

---

* The Dal-Tex Building was searched immediately after the assassination, so some suspicion must have been cast on these buildings lining the east side of Houston Street. There is no indication that any other buildings were searched, possibly since they were above reproach as housing Dallas County municipal offices.

tials at Officer Joe Marshall Smith, and after Smith
had checked the interior but *not* the trunk of the
car, the "Secret Service agent" might simply have
driven it away. According to Holland, it was an "off-
white" 1960 or 1961 Chevrolet sedan.[3]

Is this really what happened on November 22?
Is the scenario sketched above a work of history,
semihistory, or fiction? Have we finally found the
*truth* about the assassination?

In all candor it must be said that we have found
at most only part of the truth. Although we have
charted its outline, a detailed knowledge still eludes
us. It is no longer possible to doubt that shots were
fired from locations other than the Depository or
that the Governor was hit by a later bullet than the
one that struck the President. The sequence of shots,
their timing, their trajectories—all these variables
have been established within the limits of precision
allowed by the evidence. But after the overall outline
of the assassination has been defined, it is difficult to
move further with much confidence.

Was the gunman in the Depository Lee Harvey
Oswald? A later chapter will discuss the question of
Oswald's guilt and present new evidence suggesting
that two men (neither of whom was Oswald) may
have been on the sixth floor of the Depository at the
time of the shooting. But with the evidence available
it is simply not possible to reach a final conclusion as
to Oswald's guilt.

A similar answer has to be given to many questions concerning how the various assassins reached
their firing locations and made good their escapes.
We know one shot came from the east side of Houston Street. We know that no guards were stationed
in or on these buildings and that only one of them
(the Dal-Tex Building) was searched after the assassination. But the details of how an assassin made
his way along Houston Street to his sniper's nest and
subsequently escaped lie beyond our knowledge.

Much the same can be said with regard to the shot from behind the stockade fence. The evidence indicates unambiguously that a shot came from that location, but whether one or two conspirators were involved must remain an open question. The most plausible explanation has been given above: Bowers saw two men behind the fence. One fired the shot and then climbed into the trunk of an adjacent automobile. The other flashed fake Secret Service credentials and later drove his accomplice away from the scene. But other explanations cannot be ruled out. The man J. C. Price saw "run towards the passenger cars on the railroad siding after the volley of shots" (19H492) may have been the only assassin stationed on the knoll.

The scenario sketched on previous pages is thus an amalgam of hard fact and educated speculation. Although the essential outline of the assassination—four shots from three guns in 6 seconds—is now apparent, the details remain unclear. A future investigation, a sudden revelation, or the patient labors of other researchers and historians may yet fill in these details.

**NOTES**

1. Letter from Robert Hughes to his parents, Mr. and Mrs. Ray Hughes, Nov. 22, 1963.

2. William Manchester, *The Death of a President* (New York: Harper & Row, 1967), p. 154.

3. Taped interview, Nov. 30, 1966.

# IX

## THE WARREN REPORT

*I don't think the people are going to believe
this [the single-bullet theory]—this year,
next year, or a hundred years from now . . .
This thing will be challenged today, tomor-
row, and forever.—Assistant Commission
Counsel Arlen Specter.*[1]

ANY account of the assassination that claims to be
definitive must do at least two things: First, it must
offer a comprehensive and consistent picture of what
happened, thus bringing into coherence the eye- and
earwitness testimony, the evidence of the films, and
the story told by physical evidence found at the
scene. Secondly, if it is to be believed, it must offer
an equally plausible account of just how and why
the Warren Commission went wrong.

With only occasional exceptions, all the evidence
discussed in previous chapters was available to the
Commission. But the Commission, in its haste, its
uncritical evaluation of the facts, and its predisposi-
tion to prove Oswald the lone assassin, overlooked
much of this evidence.

In the final analysis, the Commission's error can
be traced to one central fact: its uncritical accept-

The Warren *Report* and its twenty-
six supporting volumes of testimony and exhibits.

ance of the autopsy's conclusion that a bullet exited from the front of the President's throat. As the evidence in the case unfolded, this one conclusion assumed crucial importance. Because of it, certain evidence had to be ignored and other evidence twisted. In stubbornly holding on to it and the single-bullet theory it gave rise to—in refusing to give up either or even to examine them—the Commission was led hopelessly astray. The story of its wanderings begins at Bethesda Naval Hospital on the evening of November 22.

## THE AUTOPSY

"The pattern was clear," Commander Humes could assert with confidence at the close of the autopsy on the evening of November 22. "One bullet had entered the President's back and had worked its way out of the body during external cardiac massage, and a second high-velocity bullet had entered the rear of the skull and had fragmentized prior to exit through the top of the skull" (*Archives,* CD 7). Apparently, the pattern remained "clear" for something less than 12 hours—the time required for Commander Humes to call Dr. Perry in Dallas and learn that there was one gunshot wound in the President's body that he had not examined.

At some point during the next 24 hours Commander Humes met with the other two autopsy surgeons (the President's body having long since been removed) to decide jointly what their conclusions would be. It is important to note who these doctors were and what they knew and did not know at the time their findings were decided upon.

Commander Humes's official title is "Director of Laboratories of the Naval Medical School at the Naval Medical Center, Bethesda, Md." (2H348). Except for one course at the Armed Forces Institute of Pathology, he had no training or experience in forensic pathology. When asked by Assistant Counsel Specter what specific experience he had with respect to gunshot wounds, he could only reply:

*My type of practice, which fortunately has been in peacetime endeavor to a great extent, has been more extensive in the field of natural disease than violence. However, on several occasions in various places where I have been employed, I have had to deal with violent death, accidents, suicides, and so forth (2H348).*

This elliptical answer from Commander Humes leaves open the question whether he had *ever* performed an autopsy on a gunshot victim, yet it was Humes who was in charge of the President's autopsy. Humes's assistant, Commander Boswell, likewise reports no special experience or training in the field of forensic pathology (2H377). Neither Humes's nor Boswell's name appears on the membership roster of the American Academy of Forensic Sciences. Only Lieutenant Colonel Finck's name appears on that list (not as a Fellow but as a "Provisional Member"[2]), yet, as I learned from Boswell, Lt. Col. Finck was called in by telephone only after the autopsy was already in progress.*

---

* Boswell interview, Jan. 11, 1967. Dr. Milton Helpern has made the following observation about the difficulty of Lt. Col. Finck's position at the autopsy and about his experience as a forensic pathologist:

*Colonel Finck's position throughout the entire proceeding was extremely uncomfortable. If it had not been for him, the autopsy would not have been handled as well as it was; but he was in the role of the poor bastard Army child foisted into the Navy family reunion. He was the only one of the three doctors with any experience with bullet wounds; but you have to remember that his experience was limited primarily to "reviewing" files, pictures, and records of finished cases. There's a world of difference between standing at the autopsy table and trying to decide whether a hole in the body is a wound of entrance or a wound of exit, and in reviewing another man's work at some later date in the relaxed, academic atmosphere of a private office. I know, because I've sweated out too many of these cases during the past thirty-five years. Colonel Finck is extremely able in the type of administrative work which has been assigned him over the years (Houts, op. cit., pp. 55-56).*

Thus, the only two doctors present throughout the autopsy were ordinary hospital pathologists, not forensic specialists. In the opinion of many this was a far-reaching mistake. "The tragic, tragic thing," Dr. Milton Helpern has said of the medico-legal aspects of the Kennedy assassination, "is that a relatively simple case was horribly snarled up from the very beginning; and then the errors were compounded at almost every step along the way."[3] And what was, in Dr. Helpern's opinion, the most grievous error of all?

> *I've already touched on the gravest of them all—the selection of a "hospital" pathologist to perform a medico-legal autopsy. This stemmed from the mistaken belief that because a man can supervise a laboratory or perform a hospital autopsy to see whether a patient died from emphysema or heart disease, he is qualified to evaluate gunshot wounds in the body. It's like sending a seven-year-old boy who has taken three lessons on the violin over to the New York Philharmonic and expecting him to perform a Tchaikovsky symphony. He knows how to hold the violin and bow, but he has a long way to go before he can make music.*[4]

Ultimately, however, the identity of the autopsy surgeons is not of critical importance for understanding their findings. What is of critical importance is a knowledge of the facts available to them when they arrived at these findings.

Their own autopsy examination had revealed a small hole in the President's back with a short lane of penetration and no exit lane. They had observed the massive defect in the President's head and the small entry hole just below this defect. From Humes's conversation with Perry they had learned of a small hole "a few millimeters in size" that had been obliterated by the tracheotomy incision (17H29). From Perry they had also learned that there had been an "injury to the right lateral wall of the trachea" and that there had been "blood and air in [the] upper mediastinum" (17H29). By this time they knew, too, the official view that Oswald, and Oswald alone, had shot the President from behind.[5]

Far more important than what they did know is what they did *not* know. They did not know, for instance, that the tear in the trachea was on the *"anterior* lateral right side" (3H370)[6]—a location that would cast some doubt on the idea of a back-to-front transit. Nor did they know anything of the "contusions and hematoma to the right of the larynx" (3H360), which also argues against a back-to-front transit and which was noted by Drs. Carrico and McClelland, neither of whom Humes had talked with. Nor, of course, had they any inkling that ballistics tests performed later by Dr. Alfred G. Olivier would show that a back-to-front transit would have punched out an exit hole twice the size as that described by Dr. Perry. Finally, since the brain examination had not been performed at this time, the doctors knew nothing of the two communicating tears in the mid-brain and left cerebral peduncle, lacerations that might have suggested another explanation of the throat wound.

Given this mixture of knowledge and ignorance, it is not difficult to understand how the autopsy surgeons made the decision they did. To explain the throat wound as an entry wound would immediately have necessitated the existence of another gunman as well as either a bullet in the body or an exit in the back of the neck—neither of which the doctors had seen. To explain the throat wound as a fragment exit from the head shot would also have caused difficulty, for the doctors had already concluded that the main force of the bullet entering the President's head had blown upward through the large skull defect. What was left, then, was a transit from back to front. True, they had been unable to find any such lane, but perhaps the bullet had slipped between two strap muscles, leaving no telltale track. Dr. Perry had noted some damage in the upper mediastinum and their own examination had revealed some bruising of the right apical pleura. By joining all these points of injury—the back wound, the bruising of the pleura, and the throat wound observed by Dr. Perry—they could infer the passage of a bullet from back to front.

Thus was born the medical conclusion of a back-to-front transit, a conclusion that in its turn would give rise to a theory of the greatest importance for the entire investigation.

## THE SINGLE-BULLET THEORY

It is unknown just when Commander Humes and his colleagues finished their deliberations. Commander Humes did testify that

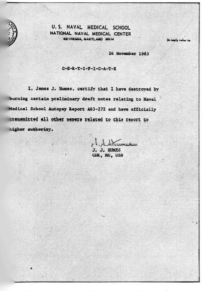

U. S. NAVAL MEDICAL SCHOOL
NATIONAL NAVAL MEDICAL CENTER
BETHESDA, MARYLAND 20014

24 November 1963

C-E-R-T-I-F-I-C-A-T-E

I, James J. Humes, certify that I have destroyed by burning certain preliminary draft notes relating to Naval Medical School Autopsy Report A63-272 and have officially transmitted all other papers related to this report to higher authority.

J. J. HUMES
CDR, MC, USN

Commander Humes's formal document certifying that he had burned preliminary notes of the autopsy. The reason, one Commission staff member believes, was that they reflected a finding contrary to the official report.

*from the time of the completion of the examination until the submission of the final report following its preparation, all of the papers pertinent to this case were in my personal custody (2H373).*

Yet, to my amazement, I learned from Commander Boswell that there was an additional autopsy face sheet (similar to CE 397 yet with additional information) that apparently disappeared somewhere between the autopsy examination room and the Commission's files.[7] Humes had testified that on Sunday morning, November 24, he burned in his fireplace "a draft of this report which I later revised" (3H373). It is unclear just what this earlier draft contained; one distinguished member of the Commission's staff told *Life* that he was "certain" Humes burned the original draft because it reflected a finding contrary to the official report.[8] It is by no means certain that this is the case (the lawyer gave *Life* no indication why he was so sure), but if it does turn out to be so, then the missing autopsy face sheet may also have disappeared up the chimney of Commander Humes's suburban fireplace. Although the final disposition of this face sheet must remain in doubt, we do know that neither it nor Humes's original draft appears

Assistant Commission Counsel Arlen Specter.

According to forensic expert Dr. Milton Helpern, the word "presumably," inserted twice (arrows) into Humes's draft of the official autopsy, "just doesn't read like the work of men in confident command of their ship."

among the documents that finally found their way into the Commission's files.

The working papers and the final autopsy report were turned over to Captain John H. Stover of the Naval Medical School on November 24.[9] Stover had them transferred to Admiral Burkley at the White House, who turned them over to the Secret Service on November 26 (*Archives*, CD 371). Copies of these documents reached the Warren Commission and the FBI about a month later.[10] When Arlen Specter came to work for the Commission in mid-January, both the typed official report and Humes's handwritten draft were on his desk.[11]

As the lawyer chiefly responsible for laying out the basic facts of the assassination—the number of shots, the trajectories, the wounds—Specter could only read this report as a key document, a document that would define the direction and limits of his whole subsequent investigation. And there in print before him he found the Bethesda pathologists' statement that the bullet that entered the President's back had exited from his throat. What to the Bethesda doctors had been originally only a plausible hypothesis (they spoke of the throat wound as one *"presumably* of exit") had been transmuted into an "official fact." Once written down in an official document, it had achieved a remarkable solidity and firmness; it was not to be doubted. The logical consequence of this hypothesis now engaged Specter's attention. If the bullet exited from the President's throat, where did it go? It was found nowhere in the car, and there was no bullet damage to the rear compartment. But Governor Connally was sitting directly in front of the President and Governor Connally had been struck by a bullet. Given these facts, surely the most plausible explanation was that the bullet had continued on to wound the Governor.

By such a train of reasoning was born the single-bullet, double-hit theory, a theory that would entail a massive twisting and reshaping of the basic facts of the assassination. For when Specter came to work in mid-January an alternative theory had already been accepted by the two government agencies investigating the assassination. The Secret Service, having already studied the Zapruder film, concluded that the Governor had been wounded by the second shot, and for at least two months this opinion was never brought into question. Both the Secret Service and the FBI submitted reports right up to the end of January that assumed as indisputable fact the wounding of the Governor by the second bullet.[12] It would have been difficult indeed for Assistant Counsel Specter to convince these two agencies they were wrong were it not for one point in his favor: the Zapruder film had also shown that the maximum time between the wounding of the two victims was less than the minimum firing time of Oswald's rifle. Either they would have to admit that Specter's single-bullet theory was correct, or they would have to confess that a second gunman had been firing in Dealey Plaza and that they had failed to turn up a single clue as to his existence or identity. Obviously, the first alternative was more palatable.

But it could not be advanced without a massive reshuffling of the evidence compiled to date. If Kennedy and Connally were hit by the same bullet, then both the Governor's and Mrs. Connally's assertions that the President had been hit first must be disregarded. So too must the testimony of S. M. Holland, Jean Hill, Dave Powers, Gayle Newman, and the Willis family—all of whom correlated the Governor's wounding with the second shot. Not one of the several hundred witnesses to the assassination saw it as a double hit by one bullet.

If Kennedy and Connally were hit by the same bullet, then only one other bullet could have struck in the car. But most witnesses heard three shots and the Commission knew that three cartridge cases had been found in the Depository. Thus a third shot must have been fired but missed the car entirely. Through the device of vagueness—by stating that a shot missed but not stating which one it was—the Commission could conceal the paucity of evidence for such a miss. By again ignoring the great weight of testimony indicating that no shots missed, a ramshackle case could be put together.

More importantly, to permit a barely plausible trajectory through both victims of the double hit, the President's back wound had to be elevated several inches from its indicated position on the autopsy face sheet. To accomplish this task a Navy corpsman who had seen neither body nor photographs of it was enlisted by Commander Humes in the preparation of sketches that would more nearly accord with the official theory (see illustration). These sketches were then shown to the Commission, which, true to its docile nature, never asked to see the original photos and X-rays even though they were in the government's possession.[13]

Finally, if the President and the Governor were hit by the same bullet, then that bullet must be CE 399, and that bullet must have been found on Governor Connally's stretcher. In trying to establish this sequence of fact, Assistant Counsel Specter revealed the character of the whole investigation. Consider the following stages in his examination of CE 399.

On March 16 the Commission heard the testimony of the chief autopsy surgeon, Commander Humes. At one point in the examination of Commander Humes, Allen Dulles interrupted Specter to indicate that he was "confused" by the line of questioning, since he had thought CE 399 had been found on the President's (not the Governor's) stretcher. Specter replied:

The position of Kennedy's back wound was sketched by Commander Boswell (above) during the autopsy. Later, when an official rendering was made (below), the wound was raised to agree with the official theory.

> *There has been other evidence, Mr. Dulles. If I may say at this point, we shall produce later, subject to sequential proof, evidence that the stretcher on which this bullet was found was the stretcher of Governor Connally (2H368).*

Just what "evidence" Specter was referring to must remain more than a little mysterious.[14] For as Edward Epstein has pointed out, he made this claim four days before going to Dallas to interview the man who found the bullet, Darrell Tomlinson.[15]

In November, 1966, Tomlinson indicated to me that he was still unhappy about Specter's treatment of him. "He seemed to be trying to get something," Tomlinson told me at Parkland Hospital.[16] When we turn to the record of Specter's questioning of Tomlinson, what the Assistant Counsel was "trying to get" becomes obvious.

First, Specter had Tomlinson draw a small sketch showing the vestibule area and the two stretchers— "A" indicating the stretcher Tomlinson wheeled off the elevator (Connally's stretcher), and "B" indicating the stretcher already present in the vestibule. Specter asked Tomlinson on which stretcher he found the bullet, and the engineer replied: "I believe that it was 'B'" (6H130). This was a devastating answer for Specter. Here was the man who found the bullet telling him it was *not* on Governor Connally's stretcher, but on a stretcher completely unrelated to the case. He asked Tomlinson if he could be "sure that it was stretcher 'A' you took out of the elevator and not stretcher 'B'?" (6H131). Tomlinson replied that he could not be "positive" since subsequent to removing the stretcher he had made several trips up and down in the elevator during which the stretchers might have been moved (6H131). Undaunted, Specter persevered:

*Specter: Now, just before we started this deposition, before I placed you under oath and before the court reporter started to take down my questions and your answers, you and I had a brief talk, did we not?*

*Tomlinson: Yes.*

*Specter: And we discussed in a general way the information which you have testified about, did we not?*

*Tomlinson: Yes, sir.*

*Specter: And at the time we started our discussion, it was your recollection at that point that the bullet came off of stretcher A, was it not?*

*Tomlinson: B (6H131).*

But even Tomlinson could not hold up under this onslaught of prosecutor's tricks forever, and Specter finally managed to extract from him the admission that "I'm just not sure of it, whether it was A or B that I took off" (6H132). Tomlinson later told me that at the beginning of the interview he had been rather clear as to what happened, but at the end, with two stretchers being moved around on the diagram, he had been reduced to confusion.[17] Specter's strategy had succeeded. If the witness would not provide the "evidence" he had earlier promised the Commission, then at least the witness could be confused so that his testimony would not count against Specter's theory. In this way an impartial search for the truth was prosecuted.

A recently declassified document from the National Archives provides an even more devastating insight into the way Specter bent the evidence concerning CE 399 to accord with his single-bullet theory. On April 21 a special showing of the Zapruder film was arranged for Specter, Governor and Mrs. Connally, Connally's Dallas doctors, three wound ballistics experts from the Army's Edgewood Arsenal, and Commission personnel. Another assistant counsel, Melvin Eisenberg, wrote up a memorandum on the conclusions that emerged from this viewing session. One conclusion mentioned in Eisenberg's memo explicitly concerns CE 399:

> *Drs. Light and Dolce [two ballistics experts from the Army's Wound Ballistics Branch, Edgewood Arsenal] expressed themselves as being very strongly of the opinion that Connally had been hit by two different bullets, principally on the ground that the bullet recovered from Connally's stretcher could not have broken his radius without having suffered more distortion. Dr. Olivier [another wound ballistics expert] withheld a conclusion until he has had the opportunity to make tests on animal tissue and bone with the actual rifle.*

The stress of logic now tightened around CE 399. Could it have caused the Connally wrist injury and remained in its undeformed state? Two ballistics specialists thought not, while the third wanted to await the results of tests with Oswald's rifle—the tests would decide the question. Moreover, these tests would provide even more crucial information with respect to CE 399. For if it did not cause the wrist wound, then, for it to be the bullet that wounded the Governor, two other hypotheses must be established: (1) a pristine bullet from Oswald's rifle *could* have caused the Governor's wrist wound, and (2) a bullet fired from Oswald's rifle through only the President's neck and Connally's chest would have been slowed sufficiently to have caused the superficial wound in the Governor's thigh.

The tests not only validated Drs. Light's and Dolce's conviction that CE 399 could not have caused the Connally wrist wound, but also invalidated each of the other two hypotheses. As an earlier chapter has shown, bullets fired from Oswald's rifle into virtually anything were grossly deformed. A bullet fired into a cadaver's wrist (closely simulating the Connally wrist injury) emerged with a flattened nose. Just as importantly, the tests indicated that a pristine bullet from Oswald's rifle *could not* have caused the Governor's wrist wound; the impact of such a bullet would have virtually amputated the Governor's hand (5H83). The second hypothesis was similarly invalidated. The tests showed that a bullet from Oswald's gun, having passed through the President's neck and the Governor's chest, would still have a velocity of just under 1,400 feet per second (5H77–78, 86). A bullet traveling at such a speed would have caused much more damage to the Governor's thigh than a superficial flesh wound.

The effect of these tests was to prove rather conclusively that CE 399 could not have caused any of the Governor's wounds. Moreover, we know from Eisenberg's memorandum that one purpose of the tests was to investigate just this point. It is profoundly revealing, then, that when Specter examined the three doctors who conducted the tests he carefully kept the whole question of CE 399 in the background. To none of these doctors did Specter address the crucial question of whether CE 399 could have caused the Governor's wounds.[18] Instead, he contented himself with showing that theoretically a bullet fired from Oswald's gun would have had sufficient penetrating power to burrow through two bodies. Having been present at the April 21 viewing conference, he knew Dr. Light's conviction "that the bullet recovered from Connally's stretcher could not have broken his radius without having suffered more distortion," and he also knew that the tests had established the truth of this conviction. Knowing, too, what a devastating effect either of these facts would have on his single-bullet theory, he carefully questioned Dr. Light only about the *theoretical* possibility that a single bullet had hit both Kennedy and Connally. He never raised the critical question whether that bullet could be CE 399, never broached the problem of the wrist wound and CE 399's undeformed state (5H94–97). Yet, as we saw, it was this question that the tests (in part) were meant to answer.

If a witness says the wrong thing, then confuse him; if a test produces the wrong result, then ignore it. This would appear to be the principle that guided Specter's investigation of bullet 399, an investigation that discloses in a particularly striking manner the biased and crippled character of the whole Warren Commission enterprise.

As critics began to nibble away at the foundation of this unstable structure Specter retreated further into fantasy. Told that the FBI reports of December 9 and January 13 indicated there was no exit from the President's back wound, Specter explained that this was due to the precipitate departure of the two FBI agents attending the autopsy. As soon as they noticed that the doctors could find no exit they "rushed out of the room" to telephone the news to their Maryland field office.[19] Only later, Specter told author Edward Epstein, "the doctors found the path, and by the time the agents submitted their reports, the FBI Summary Report had gone to press."[20] Since Specter offered this explanation, the Sibert-O'Neill report has come to light with its clear indication of Commander Humes's judgment at the conclusion of the autopsy. It was not a hurried phone conversation, but the five-page Sibert-O'Neill report that formed the basis of the FBI's Summary Report of December 9 (*two weeks* after the autopsy). And so the charade goes on. In a *U.S. News & World Report* interview Specter asserts that the single-bullet theory "is not a *sine qua non* for the conclusion that Oswald was the sole assassin,"[21] a claim that even his colleague, Assistant Counsel Norman Redlich, earlier had rejected.[22]

## THE COMMISSION

"If we are going to accept the Warren *Report* as factual then we've wasted a week of time," said Judge Bernard J. Bagert. "It is fraught with hearsay and contradiction," added Judge Matthew S. Braniff.[23] In so speaking, two New Orleans judges denied a defense motion that the Warren *Report* be introduced into evidence in the pretrial hearing of alleged conspirator Clay L. Shaw. Thus, by the spring of 1967, less than three years after the *Report* was published, it had become the butt of public scorn and derision. The legal judgment that it was inadmissible as evidence only reflected a public judgment that had already become general.

Yet it was the Commission's task to write a report that would gain and hold public confidence, that would put to rest the gnawing doubts and rumors. In this task the Commission failed utterly. Instead of quieting doubts its *Report* stimulated them; instead of killing rumors it spawned them; instead of giving peace it left unease. Who must bear the responsibility for this failure?

"Conclusions," stated Representative Gerald Ford, "were the work of the Commission."[24] And it is because conclusions were the responsibility of the Commission that the Commission must bear the ultimate weight of criticism. The Commissioners judged, and in their judging they failed. Yet perhaps their most critical failure—the act that most radically betrayed their trust—grew out of a reticence to judge at all. It was their refusal to judge the most important issue facing them that accounts for the radical failure of their *Report*.

Arlen Specter told *Life* that "the dominant thinking with many people right up to the time the *Report* was published" was that the Governor and the President were hit by different bullets.[25] Edward Epstein disclosed that in the summer of 1964 the Commission was evenly split on the single-bullet theory.[26] Senator Richard Russell had declared he would not sign a report that concluded that both victims were hit by the same bullet.[27] Both Senator John Sherman Cooper and Representative Hale Boggs tended to go along with Russell. "I, too, objected to such a conclusion," Epstein quotes Senator Cooper. "There was no evidence to show both men were hit by the same bullet."[28] Representative Boggs told Epstein, "I had strong doubts about it [the single-bullet theory]," and went on to indicate that he felt the issue was never resolved.[29]

It was in failing to resolve this issue that the Commission as a whole betrayed its trust. By late summer its members were evenly split; Ford, Dulles, and McCloy went along with Specter's single-bullet theory, while Russell, Cooper, and Boggs opposed it. In what John J. McCloy called "the battle of the adjectives," an evasion of the whole problem was worked out.[30] Instead of a judgment, the following paragraph was inserted in the *Report:*

> *Although it is not necessary to any essential findings of the Commission to determine just which shot hit Governor Connally, there is very persuasive evidence from the experts to indicate that the same bullet which pierced the President's throat also caused Governor Connally's wounds. However, Governor Con-*

*nally's testimony and certain other factors
had given rise to some difference of opinion
as to this probability but there is no question
in the mind of any member of the Commission that all the shots which caused the
President's and Governor Connally's wounds
were fired from the sixth floor window of the
Texas School Book Depository (R19).*

Had the Commission only hesitated for a moment
in that summer of 1964 to consider the problem
facing it, its inquiry might have taken a different
turn. The fact that its investigation had reached an
impasse might have been taken to indicate the need
for a reexamination of premises. As the evidence
accumulated against the single-bullet theory—the
Zapruder film, Governor and Mrs. Connally's testimony, the difficulties with CE 399—the premises of
the theory might have been reexamined. It was
founded on the presumption that a bullet exited
from the President's throat—the "official fact" con
tained in the autopsy report. Had this presumption
been brought under critical examination its suspect
character might have been revealed. Its true status
as an *inference* (not an *observation*) might have been
disclosed, and an effort been made either to validate
or invalidate it.

The Commissioners need not have been satisfied
with their investigation thus far. They might better
have decided to extend it, to fill in some of the holes,
to answer some of the important questions left unanswered. The Commission's staff could have made
the same measurements on the Zapruder film we
have made. They could have talked to some of the
witnesses, such as Marilyn Sitzman, Marilyn Willis,
and the Newmans, whom we interviewed for the first
time. And they could have talked to certain key witnesses such as James Chaney, to whom we were not
permitted to speak. They could have weighed CE 572
and thus established accurately the weight of a *fired*
6.5-millimeter projectile for comparison with CE 399;
we were denied this opportunity. They could have

performed neutron activation analyses on CE 399 and on the fragments removed from Connally's wrist to determine once and for all whether CE 399 struck the Governor. They could have viewed the autopsy photos and X-rays (in government possession up to April, 1965). They could have interviewed Agents Sibert and O'Neill (the FBI refused to tell us even where they were located). They could have submitted the Moorman photo to the image-processing lab at Scripps Oceanographic Institute in La Jolla, California, for a determination as to whether the curious shape on the fence line is a human head; we were told "this laboratory cannot undertake image processing of pictures related to the Kennedy assassination unless requested by some appropriate Government organization."[31] They could have performed audiometric soundings in Dealey Plaza. Even more important, the Commission could have asked itself a few baffling questions: Why does a shot from behind drive the President's head *backward* and to the left? If the President was shot from behind, what is a piece of occipital bone (from the *rear* of the skull) doing on the grass verge to the *left* of the car's path? And what about the conviction of Marilyn Sitzman, James Chaney, Bill and Gayle Newman (supported by the clear evidence of Zapruder frame 313) that the President was struck just behind the right temple? Or, turning to the hit on the Governor, why do all the signs of a hit appear suddenly in 1/18 second at Z238 if he was hit some eighteen or twenty frames earlier? Why do two of his doctors still believe that he was hit by a bullet other than the one that struck the President? Finally, how did CE 399 manage to pierce two people, shattering two bones and causing seven separate wounds, all the while keeping its nose in perfect shape and losing only an infinitesimal part of its substance? How did CE 399 manage to fall onto a stretcher the Governor was never on? In its singleminded devotion to the lone assassin conclusion, the Commission left all these questions unanswered and left unexplored a buried lode of evidence.

This book has attempted to perform a task of archaeology, to lay bare a whole level of contradictory evidence buried beneath the facile conclusions of the Commission's *Report*. This evidence (much of it never published) was either ignored, disregarded, or misrepresented by the Commission. Now it has been brought to light. If its introduction makes necessary the emergence of new conclusions, then so be it.

The Warren Commission: (from left to right) Mr. Allen W. Dulles, Rep. Hale Boggs, Sen. John Sherman Cooper, Chief Justice Earl Warren, Sen. Richard B. Russell, Mr. John J. McCloy, Rep. Gerald R. Ford.

## NOTES

1. Specter made these remarks to former District Attorney James C. Crumlish after returning to Philadelphia in September, 1964. Given a leave of absence by Crumlish to serve on the Commission's staff, he gave his boss a copy of the *Report* before it was published. Crumlish read it and asked Specter about the single-bullet theory. According to Crumlish, Specter made the admission cited above while trying to explain the single-bullet theory to him. He was, Crumlish recalled, "uneasy, uncertain and without complete

control of his thinking." See *The Philadelphia Inquirer,* "Specter Predicted One-Bullet Theory Would Stir Doubt," Nov. 25, 1966, p. 1. In November, 1965, Specter defeated Crumlish in the race for district attorney.

2. See "Membership Roster of the American Academy of Forensic Sciences, 1963-1964."

3. Marshall Houts, *Where Death Delights* (New York: Coward-McCann, 1967), p. 55.

4. *Ibid.,* pp. 55-56.

5. The official autopsy report contains the following statements: "Three shots were heard and the President fell forward bleeding from the head. (Governor Connally was seriously wounded by the same gunfire.) According to newspaper reports ('Washington Post' November 23, 1963) Bob Jackson, a Dallas 'Times Herald' photographer, said he looked around as he heard the shots and saw a rifle barrel disappearing into a window on an upper floor of the nearby Texas School Book Depository Building.

". . . Based on the above observations [the autopsy description of the President's wounds] it is our opinion that the deceased died as a result of two perforating gunshot wounds inflicted by high velocity projectiles fired by a person or persons unknown. The projectiles were fired from a point behind and somewhat above the level of the deceased . . ." (16H979, 983).

6. Dr. Perry first pointed this out in testimony before the Commission on Mar. 30, 1964. If we take the holes in the President's clothing as defining the location of the back wound, it would seem very unlikely that a bullet could tear the front of the trachea without also ripping the back.

7. Boswell interview, Jan. 11, 1967. Commander Boswell remembered this face sheet when I pointed out that, although the location of the small head entry wound was given as "2.5 cm. to the right and slightly above the external occipital protuberance" in the official autopsy report, no indication of its location was given in the notes preserved in CE 397. He told me it was his recollection that the missing face sheet also contained additional information.

8. Although not present at this interview I saw a report on it written up by a *Life* representative. I am not at liberty to reveal the name of the Assistant Commission Counsel who was interviewed.

9. See 17H47.

10. This fact was turned up through inquiries carried out by journalist Fletcher Knebel; see *Look* magazine, July 12, 1966, p. 71.

11. *Look* magazine, July 12, 1966, p. 71. It has sometimes been claimed that the Commission's staff was overworked, and that many of the errors that crept into the *Report* were the products of physical exhaustion. Release of the staff pay records in January, 1967, qualify this heroic picture. Arlen Specter, for example, worked an average of

3¼ days (26 hours) per week for the 10 months during which his name appears on the Commission's payroll. For this he was paid $10,719.28.

12. See *Archives,* CD 1, 87, 298.

13. According to the Treasury Department the autopsy pictures were not turned over to the Kennedy family until Apr. 26, 1965—some 7 months after publication of the Commission's *Report!* See *Saturday Evening Post,* Jan. 14. 1967, p. 69.

14. He may be referring to Secret Service or FBI reports on interviews at Parkland Hospital. In their depositions Parkland Hospital personnel mentioned a total of about thirty interviews by Secret Service or FBI agents (6H1-152). If reports on such interviews exist, they are not among those documents available for study in the National Archives. If they exist and are classified "Secret," this in itself would be an intriguing development.

15. Specter interviewed Tomlinson on Mar. 20, 1964 (6H128), 4 days *after* making the statement cited above.

16. Tomlinson interview, Nov. 3, 1966.

17. *Ibid.*

18. Specter did ask Dr. Olivier, "Do you have an opinion as to whether, in fact, bullet No. 399 did cause the wound on the Governor's wrist, assuming if you will that it was the missile found on the Governor's stretcher at Parkland Hospital?" Olivier replied, "I believe that it was. That is my feeling" (5H90)—an answer that appears to refer more to the bullet's location of discovery than to its activities.

19. Edward Jay Epstein, *Inquest* (New York: The Viking Press, Inc., 1966), p. 49.

20. *Ibid.*

21. *U.S. News & World Report,* Oct. 10, 1966, p. 56.

22. Epstein, *op. cit.,* p. 43.

23. *New York Times,* Mar. 19, 1967.

24. Epstein, *op. cit.,* p. 148.

25. Again I was not present for this interview, but saw the *Life* interview report. The quotation cited was ascribed to Specter as a direct quotation.

26. Epstein, *op. cit.,* pp. 149-50.

27. *Ibid.,* p. 149. Senator Russell now claims the distinction of having been the only member "who bucked the Report." He claims that "from the outset" he never believed in the truth of the single-bullet theory (*Esquire,* May, 1967, p. 104).

28. Epstein, *op. cit.,* pp. 149-50.

29. *Ibid.,* p. 150. Representative Boggs expressed his continuing doubts about the single-bullet theory in a recent "Face the Nation" interview.

30. *Ibid.,* p. 150.

31. Letter to the author from James L. Harris, Sr., dated Mar. 10, 1967.

# X

## ANSWERED AND UNANSWERED QUESTIONS

### ANSWERED QUESTIONS

*Question 1: Are the "missing frames" from the Zapruder film still missing?*

*Answer: No.*

Frames 208–211 of the Zapruder film are omitted from the series of frames published in Volume XVIII of the Warren Commission *Hearings*. The same frames are missing from the set of 35-millimeter slides available for viewing in the National Archives. The omission of these frames (they are the *only* ones missing from the series) seemed odd and, to many, downright suspicious. Both Mark Lane[1] and Harold Weisberg[2] called attention to this omission, Weisberg claiming outright that the government had "doctored" the Zapruder film with sinister intent.

In light of the needless controversy surrounding these "missing frames," it is fortunate that we can publish them here for the first time. Mr. George Hunt, Managing Editor of *Life,* has authorized the following statement to be made in connection with their release for publication:

Z207

Z210

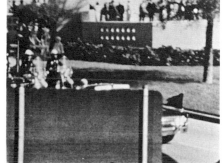

Z208

Z211

Z209

Z212

It is a fact that in handling the film of the Kennedy assassination taken by Abraham Zapruder of Dallas and purchased from him by Life we accidentally damaged not four but six frames of the original—frames 207 through 212. Before that happened, however, and before we came into possession of the original print, Zapruder had ordered three color copies made by a Dallas laboratory—two for federal agents and one for Life. These are and always have been intact. All four copy prints include the frames in question. Later the Warren Commission requested that Life supply them with color blow-ups of frames from the original film. We were unable to give them frames 207 through 212, but these were available to them on their own intact copy print. As a matter of fact, frame 210, one of those damaged, is, in copy form, printed in the Warren Commission report.

Thus, there never have been any missing frames. So, to end what has become an irrelevant discussion, we are releasing for publication frames 207 through 212, made from the intact copy print in our possession.

*Question 2: Did Julia Ann Mercer see a gunman carry a gun case onto the grassy knoll shortly before the assassination?*

*Answer: No.*

Mark Lane began his book, *Rush to Judgment*, by citing excerpts from the following affidavit of Julia Ann Mercer:

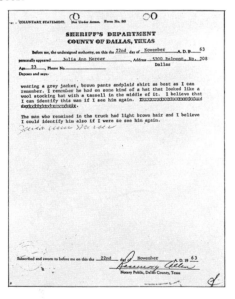

The FBI interviewed Miss Mercer the next day (November 23) and received a similar account of her adventure in Dealey Plaza (*Archives*, CD 205). On November 25 she was shown photographs of Oswald and several of his New Orleans associates. She could not identify any of the persons as having been in the pickup truck (*Archives*, CD 205). Over the next two weeks the FBI unsuccessfully canvassed local air-conditioning firms in hope of locating the truck (*Archives,* CD 205).

The break that led to the identification of the truck came from a routine interrogation of Dallas policemen present at the assassination site. Patrolman E. V. Brown, stationed on a nearby overpass (not the railroad viaduct, but a highway overpass immediately west of it), recalled the green pickup truck. On December 9, 1963, he made his report to the FBI:

> *He [Brown] advised that about 10:40 am, he recalls a green pick-up truck which was stalled on Elm Street near the overpass. This truck was a concern since they needed to get it moved prior to the Presidential motorcade. Patrolman Joe Murphy can give full facts regarding the truck and the occupants as he handled the matter and was successful in getting it removed prior to the Presidential motorcade. The persons in this truck were workmen who actually had trouble with the truck and were out of the area when the motorcade came by. He did not see anyone remove anything from this truck* (Archives, *CD* 205).

Officer Joe Murphy was immediately questioned by FBI Agents Henry J. Oliver and Louis M. Kelly. Their report, reproduced at left, effectively puts to rest any lingering doubts about the pickup truck seen by Julia Ann Mercer.

*Question 3: Was the rifle found in the Texas School Book Depository a Mauser or a Mannlicher-Carcano.*

*Answer: A Mannlicher-Carcano.*

In *Rush to Judgment* Mark Lane points out how early reports from the Dallas Police described the murder weapon as a 7.65 German Mauser. When, the following day, the FBI traced a 6.5 Mannlicher-Carcano to Oswald, the Dallas authorities corrected their earlier statements and affirmed that a Carcano, not a Mauser, had been found on the sixth floor of the Depository. Lane leaves the implication with his

100-10461
GK:mam

The following investigation was conducted by 's HENRY J. OLIVER and LOUIS M. KELLEY on December 9, 1963:

JOE MURPHY, Patrolman, Traffic Division, Police partment, Dallas, Texas, advised that on November 22, 1963, was stationed on the Triple Underpass on Elm Street to sist in handling traffic. At approximately 10:30 - 10:40 AM, pickup truck stalled on Elm Street between Houston Street the underpass. He was unable to recall the name of the pany to whom this truck belonged but stated it is the perty of the company working on the First National Bank lding at Elm and Akard in Dallas.

There were three construction men in this truck, and took one to the bank building to obtain another truck in er to assist in moving the stalled one. The other two men ained with the pickup truck along with two other officers. rtly prior to the arrival of the motorcade, the man he had en to the bank building returned with a second truck, and three of the men left with the two trucks, one pushing the er.

MURPHY noted that the men did not leave the truck ept for the one he took to the bank building, and all three t together sometime prior to the arrival of the President's rcade. He described the stalled truck as being a green kup and noted the truck had the hood raised during the time was stalled. This truck had side tool bins on it, and they a considerable amount of construction equipment in the back.

MURPHY further stated it was probable that one of e men had taken something from the rear of this truck in ffort to start it. He stated these persons were under rvation all during the period they were stalled on Elm et because the officers wanted the truck moved prior to the val of the motorcade, and it would have been impossible for of them to have had anything to do with the assassination resident KENNEDY.

- 320 -

Commission Document 205.

readers that the Dallas authorities fiddled the evidence to agree with the later FBI story.[3]

The most essential piece of ammunition in Lane's arsenal is an affidavit signed by Seymour Weitzman, one of the discoverers of the rifle. Sworn out on November 23, it describes the rifle's discovery in the following terms:

> *I was working with Deputy S. Boone of the Sheriff's Department and helping in the search. We were in the northwest corner of the sixth floor when Deputy Boone and myself spotted the rifle about the same time. This rifle was a 7.65 Mauser bolt action equipped with a 4/18 scope, a thick leather brownish-black sling on it. The rifle was between some boxes near the stairway. The time the rifle was found was 1:22 pm. Captain Fritz took charge of the rifle and ejected one live round from the chamber. I then went back to the office after this (24H228).*

On April 1, 1964, Weitzman's sworn deposition was taken by Assistant Counsel Joseph Ball:

*Ball: In the statement that you made to the Dallas Police Department that afternoon, you referred to the rifle as a 7.65 Mauser bolt action?*

*Weitzman: In a glance that's what it looked like.*

*Ball: That's what it looked like—did you say that or someone else say that?*

*Weitzman: No, I said that. I thought it was one (7H108).*

Recently, Weitzman was interviewed by CBS News reporter Eddie Barker and gave this account of his identification of the rifle:

*Barker: What kind of gun did you think it was?*

*Weitzman: To my sorrow, I looked at it and it looked like a Mauser, which I said it was. But I said the wrong one because . . . just at a glance I saw the Mauser action and,*

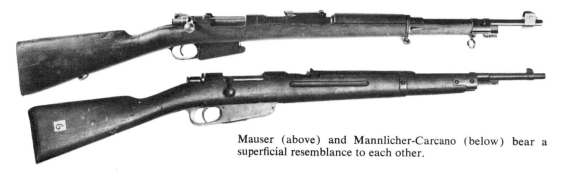

Mauser (above) and Mannlicher-Carcano (below) bear a superficial resemblance to each other.

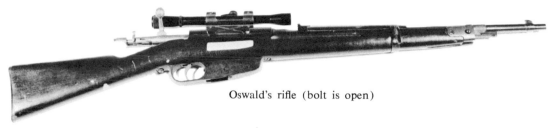

Oswald's rifle (bolt is open)

*I don't know, it just came out as a German Mauser which it wasn't. It's an Italian type gun. But from a glance it's hard to describe it, that's all I saw, was at a glance. I was mistaken and it was proven that my statement was a mistake but it was an honest mistake (CBS News, "The Warren Report," June 25, 1967).*

The Mauser and the Carcano do resemble each other. Weitzman's error would seem to be just what he called it, "an honest mistake."

We do have photographic evidence that bears on this point. Before the weapon was moved, Robert Studebaker of the Dallas Police photographed it in its cubbyhole in the Depository. Only the stock and part of the barrel are visible in this photo, but these parts of the weapon seem to resemble the relevant parts of a Mannlicher-Carcano. We also have a press photograph of Lieutenant Day removing the murder weapon from the Depository early on the afternoon of November 22. It is quite apparent in this photo that the weapon Day is carrying is a Mannlicher-Carcano carbine and not a Mauser. Furthermore, the fragments found in the front seat of the presidential

Rifle discovered in the Depository, but as yet untouched, resembles a Mannlicher-Carcano (Dallas Police Photo).

A Mannlicher-Carcano rifle being removed from the Depository on the afternoon of November 22.

limousine were matched ballistically to Oswald's Mannlicher-Carcano, not to a Mauser (3H428–437, 496–502).

*Question 4: Were the President's coat and shirt bunched at the time he was struck in the back?*

*Answer: No.*

Photographs of the President's coat and shirt show bullet holes in the upper back. Measured by Agent Robert Frazier of the FBI, these holes were found to lie 5⅜ inches (coat) and 5¾ inches (shirt) from the top of the collar (5H59). These holes define an entry into the President's upper back at a location that matches the position given in (1) the autopsy face sheet, (2) the Sibert-O'Neill report, and (3) the testimony of Secret Service Agents Greer, Kellerman, Hill, and Bennett. Such a location, however, is in contradiction with the position of the wound described in the official autopsy report—"14 cm. [5½ inches] from the tip of the right acromium process and 14 cm. [5½ inches] below the tip of the right mastoid process" (16H980). Clearly, 5½ inches below the top of the collar defines a different location than 5½ inches below the tip of the bony protuberance behind the right ear. The difference is a matter of 3 to 4 inches, a crucial 3 to 4 inches, since, if the lower location is taken, a bullet could not have continued on a downward course and still exited from the President's throat.

How can the official autopsy's description of a neck entrance wound be brought into correspondence with the holes in the President's clothing? Some have suggested that the President's shirt and coat may have been bunched at the time he was hit by the first shot. Edward Epstein discussed this suggestion in *Inquest:*

> *It is possible that President Kennedy's jacket was in some manner raised more than six inches, so that the hole in it coincided with the purported entrance wound in the "back of the neck." (The Zapruder film, however,*

*gives no indication of this.) It was, however, virtually impossible for the hole in the shirt to have coincided with an entrance wound in "the back of the neck." This could only have happened under either of the following two conditions: (1) the entire shirt, collar included, was raised six inches; or (2) a portion of the shirt was raised over the collar line (and thus doubled over). Obviously a closed shirt collar could not have been raised six inches on the neck, and therefore, for the shirt hole to have coincided with the purported entrance wound (which was above the collar line), the shirt would have to have been doubled-up over the collar. Since only one bullet hole was found in the back of the shirt, this could not have been the case.[4]*

The original color slide of this photograph, taken at the instant of the first shot, shows that the President's coat was not bunched at the time the first shot hit.

Although Epstein's estimate that the clothing must have been raised "more than six inches" is exaggerated (3 to 4 inches would suffice), his essential point seems well taken. For a shirt to move that distance it would have to have been doubled over; a bullet hit through the fold would have caused two holes, while the shirt showed only one.

We have stronger evidence, however, than this. For Philip Willis took a photograph showing the President's back at almost the exact moment when the wounding bullet struck. I have studied the original slide under a microscope. Although it is not apparent on black-and-white copies, the original color slide shows clearly that the President's clothing was *not* bunched at the time he was wounded in the back.

*Question 5: Did the fatal shot come from a "gunman" perched on a "station wagon" located near the concrete pergola?*

*Answer: No. The "station wagon" is a vehicle parked some 30 to 40 feet behind the pergola, while the "gunman" turns out to be a pattern of light and dark shadows on its west wall.*

In the fall of 1966 I first became interested in the Nix movie frames purporting to show a gunman firing at the President from the roof of a nearby station wagon. I made some measurements on the assassination site and quickly lost interest. These measurements showed that for a gunman to have fired the fatal head shot at Z313 from the supposed location, he would have to have been suspended 9 to 12 feet in the air, and would of necessity have opened fire less than half a second after the President first came into view. These conditions made such a shot extremely unlikely.

Since that time, the true identities of the "station wagon" and the "gunman" have come to light. United Press International, owner of the Nix film, requested Itek Corporation to make an exhaustive study of the relevant frames. The results of this study were released by UPI in a dispatch dated May 19, 1967:

This frame from the Nix film was thought by many to show a man firing a rifle from the roof of a station wagon (arrow).

> *Itek photographic scientists improved the quality of the film content by utilizing advanced image enhancement methods.*
>
> *Itek photogrammetrists and photointerpreters made precise measurements of a number of significant objects in the photographs to insure proper identification of the objects and to determine the feasibility of the fatal shot being fired from certain points.*
>
> *Several objects on and behind the grassy knoll were unclear in the original films and the Itek scientists were themselves at first struck by the image of a gunman.*
>
> *"The man with the rifle," however, was found to be nothing more than the shadows of tree branches and leaves on the side of the white pavilion. . . .*
>
> *The laboratory used a variety of techniques in studying the photographs. A method known as "dodging" produced an amazing clarity of light and dark tones. Use of color filters made them even sharper.*[5]

A frame from another movie, taken from a slightly different angle, reveals the "man" to be shadows and the "station wagon" to be the roof of a vehicle in the parking lot well behind the fence (arrow).

Earlier, my researches in Dallas had unearthed two motion-picture films taken from near Nix's location that validated Itek's conclusion. Taken from a slightly different angle, Robert Hughes's film showed a pattern of light and dark shapes similar to the one apparent in the Nix film. From the Hughes film, however, it was apparent that the "gunman" was between the concrete pergola and the cameraman, while the "station wagon" appeared in the background. Another film, this one taken by F. M. Bell from still a different angle, showed clearly that the "gunman" was only shadows on the concrete wall, while the "station wagon" was the roof of a vehicle (possibly a light-colored hardtop) parked in the lot behind.

The man in the doorway of the Depository (arrow).

*Question 6: Does a photograph taken by James Altgens show Oswald or Billy Lovelady (a co-worker) standing in the doorway of the Depository at the time the shots were fired?*
*Answer: Billy Lovelady.*

On April 7, 1964, Billy Lovelady's sworn deposition was taken by Assistant Counsel Joseph Ball. Ball showed Lovelady a copy of the Altgens photograph and asked him to identify himself.

*Ball: I have got a picture here, Commission Exhibit 369. Are you on that picture?*
*Lovelady: Yes, sir.*

Lee Harvey Oswald

"Man in doorway"

Billy N. Lovelady

*Ball: Take a pen or pencil and make an arrow where you are.*

*Lovelady: Where I thought the shots are?*

*Ball: No; you in the picture.*

*Lovelady: Oh, here (indicating).*

*Ball: Draw an arrow down to that; do it in the dark. You got an arrow in the dark and one in the white pointing toward you. Where were you when the picture was taken?*

*Lovelady: Right there at the entrance of the building standing on the top of the step would be here (indicating) (6H338–339).*

On the same day, Lovelady's boss, William Shelley, was also questioned by Ball. Shelley told the Assistant Counsel that at the time of the shooting he and Lovelady were standing on "the top landing of the [Depository] entrance" (6H328). In addition, Sarah Stanton and Wesley Frazier signed statements affirming that Lovelady was with them on the steps of the Depository at the time the shots were fired (22H647, 675).

This would seem to resolve the question, proving that the "man in the doorway" was not Oswald but Lovelady. Enter the FBI, and the issue became needlessly (and sensationally) clouded once again. On February 29, 1964, Lovelady was interviewed and photographed by FBI agents, and subsequently J. Edgar Hoover wrote to the Commission describing the session:

> *On February 29, 1964, Billy Nolan Lovelady was photographed by special agents of the F.B.I. at Dallas, Texas. On this occasion, Lovelady advised that on the day of the assassination of President John F. Kennedy, November 22, 1963, at the time of the assassination, and shortly before, he was standing in the doorway of the front entrance to the TSBD [Depository] where he is employed. He stated he was wearing a red and white vertical striped shirt and blue jeans (Archives, CD 457).*

The photographs of Lovelady taken that day by the FBI show him wearing a red-and-white vertical-striped shirt with short sleeves. A New York *Herald-Tribune* story of May 24, 1964, also indicated that on November 22 Lovelady was wearing "a red-and-white striped sport shirt buttoned near the neck" (22H794). But clearly, the "man in the doorway" is wearing a *long-sleeved* shirt of much the same appearance as the one in which Oswald was arrested. It is by no stretch of the imagination a red-and-white vertical-striped *short-sleeved* shirt, and it bears no resemblance to the one in the FBI photograph.

How can this apparent contradiction be reconciled? Recently, when the discrepancy between shirts was pointed out to Lovelady by CBS News, he replied, "Well, when the FBI took me in the shirt, I told them it wasn't the same shirt." The shirt Lovelady now claims to have worn on November 22 is long-sleeved and patterned in large squares.

## UNANSWERED QUESTIONS

*Question 1: Who is the "umbrella man"?*

The first shots were fired on the presidential limousine as it passed the Stemmons Freeway sign on the north side of Elm Street. Standing next to this sign was a man holding an open umbrella.

The "umbrella man" is one of the curiosities of the assassination. Dressed in a conservative dark suit, in his thirties or early forties, he stands almost as a marker of where the assassination was to occur. In photos taken immediately after the shooting we find him again: umbrella now closed, he casually watches the scramble of spectators onto the grassy knoll. When we last catch a glimpse of him, he is ambling away up Elm Street.

His is the *only* open umbrella to appear in all the photos of crowds lining the motorcade's route. It had stopped raining nearly three hours before. By noon the skies were cloudless and a gusty wind would have made holding an open umbrella somewhat of a problem.

The Umbrella Man: umbrella open.

The Umbrella Man: umbrella furled.

Could he have been shielding himself from the sun?

Such an explanation seems extremely unlikely; men in Dallas simply do not use umbrellas as parasols. Many people found the day rather brisk. Arnold Rowland and his wife, for example, were wearing topcoats and gloves. "The sun was shining," Rowland explained, "it was a fair day but the wind was blowing and it was breezy" (2H181).

Who is this man with the umbrella? Although he was one of the closest spectators to the shooting, he has never been identified. Like so many people present in Dealey Plaza that day, he vanished without a trace. If his presence there can be innocently explained (as is most likely), perhaps now he will come forward and identify himself.

*Question 2: Who owned the jacket discarded by Officer J. D. Tippit's assailant?*

A few minutes before Oswald was arrested at the Texas Theater, the following query came over the Dallas Police radio net:

> *The jacket the suspect was wearing over here on Jefferson bears a laundry tag with the letter B 9738. See if there is any way you can check this laundry tag (17H471).*

Only moments before, a young man observed running away from the Tippit shooting was seen to drop a light-colored jacket in a parking lot just off Jefferson Boulevard. If the jacket could be traced to Oswald, it would tend to prove that he was guilty of at least one murder that day. Oddly enough, in spite of exhaustive efforts by the FBI, the jacket could never be traced to Oswald. The FBI's investigation, on the contrary, tended to establish the likelihood that the jacket never belonged to Oswald.

By April 21, 1964, a canvass of all laundry and dry-cleaning establishments in the Dallas-Ft. Worth area had failed to turn up the identity of laundry mark "30 030," also found in the jacket, and dry-cleaning tag "B 9738" (*Archives,* CD 868). In all,

424 firms were contacted, with negative results (*Archives,* CD 1066, I). The search was extended to the greater New Orleans area; a canvass of 293 laundry and dry-cleaning establishments failed to turn up the identity of the tag and/or mark in question (*Archives,* CD 993, 1245). Faced with failure in what should have been a simple task, the FBI went back to Marina Oswald:

> *On April 1, 1964, Marina Oswald advised that to the best of her recollection Lee Harvey Oswald had only two jackets, one a heavy jacket, blue in color, and another light jacket, gray in color. She stated she believed Oswald possessed both of these jackets in Russia and had purchased them in the United States prior to his departure for Russia. She stated she could not recall that Oswald ever sent either of these jackets to any laundry or cleaner anywhere. She said she could recall washing them herself. She advised that to her knowledge Oswald possessed both of these jackets at Dallas on November 22, 1963.*
>
> *None of the other items of Oswald's clothing available contained any dry cleaner's or laundry markings that were similar or could be associated with the "30 030" marking and the "B 9738" dry cleaner tag appearing on the K-42 (CE 162) jacket* (Archives, *CD 868*).

Commission Exhibit 162: Jacket found near Tippit slaying.

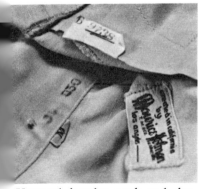

Untraced laundry mark and dry-cleaning tag.

The last paragraph of the above memorandum is not strictly accurate. An earlier FBI examination of Oswald's clothing turned up no laundry or dry-cleaning marks of any kind (*Archives,* CD 205), let alone "similar" ones. Five of his shirts, the report went on, "appear to have been laundered by hand" (*Archives,* CD 205).

From the FBI investigation it would appear that CE 162, the gray jacket discarded by Tippit's assailant, may not have belonged to Oswald. Where

Oswald's shirts carried the size "small," this jacket was marked "medium" (*Archives* CD 7, 205).

*Question 3: Which shot caused the "Tague hit"?*

James Thomas Tague was watching the motorcade from a position on Commerce Street just under the eastern edge of the railway overpass. He heard three shots and remembered that he felt something nick his cheek. After the shooting he collared a deputy sheriff (Eddy Raymond Walthers), and together they found a fresh nick on the Main Street curb some 12–15 feet from where he had been standing. Asked later which bullet of the three he heard had made the mark on the curb, Tague observed, "I would guess it was either the second or the third. I wouldn't say definitely which one" (7H555).

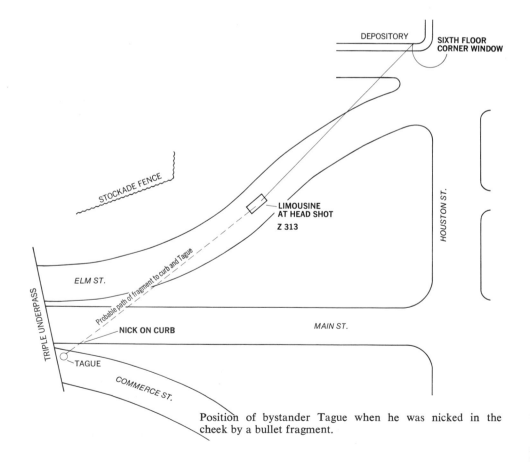

Position of bystander Tague when he was nicked in the cheek by a bullet fragment.

Bullet mark on curb of Main Street, as photographed on the afternoon of November 22.

Section of Main Street curbing removed by the FBI in July, 1964.

On the afternoon of the assassination Tom Dillard of the Dallas *Morning News* photographed the mark on the curb. A rifle enthusiast (he hand-loads his own ammunition), Dillard told me that the mark was clearly not the result of a jacketed bullet. "It couldn't have been a jacketed bullet," Dillard told me in November, 1966, "because there was no copper on the curb." He further pointed out that there was no chip in the pavement, but only a lead smear on the rounded edge of the curb.[6]

Dillard's judgment was corroborated by later FBI tests. The piece of curbing was removed and sent to Washington where it was examined in the FBI Laboratory. The results of this examination and associated spectrographic tests were forwarded to the Commission in an August 12, 1964, letter from Hoover:

*The piece of curbing containing the mark was removed on August 5, 1964, and examined in the FBI Laboratory. This curbing has been designated as Item C321 by the Laboratory. Small foreign metal smears were found adhering to the curbing section within the area of the mark. These metal smears were spectrographically determined to be essentially lead with a trace of antimony. No copper was found. The lead could have originated from the lead core of a mutilated metal-jacketed bullet such as the type of bullet loaded into 6.5 millimeter Mannlicher-Carcano cartridges or from some other source having the same composition.*

*The absence of copper precludes the possibility that the mark on the curbing section was made by an unmutilated military-type full metal-jacketed bullet such as the bullet removed from Governor Connally's stretcher, C1, or the bullet or bullets represented by the jacket fragments, C2 and C3, found in the Presidential limousine. Further, the damage to the curbing would have been much*

*more extensive if a rifle bullet had struck
the curbing without first having struck some
other object. Therefore, this mark could not
have been made by the first impact of a high
velocity rifle bullet (21H476).*

The final statement in the FBI report is the most
telling—"this mark could not have been made by
the first impact of a high velocity rifle bullet." By no
stretch of the imagination, then, could this mark be
the impact point of a shot from Oswald's rifle that
missed the limousine entirely.

If it was not the product of a missed shot, then
what caused it?

The FBI report notes that "The lead could have
originated from the lead core of a mutilated metal-
jacketed bullet"—the mark could have been caused
by the impact of a *fragment* from one of the shots that
found their mark. Of the hits, the Z313 head shot
would be the best candidate. The location of the curb
mark lies only slightly off a straight trajectory from
the Depository window through the President's head
at Z313 (see diagram). We know that other fragments from this shot flew forward, striking the front
windshield. Furthermore, Tague himself testified that
he was nicked on the cheek at the time of the second
or third shot. All this evidence would urge the conclusion that the curb mark should be seen as a product of the Z313 head impact. There is, however, one
objection to such a conclusion: the curb mark lies
almost 270 feet from the location of the President's
head at Z313. Could a bullet fragment have traveled
that far?

If this hypothesis is rejected, then we must enter-
tain the possibility that a soft-nosed lead bullet traveling at less than high velocity caused the mark.
But which shot could this have been? The first struck
the President in the back, the second the Governor,
and the third and fourth the President again. Linda
Kay Willis and James Altgens, both close to the
President at the time of the head impact, were certain that no shots followed it (7H499, 520). Yet a

miss striking the pavement at this point could only have come from a shot very late in the firing order—the FBI estimated a time of 5.3 seconds after Z313 (21H475). There is no credible evidence whatsoever to indicate such a shot was fired. There is overwhelming evidence to indicate it wasn't.

I am persuaded that the first hypothesis is much the soundest—that a fragment from the Z313 head shot caused the mark on the curb. Any other hypothesis would seem wildly improbable, unacceptable on the basis of the total evidence. Still, there are problems with this hypothesis—270 feet is a long way for a fragment to fly.

*Question 4: Did Lee Harvey Oswald shoot the President?*

The chief objections to the Commission's case against Oswald have been known for a long time. The lack of fingerprints on the rifle, the extremely small time interval between the last shot and Oswald's encounter with Superintendent Roy Truly and Police Officer Marrion Baker on the second floor of the Depository, the difficulties in accounting for when and how he brought the rifle into the building, his relatively poor skill as a marksman—all these points had long led assassination researchers to look with skepticism on the presumption of Oswald's guilt. For an equally long time, I was skeptical of the skeptics. For if Oswald was not the gunman in the Depository, then who was? Not a trace of another gunman or his means of escape had turned up. I was familiar with the reports showing that the front of the Depository remained a scene of confusion for some time,[7] and I had read Secret Service Agent Forrest Sorrels' testimony that he had found the back of the building unguarded "20 or 25 minutes" after the assassination (7H348). An assassin other than Oswald could easily have made his way out either entrance in the chaotic aftermath of the shooting. But why had no trace of such a purported other assassin ever turned up? And Oswald *was* in the building, and his gun *was* used. Surely, even in spite of the

objections raised, it seemed more reasonable to believe in Oswald's guilt than in the existence of some
shadowy "other assassin" who had made his way into
the building and escaped without leaving a trace.

Over the last year I have been forced to revise this
earlier judgment. My researches in the National Archives[8] together with discoveries in Dallas suggest
that Oswald may not have been the gunman in the
sixth-floor window, that during the shooting he was
quite likely where he said he was (on the first floor),
that two conspirators other than Oswald may well
have been on the sixth floor of the Depository during
the shooting, and finally, that both of them could
have made their escape in a light-colored Rambler
station wagon. I should point out that none of this
information *proves* Oswald's innocence. What it does
do is provide a plausible alternative to the presumption of his guilt.

Where was Oswald during the shooting? Charles
Givens testified that he saw Oswald at 11:55 A.M.
on the sixth floor with a clipboard in his hands
(6H349–351). Five minutes later Eddie Piper saw
him on the first floor (19H499; 6H383). Ten
minutes later Carolyn Arnold also thought she saw
Oswald on the first floor. An FBI report from November 26, recently discovered in the Archives, tells
her story:

> *Mrs. R. E. Arnold, Secretary, Texas School
> Book Depository, advised she was in her
> office on the second floor of the building on
> November 22, 1963, and left that office be-
> tween 12:00 and 12:15 pm, to go down-
> stairs and stand in front of the building to
> view the Presidential Motorcade. As she was
> standing in front of the building, she stated
> she thought she caught a fleeting glimpse of
> Lee Harvey Oswald standing in the hallway
> between the front door and the double doors
> leading to the warehouse, located on the first
> floor. She could not be sure that this was
> Oswald, but said she felt it was and believed*

*the time to be a few minutes before 12:15 pm*
(Archives, *CD 5*).

Mrs. Arnold's estimate of the time as "a few minutes before 12:15 pm" may have been a bit early—
in a later signed statement for the FBI she said, "I
left the Texas School Book Depository Building at
about 12:25 pm" (22H635). The time factor is critical, for at 12:15 exactly Arnold Rowland was already
observing a gunman at a sixth-floor window.

> *I noticed on the sixth floor of the building
> that there was a man back from the window.
> . . . He was standing and holding a rifle.
> This appeared to me to be a fairly high-pow-
> ered rifle because of the scope and the rela-
> tive proportion of the scope to the rifle, you
> can tell about what type of rifle it is (2H169).*

The gunman was standing at the far southwest
window, he had dark hair in a close cut, was of un-
determined height and slender build, and had on dark
pants and "a very light-colored shirt, white or a light
blue or a color such as that. This was open at the
collar" (2H169–172). Rowland was able to pinpoint the time exactly as he had just noticed the
Hertz clock atop the Depository—it was 12:15 P.M.
(2H169, 173).[9]

Clearly if Oswald was on the first floor at 12:15—
and we should note that this is where he later said he
was (R600, 605)—he could not be the gunman
Rowland saw on the sixth floor. Moreover, there is
other evidence of a far more startling sort that suggests that two men, neither of whom was Oswald,
were on the sixth floor at the time of the shooting.
On November 26 Frances Hernandez, a seamstress
in the Dal-Tex Building, was interviewed by the
FBI. Here is the full report of that interview:

> *Frances Hernandez, 1917 Annex, advised
> she, Josephine Salinas, and Henrietta Var-
> gas, all employees of McKell Sportswear*

*Company, Second Floor, 501 Elm Street, Dallas, while on their way home about 5:10 pm on November 19, 1963, and after leaving the parking lot near the Texas School Book Depository, observed two men with an automobile, about a 1956 Buick, color light blue. The older of the two men was observed to hand a rifle to the younger of the two men, who then walked from the Buick toward a white car which was a compact, but she did not know the make of it. She stated the younger man might have been Lee Harvey Oswald, but she is not able to say definitely it was Oswald. She stated she has no other information* (Archives, *CD* 205).

Josephine Salinas and Henrietta Vargas were independently interviewed and each corroborated Mrs. Hernandez' account (*Archives, CD* 205). Three items of this account stand out in light of later information: (1) Two men were involved, one older than the other, (2) "the younger man might have been Lee Harvey Oswald," and (3) the younger man took the rifle and walked toward "a white car which was a compact."

Carolyn Walther watched the motorcade from the east curb of Houston Street, 50 to 60 feet south of the Elm/Houston corner. Shortly after the assassination she gave this account of what she had seen to the FBI:

Carolyn Walther (arrow center) saw two men in an upper floor window of the Depository. Arnold Rowland (arrow right) saw a gunman on the sixth floor of the Depository at the same time another witness saw Oswald on the first floor.

*Shortly after the ambulance left [a seizure victim had just been picked up on Houston Street], she looked back toward the TSBD [Depository] building and saw a man standing on either the fourth or fifth floor in the southeast corner window. This would be the most easterly window of either the fourth or fifth floors of the windows on the south side of the building, which faces toward Elm Street. This man had the window open and was standing up leaning out the window with both his hands extended outside the window ledge. In his hands, this man was holding a rifle with the barrel pointed downward, and the man was looking south on Houston Street. The man was wearing a white shirt and had blond or light brown hair. She recalled at the time that she had not noticed the man there a few moments previously when she looked toward the building and thought that apparently there were guards everywhere. The rifle had a short barrel and seemed large around the stock or end of the rifle. Her impression was that the gun was a machine gun. She noticed nothing like a telescopic sight on the rifle or a leather strap or sling on the rifle. She said she knows nothing about rifles or guns of any type, but thought that the rifle was different from any she had ever seen. This man was standing in about the middle of the window. In the same window, to the left of this man, she could see a portion of another man standing by the side of this man with a rifle. This other man was standing erect, and his head was above the opened portion of the window. As the window was very dirty, she could not see the head of this second man. She is positive this window is not as high as the sixth floor. This second man was apparently wearing a brown suit coat, and the only thing she could see was the right side of the man, from about the waist to the shoulders.*

*Almost immediately after noticing this man with the rifle and the other man standing beside him, someone in the crowd said "Here they come," and she looked to her left, looking south on Houston Street, to see the Presidential Party. As soon as President Kennedy's car passed where she was standing, she and Mrs. Springer turned away and started walking north toward Elm Street. At*

*about the time they reached the curb at Elm
Street, she heard a loud report and thought
it was fireworks (24H522).*

It is not disturbing that she is mistaken about the
floor. Others have also been confused about which
floor they were looking at; Police Officers D. V.
Harkness, E. O. Brewer, and Charles Batchelor
called in from the scene minutes after the shooting
with reports that various witnesses had seen the
rifleman on the second, the fourth, and the fifth
floors (21H391–392). Obviously, it is easy to become confused as to the number of the floor one is
looking at. In point of fact, at that moment Harold
Norman, James Jarman, and Bonnie Rae Williams
(all three Negroes) were sitting at a southeast-corner
window on the fifth floor. Mrs. Walther may have
been mistaken about other parts of her story, too,
but the FBI made no effort to find this out. It was
three years after the assassination when Mrs. Walther
was next interviewed—this time not by the FBI, but
by representatives of Capitol Records:

*Interviewer: When you looked up at the window,
were the men talking to each other or what
were they doing?*

*Mrs. Walther: No. The man that was holding the gun
was partially leaning out, just slightly, and
he had his forearms on the window and it
was not a long rifle. This was a short gun.
Not a pistol. I had never seen one like it.
The other man was standing beside him,
but I could only see a part of his face, and
he was dressed in brown.*

*Interviewer: And was he holding anything?*

*Mrs. Walther: Not that I could see.*

*Interviewer: How was he dressed? Could you see any
items of apparel that he was wearing?*

*Mrs. Walther: A brown suitcoat was all I could see.
Just about this portion of the man's body.
And it didn't look like boxes . . .*

*Interviewer: Why, why did you say it didn't look like
boxes?*

*Mrs. Walther: Well, an agent from the FBI asked me if I thought what I had seen was boxes. And it was not boxes . . . I did not see any boxes in the building, I saw no boxes at all in the building.*

*Interviewer: When you were questioned by the FBI did they seem to be interested in finding out what everybody saw, or did they already have an idea of what had taken place?*

*Mrs. Walther: Well, they were interested in if I could identify Oswald and . . . uh, they were not interested in the other man in the window.*

*Interviewer: Were you ever asked to testify for any of the lawyers of the Warren Commission?*

*Mrs. Walther: No.*

*Interviewer: Could you have identified Oswald?*

*Mrs. Walther: No, I could not. Definitely not.*

*Interviewer: When did you first realize that the President had been shot?*

*Mrs. Walther: Almost immediately. After the series of shots, people started screaming that the President had been hit.*

*Interviewer: How many shots did you hear?*

*Mrs. Walther: I definitely feel that I heard four shots.*

*Interviewer: Now, you've been reluctant to discuss this, before this evening.*

*Mrs. Walther: Very.*

*Interviewer: Could you tell us why?*

*Mrs. Walther: Well, it's just very painful. It was a terrible thing that . . . happened and to be so close . . . to a murder. Uh . . . if I could have identified the person I would have been glad to have, you know, done so, right away. But since I couldn't and I would not say that it was Oswald . . . it . . . I'm not sure.*

*Interviewer: What does the fact that there were two men on that floor mean to you?*

*Mrs. Walther: It means that there is at least one more person free.*

*Interviewer: And there's no doubt in your mind that there were two people there.*

*Mrs. Walther: No. There's no doubt in my mind that there was two men in this window.*[10]

As we shall see in a moment, there is photographic evidence indicating that there were two men at southeast-corner windows—not on the fourth or fifth floor, but on the sixth. First we must take up the trail of the putative brown-coated accomplice.

James Worrell saw a man run out the back of the Depository shortly after the shooting. In an affidavit sworn out on November 23 he noted:

> *I got scared and ran from the location. While I was running I heard the gun fire two more times. I ran from Elm Street to Pacific Street on Houston. When I was about 100 yards from the building I stopped to get my breath and looked back at the building. I saw a w/m [white man], 5'8" to 5'10", dark hair, average weight for height, dark shirt or jacket open down front, no hat, didn't have anything in hands, come out of the building and run in the opposite direction from me. I then caught a bus to my home (16H959).*

Later, Worrell was questioned by the Commission and asked to amplify his description of the man he saw fleeing from the back entrance of the Depository.

*Specter: What clothes did the man have on?*
*Worrell: Dark, like a jacket like that.*
*Specter: Indicating a dark grey jacket?*
*Worrell: No, no. It was a jacket like that.*
*Specter: A suit jacket?*
*Worrell: Yes.*
*Specter: Or was it a sports jacket?*
*Worrell: Sports jacket.*
*Specter: Did not have on matching coat and trousers?*
*Worrell: No.*
*Specter: Was it dark in color or light?*
*Worrell: It was dark in color. I don't know whether it was blue, black, or brown, but it was dark,*

> *and he had light pants. And that is all I can*
> *say on his clothes, except his coat was open*
> *and kind of flapping back in the breeze when*
> *he was running (2H196).*

The last time Worrell saw him, this man in the dark (possibly brown) sport or suit coat was moving quickly south along Houston Street. We next pick up his trail in the testimony of Richard Randolph Carr.

Carr is a steelworker, and around noon on November 22 he was climbing a steel stairway of the new courthouse building, then under construction at the corner of Houston and Commerce Streets. Looking over toward the Depository, he saw a man at a window on the top floor.

> *This man [Carr recalled], a heavy set indi-*
> *vidual, who was wearing a hat,* a tan sport
> coat *and horn rimmed glasses, was not in the*
> *end window next to Houston Street, but was*
> *I believe in the second window over from*
> *Houston Street* (Archives, *CD 385; empha-*
> *sis added*).

Carr continued about his business, and "a minute or so later" heard the shots in Dealey Plaza. He climbed down the stairway to find out what happened. There on Houston Street he saw, walking very fast, the same tan-coated man he had seen earlier in the Depository.

> *While I was on Houston St. near the Com-*
> *merce St. intersection I saw a man whom I*
> *believe was identical with the man I had*
> *earlier seen looking out of the window of the*
> *Texas School Book Depository building.*
> *This man, walking very fast, proceeded on*
> *Houston St. south to Commerce St., then*
> *east on Commerce St. to Record St. which is*
> *one block from Houston St. This man got*
> *into a 1961 or 1962 Grey Rambler Station*
> *Wagon which was parked just north of*

*Commerce on Record St. The station wagon, which had Texas license and was driven by a young negro man, drove off in a northerly direction* (Archives, *CD 385*).

This is our last glimpse of the tan-coated man. It is not our last glimpse of a light-colored Rambler station wagon, with a Texas license plate and driven by a Negro.

Marvin C. Robinson furnished a report about such a station wagon to the FBI on November 23. Here is that report:

*Marvin C. Robinson, 5120 South Marsalis Avenue, telephone number FR 4-5834, advised that approximately between 12:30 and 1:00 p.m. on the afternoon of November 22, 1963, while traveling west on Elm Street he crossed the intersection of Elm and Houston streets shortly after the assassination of President Kennedy. Robinson stated that after he had crossed Houston Street and was in front of the Texas School Book Depository building a light colored Nash stationwagon suddenly appeared before him. He stated this vehicle stopped and a white male came down the grass covered incline between the building and the street and entered the stationwagon after which it drove away in the direction of the Oak Cliff section of Dallas. Robinson stated he does not recall the license number on the stationwagon or whether or not it bore a Texas license plate.*

*He stated further that he did not pay particular attention to the individual who entered the stationwagon and would be unable to identify him.*

*Robinson was unable to furnish any pertinent information concerning the assassination of President Kennedy* (Archives, *CD 5*).

Robinson's recollection is corroborated and added to

by the testimony of Sheriff's Deputy Roger Craig. His November 23 report to the Sheriff's Department observes:

> *About this time I heard a shrill whistle and I turned around and saw a white male running down the hill from the direction of the Texas School Book Depository Building and I saw what I think was a light colored Rambler stationwagon with luggage rack on top pull over to the curb and this subject who had come running down the hill got into this car. The man driving this station wagon was a dark complected white male. I tried to get across Elm Street to stop the car and talk with subjects, but the traffic was so heavy I could not make it. I reported this incident at once to a secret service officer, whose name I do not know, then I left this area and went at once to the building and assisted in the search of the building.*
>
> *Later that afternoon, I heard that the City had a suspect in custody and I called and reported the information about the suspect running down the hill and getting into a car to Captain Fritz and was requested to come at once to City Hall. I went to the City Hall and identified the subject they had in custody [Oswald] as being the same person I saw running down this hill and get into the station wagon and leave the scene (19H524).*

Later, Craig amplified his report before the Commission. The man running down the incline was "a white male in his twenties, five nine, five eight . . . about 140 or 150 . . . blue trousers . . . and a light tan shirt" (6H266). The man driving the station wagon "was very dark complected, had real dark short hair, and was wearing a thin white-looking jacket . . . my first glance at him he struck me as a Negro" (6H266–267). The station wagon was a light-colored Nash Rambler with a luggage rack and a Texas license (6H267).

We know Oswald could not have been the man Craig saw running down the incline—at that very moment he was riding in William Whaley's taxicab to his Beckley Street apartment.[11] Who was this individual who looked so much like Oswald that Craig mistook his identity? Richard Popkin has suggested that he may have been the "second Oswald" who figured so prominently in pre-assassination activities.[12]

What is intriguing about this pattern of evidence is the way in which the details interlock. None of these witnesses could have known of the others' reports. Yet Carolyn Walther described the two men in the window in such a way that the gunman could have been the "second Oswald" Craig saw entering the station wagon, while his accomplice could have been the tan-coated figure seen by Worrell and Carr. Worrell, moreover, described the man fleeing from the back entrance of the Depository as moving in a direction that would bring him into contact with Carr (see diagram). Finally, Carr's description of the station wagon and its driver dovetails perfectly with the description of both furnished by Robinson and Craig. And this vehicle, we recall, Carr saw headed in a northerly direction on Record Street—two blocks north, a left turn (see diagram), and it would be

Movements of two men and one station wagon:

(1) A second man besides the gunman was seen at a window by Carolyn Walther, who was standing on Houston Street. This second man, she said, had on a brown sport or suit jacket. (2) A man answering the same description was seen by James Worrell leaving a rear door of the Depository a few minutes after the assassination. (3) Richard Randolph Carr (watching from a building under construction on Commerce Street) saw a man in a tan jacket on the top floor of the Depository shortly before the assassination. Carr saw the same man a few minutes afterward walk "very fast" down Houston Street, turn the corner onto Commerce Street, and get into a light-colored Rambler station wagon (driven by a Negro) on Record Street (4). (5) Deputy Sheriff Roger Craig and motorist Richard Robinson both saw a man run down across a grassy incline in front of the Depository and get into a light-colored Rambler station wagon (6). Craig said the driver of the station wagon was either a Negro or "a dark-complected white man." The station wagon then proceeded through the triple underpass (7).

Immediately before the shooting, an unidentified figure (arrow) appears in the window next to the assassin's. These three frames from Robert Hughes's 8-millimeter movie film cover 4 seconds; the last frame coming approximately 7 seconds before the shots. Hughes stopped his camera at this point.

headed down Elm Street in front of the Depository.

There is also photographic evidence supporting the contention that there were two people on the sixth floor rather than one. Some eighty-eight frames of Bob Hughes's 8-millimeter film show what appear to be two figures on the sixth floor of the Depository within 5 seconds of the first shot. This film has been discussed in an earlier chapter, and a shape in the corner window of the sixth floor has been noted. Not recognizable as a human figure, this shape must be animate since its width changes through time—wide at first, it becomes steadily narrower as the presidential car makes its turn onto Elm Street. It may very well be the gunman in the sniper's nest getting into firing position. The other figure appears 10 or 12 feet to the left in the second pair of windows from the corner. The outline of what seems to be a head appears above the first lintel in the window frame. In some of the eighty-eight frames that picture the Depository, this figure appears clearly. In others its outlines blur, and it becomes scarcely visible. This change may be a natural function of the camera—some frames clear and others fuzzy—or it may be due to the figure's moving toward and then away from the window.

Could this "figure" be only the outline of boxes piled within the Depository?

Other photos suggest it is not. Robert Studebaker of the Dallas Police took photographs of the interior of the sixth floor shortly after the shooting. One of his photos shows the disposition of boxes behind the second pair of windows. It is clear from Studebaker's photo that the boxes would form a straight, horizontal line across the window, and that, if seen from the street, they would appear *below* the first lintel. More enlightening even than Studebaker's photo is a 35-millimeter shot of the building exterior taken only minutes after the assassination by Jim Murray. Murray took the photo from a position not far from Bob Hughes's vantage point at the corner of Main and Houston streets. It is clear from his photo that the boxes in question appear very low in the window, and that the shape appearing in the Hughes film has now disappeared (see illustrations).[13]

What does this collection of new evidence prove? It does not *prove* that the assassination was a conspiracy and that two men were together on the sixth floor of the Depository at the time the shots were fired. Nor does it *prove* Oswald's innocence. What it does suggest is that there are threads in this case that should have been unraveled long ago instead of being swept under the Archives rug. It also shows that the question of Oswald's guilt must remain—nearly four years after the event—still unanswered.

Dallas Police photo taken a short time after the assassination showing boxes in front of second window. It is evident that these boxes would not have appeared above the first lintel of the window from outside.

An enlargement from Hughes's film shows a figure in the window next to the assassin's.

This photo of the Depository windows, taken only moments after the assassination by Dallas photographer Jim Murray, shows boxes much lower in the window than the figure apparent in the Hughes film.

Robert Hughes's photo of the Depository and the presidential
motorcade taken seconds before the assassination.

In this recently discovered photograph by Jack A. Weaver, taken only seconds before the shooting, the same figure appears on the sixth floor in the second window from the corner.

## NOTES

1. Mark Lane, *Rush to Judgment* (New York: Crest Books, 1967), pp. 387-88.

2. Harold Weisberg, *Whitewash I* (Hyattstown, Md.: Harold Weisberg, 1966), p. 45; *Whitewash II* (Hyattstown, Md.: Harold Weisberg, 1966), pp. 215, 216, 220-23.

3. Lane, *op. cit.,* pp. 114-20; Crest edition, pp. 95-101.

4. Edward Jay Epstein, *Inquest* (New York: The Viking Press, Inc., 1966), pp. 55, 58.

5. Philadelphia *Inquirer,* May 19, 1967.

6. Dillard interview, Nov. 2, 1966.

7. Leo Sauvage, for example, offers the following description of the Depository's front entrance given him by Roy Truly: "Truly told me that when he came back down with the motorcycle officer he found 'a real crowd' on the ground floor, 'maybe 15 or 20 people or more.' Some, he said, were 'reporters, photographers, employees who worked on other floors.' Others were 'just people from the street, I suppose.' " Léo Sauvage, *The Oswald Affair* (Cleveland and New York: The World Publishing Company, 1966), p. 20.

8. Photocopies of all Archives documents cited or excerpted in this section may be found in Appendix G, "Documents from the National Archives."

9. Rowland provided another means for checking his estimate of the exact time when he saw the gunman. He was standing near a police motorcycle at the time, and, "right after the time I noticed him [the gunman] . . . the dispatcher came on and gave the position of the motorcade as being on Cedar Springs. This would be in the area of Turtle Creek, down in that area" (2H173). A check of the police radio logs shows that such an announcement was made between 12:15 and 12:16 P.M. (17H460, 21H390, 23H911).

10. Richard Warren Lewis and Lawrence Schiller, *The Scavengers and Critics of the Warren Report* (New York: Dell Publishing Co., Inc., 1967), pp. 126-27.

11. Whaley positively identified Oswald as the man he took from downtown Dallas to a Beckley Street address (2H256, 261). Oswald's previous landlady, Mrs. Mary Bledsoe, testified she saw Oswald get on and off a bus in downtown Dallas shortly after the assassination (6H409–410).

12. Richard H. Popkin, *The Second Oswald* (New York: Avon Books, 1966), p. 90.

13. Some corroboration for the thesis of two conspirators on the sixth floor of the Depository at the time of the shooting can be found in the strange tale of Norman Similas, a Canadian journalist. In Dallas to cover a bottlers' convention, Similas was in Dealey Plaza at the time of the assassination. He took several photographs, some showing the presidential limousine and at least one showing the Depository just after the last shot. Similas described this latter

photo in a signed statement for the Royal Canadian Mounted Police:

> *I arrived in Toronto at about 10 p.m., on November 23. Almost immediately on my arrival at home, I was contacted by a reporter from the Toronto Telegram who advised they received word from the Associated Press in Chicago that I had negatives that they might be interested in. He arrived at my home in five or ten minutes. I went over the story giving him an eyewitness account of what I had seen and heard during and following the assassination. He then examined the negatives, and while examining them he exclaimed, "There looks like two people at this window." I then went over and looked at the negative and I agreed that there were two objects in the window on the 6th floor southeast corner of the building. This window differed from the others in that it had an alcove above the window as opposed to the others on the 5th and other floors, which had a square frame. The two objects appeared to be people and the Telegram reporter thought he saw what appeared to be a rifle barrel between them. I did not make any comment on this upon looking at it as it blended into the shadow of the object on the left.*
>
> *This negative was one of a strip of three and this strip plus another strip of three was handed over to this reporter.*

The reporter in question, Colin Davies, gave a somewhat different picture of their examination of the negatives.

> *On September 19, 1964, a member of the Royal Canadian Mounted Police (RCMP) interviewed Colin Davies, reporter and photographer of the Toronto Telegram. Davies advised he was the reporter who interviewed Norman Mitchel Similas on the night of November 23, 1963, and subsequently examined the negatives in Similas' possession. Davies stated that Similas was very excited at the time of the interview. While viewing the negatives Similas was said to have pointed out the window and asked Davies if he didn't think there were two people there. Similas drew his attention to the article written by a Dallas reporter in which two people were mentioned as being in the window. Davies said he felt it was the power of suggestion and that Similas wanted to see the two people in the negative so badly that he actually believed he did. It was Davies' opinion that the negatives were worthless from a news standpoint, but due to Similas' state of excitement he did not have the*

*heart to disappoint him. Davies decided to take
the negatives and let the Photo Editor decide what
should be done. During the next day or so, the
negatives became lost and the Telegram, feeling
responsible, sent Similas a check to pay for them.
Davies did not know the amount but he later met
Similas who told him he had received $300. for his
negatives. (Actually he received $50.00.)*

One thing is certain. The negatives are lost, and until they
are recovered we cannot know whether there were "two
objects" or "two people" in the sixth-floor window.

The documents relating to Similas were discovered in the
Archives by Harold Weisberg. They are reprinted in his
book *Photographic Whitewash* (Hyattstown, Md.: Harold
Weisberg, 1967), pp. 213-40.

# APPENDIX A

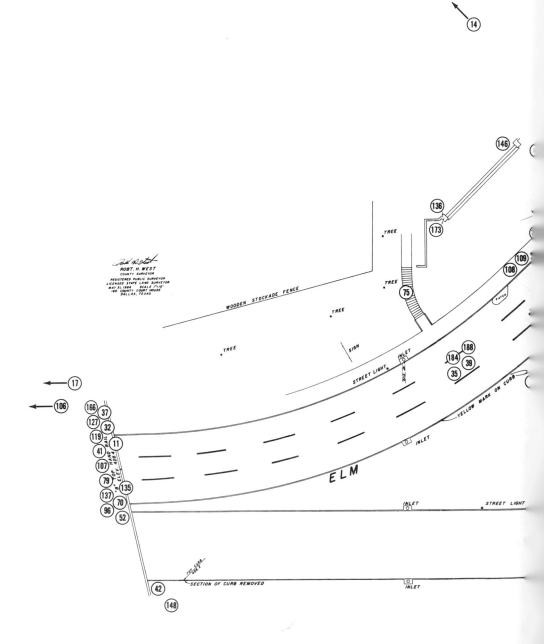

**DEALEY PLAZA CHAR**

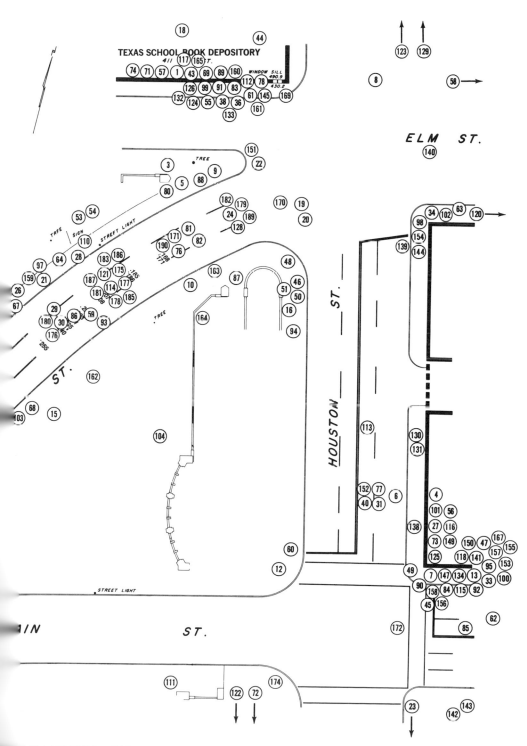

**CATION OF WITNESSES**

# MASTER LIST OF ASSASSINATION WITNESSES

| WITNESS NO. | NAME | LOCATION | NO. OF SHOTS | BUNCHING OF SHOTS | DIRECTION OF SOUND/SHOTS | TOTAL TIME OF SHOTS | DATE OF REPORT | REFERENCES | REMARKS |
|---|---|---|---|---|---|---|---|---|---|
| 1 | (Miss) Victoria Elizabeth ADAMS | 4th fl. window, TSBD | 3 | 2 & 3 | KNOLL: below & to the right | — | 3/23/64 | Archives, CD 5, p. 39; 6H388; 22H632 | Saw person resembling Ruby asking questions at Depository after shooting |
| 2 | James W. ALTGENS | Grass, S. side, Elm St. | At least 3 | "Regular intervals" | 1st shot from behind TSBD; all shots sounded alike | — | 7/22/64 | Archives, CD 1088, p. 3; 7H517-525 | Altgens' picture taken just after 1st shot; Altgens sure no shots previous to this |
| 3 | Danny G. ARCE | Grass across dead-end Elm from TSBD | 3 | — | KNOLL: RR tracks on West | — | 11/22/63; 4/7/64 | 6H365-367; 22H634 | Ran to RR area after shots |
| 4 | Cecil AULT | Criminal Cts. Bldg. | 3 | 1 & 2 | — | — | 1/10/64 | 24H534 | — |
| 5 | (Mrs.) Donald Sam BAKER (née V. RACKLEY) | Curb of Elm St., front of TSBD | 3 | — | KNOLL: RR tracks beyond monument | — | 3/19/64; 7/22/64 | 7H507-515; 22H635; Archives, CD 5, pp. 66-67 | After 2nd shot she smelled gunsmoke (probably a bit later); after shots she moved out in street; saw something hit pavement, middle of lane behind car |
| 6 | M. L. BAKER | Motorcade: Houston St. on motorcycle | 3 | even | — | 3, not over 3 sec. apart | 11/22/63 | 3H242-270; 24H199 | Said he "figured" shots came from TSBD, but told R.S. Truly that day he wanted to get to roof to look over RR yards |
| 7 | Malcolm James BARCLAY | Main St., in front of Courts Bldg. | — | — | — | — | 6/15/64 | 26H552-554 | Turned to reenter courthouse and heard "one or more loud reports" |
| 8 | Welcome Eugene BARNETT | Elm/Houston intersection | 3 | — | TSBD | — | 7/23/64 | 7H539-544 | 2nd shot sounded "high" |
| 9 | (Mrs.) Jane BERRY | Elm St., front of TSBD | 3 | — | West of her | — | 3/19/64 | Archives, CD 5, p. 42; 22H637 | — |
| 10 | Hugh William BETZNER, Jr. | Elm St., S. side, short distance down from corner | "at least" 2 | — | — | — | 11/22/63 | 19H467 | — |

| | | | | | | | | | |
|---|---|---|---|---|---|---|---|---|---|
| 11 | Curtis Freeman BISHOP | RR overpass | 3 | — | — | — | 3/19/54 | 22H834 | — |
| 12 | (Miss) Wilma BOND | NW corner, Houston/Main | 3 | — | — | — | 2/18/64 | *Archives*, CD 735, I, p. 7 | — |
| 13 | Eugene BOONE | Sheriff's Office, Main St. | 3 | 2 & 3 | — | — | 3/25/64 | 3H291-295 | — |
| 14 | Lee E. BOWERS, Jr. | RR tower | 3 | 2 & 3 | — | — | 4/2/64 | 6H284-289; 24H201 | 1st shot, car out of sight behind decorative masonry |
| 15 | Charles F. BREHM | S. side, Elm St. | 3 | — | TSBD: bldgs. at Elm/Houston corner | — | 11/25/63 | 22H837-838 | 2nd shot hit JFK head, saw hair fly up; 3rd shot followed |
| 16 | Howard Leslie BRENNAN | On wall, Houston/Elm | 2 | — | TSBD: saw man fire | — | 11/22/63; 3/24/64 | *Archives*, CD 5, pp. 12-14; CD 205, pp. 15-16; 3H143-144; 19H470 | 1st shot, something caught his eye in TSBD; 3rd shot, saw man fire; heard no 2nd shot! |
| 17 | Earle V. BROWN | Highway overpass | 3 | — | TSBD | — | 4/7/64 | 6H231-236; 22H600 | Says pigeons flew up to the left; a few minutes after shooting, smelled gunpowder |
| 18 | (Miss) Doris Fay BURNS | 3rd fl, TSBD, walking in hall | — | — | — | — | 3/19/64 | 22H637 | — |
| 19 | Mayor Earle CABELL | Motorcade: 2 cars back of V. Pres. car | 3 | 2 & 3 | TSBD | 5 sec. | 7/13/64 | 7H476-485 | Car was just making turn at 1st shot; time twice as long between 1st and 2nd shots as between 2nd and 3rd shots |
| 20 | (Mrs.) Earle CABELL | Motorcade: 2 cars back of V. Pres. car | 3 | 2 & 3 | TSBD | — | 7/13/64 | 7H485-491 | Car making turn at 1st shot; smelled gunsmoke; Congressman Roberts corroborates smell |
| 21 | (Mrs.) Gloria CALVERY | N. side Elm St., halfway to overpass | — | — | — | — | 3/19/64 | 22H638 | JFK directly in front of her on last shot |
| 22 | Ochus Virgil CAMPBELL | With Truly at signal light, Elm St. | 3 | — | KNOLL: RR tracks near viaduct | — | 11/24/63; 3/14/64 | 22H638, 845 | — |

| WITNESS NO. | NAME | LOCATION | NO. OF SHOTS | BUNCHING OF SHOTS | DIRECTION OF SOUND/SHOTS | TOTAL TIME OF SHOTS | DATE OF REPORT | REFERENCES | REMARKS |
|---|---|---|---|---|---|---|---|---|---|
| 23 | Richard Randolph CARR | 6th fl., new courthouse | 2 | — | — | — | 1/4/64 | Archives, CD 329, pp. 28-31 | Saw man on top floor, TSBD |
| 24 | Clifton C. CARTER | V. Pres. follow-up car | 3 | "evenly spaced" | — | 5-6 sec. | 5/20/64 | 7H474-475 | 1st shot, car had just made turn |
| 25 | John Arthur CHISM | In front of Stemmons Freeway sign | 2-3 | — | KNOLL: "Behind him" | — | 11/25/63 | 19H471; 24H525 | 1st shot, car in front of or just past him; 2nd shot, just after 2 men in front seat looked back |
| 26 | (Mrs.) Marion Faye CHISM | In front of Stemmons Freeway sign | 2 | — | — | — | 11/22/63 | 19H472 | 1st shot, as Pres. was "coming through"; 2 men in front of car "stood up" and then 2nd shot |
| 27 | (Mrs.) Rose CLARK | Criminal Cts. Bldg. window | 3 | — | — | — | 1/10/64 | 24H533 | 1st shot seemed louder |
| 28 | (Mrs.) Billie P. CLAY | Elm St., 150' W. of TSBD entrance | 3 | — | — | — | 3/23/64 | 22H641 | 1st shot a few seconds after car had passed |
| 29 | Gov. John CONNALLY | In car | 3 | 1 & 2 | TSBD | 10-12 sec. | 4/21/64 | 4H129-146 | 1st shot, heard; 3rd shot, heard; 2nd shot, felt but not heard |
| 30 | (Mrs.) John CONNALLY | In car | 3 | 1 & 2 | "right rear" | — | 4/21/64 | 4H146-149 | 1st shot hit JFK, he grabbed throat; 2nd shot hit CONNALLY; 3rd shot, spray from JFK's head |
| 31 | Malcolm O. COUCH | Press car motorcade | 3 | — | — | — | 4/1/64 | 6H153-162 | After 3rd shot, saw rifle being withdrawn from TSBD |
| 32 | Ewell William COWSERT | RR overpass | 2 or 3 | — | — | — | 3/19/64 | 22H836 | — |
| 33 | Roger D. CRAIG | Sheriff's Office, Main St. | 3 | 2 & 3 | — | 5-6 sec. | 11/23/63 | 6H260-273; 23H817 | Time between 1st and 2nd shots a bit longer than 2-3 sec.; time between 2nd and 3rd "not more than 2 sec." |
| 34 | James N. CRAWFORD | Corner, Elm/Houston | 3 | 2 & 3 | KNOLL: "From down the hill" | — | 1/10/64; 4/1/64 | Archives, CD 329, p. 22; 6H171-174 | — |

| # | Name | Location | Number of shots | | Source | Timing | Date | Citation | Remarks |
|---|------|----------|-----------------|---|--------|--------|------|----------|---------|
| 35 | Chief of Police Jesse E. CURRY | Motorcade: head car | 3, | certain | RR yards; then TSBD | 5-6 sec. | 4/22/64 | 4H150-202 | 1st shot, presidential car halfway to underpass |
| 36 | (Mrs.) Avery DAVIS | Lower step, entrance, TSBD | 3 | — | KNOLL: "viaduct" | — | 3/20/64 | *Archives*, CD 593, I, pp. 232-234; 22H642 | — |
| 37 | George A. DAVIS | RR overpass | — | — | — | — | 3/18/64 | 22H837 | Sounded unlike rifle fire; shots were very close together |
| 38 | (Mrs.) Joseph Eddie DEAN | Steps of TSBD | 3 | — | TSBD: "above her" | — | 11/25/63 | 22H643, 839 | — |
| 39 | Sheriff William DECKER | In lead car | 2 | — | — | — | no date | 19H458 | 1st shot, saw "spray of water" come out of rear seat of presidential car |
| 40 | Tom C. DILLARD | Motorcade: 6th car back from JFK | 3, "no more, no less" | "equally spaced" | — | — | 4/1/64 | 6H162-167 | Rather surprised to have smelled gunsmoke at Elm/Houston corner |
| 41 | Richard Calvin DODD | RR overpass | — | — | — | — | 3/18/64 | Lane, p. 40; 22H835 | "Sounds were very close together" |
| 42 | John F. DOLAN | Base of viaduct | 3 | — | — | — | 12/18/63 | *Archives*, CD 205, p. 32 | — |
| 43 | (Mrs.) Elsie T. DORMAN | 4th fl., TSBD | — | — | "area of the Records Bldg." | — | 11/24/63 | *Archives*, CD 5, p. 34 | — |
| 44 | Jack E. DOUGHERTY | 5th fl., TSBD, at work | — | — | — | — | 11/22/63 | *Archives*, CD 206, p. 11; 6H373-382; 22H645; 24H206 | Heard one shot, "sounded like it was coming from inside the building" |
| 45 | William T. DOWNEY | Corner, Main/Houston | — | — | — | — | 6/15/64 | 26H551 | "Heard one or more explosions" |
| 46 | Robert E. EDWARDS | Corner, Elm/Houston | 4 | — | — | — | 11/22/63 | *Archives*, CD 205, pp. 19-22; 6H200-205; 19H473, 647 | — |
| 47 | Harold ELKINS | Sheriff's Office, Main St | 3 | 2 & 3 | KNOLL: "Between RR yards and TSBD" | — | 3/10/64 | 19H540 | — |

| WITNESS NO. | NAME | LOCATION | NO. OF SHOTS | BUNCHING OF SHOTS | DIRECTION OF SOUND/SHOTS | TOTAL TIME OF SHOTS | DATE OF REPORT | REFERENCES | REMARKS |
|---|---|---|---|---|---|---|---|---|---|
| 48 | Amos Lee EUINS | Corner, Elm/Houston | 3/4 | — | — | — | 3/10/64 | 2H201-210; 16H963; 19H474 | — |
| 49 | Jack W. FAULKNER | Corner, Main/Houston | 3 | — | — | — | 11/22/63 | 19H511 | Says TSBD office workers said shots came from monument |
| 50 | Ronald B. FISCHER | Corner, Elm/Houston | 3 | "evenly spaced" | KNOLL: "RR tracks and area just W. of TSBD" | 6-8 sec. | 11/22/63; 4/1/64 | Archives, CD 205, pp. 19-22; 6H191-200; 19H475 | — |
| 51 | Terrence S. FORD | Near corner, Elm/Houston | 3 | — | — | — | 2/18/64 | Archives, CD 354 | — |
| 52 | J. W. FOSTER | RR overpass | 3 | 2 & 3 | "Back toward Elm/Houston corner" | — | 4/9/64 | Archives, CD 897, I, pp. 20-21; 6H248-253 | — |
| 53 | Jack FRANZEN | N. side of Elm St., near Plaza | 3 or 4 | — | — | — | 11/24/63 | Archives, CD 5, p. 46; 22H840 | After 1st shot, noticed small fragments flying inside the car |
| 54 | (Mrs.) Jack FRANZEN | N. side of Elm St., near Plaza | 3 | — | — | — | 11/25/63 | 24H525 | After 1st shot, noticed small fragments flying inside the car |
| 55 | Wesley FRAZIER | Front steps, TSBD | 3 | — | KNOLL: "Down the RR tracks there" | — | 11/22/63 | 2H210-245; 7H531; 22H647; 24H209 | — |
| 56 | E. R. GADDY | 2nd fl., Criminal Cts. Bldg. | 3 | — | — | — | 1/20/64 | Archives, CD 835, p. 13 | — |
| 57 | Dorothy Ann GARNER | 4th fl. window, TSBD | 3 | — | KNOLL: "Point to the W. of bldg." | — | 3/20/64 | 22H648 | — |
| 58 | Charles Douglas GIVENS | Record/Elm Sts., parking lot | 3 | — | — | — | 11/22/63 | 6H345-356; 22H649; 24H210 | — |
| 59 | Bobby W. HARGIS | Motorcade cycle, inboard left rear | 2+ | 2 & 3 | KNOLL: brain on windshield | — | 4/8/64 | 6H293-296 | Blood and brain spattered |

| No. | Name | Location | | | | Date | Citation | Remarks |
|---|---|---|---|---|---|---|---|---|
| 60 | D. V. HARKNESS | Main/Houston, W. side of Houston | 3 | — | — | 4/9/64 | 6H308-315 | — |
| 61 | (Mrs.) Peggy Joyce HAWKINS | Front of TSBD | 2 or 3 | — | KNOLL: RR yards | 4/1/64 | Archives, CD 337, I, pp. 35-36 | — |
| 62 | Clyde A. HAYGOOD | Motorcade cycle, several cars back of Pres. | 3 | 2 & 3 | — | 4/9/64 | 6H296-302 | — |
| 63 | (Mrs.) Ruby HENDERSON | E. side of Elm St., N. of Houston | 4 | 1 & 2; 3 & 4 | — | 11/25/63 | 24H524 | — |
| 64 | (Miss) Georgie Ruth HENDRIX | 150' W. of TSBD on Elm St. | 3 | — | — | 3/24/64 | 22H649 | — |
| 65 | Charles HESTER | N. side of Elm St. on slope | 2 | — | "Immediately behind us and over our heads" | 11/22/63; 11/25/53 | 19H478; 22H841 | — |
| 66 | (Mrs.) Charles HESTER | N. side of Elm St. on slope | 2 | — | — | 11/25/63 | 24H523 | Thinks she and husband were in the direct line of fire |
| 67 | (Mrs.) Karen HICKS | N. side of Elm St., halfway between underpass and Elm/Houston | — | — | — | 3/20/64 | 22H650 | 1st shot, car directly in front of where she was standing |
| 68 | (Mrs.) Jean HILL | S. side of Elm St. | 4-6 | 1 & 2; 3 & 4 | KNOLL | 11/22/63; 3/24/64 | 6H205-223; 19H479; 24H212 | Noticed difference in reports; Kennedy looks her way, is hit |
| 69 | Geneva L. HINE | 2nd fl. window, TSBD | 3 | — | TSBD | 4/9/64 | 6H393-397 | Came from inside building because it vibrated from the explosion |
| 70 | S. M. HOLLAND | RR overpass | 4 | 1 & 2; 3 & 4 | TSBD: N. end of Elm St.; KNOLL | 1/22/64; 4/8/64 | 6H239-248; 19H480; 24H212 | Puff of smoke coincident with last shots; Mrs. Kennedy turns late; Connally turns with right hand up, hit by 2nd shot |

| WITNESS NO. | NAME | LOCATION | NO. OF SHOTS | BUNCHING OF SHOTS | DIRECTION OF SOUND/SHOTS | TOTAL TIME OF SHOTS | DATE OF REPORT | REFERENCES | REMARKS |
|---|---|---|---|---|---|---|---|---|---|
| 71 | Mary Madeline HOLLIES | 4th fl. window, TSBD | 3 | — | — | — | 3/19/64 | 22H652 | — |
| 72 | Harry D. HOLMES | 5th fl. office 2 blocks away | 3 | — | — | — | 4/2/64 | 7H289-308 | — |
| 73 | (Mrs.) Jeannette E. HOOKER | Window in Criminal Cts. Bldg. | 3 | — | — | — | 1/10/64 | 24H533 | — |
| 74 | (Mrs.) Alvin HOPSON | Behind closed window, 4th fl., TSBD | 2 or more | — | — | — | 12/4/63 | 24H521 | Did not appear that shots were coming from her bldg. |
| 75 | Emmet Joseph HUDSON | Standing on steps leading up to monument | 3 | "evenly spaced" | KNOLL: "Above and behind me" | 2 minutes | 11/22/63; 7/22/64 | Archives, CD 5, pp. 30-31; 7H558-565; 19H481 | — |
| 76 | Hurchel JACKS | Motorcade; driver, V. Pres. car | 3 | — | 1st shot, "right rear" | — | 11/28/63 | 18H801 | — |
| 77 | Robert Hill JACKSON | Motorcade; 7th car back, Houston/Main | 3 | 2 & 3 | KNOLL: "At head of motorcade in a northwesterly direction" | 5-6 sec. | 3/10/64 | 2H155-165; 19H517; 24H117 | — |
| 78 | James JARMAN | 5th fl. window, TSBD | 3 | 2 & 3 | "Below and left" | — | 3/24/64 | Archives, CD 5, pp. 334-335; 3H198-211 | Didn't hear bolt or dropping cartridges |
| 79 | Clemon Earl JOHNSON | RR overpass | — | — | — | — | 3/14/64 | 22H836 | White smoke near pavilion; believed smoke came from motorcycle abandoned near there |
| 80 | (Miss) Judy Marie JOHNSON | SW corner, Elm/Houston | 3 | — | — | — | 3/23/64 | 22H656 | — |

| No. | Name | Location | No. of shots | Spacing | Direction | Interval | Date | Citation | Remarks |
|---|---|---|---|---|---|---|---|---|---|
| 81 | Pres. Lyndon Baines JOHNSON | Motorcade, V. Pres. car | — | — | — | — | 7/10/64 | 5H561-564 | One sharp report, then "other explosions" |
| 82 | (Mrs.) Lyndon B. JOHNSON | Motorcade, V. Pres. car | 3 | 2 & 3 | TSBD | — | 12/2/63 | 5H564-567 | 1st shot "from the right, above my shoulder, from a building" |
| 83 | Carl Edward JONES | Front steps, TSBD | 3 | — | — | — | 3/18/64 | 22H657 | — |
| 84 | C. M. JONES | In front of Sheriff's Office, Main St. | 3 | 2 & 3 | — | 4-7 sec. | 11/22/63 | 19H512 | — |
| 85 | Seth KANTOR | Motorcade; Press bus | 3 | — | — | — | 12/3/63 | 20H351, 403-421 | Notebook notes: "you could smell gunpowder in our car all the way back"; "entered right temple" |
| 86 | (Mrs.) Jacqueline KENNEDY | Motorcade; in car | 2 or 3 | — | — | — | 6/5/64 | 5H178-181 | Noise; Connally yells "oh no, no, no," looks at JFK |
| 87 | (Mrs.) Dolores Arlene KOUNAS | 15' W. of SW corner, Elm / Houston | 3 | "equally spaced" | KNOLL: "a westerly direction . . . viaduct" | "a few seconds apart" | 11/25/63; 3/23/64 | 22H659, 846 | "these shots were coming *not* from TSBD but from direction of the underpass" |
| 88 | (Miss) Patricia Ann LAWRENCE | 7' W. of SW corner, Elm / Houston | 3 | — | TSBD: "right over my head" | — | 3/20/64 | 22H660, 841 | — |
| 89 | Ray Edward LEWIS | Inside entrance, TSBD | 3 | — | TSBD: "somewhere above me" | — | 3/18/64 | 22H661 | — |
| 90 | C. L. "Lummie" LEWIS | Sheriff's Office, Main St. | 3 | — | — | — | 11/23/63 | 19H526 | — |
| 91 | Billy Nolan LOVELADY | Steps, TSBD | 3 | 2 & 3 | KNOLL: "that concrete little deal on that knoll" | — | 3/19/64; 4/7/64 | 6H336-341; 22H662; 24H214 | — |
| 92 | W. W. MABRA | In front of Criminal Cts. Bldg. | 3 | — | — | — | 11/27/64 | 19H541 | — |

| WITNESS NO. | NAME | LOCATION | NO. OF SHOTS | BUNCHING OF SHOTS | DIRECTION OF SOUND/SHOTS | TOTAL TIME OF SHOTS | DATE OF REPORT | REFERENCES | REMARKS |
|---|---|---|---|---|---|---|---|---|---|
| 93 | B. J. MARTIN | Motorcade, outboard cycle, left rear | 3 | — | — | — | 4/3/64 | 6H289-293 | Blood and brain spattered |
| 94 | John MARTIN, Jr. | Near reflecting pool | 3 | 2 & 3 | TSBD | — | 4/2/64 | Archives, CD 897, I, pp. 51-53 | — |
| 95 | A. D. McCURLEY | Front of Sheriff's Office, Main St. | 3 | — | — | — | 11/22/63 | 19H514 | Says a RR worker saw "smoke from the bullets came from the vicinity of stockade fence" |
| 96 | Austin L. MILLER | RR overpass | 3 | 2 & 3 | — | "few seconds" | 11/22/63 | 6H223-227; 19H485; 24H217; Archives, CD 205, p. 27 | Saw "smoke or steam" coming from a group of trees N. of Elm; saw shot hit street past car |
| 97 | A. J. MILLICAN | N. side of Elm, halfway to underpass | 8 | — | TSBD: (1st 3) and KNOLL (2 & 3) | — | 11/22/63 | 19H486 | First shots from TSBD, then shots from Arcade, then more shots from Arcade but farther back |
| 98 | (Miss) Mary Ann MITCHELL | SE corner, Elm/Houston | 3 | 2 & 3 | — | "few seconds" | 1/18/64; 4/7/64 | Archives, CD 329, p. 24; 6H175-177 | — |
| 99 | Joe R. MOLINA | Top step, entrance, TSBD | 3 | 2 & 3 | "sort of, kind of from the west" | — | 3/25/64 | 6H368-373 | — |
| 100 | Luke MOONEY | Sheriff's Office, Main St. | 3 | 2 & 3 | KNOLL: "the RR yard" | — | 11/23/63; 3/25/64 | 3H281-290 | — |
| 101 | Lillian MOONEYHAM | Window, Criminal Cts. Bldg. | 3 | 2 & 3 | — | — | 1/10/64 | Archives, CD 329, pp. 17-18; 24H531 | — |
| 102 | T. E. MOORE | SE corner, Elm/Houston | 3 | — | — | — | 1/10/64 | 24H534 | — |

| No. | Name | Location | No. of shots | Direction | Grouping | Interval | Date | Reference | Remarks |
|---|---|---|---|---|---|---|---|---|---|
| 103 | (Mrs.) Mary Ann MOORMAN | S. side of Elm St. | 3 or 4 | — | — | — | 11/22/'63; 11/23/63 | WFAA-TV tape; 19H487; 22H838; 24H217 | — |
| 104 | (Mrs.) Marie MUCHMORE | NW corner, Houston, Main | 3 | — | — | — | 2/18/64 | Archives, CD 735, I, p. 8 | — |
| 105 | F. Lee MUDD | N. side, Elm St., 75'-100' W. of TSBD | 2 or 3 | — | — | — | 1/28/64 | Archives, CD 385, p. 18; 24H538 | — |
| 106 | Joe E. MURPHY | Stemmons Freeway overpass | 3 | — | — | — | 4/8/64 | 6H256-260 | — |
| 107 | Thomas J. MURPHY | RR overpass | 2 | KNOLL: "spot just west of TSBD" | — | — | 3/20/64 | 22H835 | — |
| 108 | (Mrs.) Gayle NEWMAN | N. side of Elm St., halfway to overpass | 3 | KNOLL | 1 & 2 | — | 11/22/'63; 11/24/63 | Tape; WFAA-TV tape; 22H842 | 1st shot hit JFK; 2nd shot hit Connally; 3rd shot: Kennedy head shot |
| 109 | (Mrs.) Jean NEWMAN | N. side of Elm St., halfway sign to TSBD | 2+ | — | — | — | 11/22/'63; 11/28/63 | 19H489; 22H843; 24H218 | Saw JFK put up elbows after 1st shot; can't say there were more than 2 shots |
| 110 | William Eugene NEWMAN | N. side of Elm St., halfway to overpass | 3 | KNOLL: "garden directly behind me" | 1 & 2 | — | 11/22/'63; 11/24/63 | Tape; WFAA-TV tape; 22H842; 24H219 | — |
| 111 | Orville O. NIX | Near Main/Houston corner, on Main | 3 | KNOLL | — | — | 12/3/'63; 1/29/64 | Mark Lane film interview; 24H539 | — |
| 112 | Harold NORMAN | 5th fl., TSBD | 3 | TSBD: "heard shells falling" | — | — | 12/4/63 | 3H186-198; 17H208; 22H666 | — |
| 113 | Lawrence F. O'BRIEN | Motorcade, 6 cars back | 3 | — | "evenly spaced" | — | 5/26/64 | 7H457-472 | — |
| 114 | Kenneth P. O'DONNELL | Motorcade, pres. follow-up car | 3 | "right rear" | 1 & 2 | 5-6 sec. | 5/18/64 | 7H440-457 | — |

| WITNESS NO. | NAME | LOCATION | NO. OF SHOTS | BUNCHING OF SHOTS | DIRECTION OF SOUND/SHOTS | TOTAL TIME OF SHOTS | DATE OF REPORT | REFERENCES | REMARKS |
|---|---|---|---|---|---|---|---|---|---|
| 115 | J. L. OXFORD | Sheriff's Office, Main St. | — | — | — | — | 11/23/63 | 19H530 | "man told us he had seen smoke up in the corner of the fence" |
| 116 | Sam PATERNOSTRO | 2nd fl., Criminal Cts. Bldg. | 3 | 2 & 3 | — | 5-7 sec. | 1/20/64 | 24H536 | — |
| 117 | Eddie PIPER | 1st fl., TSBD | 2/3 | — | TSBD | — | 11/23/63 | 6H382-386; 19H499 | "the shots seemed to me like they came from up inside the building" |
| 118 | Charles Polk PLAYER | Inside Sheriff's Office, Main St. | 3 | — | — | — | 11/22/63 | 19H515 | — |
| 119 | Nolan H. POTTER | RR overpass | 3 | — | — | — | 3/19/64 | 22H834 | "saw smoke in front of the TSBD rising above the trees" |
| 120 | James W. POWELL | Half block E. of Elm / Houston | possibly 3 shots | — | — | — | 3/1/64 | Archives, CD 206, p. 20 | — |
| 121 | David F. POWERS | Motorcade, pres. follow-up car | 3 | — | — | 5-6 sec. | 5/18/64 | 7H472-474 | 1st impression: shots came from right and overhead; fleeting impression that noise came from front |
| 122 | J. C. PRICE | Roof, Terminal Annex Bldg. | 6 | — | — | 5+ min. | 11/22/63 | 19H492 | A volley; then 5 minutes later, another shot |
| 123 | G. W. RACKLEY, Sr. | 2 blocks N. of Elm / Houston | — | — | — | — | 4/8/64 | 6H273-277 | Saw pigeons fly up around Trinity Building |
| 124 | Madie Belle REESE | Steps, TSBD | 3 | — | — | — | 3/20/64 | 22H669 | — |
| 125 | Robert REID | Window, Criminal Cts. Bldg. | 3 | — | — | — | 1/10/64 | 24H532 | — |
| 126 | (Mrs.) R. A. REID | Adjacent to TSBD | 3 | — | — | — | 11/22/63 | Archives, CD 5, p. 27; 24H223 | — |

| | | | No. shots | Spacing | Origin | Sec. | Date | Reference | Comment |
|---|---|---|---|---|---|---|---|---|---|
| 127 | Frank E. REILLY | RR overpass | 3 | — | KNOLL: "trees on N. side Elm St." | — | 12/19/63; 4/8/64 | *Archives*, CD 205, p. 29; 6H227-231 | — |
| 128 | Joe Henry RICH | Motorcade, V. pres. follow-up car | 3+ | — | — | — | 11/28/63 | 18H800 | — |
| 129 | James Eliot ROMACK | Houston/Ross construction work | 3 | "spaced evenly" | TSBD | 6-8 sec. | 4/8/64 | *Archives*, CD 897, I, pp. 35-36; 6H277-284 | — |
| 130 | Arnold Louis ROWLAND | Houston St., 200' from corner, Elm/Houston | 3 | 2 & 3 | KNOLL: "RR yards" | 7-12 sec. | 11/23/63 | 24H224; 26H166 | — |
| 131 | (Mrs.) Barbara ROWLAND | Houston St., 200' from corner, Elm/Houston | 3 | Conflict | — | — | 11/22/63; 4/7/64 | 6H177-191; 19H493 | — |
| 132 | (Mrs.) Robert E. SANDERS | Door of TSBD | 3 | — | TSBD: "building above her" | — | 11/24/63 | 22H844 | — |
| 133 | William H. SHELLEY | Entrance of TSBD | 3 | 2 & 3 | KNOLL: "came from the west" | — | 11/22/63; 4/7/64 | 6H327-334; 24H226 | — |
| 134 | Edward SHIELDS | 601 Main St., on sidewalk | 3 | — | — | — | 3/23/64 | 22H674 | — |
| 135 | James L. SIMMONS | RR overpass | 3 | — | TSBD | — | 3/19/64 | 22H833 | "saw exhaust fumes or smoke near embankment in front of TSBD" |
| 136 | (Miss) Marilyn SITZMAN | On wall of colonnade | 2 | — | — | — | 11/23/63 | Tape; 19H535 | Saw 1st shot hit JFK; saw 3rd head shot; missed Connally shot |
| 137 | Royce SKELTON | RR overpass | 4 | 1 & 2; then 3 & 4 | — | — | 11/22/63; 12/18/63; 4/8/64 | *Archives*, CD 205, p. 26; 6H236-238; 19H496 | "saw 2 shots or fragments hit the pavement" |
| 138 | Garland Glenwill SLACK | On Houston St. | 2 | — | — | — | 11/22/63 | 19H495 | Shots sounded like they came from deep within a building |

| WITNESS NO. | NAME | LOCATION | NO. OF SHOTS | BUNCHING OF SHOTS | DIRECTION OF SOUND/SHOTS | TOTAL TIME OF SHOTS | DATE OF REPORT | REFERENCES | REMARKS |
|---|---|---|---|---|---|---|---|---|---|
| 139 | Edgar Leon SMITH | Houston St., near Houston / Elm corner | 3 | — | KNOLL: "monument" | — | 7/24/64 | 7H565-569; 22H604 | — |
| 140 | Joe Marshall SMITH | Facing traffic on Elm St. | — | — | KNOLL: "behind the concrete structure" | — | 7/23/64 | 7H531-539; 22H600 | — |
| 141 | L. C. SMITH | Sheriff's Office, Main St. | 3 | — | — | — | 11/22/63 | 19H516 | Woman told him shots came from fence on N. side of Elm St. |
| 142 | (Mrs.) Ruth SMITH | 2nd fl., old courthouse | 3 | 2 & 3 | — | — | 12/21/63 | Archives, CD 206 | — |
| 143 | John J. SOLON | Entrance to old courthouse | 3 | 2 & 3 | — | 5 1/2 sec. | 1/8/64 | 24H535 | "fast shot, pause; 2 shots; then echoes of shots" |
| 144 | (Mrs.) Pearl SPRINGER | Houston, near Elm / Houston | 3 | 2 & 3 | — | — | 12/5/63 | 24H523 | — |
| 145 | Sarah D. STANTON | Steps, TSBD | 3 | — | — | — | 3/18/64 | 22H675 | — |
| 146 | Malcolm SUMMERS | Terrace of park N. of Elm St. | — | — | — | — | 11/23/63 | 19H500 | Saw Pres. slump after 1st shot |
| 147 | Allan SWEATT | Main St., 30' E. of Houston / Main | 3 | 2 & 3 | "vicinity of Elm / Houston" | 9-11 sec. | 11/23/63 | 19H531-533 | — |
| 148 | James Thomas TAGUE | E. of underpass on Main St. | 3 | — | KNOLL: "over at monument to his left" | — | 7/23/64 | 7H552-558 | Thinks 2nd or 3rd shot nicked him |
| 149 | (Mrs.) Ruth THORNTON | 2nd fl., Criminal Cts. Bldg. | 3 | 2 & 3 | — | — | 1/20/64 | 24H537 | — |

| No. | Name | Location | Floor | Number/Spacing | Direction | Date | Reference | Remarks |
|---|---|---|---|---|---|---|---|---|
| 150 | L. C. TODD | Sheriff's Office, Main St. | 3 | — | — | 11/27/63 | 19H543 | — |
| 151 | Roy Sansom TRULY | Near front of TSBD | 3 | 2 & 3 | KNOLL: "vicinity of RR or WPA project" | 11/23/63; 3/24/64 | 3H219-222; 24H227 | — |
| 152 | James R. UNDERWOOD | Motorcade, Press car, halfway between Main & Elm | 3 | — | "overhead" | 4/1/64 | 6H167-171 | — |
| 153 | Ralph WALTERS | Sheriff's Office, Main St. | 2 | — | — | 11/23/63 | 19H505-506 | — |
| 154 | (Mrs.) Carolyn WALTHER | Houston St., 50'-60' from Elm/Houston | 4 | 1-2; 3, 4 | TSBD | 12/5/63 | 24H522 | — |
| 155 | Eddy Raymond WALTHERS | Sheriff's Office, Main St. | 3 | — | — | 11/22/63 | 7H544-552; 19H518-521 | — |
| 156 | Jack WATSON | Main St., 30' E. of Houston/Main | 3 | "evenly spaced" | — | 11/22/63 | 19H522 | — |
| 157 | Harry WEATHERFORD | Sheriff's Office, Main St. | 3 | — | KNOLL: "RR yards" | 11/23/63 | 19H502-504 | — |
| 158 | Seymour WEITZMAN | Near Main/Houston | 3 | 2 & 3 | KNOLL | 11/23/63; 4/1/64 | *Archives*, CD 5, pp. 126-127; 7H105-109; 24H228 | Picked up piece of skull 8-12" from S. curb of Elm St. |
| 159 | (Miss) Karen WESTBROOK | N. side of Elm St., halfway to underpass | — | — | — | 3/19/64 | 22H679 | Car "almost directly in front of where I was standing when I heard the first explosion" |
| 160 | Bonnie Ray WILLIAMS | 5th fl. window, TSBD | 3 | 2 & 3 | TSBD | 11/22/63; 3/24/64 | *Archives*, CD 5, pp. 330-333; 3H161-184; 24H229 | In Nov. 22 statement speaks only of 2 shots; "sounded like they came from just above us" |

| WITNESS NO. | NAME | LOCATION | NO. OF SHOTS | BUNCHING OF SHOTS | DIRECTION OF SOUND/SHOTS | TOTAL TIME OF SHOTS | DATE OF REPORT | REFERENCES | REMARKS |
|---|---|---|---|---|---|---|---|---|---|
| 161 | Otis Neville WILLIAMS | Steps, TSBD | 3 | — | Courthouse | — | 3/19/64 | *Archives,* CD 5, p. 64; 22H683 | — |
| 162 | (Miss) Linda Kay WILLIS | S. side of Elm St., near corner | 3 | Conflict | — | — | 7/22/64 | Tape; 7H498-499 | 1st shot hit JFK; 2nd, couldn't see; 3rd hit JFK head. No more after 3rd! |
| 163 | Philip L. WILLIS | S. side of Elm St., near corner | 3 | 3 shots, 2 sec. apart | TSBD: "high up, across street" | 6 sec. | 7/22/64 | Tape; CD 1245, pp. 44-48; 7H492-497 | — |
| 164 | (Mrs.) Philip L. WILLIS | Dealey Plaza Pavilion | 3 | "evenly spaced" | — | — | 6/19/64 | Tape; CD 1245, pp. 44-45 | — |
| 165 | Steven F. WILSON | 3rd fl., TSBD; window shut | 3, no more, no less | 1 & 2 | "west end of building or colonnade" | less than 5 sec. | 3/19/64; 3/25/64 | *Archives,* CD 329, p. 27; 22H685-686 | "shots did not sound like they came from above me" |
| 166 | Walter Luke WINBORN | RR overpass | 3 | — | — | — | 3/18/64 | 22H833 | — |
| 167 | John WISEMAN | Sheriff's Office, Main St. | 3 | — | — | — | 11/23/63 | 19H535 | — |
| 168 | Mary Elizabeth WOODWARD | 2nd lamp post on Elm St. | 3 | 2 & 3 | — | — | 12/7/63 | 24H520 | 1st reaction: above and behind her; 2nd reaction: shots from overpass |
| 169 | James Richard WORRELL | Southwest corner, Elm/Houston | 4 | — | TSBD | 5-6 sec. | 11/22/63; 3/10/64 | *Archives,* CD 19, p. 5; 2H190-201; 16H959 | — |
| 170 | Milton T. WRIGHT | Motorcade, Mayor Cabell's car | — | — | — | — | 11/28/63 | 18H802 | 1st shot, car had turned corner |
| 171 | Senator Ralph YARBOROUGH | Motorcade, V. Pres. car | 3, no more! | Conflict | TSBD: "backward and to the right" | 4½-5 sec. | 7/10/64 | 7H439-440 | — |
| 172 | (first name unknown) YATES | Motorcade, corner of Houston/Main | 3 | — | — | — | 11/30/63 | 21H423 | "what sounded like 3 firecrackers which might have been thrown off the overpass" |

| # | Name | Location | No. shots | Which shots | Direction | Seconds | Date | Reference | Remarks |
|---|------|----------|-----------|-------------|-----------|---------|------|-----------|---------|
| 173 | Abraham ZAPRUDER | On wall of colonnade | 2 | — | KNOLL: "back of me" | — | 7/22/64 | WFAA-TV tape; 7H569-576 | Saw 1st shot hit JFK; saw third, head shot; missed Connally shot |
| 174 | F. M. BELL | SW corner, Main/Houston | 3 | *not evenly spaced* | — | — | — | Interview | — |
| | Secret Service: | | | | | | | | |
| 175 | Glen A. BENNETT | Motorcade, follow-up car | 3 | — | — | — | 11/22/63 | 18H760 | 2nd shot hit Kennedy in back 4" down from shoulder; 3rd shot hit Kennedy's head |
| 176 | William R. GREER | Motorcade, driver of Pres. car | 3 | 2 & 3 | TSBD: "from right rear" | — | 11/28/63; 3/9/64 | *Archives*, CD 7, pp. 3-11; 2H112-132; 18H723 | — |
| 177 | George W. HICKEY | Motorcade, follow-up car | 3 | 2 & 3 | — | 4-5 sec. | 11/22/63; 11/30/63 | 18H761-764 | 2nd two shots different in sound |
| 178 | Clinton J. HILL | Motorcade, follow-up car | 2 | — | — | 5 sec. | 11/30/63 | 2H132-144; 18H740-745 | 1st shot right rear into JFK; 2nd shot into head |
| 179 | Thomas L. JOHNS | Motorcade, V. Pres. follow-up car | 3 | — | — | — | 11/29/63 | 18H773-775 | — |
| 180 | Roy H. KELLERMAN | Motorcade, in Pres. car | 3+ | 2 & 3 | — | 5 sec. | 11/29/63; 3/9/64 | 2H61-112; 18H724-727 | — |
| 181 | Samuel A. KINNEY | Motorcade, driver, follow-up car | 3 | — | — | — | 11/22/63; 11/30/63 | 18H730-731 | — |
| 182 | Jerry D. KIVETT | Motorcade, V. Pres. follow-up car | 3 | — | — | — | 11/29/63 | 18H778-781 | — |
| 183 | Paul E. LANDIS | Motorcade, follow-up car | 2 | — | — | 4 or 5 sec. | 11/27/63; 11/30/63 | 18H751-757 | 1st shot, over right shoulder; 2nd (head) shot "somewhere towards the front right hand side" |
| 184 | Winston G. LAWSON | Motorcade, lead car | 3 | 2 & 3 | — | 5 sec. | 11/23/63; 12/1/63 | 4H317-358; 17H628-629 | — |

| WITNESS NO. | NAME | LOCATION | NO. OF SHOTS | BUNCHING OF SHOTS | DIRECTION OF SOUND /SHOTS | TOTAL TIME OF SHOTS | DATE OF REPORT | REFERENCES | REMARKS |
|---|---|---|---|---|---|---|---|---|---|
| 185 | William T. McINTYRE | Motorcade, follow-up car | 3 | — | — | — | 11/29/63 | 18H746-747 | 3rd and last shot hits Pres. in head |
| 186 | John D. READY | Motorcade, follow-up car | — | — | — | — | 11/22/63 | 18H749 | Shots appeared to come from right rear side, but not certain |
| 187 | Emory P. ROBERTS | Motorcade, follow-up car, front seat | 3 | — | — | — | 11/29/63 | 18H734-739 | — |
| 188 | Forrest V. SORRELS | Motorcade, lead car | 3, no more, no less | 2 & 3 2:1 ratio | KNOLL: "look up on the terrace there" | 6 sec. | 11/28/63; 5/7/64 | 7H332-360; 21H548 | — |
| 189 | Warren W. TAYLOR | Motorcade, V. Pres. follow-up car | 3 | 2 & 3 | — | | 11/29/63 | 18H782-784 | — |
| 190 | Rufus W. YOUNGBLOOD | Motorcade, V. Pres. car | 3 | 2 & 3 | TSBD: "right rear" | 5 sec. | 11/29/63 | 2H144-155; 18H766-772 | — |

## OTHER WITNESSES MENTIONED IN PRESS REPORTS

| | | | | | | | |
|---|---|---|---|---|---|---|---|
| 191. | Jack BELL | N. Y. Times | 11/23/63 | 197. | Ed JOHNSON | Ft. Worth Star Telegram | 11/23/63 |
| 192. | Richard O. BOTHUN | Dallas Morning News | 11/23/63 | 198. | Robert McNEILL | N. Y. Times | 11/23/63 |
| 193. | Jerry BROSEH | Dallas Morning News | 11/23/63 | 199. | Barbara RICHARDSON | Ft. Worth Star Telegram | 11/23/63 |
| 194. | Peggy BURNEY | Dallas Times | 11/23/63 | 200. | Norman SIMILAS | N. Y. Times | 11/23/63 |
| 195. | Robert CLARK | N. Y. Times | 11/23/63 | 201. | Alan SMITH | N. Y. Times | 11/23/63 |
| 196. | Robert HILBURN | Ft. Worth Star Telegram | 11/23/63 | | | | |

## OTHER WITNESSES MENTIONED IN GOVERNMENT REPORTS

Although the names of the following witnesses appear in official government reports, the witnesses were either not questioned by any investigative agency, or were questioned so superficially as not to elicit significant data.

| | | | |
|---|---|---|---|
| 202. | J. B. ALLEN 22H601 | 207. | Robert BENEVIDES 19H512 |
| 203. | Aurelia ALONZO 24H520 | 208. | Jack BROOKS 17H616 |
| 204. | Thomas ALYEA 25H875 | 209. | Margaret BROWN 24H520 |
| 205. | Carolyn ARNOLD 22H635 | 210. | Edna CASE 22H639 |
| 206. | Lindley BECKWORTH 17H616 | 211. | James M. CHANEY 3H266 |

# APPENDIX B

(This appendix was prepared by William Hoffman)

# CALCULATIONS FROM ZAPRUDER FRAMES 301–330

## INTRODUCTION

The original objective of the study of the Zapruder film was to determine quantitatively the three-dimensional motion of the President's head from frames 301 to 330. However, due to the position of the photographer relative to his subject, precise measurements were possible only along a longitudinal axis through the presidential vehicle. The calculations based upon these one-dimensional measurements therefore yield only minimum values: the actual values of the velocity and acceleration, which are vector quantities, are probably larger.

## THEORY

### OPTICS

The methods of photographic measurement used in this study are the same as those used in photographic analysis during the past seventy years.* As the photographic plate is a perspective view of the object it represents, it is a two-dimensional copy of the original that differs from it only in scale. Once this has been determined, the measured image of the object under study can be used to compute its actual dimensions. The law governing this relationship is

$$l = l' \ (L/L'), \qquad (1)$$

where $l$ is the actual length of the unknown object, $l'$ is the length of its photographic image, $L$ is the actual length of the reference unit, and $L'$ is the length of its photographic image.

This formula is strictly valid only when the object of unknown dimensions and the reference unit are located at the same distance from the camera lens and have the same orientation. If these "object distances" are not equal, a correction to the above formula must be made.

Let $L''$ be the length the reference unit would have if both it and the unknown object were at an equal distance from the photographic lens. Then, application of a fundamental principle of geometry (corresponding parts of similar triangles are proportional) to Figure I shows that

$$L''/L = (H - d)/H \qquad (2)$$

or, after rearrangement, that

$$L'' = L(1 - d/H). \qquad (3)$$

Substituting $L''$ for $L$ in Equation (1) yields the following expression for the actual length of the object:

$$l = l'(L/L') \ (1 - d/H). \qquad (4)$$

From this equation it is apparent that as the object approaches the reference unit, the above expression reduces to Equation (1). This fact shows that the first equation is a special form of the more general case. Equation (4) remains valid even when the surfaces of the object being measured are not perpendicular to the focal axis, because the ratio of line segments remains constant for any perspective view of that line.

### DYNAMICS

Newton's second law states that acceleration is directly proportional to the resultant force and *is in the same direction as that force.*\* To determine the direction of the resultant force applied to the President's head in the small time interval centered about frame 313, it was therefore necessary to calculate the acceleration of the President's head through successive frames. Because the photographs were actually made at small time intervals (.0546 second in duration), the parameters calculated from them are time averages; the actual acceleration

---

* E. Deville (ed.), *Photographic Surveying* (Ottawa, 1895).

* Keith R. Symon, *Mechanics* (2nd ed.; Reading, Mass.: Addison-Wesley Publishing Co., Inc., 1960), p. 7.

during this time interval is greater * than the results presented here, but due to the discrete nature of the data, the resolution cannot be improved. Our results, then, yield *minimum* values for velocity and acceleration.

As acceleration is defined as the time rate of change of velocity, it is necessary to calculate the velocity immediately before and after the frame under study to determine the average acceleration at this point. The velocity along the axis of the car (the axis along which the measurements were made) can be calculated from the equation

$$V_{n,n+1} = (l_{n+1} - l_n)/.0546, \quad (5)$$

where $n$ is the number of the frame under study, $V_{n,n+1}$ is the velocity between frame $n$ and $n+1$, $l_n$ and $l_{n+1}$ are the distances between the back of the President's head and a fixed point on the car in frames $n$ and $n+1$ respectively, and .0546 is the elapsed time between consecutive frames measured in seconds.

After Equation (5) has been used to calculate the velocity between successive frames, the acceleration can be determined theoretically from the relation

$$a_n = [(V_{n+1,n} - V_{n,n-1})^2$$
$$+ (V_{n+1,n}^\perp - V_{n,n-1}^\perp)^2]^{1/2}$$
$$\times (1/.0546), \quad (6)$$

where $a_n$ is the acceleration in frame $n$ and $V_{n+1,n}^\perp$ and $V_{n,n-1}^\perp$ are the components of the velocity along an axis perpendicular to the longitudinal axis of the car.

Because precise measurements of the transverse motion could not be made, this component was neglected and only a *minimum* value for the acceleration was calculated. This procedure assumes that

$$V_{n+1,n}^\perp = V_{n,n-1}^\perp = 0. \quad (7)$$

Combining Equations (5) and (7) gives

$$a_n = (l_{n+1} + l_{n-1} - 2l_n) \times (1/.0546)^2. \quad (8)$$

This equation yields a minimum value of

---

* Because a collision between the President's head and a bullet would take place in a few milliseconds, the values may be as much as 30 times too small.

the average acceleration because of the implicit assumption of one-dimensional motion.

Viewed as a motion picture, however, the film gives the distinct impression that while the initial velocity is in the forward direction, the final velocity is more nearly at an angle of 45 degrees to the longitudinal axis of the car. If this were the case, then for frame 313

$$V_{n+1,n}^\perp = V_{n+1,n}$$
$$V_{n,n-1} = 0. \quad (9)$$

Using these values in Equation (6) gives

$$a_n = [(V_{n+1,n} - V_{n,n-1})^2$$
$$+ (V_{n+1,n})^2]^{1/2} \times (1/.0546). \quad (10)$$

## METHOD

### OPTICS

To determine the parameters necessary to calculate the motion of the President's head from frame 301 to frame 330, three sets of measurements were made on 8-x-10-inch enlargements of the 8-millimeter Zapruder film. (Frame 318 was too blurred for exact measurements to be made, so that no data were obtainable for this frame.) First the length of the reference unit, the distance between the most forward point on the left-rear hand-hold and the upper edge of the back seat directly in front of it (the line $AB$), was measured. Then the distance between the back of the President's head and each of the same two fixed points on the car was determined (lines $AC$ and $BC$ respectively). Two measurements of the head position were made in order to procure an independent, internal verification of the data. The same two fixed points were used in order to minimize the error inherent in attempting to fix a location.

To make the measurements as precise as possible, the endpoints of each line were first marked with pinholes. This procedure is necessary as all perception of detail is lost in the blur of the emulsion when photographs are viewed under a microscope. A strip of Codex millimeter graph paper was then attached to the photograph so that one edge connected the two pinholes. At this point the entire photograph was placed on the stage of a Bausch and Lomb dissecting microscope. A scale, also manufactured by Bausch and Lomb, with divisions at every tenth of a millimeter was then aligned with the graph paper over one of the pinholes, and with the microscope adjusted for maximum magnification ($\times 45$), the hole was located to within 25 microns (1 meter is equivalent to 1 million microns). The scale was then aligned with the graph paper at the other pinhole to complete the measurement. This same technique was used to determine the length of the three distances on each of the twenty-nine frames.

The perpendicular distance from the camera to the reference unit (represented previously as the quantity $(H - d)$) was obtained from the chart of Dealey Plaza used by the Warren Commission, and was found to be 72.7 feet.

The perpendicular distance between line $AC$ (a line drawn from the President's head to the fixed point on the car) and line $AB$ (the reference unit) was taken from a scale drawing of the presidential vehicle obtained from the National Archives; this distance, previously symbolized as $d$, is 3.30 feet. The actual length of the reference unit (represented as $L$) was also taken from this drawing.

## RESULTS

When all the measurements were completed, the data were processed on an IBM 1620 computer. A numerical example may make these calculations more meaningful. Using values for the constants $L$, $d$, and $H$ (50.141 inches, 3.30 feet, and 72.7 feet respectively) in addition to the values of $l'$ (line $AC$) and $L'$ (line $AB$) for frame 301 (59.250 millimeters and 50.350 millimeters respectively) in Equation (4) gives

$$l = l' \, (L/L') \, (1 - d/H)$$

$$= 59.250 \text{ mm.} \times (50.141 \text{ in.}/50.350 \text{ mm.})$$

$$\times (1.0 - 3.30 \text{ ft.}/7.60 \text{ ft.}) = 56.467 \text{ in.}$$

for the real distance between the back of the President's head and the leading edge of the left rear handhold. Using a method analogous to that outlined above, the computer processed the raw data to obtain actual lengths: the data and the results are summarized in the chart below.

| | DATA: Photographic Measurements (Millimeters) | | RESULTS: Actual Lengths (Inches) | |
|---|---|---|---|---|
| Frame No. | Line AB | Line AC | Line AC | Line BC |
| 301 | 50.350 | 59.250 | 56.467 | 8.482 |
| 302 | 50.775 | 59.770 | 56.486 | 8.501 |
| 303 | 51.325 | 60.350 | 56.423 | 8.438 |
| 304 | 51.875 | 60.825 | 56.264 | 8.279 |
| 305 | 52.275 | 60.625 | 55.650 | 7.665 |
| 306 | 52.550 | 61.050 | 55.747 | 7.762 |
| 307 | 52.700 | 61.450 | 55.952 | 7.967 |
| 308 | 53.075 | 62.075 | 56.122 | 8.137 |
| 309 | 54.050 | 62.575 | 55.553 | 7.568 |
| 310 | 54.250 | 63.100 | 55.813 | 7.828 |
| 311 | 54.625 | 63.200 | 55.518 | 7.533 |
| 312 | 51.300 | 59.525 | 55.678 | 7.693 |
| 313 | 55.400 | 66.800 | 57.859 | 9.874 |
| 314 | 55.125 | 65.850 | 57.321 | 9.336 |
| 315 | 55.025 | 64.500 | 56.248 | 8.263 |
| 316 | 55.500 | 63.640 | 55.023 | 7.038 |
| 317 | 56.225 | 62.475 | 53.319 | 5.334 |
| 318 | NO DATA AVAILABLE | | | |
| 319 | 56.333 | 59.008 | 50.264 | 2.279 |
| 320 | 56.350 | 58.575 | 49.880 | 1.895 |
| 321 | 55.525 | 57.175 | 49.411 | 1.426 |
| 322 | 55.525 | 57.625 | 49.800 | 1.815 |
| 323 | 52.950 | 55.900 | 50.658 | 2.673 |
| 324 | 51.325 | 55.850 | 52.215 | 4.231 |
| 325 | 50.300 | 55.200 | 52.659 | 4.674 |
| 326 | 50.275 | 56.600 | 54.022 | 6.037 |
| 327 | 49.350 | 56.650 | 55.083 | 7.098 |
| 328 | 48.100 | 56.900 | 56.764 | 8.779 |
| 329 | 47.350 | 57.900 | 58.676 | 10.691 |
| 330 | 45975 | 58.950 | 61.527 | 13.542 |

To calculate a value for the average velocity, one need only apply Equation (5) to the above results. For frames 301 and 302,

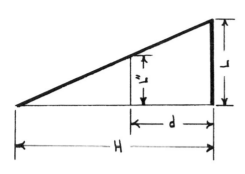

Figure I

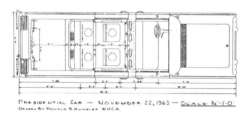

PRESIDENTIAL CAR — NOVEMBER 22, 1963 — SCALE ¾"·1'-0"
DRAWN BY RONALD S. KNOBLES WHCA

Secret Service drawing of presidential limousine.

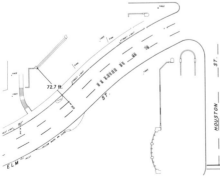

Dealey Plaza. Distance between Zapruder's camera and the President at frame 313.

$$V_{301,302} = (l_{302} - l_{301})/.0546$$
$$= (56.486 - 56.467)/.0546$$
$$= .344 \text{ in./sec.}$$
$$= .0287 \text{ ft./sec.}$$

The same calculations for frames 302 and 303 give

$$V_{302,303} = -.0962 \text{ ft./sec.}$$

These velocity figures can be used in Equation (6) to derive the average acceleration at frame 302.

$$a_{302} = (V_{303,302} - V_{302,301}) \times 1/.0546$$
$$= (-.0962 - .0287) \times 1/.0546$$
$$= -2.26 \text{ ft./sec.}^2$$

Graphs showing the position of the President's head relative to each of the two fixed positions on the car as a function of time are given on page 91. These plots show that until frame 313 the President's head remains almost stationary relative to the limousine in which he is riding. Suddenly, between frames 312 and 313, his head is impelled forward 2.2 inches, which corresponds to a minimum average velocity of 3.3 ft./sec. The average forward acceleration, as calculated over the time interval from frame 311 to frame 313, is at least 69.6 ft./sec.[2] By frame 314 this forward motion has been reversed, and the President's head has a velocity in the opposite direction. Between frames 313 and 314 its average velocity is −0.8 ft./sec., and its average backward acceleration (measured over the corresponding time interval) is at least −75.6 ft./sec.[2] This movement toward the rear of the car remains uniform until frame 319, when the President's left shoulder first contacts the seat cushion, reversing the rearward movement.

A graph of the acceleration in frames 306 to 317 was .constructed from Equations (6) and (8), and is presented on page 93. The profile of this graph indicates tnat both forward and backward movements are the products of impulsive forces.* Therefore, the acceleration as

---

* For a more detailed explanation of this point see David Halliday and Robert Resnick, *Physics* (New York: John Wiley & Sons, Inc., 1963).

calculated from initial and final velocities averaged over larger time intervals is more representative than the previous calculations of the resultant forces. This is due to the statistical uncertainty in the location of any particular point. Using a value for the final velocity averaged over frames 313 to 319, the average backward acceleration is found to be $-94.7$ ft./sec.$^2$ for one-dimensional motion, and $-100.3$ ft./sec.$^2$ for a final velocity, which is at an angle of 45 degrees to the longitudinal axis of the car.

The calculations show an initial forward acceleration followed immediately by a backward acceleration. According to Newton's second law, these accelerations are directly proportional to and, more important, in the *same direction* as the resultant impressed forces that caused them. Therefore, these calculations prove that two impressed forces acted on the President's head within 100 milliseconds of each other. The first force drove his head forward along the longitudinal axis of the car, while the second drove it backward and to his left. This second force has terminated by frame 314.

## VARIANCE

To estimate the variance associated with the measurement process, twenty lengths were selected at random to be remeasured. The standard deviation was 21 microns. This sets the 95 percent confidence limits at $\pm 41$ microns.

The second series of measurements did not involve a replacement of the pinholes. The variance associated with this process must therefore be examined separately. As the validity of the results depends upon the degree to which they accurately reflect the time rate of change of position, and not the position itself, it is only the reproducibility of the positioning of the pinhole that determines the error. After a pinhole had been placed on the photograph the experimenter occasionally found it necessary to relocate it in order to make it more accurately reflect the true position of the endpoint. As these shifts were sometimes as small as 100 microns, this length was used as the upper limit of the variance associated with each hole. As two holes define a distance, the total variance associated with each length* is about 153 microns. When this figure is used to compute the maximum total uncertainty in $l$, the result is

$$\triangle l = .132 \text{ in.} \qquad (11)$$

This value means that the maximum uncertainty in any value of the average acceleration due to the process of measurement is 7.35 ft./sec.$^2$ That these variance estimates are extremely conservative is shown by the fact that calculations based upon each of the two independent reference points agree to within 2 percent.

* W. E. Demings, *Statistical Adjustment of Data* (New York: John Wiley & Sons, Inc., 1943).

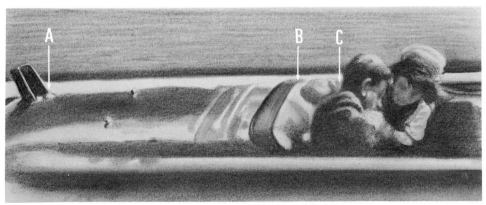

Z312      Zapruder frame 312 with points A, B, and C.    SKETCH

# APPENDIX C

(This appendix was prepared by William Hoffman.)

## CALCULATION OF VELOCITY OF PRESIDENTIAL VEHICLE FROM ZAPRUDER FRAMES 301–330

### INTRODUCTION

A secondary objective of the study of the Zapruder film was to obtain a quantitative description of the motion of the President's car during the time interval centered about frame 313.

The methods used for this analysis are essentially the same as those discussed in Appendix B. Several fixed objects were located in the background of each frame. The distances between these objects and a fixed reference point on the car itself was measured along an axis parallel to the direction of motion.

As the experimenters had no means of measuring the distance from the photographic lens to the background references (symbolized by $H$ in Appendix B), Equation (4) of that section could not be applied to the data. Nevertheless, the results are completely adequate to determine accurately ratios of car velocities at different times, and hence whether the velocity is constant over the interval Z301-330. The direct use of Equations 1 and 5 of Appendix B gives only an approximate value for the car's average velocity.

The dynamical analysis was completed in the light of the results found in Appendix B. To determine the degree to which the reported acceleration figure for the President's head reflects the mo-tion of the car, the acceleration of this vehicle was calculated at frame 313.

### RESULTS

The results are presented in the graph shown below. They indicate that, to within experimental variance the car maintained a uniform velocity during this time interval. The velocity on the graph is about 8 mi./hr., and the average acceleration from frame 313 to frame 325 is 3.18 ft./sec.[2] Rough estimates of $d$ and $H$ in the correction factor $(1 + d/H)$ suggest that the actual figures are closer to 11 mi./hr. and 4.2 ft./sec.[2] respectively.*

### VARIANCE

Experimental variance in these calculations is due largely to the number of measurements involved and to the use and alignment of several sets of axes. A measurement of the standard deviation was made by using several sets of objects in the background as references simultaneously. As $\sigma = 475$ microns, the 95 percent confidence limits are ±930 microns, which corresponds to a maximum uncertainty of about 1 mi./hr. and 27 ft./sec.[2]

---

* The subtraction sign in Equation (4) of Appendix B has been replaced with a plus sign as the reference unit must now be 'moved" in the opposite direction.

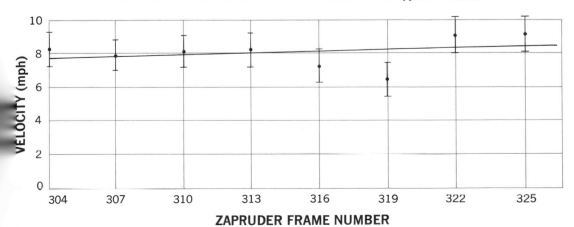

# APPENDIX D

# A CRITIQUE OF PRESIDENT KENNEDY'S AUTOPSY
## by
## Cyril H. Wecht, M.D., LL.B.

Had President Kennedy been a European head of state, his government would have appointed the most eminent forensic pathologist in the country to conduct the autopsy. As assistants, such a man would have had two or three other forensic experts or heads of medico-legal institutes. It is history's profound loss that men of this caliber were not appointed to perform the President's autopsy. Had they been, nearly all the troubling questions about the assassination which continue to vex us today could have been settled at the outset with scientific precision.

## CHOICE OF PATHOLOGISTS

The specialty of forensic pathology is recognized by the American Board of Pathology, which gives subspecialty examinations in this field. The practice, experience, and knowledge of a forensic pathologist are to a great extent quite different from those of a general "hospital" pathologist. The hospital pathologist spends much of his time examining organs or tissue slides as a means to establishing diagnoses on living patients. When he is called upon to do an autopsy, it usually concerns a patient who has succumbed in the hospital from some natural disease. The autopsy most often is performed to confirm a diagnosis already arrived at, or for research purposes.

The forensic pathologist operates within quite a different setting. Often associated with the medical examiner's office, his job is not to verify an already arrived at diagnosis, but to establish independently the exact cause and manner of death.

Dr. Wecht is Research Professor of Law and Director, Institute of Forensic Sciences, Duquesne University School of Law, and Chief Forensic Pathologist, Allegheny County Coroner's Office. In February 1967 he was elected Secretary of the Pathology and Biology Section of the American Academy of Forensic Sciences. Dr. Wecht is also Director of the Pittsburgh Institute of Legal Medicine.

Whereas the hospital pathologist's milieu is natural disease, the forensic pathologist's setting is very often violent death. The expertise and tasks of the two specialties are quite distinct. As my colleague Dr. Milton Helpern, Chief Medical Examiner of New York City, has noted, to give a hospital pathologist a gunshot wound case is "like sending a seven-year-old boy who has taken three lessons on the violin over to the New York Philharmonic and expecting him to perform a Tchaikovsky symphony. He knows how to hold the violin and bow, but he has a long way to go before he can make music."[1]

It is troubling in the extreme, then, to learn that a hospital pathologist was in charge of the President's autopsy. Commander [now Captain] James J. Humes of Bethesda Naval Hospital directed the autopsy. With the exception of a single course at the Armed Forces Institute of Pathology, Commander Humes had no special knowledge or expertise in forensic pathology (2H348). His official title was "Director of Laboratories of the Naval Medical School at Naval Medical Center, Bethesda, Md." (2H348). He was assisted by Navy Commander J. Thornton Boswell, like Humes a hospital pathologist with no special experience in medico-legal autopsies. After Commanders Humes and Boswell saw the body and realized how difficult their job would be, Lt. Col. Pierre Finck of the Armed Forces Institute of Pathology was called in to assist. Lt. Col. Finck is an able forensic pathologist, but his experience as of November 1963 had been mainly administrative — limited chiefly to reviewing files, pictures, and records of finished cases. More importantly, his position at the autopsy table on November 22 was extremely difficult. He had been summoned only after the autopsy had begun, and he was working in a Navy hospital under the direction of a Navy doctor.

Given the circumstances, what seems so inexplicable is the fact that not one of a score of available civilian forensic experts was called in to perform the autopsy on President Kennedy. When Presidents Eisenhower or Johnson had medical problems, civilian experts were immediately summoned. In this case, however, a case which might take on the most awesome international political significance, the decision was made to get by with three military pathologists. Yet within one hour's flying time were some of the greatest forensic pathologists in the world. Dr. Russell S. Fisher in Baltimore, Dr. Milton Helpern in New York City, Dr. Joseph W. Spelman in Philadelphia, Dr. Geoffrey T. Mann in Virginia, and Dr. Alan R. Moritz in Cleveland are only some of the people who are located in areas quite close to Washington, D.C., and who could have been called upon by the government to assist. The irony of the situation is that these experts are men the military has called upon countless times in the past. They have lectured at the Armed Forces Institute of Pathology on forensic pathology. These are men the government uses to teach, yet in this autopsy—probably the most important of the century—the government chose not to call on them. Much of the controversy and mystery which enfolds the case owes its origin to this tragic choice.

## CONSEQUENCES OF THE CHOICE

Cdr. Humes's final autopsy report and his subsequent testimony before the Warren Commission reveal mistakes of procedure and technique which only an inexperienced person could make in performing a medico-legal autopsy.

Experienced forensic pathologists do not probe bullet wounds with their fingers, as Cdr. Humes did (2H367), nor do their autopsy reports include newspaper articles as relevant to their findings.[2] The location of the controversial back wound is given from rather unorthodox reference points: "14 cm. from the tip of the right acromion process and 14 cm. below the tip of the right mastoid process" (16H980); experienced forensic patholo-

gists would use the top of the head and the midline of the body to locate such a wound. These technical errors are not important in themselves, but they do reveal the unconventional character of the whole report. Other errors of procedure have greater importance and wider ramifications.

The Bethesda surgeons knew by 4:00 P.M. on the afternoon of November 22 that they would be performing the President's autopsy. The first move of any experienced forensic pathologist at that time would have been to get in touch with the Dallas doctors who had tried to save the President's life. Such a call would have alerted the Bethesda doctors to the existence of a small throat wound, a wound they only learned of the next day (*after* the body was out of their hands) when Humes belatedly called Dr. Malcolm Perry in Dallas. Had they known of this wound on Friday night they might have been more zealous in tracing the course of the bullet which entered the President's back. As it was, when the body left their hands on Friday night they held the *hypothesis* that the bullet that entered the back had fallen out of the wound, an hypothesis they later felt bound to reject. An experienced forensic pathologist does not settle for hypotheses or inferences. Had an experienced forensic pathologist been in the Bethesda autopsy room, he would not have permitted the body to be taken away until he had *traced out* (most likely by dissection) the actual course of the bullet that had entered the President's back.

The official autopsy report contains two omissions which cast a shadow over the whole proceeding. First, the failure to mention the adrenal glands, either grossly or microscopically. There can be no doubt that the adrenal glands were identified and examined; Cdr. Boswell himself has admitted this.[3] I should stress that these glands played no role whatsoever in President Kennedy's death and from that standpoint have no significance. The import of their omission lies in the fact that it makes the entire report susceptible to sincere and serious challenge inasmuch as it is incomplete. Any competent forensic pathologist knows that he cannot afford to have such a glaring omission in his report. Otherwise, his entire examination may become worthless in the eyes of the jury and the judge when such an oversight is pointed out by a skilled defense attorney on cross-examination.

Another deficiency in the overall report (and one directly associated with the murder) concerns the examination of the President's brain. A reading of the supplementary autopsy report on the brain examination discloses that the entire brain was not cut into coronal sections (16H987). Although one small section was excised from the front on the left side, the description indicates that no examination of the brain's left side was performed. This is appalling. We cannot know what injuries were present in the left cerebral hemisphere if no examination was made. No competent forensic pathologist would examine only half a brain, particularly in a case where it had been injured by one or more bullets.

Either way we consider these deficiencies, the picture is not reassuring. If the military pathologists on their own decided not to examine the adrenal glands and the left cerebral hemisphere, then they are to be soundly condemned, and their report is to be strongly criticized. If they were told by their military superiors to make the omissions and obeyed that order, then two things follow: (1) The pathologists and their report are totally discredited, and (2) it becomes comprehensible why civilian medico-legal experts were excluded from the autopsy—they could not have been controlled in this way.

## WHAT CAN WE KNOW?

Given the incomplete and flawed character of the whole autopsy, what can we know of the nature of the President's wounds?

Histological slides taken from the periphery of the bullet holes in the President's upper back and the occipital region of the skull apparently show "coagulation necrosis of the tissues at the wound margins" (16H988). This would be a sure

sign that the holes in question were bullet entry holes (the speed of an entering projectile almost always produces this effect in the immediately surrounding tissue), and that two bullets entered the President's body at these points.

But with the exception of these two facts, everything else—whether the President was hit in the head by one or two bullets, whether the throat wound was caused by a fragment from the head impact, from an entering bullet, or from a transiting one—must remain open to question on the basis of medical evidence alone. Other evidence must be brought to bear if any of these puzzles are to be solved. However, as other evidence accumulates and as the medico-legal expert can begin to weigh the plausibility of alternative hypotheses, two conclusions of the Commission become less plausible.

The first concerns the nature of the head wound or wounds. On the basis of the autopsy report we cannot rule out the possibility that the President was struck on the right front side of the head. Although the official report mentions the microscopic examination of the periphery of the small occipital wound, no mention is made of a similar examination of the periphery of the large gaping wound on the right side of the head. Without such an examination (or, for that matter, without a careful scrutiny of the remaining scalp and hair, which might easily mask a bullet hole) we cannot be sure that there was not a second wound of entrance in the head forward on the right side. I mention this only because of the extremely persuasive evidence on this point in the Zapruder film. I have seen this film in the superior copy owned by *Life* magazine. Quite clearly, the President's body moves sharply backward and to the left under the impact of the fatal shot. It seems to me extremely unlikely that his body would have moved in this direction if he had been struck from above and behind as concluded by the Warren Commission.

The second concerns the back wound. The official conclusion of the military pathologists that a bullet entered the back of the President's neck and emerged from his throat, along with the "single-bullet theory" which it spawned, is brought into question by four different clusters of evidence:

(1) *The location of the back wound.* As mentioned earlier, Humes's official report locates the back wound with respect to two unorthodox reference points—the acromion and the mastoid process. The difficulty with using these two points is that measurements taken from them locate positions which vary from person to person. The same measurements will define different points depending upon the length of neck and width of shoulders of the person involved. Still, it is clear that the location of the back wound as given in the official autopsy report is much higher than the location drawn on the face sheet during the autopsy by Cdr. Boswell. When this discrepancy was pointed out to Boswell, he ascribed it to carelessness. "If I had known at the time that this sketch would become public record," he remarked, "I would have been more careful."4 Clearly, his excuse is unacceptable. It is true that pathologists do not make such sketches on an accurate-scale basis at the time of the autopsy. No one would dispute a matter of an inch or so. But in this case we are talking about completely different parts of the body—his sketch shows a hole in the back, not in the lower neck. In addition, we should remember that Boswell managed to locate properly all the other scars or wounds on the President's body. Why should he make a mistake on only this one wound? And why should his "mistake" align perfectly with the location defined by the holes in the President's clothing, the report of FBI agents Sibert and O'Neill, and the testimony of Secret Service agents Hill, Kellerman, and Greer?

The problem, of course, is that this overwhelming body of evidence marks an entrance hole in the back substantially *lower* than the purported exit in the throat—clearly an impossibility if the shot came from behind and *above* the President.

One additional consideration germane to this point has never before been raised. Both the Secret Service and FBI agents present at the autopsy and Cdr. Humes

himself have pointed out that on November 22 the military doctors thought the bullet that entered the President's back had fallen out during closed chest cardiac massage at Parkland Hospital in Dallas. External cardiac massage is applied on the anterior chest wall at the level of the breast bone. This would define a location more or less directly in front of the spot where all the evidence except the official autopsy report places the back wound. A question which has never been asked Humes and his colleagues is how they concluded the bullet had been forced out during cardiac massage if indeed the hole was not in the back but in the lower neck.

(2) *Size of the throat wound.* Subsequent experiments performed at Edgewood Arsenal disclosed that a bullet fired from Oswald's rifle through sufficient goat flesh to simulate a transit of the President's neck left exit holes over twice the size of entry holes (5H77-78). But the hole in the President's throat (the putative exit hole) was actually smaller (3 to 5 mm. in largest diameter) than the back entry wound (4 by 7 mm.). It is true that exit wounds may sometimes be smaller than entrance wounds, but in this case the very tests ordered by the Commission to buttress the contention of a back to front transit actually militated against the autopsy report's conclusion.

(3) *Lack of metal traces on the President's tie and shirt front.* An FBI examination of a slit in the President's shirt near the collar button and a nick in the tie failed to disclose the presence of any metallic traces (5H60-62). It seems unlikely that a bullet could have transited from back to front without leaving some evidence of its passing at the point of exit.

(4) *The Zapruder film.* My viewing of the Zapruder film at *Life* would suggest that Governor Connally is most likely correct when he says he was hit by a different bullet than the one which struck the President. On the film, the Governor appears to be hit at frame 238—at least ¾ second after the President first shows signs of injury. Clearly, if the President and the Governor were hit by different

bullets, the bullet which struck the President could not have transited his (the President's) body as the Commission concluded.

All this indicates that the autopsy conclusion of a back to front transit has become progressively more unacceptable as the evidence accumulates. Unfortunately, this same evidence does not dictate unambiguously an alternative hypothesis. Any attempt to formulate an alternative hypothesis should take into account the following possibility:

At the beginning of his testimony Cdr. Humes observed that "the photographs and X-Rays were exposed in the morgue of the Naval Medical Center on this night [November 22], and they were not developed, neither the X-Rays nor the photographs" (2H351). Somewhat later in his testimony Humes speaks as if the X-Rays had been developed and were used in the course of the autopsy (2H364, 372). Yet his assertion here that the autopsy was done without their benefit raises the very real possibility that a bullet or bullets may still remain in the President's body. Bullets have a curious way of moving around in the body. Any experienced forensic pathologist can cite a long list of stories of bullets turning up in the oddest places. In many cases total body X-Rays are the only means by which wandering bullets can be located. With respect to the Kennedy autopsy there is conflicting testimony as to whether such X-Rays were developed and used on November 22, and even if they were used it is doubtful whether either of the Bethesda pathologists was experienced enough in gunshot cases to interpret them correctly. Thus the possibility that a bullet or bullets may still remain in the President's body cannot be ruled out. If this were shown to be the case, many problematical aspects of the assassination would become clear.

## THE FUTURE

Can anything be done at this point to clarify the situation?

The autopsy photos and X-Rays are critical. Their examination by qualified experts might throw great light on some of the questions that continue to puzzle us today. If a photograph of the President's back exists, it would definitely settle the controversy over the location of the back wound. Total body X-Rays might reveal the presence of other missiles still in the body. Head X-Rays might help us decide whether or not the President was struck more than once in the head.

The treatment of these photos and X-Rays by the government has been extremely irresponsible. Although they constituted primary evidence of a critical sort, they were never viewed by any member of the Warren Commission or its staff —and this in spite of the fact that they remained in government custody until April 1965.[5] At that time they were turned over to the Kennedy family. In November 1966 this material returned to government custody under an agreement with the family which prohibits non-governmental experts from viewing it until 1971.

Has anyone seen this material?

William Manchester, in an early draft of his book *The Death of a President,* implied that he had examined it.[6] When Richard Goodwin learned that this was false, that Manchester had actually been denied permission to see it, he pressured the author to remove the offending paragraph.[7] The result was a mystifying footnote in the present edition in which Manchester admitted that he had not seen the X-Rays and photos, but had discussed them with three men, each a stranger to the others, who carried "special professional qualifications," and who had examined the material.[8] It would be interesting to know just what "special professional qualifications" these shadowy experts hold. Not one of them is known to either Dr. Milton Helpern or myself, or for that matter (as far as I know) to any other member of the American Academy of Forensic Sciences.

On the day the photos and X-Rays were turned over to the Archives they were viewed by the two Bethesda pathologists, Humes and Boswell, who proudly announced that they confirmed their earlier autopsy findings. However, both are interested parties to the growing controversy surrounding the autopsy, and the earlier cited omissions and deficiencies in the official report render their judgments suspect. More importantly, they are not forensic pathologists and thus are unequipped by either training or experience to interpret the photos and X-Rays correctly.

At the present time, then, there is no credible evidence that any qualified expert has in fact examined these photos and X-Rays. Surely such a situation should be remedied with all due speed. A move in this direction was made by Representative Theodore R. Kupferman of New York. In letters to the Archivist of the United States (Dec. 27, 1966) and to President Johnson (Feb. 16, 1967) he requested permission to view the autopsy photos and X-Rays in company with Dr. Milton Helpern and me.[9] Representative Kupferman's request was turned down both by the executive branch of the government and by Burke Marshall, a lawyer for the Kennedy family.

This refusal to let qualified experts examine the material raises many interesting questions. If the bullet wound in the back is where the autopsy report says it is, then why won't the present administration permit qualified experts to verify this fact? The request was made in a proper and official way by a respected member of the Congress. No one could dispute the fact that Milton Helpern is very likely the most respected forensic pathologist in the world. Clearly, nothing is gained by keeping this evidence sequestered and unexamined when qualified experts are available. Why then are we not permitted to examine it? The present administration in Washington may be able to answer this question. I cannot.

## CONCLUSION

In February 1966 I gave a talk to the American Academy of Forensic Sciences which covered many of the points touched on in this paper. At that time, in spite of the omissions and deficiencies already apparent in the official autopsy report, I nevertheless concluded my talk by saying that I agreed with the essential findings of the Warren Commission. Some eighteen months later, I must now say that I wish I had not written that final paragraph. For no longer can I agree with the essential findings of either the Warren *Report* or the autopsy on which it was based.

The more one analyzes the critical area of the autopsy the more one comes to recognize that the government's handling of the case is fraught with irregularities. The inexplicable unwillingness of officials to permit civilian forensic experts to participate in the autopsy, Humes's burning of his autopsy draft notes on November 24, the omissions and deficiencies which plague the official report itself, the mysterious transmutation of a wound in the upper back into a wound in the lower neck, the Commission's reticence to view the autopsy photos and X-Rays even though they were in government possession, and finally, the refusal of the present administration to permit qualified experts to examine these same photos and X-Rays —it is this concatenation of facts which nurtures the reasonable man's suspicions.

Nor is the autopsy the only part of the case where the government's handling of evidence and testimony lends itself to suspicion. Commission Exhibit 399 is another case in point.

Although this bullet is nearly pristine in appearance and lacking only 2.4 grains of its substance, the Commission concluded that it smashed through both President Kennedy and Governor Connally, causing seven separate wounds, and shattering the Governor's fifth rib and right wrist. From a medico-legal standpoint such a conclusion is utterly unacceptable —bullets which strike two large bones do not remain undeformed. Its unacceptability, moreover, was shown by the Commission's own tests and echoed in the opinions of its ballistic experts. The conclusion was accepted in spite of overwhelming contrary evidence because the single-bullet theory—the keystone of the Commission's case—required it.

Photographs of CE 399 show a slice missing from the nose where a sliver of metal was removed for spectrographic analysis. Had a similar examination of

Governor Connally's clothes been possible, a firm conclusion might have been reached as to whether CE 399 was the bullet which wounded him or whether, alternately, his wounds had been caused by a pristine bullet. Yet Connally's clothes were not available for such a comparison —his suit was dry cleaned and his shirt laundered before any of the investigating officials thought to have them examined by the FBI. It is hard to believe that the FBI would not have wanted the clothes of the victims immediately, inasmuch as this is a cardinal rule in the investigation of any shooting. As with so many other aspects of the federal investigation of the crime, one is driven to believe that this oversight was due more to premeditated deliberation than to innocent, albeit negligent, omission.

The list of irregularities and evasions in the official report may be multiplied at will. As the person trained in criminological procedures delves more deeply into the case, the more certain he becomes that

the truth about the Kennedy assassination is not the "official truth" contained in the Warren *Report*. Truth was not the aim of the Commission, nor was truth the end product of its labors. We will know the real truth about the assassination only when impartial and scientific investigation replaces governmental promulgation and official obfuscation.

## NOTES

1. Marshall Houts, *Where Death Delights* (New York: Coward-McCann, Inc., 1967), p. 55.
2. See 16H979.
3. See *Kansas City Times,* July 29, 1967.
4. *Philadelphia Inquirer,* November 25, 1966.
5. *Saturday Evening Post,* January 14, 1967, p. 69.
6. Edward Jay Epstein, "Manchester Unexpurgated," *Commentary,* Volume 44, No. 1 (July 1967), p. 30.
7. *Ibid.*
8. William Manchester, *The Death of a President* (New York: Harper & Row, 1967), pp. 156-157.
9. This correspondence is reproduced in Appendix E of this book.

# APPENDIX E

## OFFICIAL CORRESPONDENCE
## OF REPRESENTATIVE
## THEODORE R. KUPFERMAN

Representative Theodore R. Kupferman (R.-N.Y.) has made available the following documents pertaining to his unsuccessful effort to have the Kennedy autopsy photos and X-rays examined by two medico-legal experts, Dr. Milton Helpern of New York City and Dr. Cyril Wecht of Pittsburgh. On September 28, 1966 Representative Kupferman introduced a concurrent resolution to establish a joint committee of the Congress to determine the necessity of a congressional investigation of the assassination of President Kennedy.

First, Representative Kupferman's statement on the floor of the House of Representatives, April 13, 1967.

STATEMENT BY REP. THEODORE R. KUPFERMAN (R. - N.Y.) IN THE HOUSE OF REPRESENTATIVES UPON THE INTRODUCTION OF A CONCURRENT RESOLUTION TO ESTABLISH A JOINT COMMITTEE TO DETERMINE THE NECESSITY OF A CONGRESSIONAL INVESTIGATION OF THE ASSASSINATION OF PRESIDENT KENNEDY, SEPTEMBER 21, 1966.

THE KENNEDY ASSASSINATION
and
THE WARREN COMMISSION

Pursuant to Executive Order 11130 dated November 29, 1963, the President's Commission on the Assassination of President Kennedy investigated the assassination which took place one week before on November 22, 1963, of President Kennedy, and the subsequent killing of the alleged assassin, and reported to President Lyndon B. Johnson.

The President's Commission, more popularly referred to as the Warren Commission because the Chief Justice of the United States Supreme Court, Earl Warren, was designated by the President to serve as its Chairman, was directed to evaluate all the facts and circumstances surrounding the assassination of President Kennedy and the shooting of Governor Connally and the subsequent killing of the alleged assassin Lee Harvey Oswald.

Following ten months of exhaustive investigation, and after reviewing testimony of 552 witnesses, 25,000 FBI interviews, 1550 Secret Service interviews and other documents which compose a stack of papers that is said to fill 300 cubic feet in the National Archives, the seven-man Warren Commission publicly submitted its report to the President on September 24, 1964. On September 20, 1964, the Warren Report was made public.

It was the the conclusion of the Commission, among other things, that Lee Harvey Oswald, acting alone, killed the President. The shots which killed President Kennedy and wounded Governor Connally, the Commission found, were fired from the sixth floor window at the southeast corner of the Texas School Book Depository. The Commission concluded that of the evidence indicates that there were three shots fired. The Commission held that it was not necessary to any of its essential findings to determine just which shot hit Governor Connally, but that very persuasive evidence from the experts indicates that the same bullet which pierced the President's throat also caused Governor Connally's wounds. While the third conclusion of the Commission states that Governor Connally's testimony and certain other factors have given rise to some difference of opinion as to this probability, the Commission states there is no question in the mind of any member of the Commission that all the shots which caused the President's and Governor Connally's wounds were fired from the sixth floor window of the Texas School Book Depository, and that which killed President Kennedy and wounded Governor Connally were fired by Lee Harvey Oswald.

The Commission found no evidence that either Lee Harvey Oswald or Jack Ruby was part of any conspiracy, domestic or foreign, to assassinate President Kennedy. Moreover, it concluded that in its entire investigation the Commission found no evidence of conspiracy, subversion, or disloyalty to the U. S. Government by any Federal, State, or local official.

The stated purpose of the Commission was to investigate all the facts and circumstances surrounding the assassination and the subsequent killing of the alleged assassin. But, as a practical matter, no doubt President Johnson knew the value of reinforcing the public confidence in its institutions and Governmental agencies.

There was a natural outburst of public emotion following the tragic and shocking events which took place so rapidly on November 22, 1963, and an increasing wave of speculation in this country, and even across in Europe and Latin America, concerning the possibilities of conspiracy and plotting of right or left-wing elements.

---

2

I wrote to President Johnson on February 16, 1967. His Office stated:

THE WHITE HOUSE
Washington
February 17, 1967

Dear Congressman:

For the President, may I acknowledge your letter of February 16 to the President regarding your request to examine the X-rays and photographs taken during the autopsy of President Kennedy.

Your letter and enclosures will be given careful attention.

Sincerely yours,
(signed)
Henry H. Wilson, Jr.
Administrative Assistant
to the President

Honorable Theodore R. Kupferman
House of Representatives
Washington, D. C.

The matter was then referred back to the General Services Administration by the President's Office, where the Administrator gave me the same answer that I had previously received. It is ironical that the Administrator in his letter of reply states:

The public interest in the X-rays and photographs as a part of the historical record of the assassination of President Kennedy is appropriately served, not only by their deposit and preservation in National Archives, but also by the provision for unrestricted access by any official government body, including committees of the Congress, having authority to investigate matters relating to the assassination.

This, of course, was on the basis of my request in my letter to President Johnson. This correspondence, hereinafter attached, is an exercise in bureaucracy and futility. More significantly, it amounts to deliberate failure on the part of the Executive Branch to inform the American people in a vital area, one about which the public has a right to know more.

Inasmuch as the Executive Branch will not face its responsibilities and take necessary action, only the Congress of the United States, with its investigative powers, remains available to do the job that must be done.

Attached hereto is my original statement on the introduction of my original Resolution, H.Con.Res. 1023, and my correspondence relative to the X-rays and photographs.

#########

---

STATEMENT BY REP. THEODORE R. KUPFERMAN (R.-N.Y.) IN THE HOUSE OF REPRESENTATIVES UPON REINTRODUCTION OF A CONCURRENT RESOLUTION TO ESTABLISH A JOINT COMMITTEE TO DETERMINE THE NECESSITY OF A CONGRESSIONAL INVESTIGATION OF THE ASSASSINATION OF PRESIDENT KENNEDY -- APRIL 13, 1967.

Mr. Speaker, I am today reintroducing my Concurrent Resolution for a Joint Congressional Committee to determine the necessity for reinvestigating the assassination of President Kennedy.

In the 89th Congress on September 28, 1966, the second anniversary of the Warren Commission Report (see Congressional Record, page 23205), I introduced H.Con.Res. 1023, pointing out that the official Report, with respect to the assassination of President Kennedy, had created more doubts than it had settled. Subsequent polls proved that this was so (see Congressional Record of October 4, 1966, page 24043).

The alleged truths of the Warren Commission Report can no longer, if ever, be considered self-evident.

The reason the Congress must now act is that the Executive Branch, in the most obvious areas of doubt, has engaged in a conspiracy of silence and inaction, when clearly there is a need for sound action and high-level investigation.

The refusal of the Executive Branch to take necessary action has been demonstrated in the situation involving the X-rays and the photographs of the autopsy of the late President Kennedy. It has become increasingly clear to me, throughout the rising controversy subsequent to the publication of the Warren Commission Report, that this material, which the Warren Commission as a matter of non-feasance had failed to examine, should be officially examined.

Accordingly, on December 27, 1966, I wrote to the Chief Archivist of the United States requesting an opportunity, together with some outstanding and knowledgeable people in the field, to view these materials. Copies of the correspondence with the National Archives, as well as copies of the replies received in this regard, follow at the end of this statement.

There have been many doubts raised about the findings contained in the Warren Report, but in my opinion the most vulnerable is that known as the "single bullet theory". One cannot read the Warren Report without realizing the importance of this theory to its conclusion that Lee Harvey Oswald, acting alone, killed President Kennedy.

If the first bullet entered just below President Kennedy's shoulder, and failed to exit, then the single bullet theory, the cornerstone of the Warren Commission Report, is not substantiated. If the bullet in question entered at the rear of the neck, passed completely through the neck, and exited through the throat, then the theory may be sustained. The answer may well be contained in the films and X-rays of the autopsy report.

Governor Connally of Texas, who was directly involved, and others do not accept the single bullet theory.

There has been so much confusion and ambiguity over this and many of the other basic findings of the Commission that, under the circumstances, and with my request, reason would dictate that the Executive Branch would have at least asked for an official report with an analysis of the X-rays and photographs. Rather, the response to my request can only resemble the Warren Report itself in the mountain of paperwork, but lack of a valid conclusion. The circuitousness involved is the equivalent of the circular file.

Upon receipt of my request, the Chief Archivist referred the matter to Burke Marshall, who has been designated by the Kennedy family to act in its behalf in matters relating to these materials. He denied my request by letter of January 25, 1967.

It was obvious in President Johnson's approach to selecting the composition of the Commission, that he wanted men of the highest integrity and national reputation so that the Commission's findings would have the necessary standing to ensure quick acceptance of its findings and thus provide what some have called 'domestic tranquility."

This view is epitomized by the fact that President Johnson chose the Chief Justice of the United States, Earl Warren, to act as Chairman of the Commission. Indeed, all of the seven members of the Commission are men of national reputation for intelligence, competence and integrity.

The difficulty comes in the fact that many people feel that the findings of the Warren Commission have not been accepted. In this regard, Fletcher Knebel writing in Look Magazine, July 12, 1966, reports that a Harris Survey taken in the fall of 1964, soon after the publication of the Warren Report, showed that 31% of Americans still believed Oswald had accomplices, and that less than half the people believed the Commission told the full story.

It is obvious that it would be an impossible task for the seven-member Commission to persuade even a majority of the American people as to the exact nature and circumstances of all the horrible events that took place on that Friday. But, the fact remains that if the purpose of the Warren Commission was to allay or set at rest doubts that a great many people naturally had following that event, and to restore a feeling of relative security and calm as a result of its search for the facts, then it is at least questionable whether it succeeded.

Of course, there was a rash of activity by writers and critics immediately following the publication of the Report who played on difficult and unanswered questions, thus feeding fuel to the fires of speculation in the minds of the doubters and adding to the uneasiness of the people. The obvious difficulty with the products of this first wave of critics is that they played heavily on insinuations and rhetorical questions while failing to answer or offer alternative theories based on reasoned judgments after weighing all the evidence, such as the Warren Commission purportedly did.

However, it is now two years after the publication of the Warren Commission report and a new wave of criticism has developed concerning the work of the Warren Commission. The critics who make up the second wave are not addressing themselves, for the most part, to the integrity of the Warren Commission, or even to the soundness of many of its conclusions.

The serious question raised by the second wave of critics is whether the members of the Warren Commission took the necessary time to examine thoroughly all the available material and evidence to come to an accurate and independent conclusion as to what happened, or whether they were disposed to satisfy a certain view, being persuaded in the public interest to come to a speedy decision.

Those who criticized the Warren Commission or the Warren Report along these lines would find possible support in the fact that President Johnson selected highly competent but busy men to act as Members of the Commission.

One of the many recent books critical of the Commission was written by Edward J. Epstein as an outgrowth of his masters thesis in Government for Cornell University. In the introduction to Mr. Epstein's book entitled, "Inquest: The Warren Commission and the Establishment of Truth," Richard H. Revere, a respected writer, notes in the foreword that Epstein amply demonstrates that the Commission's quest for truth was also a quest for domestic tranquility, and that the second quest often got in the way of the first. Mr. Epstein says the Commission's probe was hampered by an impossible deadline imposed by Chief Justice Warren, by lack of investigation and manpower, and by absenteeism of the busy commissioners. He calculates only three commissioners heard more than half the testimony and measured the attendance at the hearings as ranging from a low of about six percent to a high of about seventy-one percent. Mr. Epstein states that the Commission ignored possible witnesses, sifted the testimony to suit its purposes, and omitted contradictory evidence and inconsistent details.

Finally, the critics suggest as typical of the superficial nature of the Commission's work, that the Commission never independently investigated rumors, whether Oswald was a paid informant of the FBI, but merely took the word of FBI officials, principally J. Edgar Hoover, that he was not. They say the question that the public is left with now is whether the Commission's commitment from the onset of its assignment was ~~less to the discovery of~~ revelation and truth than to dispelling rumors that would damage the national interest.



In an article entitled "Round Two," written by Fred Graham, which appeared in the New York Times Book Review of August 28, 1966, it was stated that,

> Unfortunately, many people may confuse the doubts about the commission with doubts about its conclusion. One of the earliest and most perceptive critics of the Warren Commission, Paul L. Freese of the California Bar, remarked in the Columbia Law Review that the commission was vulnerable because its real task "was not to find the truth but to appear to have found the truth." Mr. Graham says with respect to this statement of Paul Freese, "The pity is that it may have done the opposite." *

Fletcher Knebel, the author of the "Warren Commission Report on the Assassination Is Struck by a New Wave of Doubt" which appeared in Look Magazine on July 12, 1966, examined Mr. Epstein's writing carefully and "...soon became convinced that Epstein was guilty of the very sins of which he accused the Warren Commission: distortion, ignoring testimony, sifting the evidence, and adroitly selecting it to fit its theories and assumptions." Mr. Knebel states with respect to "Inquest: The Warren Commission and the Establishment of Truth," "At the worst, Epstein has written a dangerously deceptive book. At the best, he is guilty of precisely what he lays at the door of the Warren Commission--a "superficial" investigation."

Richard N. Goodwin, a former assistant to President Kennedy, in a review written for Book Week of the World Journal Tribune (then on strike) and appearing in New York City in the Village Voice of August 4, 1966, considered Edward J. Epstein's book. In the early part of Mr. Goodwin's review he states,

> ...those who worked with President Kennedy, even those in the outer rings of relationship such as myself, welcomed with such swift acceptance the conclusions of the Warren Report; even though few had read it thoroughly and almost no one had examined the evidence on which it was based. There was, of course, the fact that the integrity and purpose of the Commission were beyond question and its members were men of skill and intelligence. There was the almost unanimous praise of newspapers and commentators who we assumed, if we thought about it at all, had followed the course of investigation and studied the answers. This would not ordinarily have been enough for those who had learned the lesson of the Bay of Pigs: that neither position, conviction, sincerity nor expert knowledge precluded the need for independent judgment of the evidence. This time, though, there was only room for grief; and a lone madman compelled neither hatred nor effort nor calculation.

Speaking of Epstein's harsh criticism of both the substantive portion of the Warren Commission's findings, as well as the procedures employed, and the lack of thoroughness of the Warren Commission, Mr. Goodwin states:

> ...None of this prove or even forcefully indicates that a single disturbed human being was not the cause of President Kennedy's death. Perhaps all the specific examples Epstein uses to strengthen his case will be easily refuted. If there are gaps, further study may swiftly close them. However, the attack on the nature and adequacy of the Commission's work is not easily dismissed. Even if Mr. Epstein is totally wrong in every discussion of specific evidence, and yet if he is right that the investigation itself was seriously incomplete, then we have not established to the limit the possibility that Lee Harvey Oswald acted alone to kill John F. Kennedy.

* The reference to Columbia Law Review must be inadvertent. It is actually at 40 NYU Law Review page 459 (May 1965).



Mr. Goodwin further states:

> I find it hard to believe that the investigation was seriously flawed, but here is a book which presents such a case with a logic and a subdued and reasonable tone which have already disturbed the convictions of many responsible men. It may all rest on quicksand, but we will not know that until we make an even more extensive examination than the author has made. An independent group should look at these charges and determine whether the Commission investigation was so defective that another inquiry is necessary. Such a procedure will, perhaps unnecessarily, stimulate rumors and doubts and disturb the political scene. Yet there seems to be no other course if we want to be sure that we know as much as we can about what happened on November 22, 1963.

There have been a host of other writers concerned with the Kennedy Assassination and the Warren Commission including Thomas Buchanan's "Who Killed Kennedy," Penn Jones Jr's "Forgive My Grief," Harold Weisberg's "WHITEWASH: The Report on the Warren Commission," Mark Lane's "Rush to Judgment," and most recently, "The Second Oswald" by Richard H. Popkin. At the end of this statement I have included as complete a listing as the Library of Congress has been able to compile to date of various articles and books dealing with the Warren Report and the assassination of President Kennedy.

It would seem that the relevant inquiry at this time should not be whether the Warren Commission maintained the expected degree of integrity in its investigations and findings, nor whether Lee Harvey Oswald was actually the lone assassin of President Kennedy, but rather whether the people of the United States feel the desired confidence and finality in the authoritative work that has been done to date. In other words, is the Warren Commission's report enough.

In the past, we find that our country, in the words of the noted attorney Louis Nizer, "has not resorted to commissions as a regular procedure, but chiefly in great emergencies, and, fortunately, therefore infrequently."* A review of American history tells us that one such great emergency was the debacle at Pearl Harbor, which not only shattered our fleet, but to a great extent our confidence and pride. President Roosevelt knew that a report was required following the international disaster of Pearl Harbor on December 7, 1941, that would tell the people the truth which they wanted and needed so desperately to know. He knew that the people could bear up under the truth, but that uncertainty and rumor of plots and conspiracies would, above all, undermine their confidence and destroy their will.

Thus, on December 18, 1941, President Roosevelt created the Roberts Commission. The President designated Justice Owen J. Roberts of the United States Supreme Court as its Chairman. He appointed Admiral William H. Stanley, U.S. Navy, retired, Rear Admiral Joseph M. Reeves, U.S. Navy, retired, Major General Frank McCoy, U.S. Army, retired, and Brigadier General Joseph T. McNarney of the Army to serve with Justice Roberts as members of the Commission.

Many criticized President Roosevelt and the Roberts Commission at the time for the fact that the heavy military composition of the Committee would not be likely to ensure an impartial report on their own services. Those critics were substantially quieted when the Roberts Commission publicly reported to the President on January 23, 1942, and in terms of dereliction of duty and errors of judgment placed a good deal of the blame for the Pearl Harbor disaster upon the Joint Commanders of the Army and Navy who were stationed in Hawaii at that time. The Roberts Commission's 21-page report is listed as Senate Document No. 159, 77th Congress, 2nd Session (1942).

The integrity of the members of the Roberts Commission was uncompromised and its impartiality was beyond question. Thus, it could be a very persuasive report. But, it is important to note that the purpose of the Roberts Commission was to provide a basis for sound decisions as to whether any derelictions of duty or errors of judgment on the part of the United States Army or Navy personnel contributed to such successes as were achieved by the enemy on December 7, 1941. In other words, the Roberts Commission inquiry was inherently narrow in its purpose, if not in its scope.

* An analysis and commentary of the Warren Report by Louis Nizer is found in the foreword of the Doubleday & Company, Inc. printing of the Warren Report at pg. iii-a thru pg. xxviii-a.

5

The Roberts Commission was followed by six other investigations of the Pearl Harbor incident: Immediately following the Roberts Commission was the Hart Inquiry, initiated by order from Secretary of the Navy Knox on February 12, 1944, and concluded June15, 1944. Following the Hart Inquiry, the Army Pearl Harbor Board was appointed pursuant to provisions of Public Law 339, 78th Congress, and was directed to make such recommendations as it may deem proper. The Board held sessions beginning July 20, 1944, and concluded its investigation on October 20, 1944. Following the Army Pearl Harbor board was the Navy Court of Inquiry pursuant to Public Law 339, 78th Congress. It held sessions July 24, 1944, and concluded its inquiry on October 19, 1944. The Clarke Inquiry was next, conducted from September 14 to 16, 1944, and from July 13 to August 4, 1945. This inquiry was more specific in its scope and testimony being taken concerning the handling of intercepted Japanese messages and the handling of intelligence material by the Military Intelligence Division of the War Department. Finally, there was the Clausen Investigation (Commenced November 23, 1944, and concluded on September 12, 1945) and the Hewitt Inquiry (Commenced May 14, 1945 and concluded on July 11, 1945).

Notwithstanding the work of the Roberts Commission and the six other investigations of the facts and circumstances relating to the attack on Pearl Harbor by the Japanese on December 7, 1941, serious questions, doubts and inconsistencies remained. Finally the Congress of the United States found it necessary to establish a Joint Legislative Committee on the Investigation of the Pearl Harbor Attack. The Concurrent Resolution, No. 27 (as extended), 79th Congress, 1st Session, establishing the Joint Legislative Investigation Committee composed of five members of the Senate and five members of the House, passed the Senate on September 6, 1945. The House concurred on September 11, 1945.

Ten months later, on July 20, 1945, the exhaustive and credible work of the Joint Congressional Committee was reported to the President of the Senate and Speaker of the House. The work is found in a bound Senate volume entitled, "Pearl Harbor Attack."

It is against this background that I propose that a Joint Congressional Committee be created to re-investigate thoroughly all of the facts and circumstances surrounding the events that ended in the assassination of President Kennedy, the subsequent killing of his alleged assassin, and the shooting of Governor John B. Connally.

Should the Joint Congressional Committee determine, after a preliminary investigation of all the accounts, writings and reports, including but not limited to the Warren Report, of the facts and circumstances relating to the Kennedy assassination, that an additional investigation is necessary regarding the same, then that Joint Committee would proceed to investigate fully the entire facts and circumstances surrounding the events of November 22, 1963.

The Concurrent Resolution, which I have introduced today and which follows at the end of this statement, would establish a Joint Congressional Committee composed of five members of the Senate (not more than three of whom shall be members of the Majority Party) to be appointed by the President pro tempore, and five members of the House (not more than three of whom shall be members of the Majority Party), to be appointed by the Speaker of the House.

As the Warren Commission states, it was created in recognition of the right of people everywhere to a full and truthful knowledge concerning these events. The report, in its own words, "has been prepared with a deep awareness of the Commission's responsibility to present to the American people an objective report of the facts relating to the assassination."

We must not hide from all the facts whatever they are, and whatever they indicate. In light of the current and mounting criticism of its findings we must now objectively evaluate the findings of all those who would have us believe the Warren Commission in one way or another did not do all that it could have . In this way the volume of work of the Warren Commission will be called upon to stand a true test. But so will the conclusions and rationality of those who would attack the Warren Commission be put to an equally objective test.

There appeared in the New York Times magazine section on September 11, 1966, an article written by an English political commentator, Henry Fairlie, entitled, "No Conspiracy. But--Too Assassins, Perhaps?" Mr. Fairlie writes that...

6

The Report of the Warren Commission is now under severe and, in some cases, persuasive attack. It is hard to disagree with the general judgment of its critics that it did a hurried and slovenly job, it seems to have been less than skeptical of some of the official evidence with which it was supplied, less than careful to consider in detail every possible explanation of the assassination other than Lee Harvey Oswald's sole guilt.

Following a discussion of the events and circumstances of the assassination of President Kennedy and Lee Harvey Oswald, Mr. Fairlie states :

At some point, it is clear, there will have to be another independent inquiry. But, even if this is agreed, it is by no means equally clear that the time for such an investigation is now. A portion of the investigative reports in the United States National Archives is not yet declassified. The whereabouts of other important evidence have still not been ascertained. In these circumstances the chances of a further inquiry producing a report which would carry conviction are slight.

And further, Mr. Fairlie quotes the following conclusion of Harold Weisberg, author of "WHITEWASH:", the report on the Warren Report:

A crime such as the assassination of the President of the United States cannot be left as the report of the President's Commission has left it, without even the probability of a solution, with assassins and murderers free, and free to repeat their crimes and enjoy what benefits they may have expected to derive therefrom. No President is ever safe if Presidential assassins are exculpated. Yet this is what the Commission has done.

According to Mr. Epstein, 22 Governmental agencies furnished more than 300 cubic feet of papers to the Warren Commission and there were over 1500 Secret Service interviews or reports and thousands of papers connected with the investigation of the facts and circumstances relating to the assassination of President Kennedy. In addition, the FBI alone sent the Commission 25,000 reports and papers.

I am informed that at the present time two-thirds of the available papers and documents in the National Archives are declassified and open to the public for research purposes.

The remaining one-third of the available documents and papers at the National Archives is composed, in part, of the administrative records and working papers of the Warren Commission. Additional housekeeping records are mixed in with these papers and records and have to be sorted.

The records, reports and papers concerning the facts and circumstances relating to the assassination of President Kennedy which are at the National Archives and are presently classified should be made available to the public at the earliest possible time.

In keeping with the National Freedom of Information policy embodied in Senate Bill 1160, which I supported in the House of Representatives when it passed here on June 20th, and which President Johnson signed on July 4 of this year, we must make every effort to remove the veil of secrecy over papers and documents which can be revealed without violating the public interest.

As President Johnson said upon signing this Federal public records law (P.L. 89-492):

I am instructing every official in this Administration to cooperate...and to make information available to the full extent consistent with individual privacy and the national interest.

7

There are nine exemptions to the National Freedom of Information Law. With respect to the papers and documents containing facts or circumstances relating to the assassination of President Kennedy which are at the National Archives, the first exemption should be examined. It reads as follows:

Sec. 3. Every agency shall make available to the public the following information:

(e) Exemptions. The provisions of this section shall not be applicable to matters that are (1) specifically required by Executive Order to be kept secret in the interest of the National defense or foreign policy;

As Mr. Bert Mills points out in an article entitled, "What Next on FOI?", published in the National Publisher, September, 1966,

The key phrase here is "by Executive Order." No minor official will make the decision, only the President, and his action in issuing such an order is publicised...

Although the Freedom of Information Law does not become effective until Independence Day, 1967, based upon it and the expressed intent by President Johnson in signing it, I believe the exemption cited above should not be applicable to the materials relating to the assassination of President Kennedy which are presently being held as classified in the National Archives. This view is further supported by the fact that President Johnson asked the Attorney General over one year ago to coordinate an overall agency review of the records and papers furnished to the Commission and in turn deposited with the National Archives in order to make as much of this material available to the public as they possibly could.

On August 17, 1966, the Office of the Attorney General asked the National Archives to apply the same standard of public accessibility to the working papers and administrative reports which it has received from the Warren Commission itself.

To the extent that any doubt remains, the President should be requested to free for scrutiny all documents and evidence of any kind in this area.

It is not, nor has it been, my desire to rush to verdict concerning the outcome of the question. However, I feel that these questions which the critics say were allegedly left unanswered should not be superficially answered nor should they be left unanswered. Let an independent body make a thoroughly dispositive and exhaustive evaluation of all that has been said and written to date concerning the events surrounding the assassination and the Report of those events, just as the Joint Congressional Committee reviewed Pearl Harbor and the findings of the Roberts Commission four years later.

Moreover, it is just as likely that the work and conclusions of the Warren Commission will emerge further justified and supported. In this way the confidence of the people may be restored and for all the majority of doubters should be satisfied that all there is to be known about the events of November 22, 1963, is known, and the tragedy of that day may be allowed to rest with dignity. And if a thorough and objective examination should shed new light on the happenings of that day, then we can only benefit by coming closer to the truth.

---

Burke Marshall

Old Orchard Road, Armonk, New York 10504

January 26, 1967

Honorable Theodore R. Kupferman
House of Representatives
Washington, D. C. 20515

Dear Congressman:

This will acknowledge your letter of December 27 regarding the material placed in the Archives last November by the executors of President Kennedy's estate. I regret the delay in answering; I have been away from my office.

The wishes of the Kennedy family, as reflected in the agreement by which the material was given to the United States, are that there be no examination of the material for at least five years, except by a properly authorized federal government agency. Thereafter inspection will be limited to persons professionally qualified to evaluate medical evidence, for serious historical purposes. The reasons for these restrictions are obvious.

While the first of these provisions could be waived, I have concluded that I should not do so. I have given careful consideration, because of your official position, to the question whether an exception should be made in your case, and have decided that there is no basis for that, particularly in the light of the second restriction referred to. It would then be at least very difficult to refuse other requests, and the consequences would be very painful for Mrs. Kennedy and the family.

I fully appreciate that in your case, there is absolutely no question of personal gain, or mere curiosity, but I am sure you will understand the compelling reasons against making distinctions based on my personal evaluation of someone's motives.

Sincerely,
[signature]

JAN 26 1967

---

GENERAL SERVICES ADMINISTRATION

National Archives and Records Service
Washington, D.C. 20408

January 6, 1967

IN REPLY REFER TO:

Honorable Theodore R. Kupferman
House of Representatives
Washington, D. C. 20515

Dear Mr. Kupferman:

This is in reply to your letter of December 27, 1966, concerning the x-rays and photographs taken during the autopsy of President Kennedy.

We have forwarded your request for access to the autopsy materials to Mr. Burke Marshall, who has been designated by the Kennedy family to act in its behalf in matters relating to these materials.

As you may know, these materials were accepted for deposit in the National Archives under authority of 44 USC 397(e). Conditions imposed by the Kennedy family pursuant to this authority provide that, for a period of five years these items, unless otherwise determined by Mr. Marshall, may be made available only to persons authorized to act for a committee of the Congress or a committee or agency in the Executive Branch vested with authority to investigate matters relating to the death of President Kennedy.

Sincerely yours,
[signature] Robert K. Bahmer
Robert H. Bahmer
Archivist of the United States

*Keep Freedom in Your Future With U.S. Savings Bonds*

---

THEODORE R. KUPFERMAN
17th District, New York

INTERIOR AND INSULAR AFFAIRS COMMITTEE
VETERANS' AFFAIRS COMMITTEE

CONGRESS OF THE UNITED STATES
HOUSE OF REPRESENTATIVES
WASHINGTON, D.C.

December 27, 1966

Mr. Robert H. Bahmer
Chief Archivist of the United States
National Archives and Records Section
8th Street & Pennsylvania Ave., N.W.
Washington, D. C.

Dear Mr. Bahmer:

You are undoubtedly familiar with the fact that on September 28, 1966 I introduced, in the House, H.Con.Res. 1023, my statement in connection with it is found at page 23303 of the Congressional Record of that date. I am enclosing a copy of the statement.

I have been much concerned about the fact that there was no opportunity given the Warren Commission to examine the X-rays and photographs taken during the autopsy of President Kennedy.

In my opinion, these could have a significant bearing on the question of whether it was a single bullet that hit both President Kennedy and wounded Governor Connally.

Accordingly, I would like to arrange for an opportunity to examine the X-rays and photographs, which I am informed are now in the Archives, when I return to Washington for the 90th Congress. I would prefer some time in the middle of January.

In order to have an informed judgment on the subject, I would have with me Dr. Milton Halpern, New York City's Chief Medical Examiner, and Dr. Cyril H. Wecht, who is the Chief Deputy Coroner and Chief Forensic Pathologist of Allegheny County (Pittsburgh), Pennsylvania, and Silvia Meagher, 302 West 12th Street, New York City, who has studied the Warren Commission Report and prepared an index to the 26 volumes of exhibits, etc. Her presence would be needed, so that we would have the various factual matters available as we examine the photographs and X-rays.

If you could also arrange for a suitable viewing room, that would be appreciated.

May I hear from you as soon as possible on this so that I can make the necessary arrangement for the other three parties all to be present.

Thank you for your courtesy.

Sincerely yours,
[signature]
Theodore R. Kupferman, M.C.

Exhibit "A"

THEODORE R. KUPFERMAN
17th District, New York

JAMES J. KAUFMAN
Legislative Assistant

BRIAN C. SMITH
Office Manager

INTERIOR AND INSULAR AFFAIRS COMMITTEE
VETERANS' AFFAIRS COMMITTEE

DISTRICT OFFICE:
30 West 44th Street
New York, N.Y. 10036
Telephone YUkon 6-5135

CONGRESS OF THE UNITED STATES
HOUSE OF REPRESENTATIVES
WASHINGTON, D.C.

February 16, 1967

The Honorable Lyndon B. Johnson
President of the United States
The White House
Washington D. C.

Dear Mr. President:

I write to you in the hope that a serious situation, which has become almost ludicrous, may finally be resolved.

On September 28, 1966, I introduced my resolution (H.Con.Res. 1022) for the establishment of a joint committee of the House and Senate to review the findings of the Warren Commission on the Kennedy assassination.

My statement in connection therewith, which you received at the time, is set forth at page 23203 of the Congressional Record of that date.

There have been many doubts raised about the findings contained in the Warren Commission Report, but, in my opinion, the most vulnerable of the findings is that known as the "single bullet" theory.

If the theory is rejected, then it is possible that there was more than one assassin. If the theory is sustained, then there is a possibility that reasonable people can consider the case closed.

As you well know, Governor Connally insists that he was not hit by the same shot that hit President Kennedy, although, strangely enough, Governor Connally accepts the conclusions of the Commission's Report.

As a result of the research done by Edward J. Epstein published in his book entitled "Inquest", a great deal of information has been brought to light about the methods of the Warren Commission. You will recall that Senator Russell was merely willing to call the "single bullet" theory "credible", while the drafters of the Report wanted to call it "compelling", and compromise was found in the word "persuasive". See Life Magazine of November 25, 1966 at page 53.

In all the discussions about the single bullet theory, I have been amazed to find that the X-rays and photographs taken at the autopsy of the late President Kennedy were not made available to the Commission. Arlen Specter, who worked on this phase of the investigation, in his interview in U. S. News and World Report of October 10, 1966, at page 53, states that the Commission did not press for the photographs and X-rays because they did not consider them "indispensable" and would merely corroborate what the autopsy surgeons had testified to under oath.

That the autopsy surgeons were not necessarily well informed is detailed at page 53, among others, of the Life Magazine article above mentioned.

---

Letter to President Johnson
February 16, 1967
Page Two

It became increasingly clear to me that the X-rays and photographs should be officially examined, and, accordingly, I addressed a communication to the National Archives requesting an opportunity, together with some outstanding and knowledgeable people in the field, to view these items.

Attached hereto as Exhibit "A" is a copy of my letter of December 27, 1966 to the Chief Archivist of the United States and his reply of January 6, 1967 (Exhibit "B").

I then followed up with Burke Marshall and received the reply dated January 25, 1967, copy of which is attached hereto as Exhibit "C".

I had thought that deposit with the Archives, in view of the public fanfare, had some significance. In the absence of official investigation, this is all illusory.

It is inconceivable to me that a matter of personal preference, no matter how delicate to the parties involved, should stand in the way of the public's right to know.

William Manchester, in the second installment of his book "The Death of a President", as it appears in Look Magazine of February 7, 1967, at page 45 states as follows:

In the summer of 1966, a former Cornell graduate student published a dissertation that suggested that this first bullet followed a different trajectory. The implication was that a second assassin had aided Oswald. The issue is resolved by the X-rays and photographs which were taken from every conceivable angle during the autopsy on the President's body. Robert Kennedy has decided that this material is too unsightly to be shown to anyone, including qualified scholars, until 1971. He has turned it over to the National Archives with that restriction. Although this writer has not seen the material, he interviewed three people with special qualifications who examined it before it was put under seal. None of them saw the other two, but all three gave identical accounts of what they had seen in the photographs and X-rays. The X-ray show no entry wound "below the shoulder," as argued by the graduate student. Admittedly, X-rays of active projectiles passing through soft tissue are difficult to read. However, the photographs support them in this case—and clearly reveal that the wound was in the neck. Finally, the recollections of all doctors present during the autopsy, including the President's personal physician, agree unanimously with this overwhelming evidence.

---

Letter to President Johnson
February 16, 1967
Page Three

You are, no doubt, aware of the controversy involved with respect to the publication of the Manchester Book, but that was complicated by a matter of a private contract.

In my opinion, the question of the X-rays and photographs, certainly to the extent of a proper analysis for a public report as to the specific item of where the entry wound was with respect to the first bullet, is a public matter for which there must be an official examination and analysis.

You have heretofore stated that you expect all of this material to be made available to the public, and in your comments on the Freedom of Information Act, which you supported, you made similar statements.

I now ask you for the right to examine the X-rays and photographs, as stated in my letter of December 27, 1966 to the Chief Archivist and, failing that, I call upon you to direct forthwith that there be an official examination of the X-rays and photographs with a public statement by those examining them as to their findings and conclusion.

Most respectfully,

Theodore R. Kupferman, M.C.

TRK:ejc
Enclosures

THE WHITE HOUSE
WASHINGTON

April 13, 1967

Dear Congressman:

May I acknowledge for the President your letter of April 12 enclosing a copy of your statement on reintroducing a Concurrent Resolution to establish a Joint Congressional Committee to consider a reinvestigation of the assassination of President Kennedy.

Your courtesy in making available an advance copy of your remarks is appreciated.

Sincerely,

Henry H. Wilson, Jr.
Administrative Assistant
to the President

Honorable Theodore R. Kupferman
House of Representatives
Washington, D. C.

---

GENERAL SERVICES ADMINISTRATION

Washington, D.C. 20405

MAR 8 1967

Honorable Theodore R. Kupferman
House of Representatives
Washington, D.C. 20515

Dear Mr. Kupferman:

Since the National Archives is a part of the General Services Administration, the President has referred to me your letter of February 14, 1967, concerning the x-rays and photographs made during the autopsy of President Kennedy.

As you know, the photographs and x-rays were deposited in the National Archives by the Kennedy family under certain conditions, which were accepted by me pursuant to Section 507 of the Federal Records Act of 1950, as amended (44 U.S.C. 397). This statute provides for the acceptance of such materials by the Administrator of General Services subject to restrictions on availability specified by the donors or depositors.

The condition specified by the donors and depositors relating to the autopsy materials that is most directly applicable to your request states that access shall be permitted only to

"Any person authorized to act for a committee of the Congress, for a Presidential committee or commission, or for any other official agency of the United States Government, having authority to investigate matters relating to the death of the late President, for purposes within the investigative jurisdiction of such committee, commission or agency."

Related conditions provide that examination by any person not authorized to act for a congressional committee or other official

*Keep Freedom in Your Future With U.S. Savings Bonds*

---

2

body having authority to investigate the assassination is barred for five years except with the consent of the Kennedy family representative, Mr. Burke Marshall. Following the five-year period and during the lifetime of the late President's immediate family, access to unofficial persons is limited to experts in the field of pathology or related sciences for serious purposes relevant to investigation of the assassination.

The General Services Administration has no authority to make any exceptions to the foregoing conditions. Your letter indicates that you have already sought an exception from Mr. Marshall and that he has considered your request but declined to make an exception.

The law cited above, which was enacted to encourage voluntary deposit in the National Archives of Presidential papers and other historical materials relating to a President or former President, requires that the Government comply with the restrictions under which such materials are deposited. We accepted the autopsy photographs and x-rays on the terms described above because we concluded that it was in the public interest to assure acquisition and preservation of these materials.

The public interest in the x-rays and photographs as a part of the historical record of the assassination of President Kennedy is appropriately served, not only by their deposit and preservation in National Archives, but also by the provision for unrestricted access by any official governmental body, including committees of the Congress, having authority to investigate matters relating to the assassination.

Sincerely yours,

Lawson B. Knott, Jr.
Administrator

# APPENDIX F

## A CRITIQUE OF THE CBS NEWS DOCUMENTARY "THE WARREN REPORT"

The essence of CBS News's defense of the Warren *Report,* televised June 25, 26, 27, and 28, 1967, was summarized in these words by Walter Cronkite:

*To the account given in the Warren Report we have made three additions, each of which rests on evidence at least as persuasive as any provided by the Commission. Our analysis of the Zapruder film suggests strongly that the first shot was fired at frame 186; the Commission said only that the first shot to hit came between frames 210 and 225. Something startled Mr. Zapruder earlier, and the evidence is that a rifle shot was what startled him. We have shown that the Zapruder camera was quite possibly running slower than the Commission thought. The earlier shot and the slow camera together mean that the rifleman may have had additional time to get off three shots. We have shown by carefully controlled experiments that a Mannlicher-Carcano rifle can be fired more rapidly and accurately than the Commission believed. These points strengthen the Warren Report's basic finding. They make it more likely that Oswald shot the President. They significantly weaken a central contention of the critics—their contention that Oswald could not have done it because he did not have enough time to fire . . .*

*Did Lee Harvey Oswald shoot President Kennedy? CBS News concludes that he did.*

By stretching the time available to Oswald and by claiming that the Carcano could be fired faster and more accurately than was commonly believed, CBS News sought to make it appear *"more likely that Oswald shot the President."* Let us scrutinize each of the principal supports on which the CBS case rests.

*(1) "Our analysis of the Zapruder film suggests strongly that the first shot was fired at frame 186."*

Quite independent of the Zapruder film, there is considerable evidence to indicate that no shot was fired as early as Z186. As Chapter III of this book has shown, a triangulation of witness reports would place the first shot in the interval picked by the Warren Commission—Z210–225. Photographic evidence, as we have seen, tends to corroborate such a finding, as does the on-site FBI investigation. If a shot was fired at Z186 and missed the car entirely (as CBS believes), the FBI was unable to find any trace of it (R116).

But what of the CBS claim that "the Zapruder film suggests strongly" that a shot was fired this early? The Zapruder film shows unequivocally that the President was struck in the head at frame 313. Five frames later, Z318, the film blurs and remains blurred through the next two frames. The characteristics of the blurring indicate that the camera was moved quite violently at this point, very likely because something had startled the cameraman, Abraham Zapruder.

Can this startle reaction be used to identify the timing of the earlier shots? Zapruder himself cannot be of much help here—he heard only two shots, one of which was the Z313 head impact (7H571). But perhaps, as CBS claimed, his film shows other "jiggles" that pinpoint the timing of the earlier shots. CBS claimed to have located two additional jiggles—one at Z190 and the other at Z227. But what CBS did not tell its viewers was that there were other jiggles as well in the Zapruder film, both before and after the shooting. If we choose to correlate every jiggle with gunfire, then we must believe that shots were fired while the car was still on Houston Street, and also later after Clint Hill had climbed onto the back of the limousine. Given the overall evidence, such a belief is preposterous.

Even with respect to the interval studied by CBS (frames 170–334), that network was less than candid with its viewers. For anyone who cares to check Volume XVIII of the *Hearings* can verify for himself that Z190, Z227, and Z318 are not the only spots where jiggles are visible in this interval. At Z197 there is a jiggle of much greater magnitude than the one at Z190. Again at Z210 and Z331, jiggles not mentioned by CBS appear on the film. The Z227 blur (singled out by CBS as caused by the shot that supposedly struck both Connally and Kennedy) is clearly not caused by a movement of the camera, since, although the foreground automobile is blurred, the background is in focus. If each of the jiggles in the Zapruder film is to be correlated with a shot, then at least six shots were fired in the Z170–334 interval alone. This is not counting the jiggles (shots?) that appear both earlier and later. What is the cause of these momentary blurs on the Zapruder film? When this "jiggle theory of the assassination" was discussed and rejected at *Life* last November, it was concluded that Z318 is most likely a genuine startle reaction—the only one on the film. The other blurs are most probably caused by imperfections in the camera mechanism that permit the film to move a short distance either toward or away from the lens. The unusual clarity of certain other frames (Z183, Z200, Z230, Z312, and Z323, for example) is a product of the same phenomenon.

CBS offered its viewers a "scientific" theory based on an arbitrary selection of data. Why not admit as evidence the jiggles at Z197, Z210, and Z331 as well as those occurring much earlier and much later? For the simple reason that to do this would conflict with the basic purpose of the broadcast, which was to defend the Warren *Report*. "Scientism" replaces science.

*(2) "We have shown that the Zapruder camera was quite possibly running slower than the Commission thought."*

Photo expert Lyndal L. Shaneyfelt of the FBI testified before the Commission on how he established the running speed of the three movie cameras that pictured the assassination:

*We obtained from Mr. Zapruder, Mr. Nix, Mrs. Muchmore; their cameras for examination, and in the FBI laboratory exposed film in all three cameras, aiming, focusing the camera on a clock with a large sweep second hand. We then ran the camera at the speed and conditions as described by the people who used the cameras. We ran through several tests of film, and then after the film was developed it was studied under magnification, and frames were counted for a period of 2 to 3 seconds or for the full running time, and averages were taken.*

*Mr. Zapruder has stated that his camera was fully wound. Most of the others have stated their cameras were fully wound, so we were able to more or less eliminate the very slow time that occurs when the cameras are approximately run down, and all of these things were taken into consideration and were averaged.*

*The Zapruder camera was found to run at an average speed of 18.3 frames per second (5H160).*

Abraham Zapruder's camera was independently tested by the Bell & Howell Company and was found to run at the same speed established in the FBI tests.

Faced with this rather imposing evidence on the speed of the Zapruder camera, how did CBS arrive at the conclusion that "the Zapruder camera was quite possibly running slower than the Commission thought"? Using the same technique employed by Shaneyfelt, CBS tested five *other* cameras of the same make and model as Zapruder's. They were all run against a clock, and the time required to grind through 128 frames was measured. CBS gave the times for the five cameras as 6.90, 7.30, 6.70, 8.35, and 6.16 seconds. What CBS did not tell its audience was that Zapruder's camera (running at 18.3 frames per second) would have run through the same 128 frames in 7 seconds flat. In other words, three of the five cameras were running *faster* than the FBI-established rate for Zapruder's camera. Simple arithmetic permits one to calculate the varying rates at 18.55, 17.53, 19.10, 15.33, and 20.77 frames per second. The average for the CBS five was 18.256 frames per second—within 0.044 frames per second of the figure established for Zapruder's camera by the FBI and Bell & Howell.

CBS's test, of course, proved nothing. The critical question concerns the rate of Zapruder's camera, and no other, and this was tested independently by the FBI and Bell & Howell and found to run at 18.3 frames per second. CBS's test of other cameras proved nothing about Zapruder's camera, although its average figure for the five cameras came very close to 18.3 frames per second. Once again a so-called scientific test was used by CBS to throw dust in the eyes of its viewers.

*(3) "We have shown by carefully controlled experiments that a Mannlicher-Carcano rifle can be fired more rapidly and accurately than the Commission believed."*

Assuming with the Commission that Oswald was the only gunman firing on the motorcade, how much time did he have to get off three shots?

As previous chapters have shown, the first shot was fired in the interval Z210-224, while the last shot struck the President in the head at Z313. Simple subtraction tells us that the total time span of the shots varied anywhere from a minimum of 4.8 seconds to a maximum of 5.6 seconds. In this time period Oswald supposedly got two hits, one entering the President's lower neck and the other hitting Mr. Kennedy's head. The Commission also developed information that Oswald had not practiced with the rifle in the months preceding the assassination (R125, 192), and that his scope had a built-in defect that would throw shots high and to the right (R194, 3H405–406, 26H103–104).

CBS went to great pains to simulate Oswald's shooting situation on the sixth floor of the Depository. A tower of the same height was constructed, and below it a ramp duplicated the exact contours of Elm Street as it swept away from the building. A motor-driven dolly rode this ramp at the exact speed of the presidential limousine. Borne on the dolly was an FBI target simulating a man's head and upper trunk. The volunteers selected for the firing tests were all expert marksmen. Of the eleven who fired, three were Maryland State Troopers, three were employees of the H. P. White Ballistics Laboratory, one was a "weapons engineer," one a "ballistics technician," two "sportsmen," and one was an ex-paratrooper who had just returned from Vietnam. They all used a Carcano of the same year and model as Oswald's. A duplicate of Oswald's scope was fitted to the rifle and sighted in. All marksmen were permitted to practice with the rifle at a nearby indoor range.

What were the results of the tests? Two gates were set up along the dolly's track, one simulating Z210 and the other a point reached by the dolly 7.5 seconds later. The marksmen were told to hold their fire until the target reached the first gate, and to cease firing when it reached the second gate 7.5 seconds later. Thirty-seven firing runs of three shots each were made, but of these only twenty runs were fired within the constraint of 7.5 seconds. Of the thirty-seven firing runs only ten (27 percent) were fired in 5.6 seconds or less. On these runs the marksmen made anywhere from zero to three hits—their average was 1.3 hits for every three shots fired. Taking into account all the runs fired in less than 7.5 seconds, the average was 1.2 hits for every three shots fired.

These tests showed that trained marksmen who had practiced with the Carcano and had perfect sights were able to equal Oswald's maximum time of 5.6 seconds *in only one-quarter of their attempts.* Their hit ratio was 1.2–1.3 hits for every three shots. Oswald, we recall, firing with no practice and defective sights, was purported to have gotten two hits in a time period estimated as between 4.8 and 5.6 seconds. Could Oswald have fired his rifle fast enough and accurately enough to have accomplished the feat ascribed to him? From the results of its tests, CBS drew the following conclusion:

> *From our tests we were convinced that a rifle like Oswald's could be fired in 5.6 seconds or less, and with reasonable accuracy at a target moving much the same as the Presidential limousine was traveling away from the Book Depository's sixth floor window. But clearly, there is no pat answer to the question of how fast Oswald's rifle could be fired. In the first place, we did not test his own rifle. It seemed reasonable to say that an expert could fire that rifle in five seconds. It seems equally reasonable to say that Oswald under normal circumstances would take longer. But the circumstances were not normal—he was shooting at a president. So our answer is: probably fast enough.*

Need anything else be said?

# APPENDIX G

## DOCUMENTS FROM THE
## NATIONAL ARCHIVES

1
DL 89-43
KCH:rmb

<u>RESULTS OF AUTOPSY ON JOHN F. KENNEDY</u>

On November 23, 1963, an autopsy was performed on the body of former President JOHN F. KENNEDY at the National Naval Medical Center, Bethesda, Maryland. A total body X-ray and autopsy revealed one bullet hole located just below shoulders to right of spinal column and hand-probing indicated trajectory at angle of 45 to 60 degrees downward and hole of short depth with no point of exit. No bullet located in body.

A second bullet entered back of head and thereafter emerged through top of skull. Two metal fragments removed from brain area, the first 7 x 2 millimeters and the other 3 by 1 millimeters in size.

The above two metal fragments were turned over to Agents of the FBI for delivery to the FBI Laboratory.

A piece of skull measuring 10 by 6.5 centimeters had been flown in to Bethesda from Dallas hospital and this disclosed minute metal fragments where bullet emerged from skull.

With respect to the bullet hole located in the back, pathologist at National Naval Medical Center was of the opinion this bullet worked its way out of the victim's back during cardiac massage performed at Dallas hospital prior to transportation of the body to Washington.

With respect to this situation, it is noted that Secret Service Agent RICHARD JOHNSON turned over to the FBI Laboratory one 6.5 millimeter rifle bullet (approximately .25 caliber), copper alloy, full jacket, which he advised was found on a stretcher in the emergency room of the Dallas hospital to which the victim was taken. JOHNSON was unable to advise whether stretcher on which this bullet was found had been used for the President.

The above information was received by communication from the Baltimore Office, dated November 23, 1963.

*149*

CD 5

---

CD-7

DL 100-10461/cv

A.  AUTOPSY OF BODY OF PRESIDENT
    JOHN FITZGERALD KENNEDY

CD 7

FD-302 (Rev. 1-25-60)    FEDERAL BUREAU OF INVESTIGATION

1                                    Date ___11/26/63___

At approximately 3 p.m. on November 22, 1963, following the President's announced assassination, it was ascertained that Air Force One, the President's jet, was returning from Love Field, Dallas, Texas, flying the body back to Andrews Air Force Base, Camp Springs, Maryland. SAs FRANCIS X. O'NEILL, JR. and JAMES W. SIBERT proceeded to Andrews Air Force Base to handle any matters which would fall within the jurisdiction of the Federal Bureau of Investigation, inasmuch as it was anticipated that a large group of both military and civilian personnel assigned to the Base would congregate at Base Operations to witness the landing of this flight.

Lt. Col. ROBERT T. BEST, Director of Law Enforcement and Security, advised the President's plane would arrive at 5:25 p.m. Subsequently, Col. BEST advised that the plane would arrive at 6:05 p.m.

At approximately 5:55 p.m. agents were advised through the Hyattsville Resident Agency that the Bureau had instructed that the agents accompany the body to the National Naval Medical Center, Bethesda, Maryland, to stay with the body and to obtain bullets reportedly in the President's body.

Immediately agents contacted Mr. JAMES ROWLEY, the Director of the U. S. Secret Service, identified themselves and made Mr. ROWLEY aware of our aforementioned instruction. Immediately following the plane's landing, Mr. ROWLEY arranged seating for Bureau agents in the third car of the White House motorcade which followed the ambulance containing the President's body to the Naval Medical Center, Bethesda, Maryland.

On arrival at the Medical Center, the ambulance stopped in front of the main entrance, at which time Mrs. JACQUELINE KENNEDY and Attorney General ROBERT KENNEDY embarked from the ambulance and entered the building. The ambulance was thereafter driven around to the rear entrance where the President's body was removed and taken into an autopsy room. Bureau agents assisted in the moving of the casket to the autopsy room. A tight security was immediately placed around the autopsy room by the Naval facility and the U. S. Secret Service. Bureau agents made contact with Mr. ROY KELLERMAN, the Assistant Secret Service Agent in Charge of the White House Detail, and advised him of the Bureau's interest in this matter.

On __11/22/63__ at __Bethesda, Maryland__ File # __89-30__

by __SAs FRANCIS X. O'NEILL, JR.;__    Date dictated __11/26/63__
    __JAMES W. SIBERT : dfl__
This document contains neither recommendations nor conclusions of the FBI. It is the property of the FBI and is loaned to your agency; it and its contents are not to be distributed outside your agency.

CD 7

---

BA 89-30
FXO/JWS:dfl
2

He advised that he had already received instructions from Director ROWLEY as to the presence of Bureau agents. It will be noted that aforementioned Bureau agents, Mr. ROY KELLERMAN, Mr. WILLIAM GREER and Mr. WILLIAM O'LEARY, Secret Service agents, were the only personnel other than medical personnel present during the autopsy.

The following individuals attended the autopsy:

Adm. C. B. HOLLOWAY, U. S. Navy, Commanding Officer of the U. S. Naval Medical Center, Bethesda;

Adm. BERKLEY, U. S. Navy, the President's personal physician;

Commander JAMES J. HUMES, Chief Pathologist, Bethesda Naval Hospital, who conducted autopsy;

Capt. JAMES H. STONER, JR., Commanding Officer, U. S. Naval Medical School, Bethesda;

Mr. JOHN T. STRINGER, JR., Medical photographer;

JAMES H. EBERSOLE;

LLOYD E. RAHE;

J. T. BOZWELL;

J. G. RUDNICKI;

PAUL K. O'CONNOR;

J. C. JENKINS;

JERROL F. CRESTER;

EDWARD F. REED;

JAMES METZLER.

During the course of the autopsy, Lt. Col. P. FINCK, U. S. Army Armed Forces Institute of Pathology, arrived to assist Commander HUMES in the autopsy. In addition, Lt. Cmdr. GREGG CROSS and Captain DAVID OSBORNE, Chief of Surgery, entered the autopsy room.

Major General WEHLE, Commanding Officer of U. S. Military District, Washington, D.C., entered the autopsy room to ascertain from the Secret Service arrangements concerning the

CD 7

---

BA 89-30
FXO/JWS:dfl
3

transportation of the President's body back to the White House. AMC CHESTER H. BOYERS, U. S. Navy, visited the autopsy room during the final stages of such to type receipts given by FBI and Secret Service for items obtained.

At the termination of the autopsy, the following personnel from Gawler's Funeral Home entered the autopsy room to prepare the President's body for burial:

JOHN VAN HAESEN
EDWIN STROBLE
THOMAS ROBINSON
Mr. HAGEN

Brigidier General GODFREY McHUGH, Air Force Military Aide to the President, was also present, as was Dr. GEORGE BAKEMAN, U. S. Navy.

Arrangements were made for the performance of the autopsy by the U. S. Navy and Secret Service.

The President's body was removed from the casket in which it had been transported and was placed on the autopsy table, at which time the complete body was wrapped in a sheet and the head area contained an additional wrapping which was saturated with blood. Following the removal of the wrapping, it was ascertained that the President's clothing had been removed and it was also apparent that a tracheotomy had been performed, as well as surgery of the head area, namely, in the top of the skull. In all probability with the exception of medical officers needed in the taking of photographs and X-Rays were requested to leave the autopsy room and remain in an adjacent room.

Upon completion of X-Rays and photographs, the first incision was made at 8:15 p.m. X-Rays of the brain area which were developed and returned to the autopsy room disclosed a path of a missile which appeared to enter the back of the skull and the path of the disintegrated fragments could be observed along the right side of the skull. The largest section of this missile as portrayed by X-Ray appeared to be behind the right frontal sinus. The next largest fragment appeared to be at the rear of the skull at the juncture of the skull bone.

The Chief Pathologist advised approximately 40 particles of disintegrated bullet and smudges indicated that the projectile had fragmentized while passing through the skull region.

CD 7

---

BA 89-30
FXO/JWS:dfl
4

During the autopsy inspection of the area of the brain, two fragments of metal were removed by Dr. HUMES, namely, one fragment measuring 7 x 2 millimeters, which was removed from the right side of the brain. An additional fragment of metal measuring 1 x 3 millimeters was also removed from this area, both of which were placed in a glass jar containing a black metal top which were thereafter marked for identification and following the signing of a proper receipt were transported by Bureau agents to the FBI Laboratory.

During the latter stages of this autopsy, Dr. HUMES located an opening which appeared to be a bullet hole which was below the shoulders and two inches to the right of the middle line of the spinal column.

This opening was probed by Dr. HUMES with the finger, at which time it was determined that the trajectory of the missile entering at this point had entered at a downward position of 45 to 60 degrees. Further probing determined that the distance travelled by this missile was a short distance inasmuch as the end of the opening could be felt with the finger.

Inasmuch as no complete bullet of any size could be located in the brain area and likewise no bullet could be located in the back or any other area of the body as determined by total body X-Rays and inspection revealing there was no point of exit, the individuals performing the autopsy were at a loss to explain why they could find no bullets.

A call was made by Bureau agents to the Firearms Section of the FBI Laboratory, at which time SA CHARLES L. KILLION advised that the Laboratory had received through Secret Service Agent RICHARD JOHNSON a bullet which had reportedly been found on a stretcher in the emergency room of Parkland Hospital, Dallas, Texas. This stretcher had also contained a stethoscope and pair of rubber gloves. Agent JOHNSON had advised the Laboratory that it had not been ascertained whether or not this was the stretcher which had been used to transport the body of President KENNEDY. Agent KILLION further described this bullet as pertaining to a 6.5 millimeter rifle which would be approximately a 25 caliber rifle and that this bullet consisted of a copper alloy full jacket.

Immediately following receipt of this information, this was made available to Dr. HUMES who advised that in his opinion this accounted for no bullet being located which had entered

CD 7

BA 89-30
FCO/JWS:dfl
5

the back region and that since external cardiac massage had been performed at Parkland Hospital, it was entirely possible that through such movement the bullet had worked its way back out of the point of entry and had fallen on the stretcher.

Also during the latter stages of the autopsy, a piece of the skull measuring 10 x 6.5 centimeters was brought to Dr. HUMES who was instructed that this had been removed from the President's skull. Immediately this section of skull was X-Rayed, at which time it was determined by Dr. HUMES that one corner of this section revealed minute metal particles and inspection of this same area disclosed a chipping of the top portion of this piece, both of which indicated that this had been the point of exit of the bullet entering the skull region.

On the basis of the latter two developments, Dr. HUMES stated that the pattern was clear   that the one bullet had entered the President's back and had worked its way out of the body during external cardiac massage and that a second high velocity bullet had entered the rear of the skull and had fragmentized prior to exit through the top of the skull. He further pointed out that X-Rays had disclosed numerous fractures in the cranial area which he attributed to the force generated by the impact of the bullet in its passage through the brain area. He attributed the death of the President to a gunshot wound in the head.

The following is a complete listing of photographs and X-Rays taken by the medical authorities of the President's body. They were turned over to Mr. ROY KELLERMAN of the Secret Service. X-Rays were developed by the hospital, however, the photographs were delivered to Secret Service undeveloped:

    11 X-Rays
    22 4 x 5 color photographs
    18 4 x 5 black and white photographs
    1 roll of 120 film containing five exposures

Mr. KELLERMAN stated these items could be made available to the FBI upon request. The portion of the skull measuring 10 x 6.5 centimeters was maintained in the custody of Dr. HUMES who stated that it also could be made available for further examination. The two metal fragments removed from the brain area were hand carried by SAs SIBERT and O'NEILL to the FBI Laboratory immediately following the autopsy and were turned over to SA KURT FRAZIER.

## CD 7

---

U. S. Secret Service

Chief                                                    November 28, 1963

Inspector Kelley

Preliminary Special Dallas Report #1. Assassination of the President (Assassination Scene)

At approximately 12:30 PM on November 22, 1963, a car bearing the President, Mrs. Kennedy, Governor John Connally of Texas and Mrs. Connally, was proceeding west enroute to the Trade Mart Building, 2100 Stemmons Freeway, to a Luncheon sponsored by the Dallas Citizens Council scheduled for 12:30 PM. The car owned and operated by the Secret Service was driven by Special Agent William R. Greer. The right front seat was occupied by ASAIC Roy H. Kellerman. At the foot of Elm Street, at a point approximately 200 feet east of the Houston Street Triple Underpass, on the approach to the Stemmons Freeway, President Kennedy, who was seated on the right rear seat, was shot. Immediately thereafter Governor Connally, seated in the right jump seat, was shot once. The President was then shot the second time. The car carrying the wounded President and the Governor proceeded immediately to the Parkland Memorial Hospital at 5201 Harry Hines Boulevard where the President was pronounced dead by Dr. Kemp Clark, Chief of Neurosurgery at 1 pm. Governor Connally, critically wounded, survived.

Witnesses identified the source of the shots as the sixth floor of the Texas School Book Depository Building at 411 Elm Street. A search of the building disclosed a number of open windows on the south side of the building. Officers Capt. J. W. Fritz and Detectives R. M. Sims and E. L. Boyd of the Dallas Homicide Division of the Police Department found, in an area on the sixth floor near an open window on the southeast corner of the building, three expended shells of 6.5 MM caliber rifle ammunition. An immediate search of the room disclosed an Italian Mainlicher-Carcano rifle 6.5 MM with a 4X Scope, hidden among the boxes on opposite side of this room near the staircase. One loaded shell was found in the chamber of the rifle.

ATTACHMENTS:
see Document    Photographs of the area from which the assassin fired the shots.
No. 40          Photographs of the street being traveled by the President when assassinated
For Photos      Interviews of witnesses taken by Dallas Police Officers on their
                arrival at the Texas Schoolbook Depository.

TJK:VS
Encls- 31

## CD 87

---

FD-302 (Rev. 3-3-59)            FEDERAL BUREAU OF INVESTIGATION

                                        Date    11/29/63

1

        SA JOHN JOE HOWLETT, U. S. Secret Service, Dallas, advised that with the aid of a surveyor and through the use of 8 millimeter movie films depicting President JOHN F. KENNEDY being struck by assassin's bullets on November 22, 1963, HOWLETT was able to ascertain that the distance from the window ledge of the farthest window to the east in the sixth floor of the Texas School Book Depository Building, 411 Elm Street, to where the President was struck the first time in the neck was approximately 170 feet. He stated this distance would be accurate within two or three feet. The distance from the same window ledge to the spot where President KENNEDY was struck in the head by the assassin's bullet was approximately 260 feet. Mr. HOWLETT stated that Secret Service Agents, using the 8 millimeter film had been unable to ascertain the exact location where Governor JOHN B. CONNALLY was struck.

        SA HOWLETT advised that it had been ascertained from the movies that President KENNEDY was struck with the first and third shots fired by the assassin, while Gov. CONNALLY was struck with the second shot. SA HOWLETT stated the window referred to above was the one from which the shots were fired and faces south.

on  11/29/63  at  Dallas, Texas            File # Dallas 89-43
    ROBERT M. BARRETT

## CD 5

---

- 44 -

time he heard two more shots. He doesn't know if they came after he was on top of the Vice President, but Mr. Johnson told him that was so. Agent Johns in the Vice-Presidential follow-up car jumped out and ran to the Vice President's car, but the vehicles speeded up suddenly. He was left in the street and caught a ride to the Hospital with a press car.

E. Information Not Included in Statements

    No member of the Secret Service saw where any shots were fired from. None saw a rifle or any type of weapon in a window of the School Book Depository Building. None heard any person identify, or purport to identify, the source of the shots. None fired his own or any other weapon.

    All the Secret Service agents assigned to the motorcade stayed with the motorcade all the way to the Hospital. None remained at the scene of the shooting, and none entered the School Book Depository Building at or immediately after the time of the shooting. (This was consistent with Secret Service procedure which requires that each agent stay with the President and Vice President and not be diverted by any distractions unless he must do so in order to protect the President and Vice President.)

III. SUBSEQUENT EVENTS

    The events following the shooting of the President from the high-speed trip to Parkland Hospital to the landing of the

## CD 3

FD-302 (Rev. 3-3-59)

FEDERAL BUREAU OF INVESTIGATION

Date _11/24/63_

1

OTIS N. WILLIAMS, 3429 South Western Avenue, Dallas, Texas, furnished the following information:

WILLIAMS is an employee of the Texas School Book Depository, Elm at Houston Street, Dallas, Texas and has been for the past 12 years.

On November 22, 1963 at the time the Presidential Procession passed the Texas School Book Depository Building, WILLIAMS was on the front steps of the building. The Presidential car had just passed the building a few seconds and was out of sight over the embankment when WILLIAMS heard three loud blasts. He thought these blasts came from the location of the court house. He did not look up and immediately went back into the building into his office on the second floor. A few minutes later, Detectives came into the building and he went with a Detective to check the second floor of the building. WILLIAMS remained in the building until approximately 3 PM, at which time the building was closed.

WILLIAMS is not acquainted with LEE HARVEY OSWALD, an employee of the Texas School Book Depository. He has possibly seen OSWALD in the building, but cannot recall him.

on _11/23/63_ at Dallas, Texas ___ File # _DL 89-43_

by Special Agent PAUL J. SCOTT & EDMOND C. HARDIN/sbr Date dictated _11/24/63_

This document contains neither recommendations nor conclusions of the FBI. It is the property of the FBI and is loaned to your agency; it and its contents are not to be distributed outside your agency.

CD 5

---

FD-302 (Rev. 3-3-59)

FEDERAL BUREAU OF INVESTIGATION

Date _11/24/63_

1

Mrs. JOHN T. (ELSIE) DORMAN, 1233 East Louisiana, Dallas, Texas, advised that she is employed in a clerical capacity for the Scott-Foresman Company, educational publishers, offices located on the fourth floor of the Texas School Book Depository Building.

She stated she had never seen LEE HARVEY OSWALD in the building and failed to recognize his photographs when shown on television.

When the President's motorcade passed, Mrs. DORMAN advised she was looking out the window on the fourth floor. The window was raised and she was taking pictures. It was at this time she heard sounds which sounded like shots. She felt that these shots were coming from the area of the Records Building. She stated she had seen no one whom she could associate with the shots during or after the shots were fired and was unable to provide any additional information.

on _11/22/63_ at Dallas, Texas ___ File # _DL 89-43_

by Special Agent DAVID H. BARRY & LOUIS M. KELLEY/sih Date dictated _11/24/63_

This document contains neither recommendations nor conclusions of the FBI. It is the property of the FBI and is loaned to your agency; it and its contents are not to be distributed outside your agency.

CD 5

---

FD-302 (Rev. 3-3-59)

FEDERAL BUREAU OF INVESTIGATION

Date _6/22/64_

PHILLIP L. WILLIS, 2824 Ava Lane, telephone No. EV 1-1326, advised he is self-employed as a real estate broker and has his office in his home. He stated he was born August 2, 1918, in Kaufman County, Texas. WILLIS stated he is a retired Air Force Major, was a Senior Pilot, and had 23 months combat experience in the South Pacific from 1941 to 1943. WILLIS advised he served in the Texas State House of Representatives from 1946 to 1950 from Kaufman County.

On November 22, 1963, WILLIS advised he was employed by Downtown Lincoln Mercury, Incorporated, 118 Commerce Street, Dallas, Texas, as an executive salesman for the Lincoln Continental. He said he was jointly employed by both the Downtown Lincoln Mercury, Incorporated, and the Ford Motor Company. WILLIS advised that on November 22, 1963, his wife, MARILYN; his two daughters, ROSEMARY, age 10, and LINDA KAY, age 14, his mother-in-law and father-in-law, Mr. and Mrs. WILLIAM H. STUBBLEFIELD, met him at Downtown Lincoln Mercury, Incorporated, so they could all watch the Presidential motorcade together. He advised they all left Downtown Lincoln Mercury, Incorporated, about noon on November 22, 1963, and arrived at the northwest corner of Main and Houston Streets at about 12:05 p.m. He said his daughters remained at that location with him and his wife and her parents moved down to the colonnade area on the north side of Elm Street. WILLIS stated that a little before 12:30 p.m., the Presidential motorcade approached his position and he took approximately four pictures as it approached with his 35 mm camera loaded with Kodachrome film. After the motorcade passed this position, WILLIS said he ran north on Houston Street, stopped opposite the Dallas County Jail, and took another snapshot of the Presidential motorcade. WILLIS stated he then ran from Houston Street to the south side of Elm Street across from the Texas School Book Depository building and took four pictures from this position as the Presidential motorcade proceeded west on Elm Street toward the triple underpass.

WILLIS advised that at just about the same time that the limousine carrying President KENNEDY was opposite the Stemmons Freeway road sign he heard a loud report and knew immediately it was a rifle shot. He knew also the shot "had hit." He stated he exclaimed "Someone is

on _6/18/64_ at Dallas, Texas ___ File # _DL 100-10461_

by Special Agent A. RAYMOND SWITZER:vm ___ Date dictated _6/19/64_

This document contains neither recommendations nor conclusions of the FBI. It is the property of the FBI and is loaned to your agency; it and its contents are not to be distributed outside your agency.

CD 1245

---

2
DL 100-10461

shooting at him," meaning President KENNEDY. About two seconds later, he heard another rifle shot which also hit as did the third shot which came approximately two seconds later. WILLIS said he knows from his war experience the sound a rifle shot makes when it finds its mark and he is sure all three shots fired found their mark. Further, WILLIS stated he knew the shots came from the Texas School Book Depository building and they should "ring the building." He said he meant by this the police should prevent anyone from leaving or entering the Texas School Book Depository building. WILLIS advised his two daughters ran up to him, and they were crying and saying "They've killed him." He said they told him "His head exploded; it looked like a red halo."

WILLIS advised he and his family remained in the area approximately an hour or so and he took additional pictures of the assassination site. He said he and his wife then drove directly to the Eastman Kodak Processing Laboratory to have his film developed. WILLIS stated shortly after he arrived at the Eastman Kodak Processing Laboratory a Mr. ZAPRUDER arrived with some 8 mm color film. At about the same time, WILLIS stated Mr. FORREST V. SORRELS of the Secret Service arrived and inquired of the Eastman Kodak Processing Laboratory concerning any film received by them taken at the site and at the time of the assassination of President KENNEDY.

About one half hour after arriving at the Eastman Kodak Processing Laboratory, WILLIS advised both his and ZAPRUDER's film had been developed and he, his wife, Mr. ZAPRUDER, and Mr. SORRELS viewed both his film and ZAPRUDER's film. Following this, WILLIS stated Mr. SORRELS asked if he could borrow WILLIS' film and WILLIS stated he turned his film over to Mr. SORRELS.

WILLIS stated around the latter part of December, 1963, or early January, 1964, Mr. SORRELS returned his film to him. He said he does not know what use SORRELS made of his film or if it had been viewed by the President's Commission. WILLIS stated he has determined

47

CD 1245

**300**

---

FD-302 (Rev. 3-3-59)

FEDERAL BUREAU OF INVESTIGATION

Date ___11/23/63___

1

BONNIE RAY WILLIAMS, residence 1502 Avenue B, Apartment B, employed at the Texas School Book Depository, furnished the following information:

During the past three weeks he has been putting in new flooring on the fourth floor of the Texas School Book Depository Building at the corner of Houston and Elm Streets. During that time, he became acquainted with a young man known to him as LEE.

WILLIAMS stated on November 22, 1963, he worked installing flooring on the sixth floor of the building until about 11:30 a.m. At that time, he went down on an elevator from the sixth floor to the first floor. At the same time, CHARLES GIVENS was on the other elevator, descending at the same time. As they were going down, he saw LEE on the fifth floor. He had previously seen LEE at least once that morning at about 8 a.m. on the first floor, filling orders.

At approximately 12 noon, WILLIAMS went back upstairs in the elevator to the sixth floor with his lunch. He stayed on that floor only about three minutes, and seeing no one there, he descended to the fifth floor, using the stairs at the west end of the building. There he joined two other men known to him as HANK and JUNIOR. They were looking out windows on the south side of the building approximately at the middle of the building and saw the car of President JOHN KENNEDY come north on Houston Street and then make a turn going west on Elm Street down into the triple underpass and passing directly in front of the Texas School Book Depository. While they were watching this car pass, WILLIAMS heard two shots which sounded like they came from right over his head. He stated he was not hanging out the window, but did glance up and saw no one. He stated he and the other two then ran to the west end of the building where they looked out and they did not realize that the President had been shot and WILLIAMS did not see him shot. While they were standing at the west end of the building on the fifth floor, a police officer came up on the elevator and looked all around the fifth floor and left the floor. WILLIAMS stated he and HANK and JUNIOR were standing where they would have seen anyone coming down from the sixth floor via the stairs and that they did not see anyone coming down. He

330

on __11/23/63__ at __Dallas, Texas__ _____ File # __Dallas 89-43__

BARDWELL D. ODUM and
by Special Agent __WILL HAYDEN GRIFFIN/sl__ ___ Date dictated __11/23/63__

CD 5

---

DL 89-43

2

stated someone might have been coming down on the elevator and they would not have noticed them. He stated that after the police officer left the fifth floor, WILLIAMS went down to the fourth floor where there were a lot of women around the west end of the floor. BILL SHELLEY asked about LEE, but no one had seen him.

WILLIAMS stated that while working on the sixth floor until 11:30 a.m. on November 22, 1963, he did not see LEE or anyone else in the southeast corner of the building. He stated there are a number of shelves stacked with books in this area and he would have been unable to see this corner from where he was working. He pointed out, however, that he did go to the windows on the south side of the sixth floor, middle of the building, about three minutes after 12 and did not see anyone standing at any of the windows at that time.

WILLIAMS stated that LEE was always reading the newspapers, but that he did not read the sport pages like many men do, but read "politics." He stated LEE would read something in the paper and then laugh about it. On one occasion he looked at the paper LEE was reading when he laughed and noticed LEE was reading something from the front page of the newspaper.

WILLIAMS advised that LEE did not seem to have any close friends or associate with anyone else on the job. He recalled LEE at one time rode to work with a boy named WESLEY who works in the Depository. He last saw WESLEY between 10 and 11 a.m. on November 22, 1963, on the sixth floor of the Depository, talking to Mr. SHELLEY.

WILLIAMS stated he had seen numerous pictures of LEE HARVEY OSWALD on television and that OSWALD was identical with LEE referred to above.

331

CD 5

---

FD-302 (Rev. 3-3-59)

1

FEDERAL BUREAU OF INVESTIGATION

Date ___11/23/63___

HOWARD LESLIE BRENNAN, 6814 Woodard (EV 1-2713), employed by Wallace and Beard Construction Company as a steamfitter, and engaged in doing prefabrication work at a location near the rear of the Texas School Book Depository building at 411 Elm Street, Dallas, advised he was at this location near the rear of the Texas School Book Depository building at 411 Elm Street, Dallas, for the purpose of eating lunch. He had lunch alone at a cafeteria at the northeast corner of Main and Record Streets in Dallas.

After finishing lunch, he walked back to the front of the Texas School Book Depository building and on Elm Street, directly across from the above building, took a seat on a retainer wall some 4 feet in height. He explained the place where he was seated was on the south side of Elm Street, about 20 feet west of the southwest corner of the intersection of Elm and Houston Streets, and about 5 feet from the curb.

He estimated he seated himself at this point some 3 to 5 minutes after having left the cafeteria about 12:18 PM, on November 22, 1963. He recalled noting the time as he left the cafeteria, since he was supposed to be away from the job for lunch only one-half hour. He estimated he had been seated on the retainer wall about 10 minutes before the automobile carrying President KENNEDY passed in front of him, at which time he observed the President and his wife sitting on the back seat of the vehicle. He said the automobile had passed down Elm Street (going in a westerly direction) approximately 30 yards from the point where he (BRENNAN) was seated, when he heard a loud report which he first thought to be the "backfire" of an automobile. He said he does not distinctly remember a second shot but he remembers "more than one noise", as if someone was shooting fire crackers, and consequently he believes there must have been a second shot before he looked in the direction of the Texas School Book Depository building.

Upon hearing the report, or reports, he looked across the street to the Texas School Book Depository building, where he saw a man in a window on the sixth floor near the southeast corner of the building. The man he observed in the window had what appeared to be a "heavy" rifle in his hands. He could not

on __11/22/63__ at __Dallas, Texas__ _____ File # __DL 89-43__

GASTON C. THOMPSON and
by Special Agent __ROBERT C. LISH__ /rmb __ Date dictated __11/22/63__

12

CD 5

---

2
DL 89-43

tell whether or not this rifle had a telescopic sight, as the rifle was protruding only about half its length outside the window.

He was positive that after he had observed this man in the window, he saw this person take "deliberate aim" and fire a shot. He then observed this person take the rifle from his shoulder and hold it by the barrel of the rifle, as if he were resting the butt of the rifle on the floor. He said this individual observed the scene on the street below, momentarily, and then stepped back from the window. He said the rifle was pointed in the direction of the President's car when he saw it fired.

He advised there was nothing to obstruct his line of vision between the place where he was seated and the window on the sixth floor of the Texas School Book Depository building where he saw the man with the rifle. He estimated distance between the point where he was seated and the window from which the shots were fired to be approximately 90 yards.

He noticed there appeared to be a stack of heavy cartons visible in the window and slightly to the rear of the place where the man stood with the rifle. He stated he saw two Negro men on the next lower floor, immediately beneath the window where the man was observed with the rifle. One of these men (on the floor below) was looking out a window directly beneath the window in which the rifleman stood. The other Negro was in a window immediately to the west of the first Negro mentioned above. He observed these two men glance upward, as if they were trying to determine the spot from which the rifle shots were being fired.

BRENNAN described the man with the rifle as a white male, who appeared to be in his early 30's, about 5'10" tall and around 165 pounds in weight. He stated this individual was not wearing a hat and was dressed in "light color clothes in the khaki line". He added this individual may have been wearing a light-weight jacket or sweater; however, he could not be positive about the jacket or sweater.

He advised he attended a lineup at the Dallas Police Department on November 22, 1963, on which occasion he picked LEE HARVEY OSWALD as the person most closely resembling the man he had observed with the rifle in the window of the Texas School Book Depository building. He stated, however, he could not positively identify OSWALD as the person he saw fire the rifle.

He volunteered he has been informed by his optometrist, Dr. HOWARD F. BONAR, Port Lavaca, Texas, that he (BRENNAN) has

13

CD 5

3
DL 89-43

"perfect" vision at a distance or, in other words, he is far-sighted. He advised he wears glasses for reading purposes only.

*14*

## CD 5

---

FD-302 (Rev. 3-3-59)

ᴎEDERAL BUREAU OF INVESTIGATE

1

Date ___12/18/63___

HOWARD LESLIE BRENNAN, 6814 Woodard, advised that he furnished information previously to the Federal Bureau of Investigation regarding his having observed activity at the window in the Texas School Book Depository (TSBD) from which shots were allegedly fired at President KENNEDY on November 22, 1963, at Dallas. He advised that at about 7 p.m., November 22, 1963, when he observed a line-up of individuals at the Dallas Police Department he selected LEE HARVEY OSWALD as the individual most closely resembling the person whom he had seen with a rifle in the window of the TSBD Building. He said this was the extreme east window of the sixth floor on the front side of the TSBD Building where he observed this individual. He noted that he was seated on a wall across Elm Street from the TSBD at the time the Presidential motorcade passed. He stated that he now can say that he is sure that LEE HARVEY OSWALD was the person he saw in the window at the time of the President's assassination. He pointed out that he felt that a positive identification was not necessary when he observed OSWALD in the police line-up at the Dallas Police Department at about 7 p.m., November 22, 1963, since it was his understanding OSWALD had already been charged with the slaying of Dallas Police Officer J. D. TIPPIT. He said that another factor which made him hesitate to make a positive identification of OSWALD in the police line-up was that prior to appearing at the police line-up on November 22, 1963, he had observed a picture of OSWALD on his television set at home when his daughter asked him to watch it. He said that he felt that since he had seen OSWALD on television before picking OSWALD out of the line-up at the police station that it tended to "cloud" any identification he made of OSWALD at that time.

BRENNAN stated that he is not a publicity seeker and that on the contrary he would prefer not to have it known that he had made any identification of OSWALD as the person who had fired shots from the window of the TSBD. He stated that if it became necessary that his identity be known in this matter in connection with any subsequent hearings or Governmental review of reports regarding this matter he would be willing to have his name known and, therefore, he is identified herein as having furnished at

on ___12/17/63___ at ___Dallas, Texas___ _____ File # __DL 100-10461__

by Special Agent __KENNETH D. JACKSON__ /cv _____ Date dictated __12/18/63__

## CD 205

---

DL 100-10461
KBJ:cv
2

this time a positive identification of OSWALD as the person who fired a rifle from the window of the TSBD on November 22, 1963, when the motorcade of President KENNEDY was passing the building. BRENNAN stated that he was able to observe OSWALD's head and shoulders in the window and possibly down as far as OSWALD's belt. He stated that he had earlier pointed out that he has especially good vision at a distance through being farsighted although he wears glasses for reading.

## CD 205

---

FD-302 (Rev. 3-3-59)

FEDERAL BUREAU OF INVESTIGATION

Date ___11/26/63___

1

WILLIAM ALLEN HARPER, a student at Texas Christian University, Ft. Worth, Texas, but who lives in Dallas, at 2378 E. Ledbetter Street, was taking photographs during the afternoon of November 23, 1963, approximately 5:30 PM in the area just south of the spot where President KENNEDY was assassinated and had found a piece of bone. The bone was located approximately 25 feet south of the spot where President KENNEDY was shot. Dr. HARPER stated that his nephew immediately brought the bone to him and he and the Chief Pathologist at Methodist Hospital, Dr. C. E. KERNS, had examined the piece of bone and both definitely felt that it is a piece of human skull.

Dr. HARPER felt that in view of the proximity of the place where the piece of bone was located it might possibly be part of President KENNEDY's skull.

WILLIAM ALLEN HARPER made this piece of bone available to SA JAMES W. ANDERTON of the Dallas FBI Office for what ever disposition the FBI desired.

*150*

on ___11/26/63___ at ___Dallas, Texas___ _____ File # __DL 89-43__

by Special Agent __JAMES W. ANDERTON__/atd _____ Date dictated __11/26/63__

## CD 5

DL 89-43

On November 27, 1963, the FBI Laboratory advised that a piece of bone reportedly located near where President KENNEDY was shot had been x-rayed and examined microscopically for bullet metals but none were found.

A small amount of blood appearing on the surface of the bone was determined to be of human origin but was too limited in amount for grouping purposes. This bone fragment was delivered to Admiral GEORGE BURKLEY, Physician to the President at the White House, according to the FBI Laboratory letter.

/51/

**CD 5**

---

FD-302 (Rev. 3-3-59)          FEDERAL BUREAU OF INVESTIGATION

1

Date    7/13/64

A. B. CAIRNS, M.D., 5027 Lahoma, telephone number LA 8-3256, advised he is the Chief Pathologist at Methodist Hospital of Dallas, 301 West Colorado Boulevard, Dallas, Texas.

Dr. CAIRNS advised that on November 25, 1963, he received a telephone call from Dr. JACK C. HARPER, who asked if he would take a look at a piece of bone. Dr. CAIRNS stated that Dr. HARPER had informed him that this piece of bone was found by his nephew, BILLY A. HARPER, near the site where President KENNEDY was assassinated.

Dr. CAIRNS advised that he and Dr. HARPER examined the bone at Methodist Hospital of Dallas. Dr. CAIRNS stated the bone specimen looked like it came from the occipital region of the skull. He said he performed no tests on this piece of bone and evaluated it purely from its gross appearance.

Dr. CAIRNS said that after he examined the bone, he went about his own business, after suggesting to Dr. HARPER that he report the matter to the Federal Bureau of Investigation.

Dr. CAIRNS advised that he does not know if any pictures were taken of this bone specimen, but believes that a week or so after he and Dr. HARPER had examined the bone, Dr. HARPER may have shown him a color slide of the bone specimen.

on   7/10/64   at Dallas, Texas                    File #   DL 100-10461

by Special Agent  A. RAYMOND SWITZER/ds            Date dictated   7/11/64

This document contains neither recommendations nor conclusions of the FBI. It is the property of the FBI and is loaned to your agency; it and its contents are not to be distributed outside your agency.

**CD 1395**

---

FD-302 (Rev. 3-3-59)          FEDERAL BUREAU OF INVESTIGATION

1

Date    7/13/64

JACK C. HARPER, M.D., with offices located at 526 East Jefferson, telephone number WH 1-0323, advised he resides at 534 Monssen Drive, Dallas, Texas, telephone number WH 2-2878.

He advised he had been interviewed previously by a representative of the FBI. During the course of this interview, Dr. HARPER stated he advised that his nephew, BILLY A. HARPER, 2378 East Ledbetter, Dallas, Texas, who at that time was a pre-medical student at Texas Christian University, Fort Worth, Texas, had been taking photographs in the area where President KENNEDY was assassinated, and had found a piece of human bone. Dr. HARPER stated his nephew indicated he had found this piece of bone at approximately 5:30 P.M. on November 23, 1963, in the area approximately twenty-five feet south of the site where President KENNEDY was assassinated.

Dr. HARPER stated his nephew immediately brought the bone to him and he and the Chief Pathologist at Methodist Hospital of Dallas, Dr. A. B. CAIRNS, had examined the piece of bone and both definitely felt that it was a piece of human skull.

Dr. HARPER advised that he felt in view of the proximity of the place where the piece of bone was located, it might possibly be a part of President KENNEDY's skull.

Dr. HARPER advised that after he and Dr. CAIRNS had examined the above piece of bone, he had M. WAYNE BOLLETER, Chief Medical Photographer, Medical Photography Department, Methodist Hospital of Dallas, make two 35 millimeter color slides of this piece of bone, one slide being a photograph of the concave side and the other slide being a photograph of the convex side.

Dr. HARPER stated he would make available these slides to the FBI, but requested that they be returned to him.

on   7/10/64   at Dallas, Texas                    File #   DL 100-10461

by Special Agent  A. RAYMOND SWITZER/ds            Date dictated   7/11/64

This document contains neither recommendations nor conclusions of the FBI. It is the property of the FBI and is loaned to your agency; it and its contents are not to be distributed outside your agency.

**CD 1395**

---

FD-302 (Rev. 3-3-59)          FEDERAL BUREAU OF INVESTIGATION

Date   September 29, 1964

1

On September 29, 1964, EUGENE P. ALDREDGE, 9304 Lenel, Dallas, Texas, telephonically advised that he disagreed with the President's Commission report that OSWALD did not have help in the assassination.

ALDREDGE stated he saw a television program shortly after the assassination, believed to be on Channel Four, in which a mark on the sidewalk was pointed out.

Approximately three months ago, he stated he viewed such mark, which he is sure was caused by a bullet, and that this mark is approximately six inches long. He described the location of this mark as being in the middle of the sidewalk on the north side of Elm Street, which side is nearest the Texas School Book Depository Building. He stated there is a lamp post near the sidewalk, which is about even with the west end of the Texas School Book Depository Building and that the above-described mark is approximately eight feet east of the lamp post on the sidewalk. He stated that a reporter for "The Dallas Morning News", CARL FREUND, has also stated this is a bullet mark.

When asked as to why he had waited until this time to furnish the foregoing information, he stated he felt that such an important point would be covered in the President's Commission report and did not want to become involved by furnishing the information at this time, but felt that such information, if overlooked, should be made available.

on   9/29/64   at   Dallas, Texas                  File #   DL 100-10461

by Special Agent  ROBERT P. GEMBERLING /jtf        Date dictated   9/29/64

This document contains neither recommendations nor conclusions of the FBI. It is the property of the FBI and is loaned to your agency; it and its contents are not to be distributed outside your agency.

**CD 1546**

DL 100-10461
RPG/ds

Under date of June 10, 1964, the FBI Laboratory furnished the following information concerning a firearms examination requested by the Dallas Office on May 12, 1964:

Specimens received 11/23/63

Q6  C6  6.5 mm Mannlicher-Carcano cartridge case from Texas School Book Depository

Q7  C7  6.5 mm Mannlicher-Carcano cartridge case from Texas School Book Depository

Q8  C8  6.5 mm Mannlicher-Carcano cartridge from Texas School Book Depository

Evidence received 11/27/63

Q48  C38  6.5 mm Mannlicher-Carcano cartridge case from Texas School Book Depository

Results of examination:

An examination was made of the cartridge cases, C6, C7 and C38 and the cartridge, C8, for loading, chambering, extraction and/or ejection marks for the purpose of determining if these specimens had been loaded into and extracted from Oswald's rifle, C14, more than once.

Marks were found on the C6 cartridge case indicating that it has been loaded into and extracted from a weapon at least three times. One set of marks was identified as having been made by the magazine follower of the C14 rifle. It is pointed out that the extractor and ejector marks on C6 as well as on C7, C8 and C38 did not possess sufficient characteristics for identifying the weapon which produced them. There are also three sets of marks on the base of this cartridge

CD 1245

---

2

DL 100-10461

case which were not found on C7, C8, C38 or any of the numerous tests obtained from the C14 rifle. It was not possible to determine what produced these marks.

Marks were found on the C7 cartridge case indicating that it has been loaded into and extracted from a weapon at least twice. One set of marks was identified as having been produced by the chamber of the C14 rifle and one set of marks was identified as having been produced by contact with the bolt of C14; however, it was not possible to determine whether the two sets of marks which were identified were produced by one or two loading operations in the C14 rifle.

Two sets of marks were found on the C8 cartridge (found in the C14 rifle) which were identified as having been produced by the magazine follower of the C14 rifle. Another set of follower marks was found on C8. The fragmentary nature of this set of marks could possibly account for the fact that these marks were not identified with the C14 rifle.

Marks were found on the C38 cartridge case indicating that it had been loaded into and extracted from a weapon at least twice. One set of marks was identified as having been produced by the magazine follower of the C14 rifle and one set of marks was identified as having been produced by the chamber of C14; however, it was not possible to determine whether the two sets of marks which were identified were produced by one or two loading operations in the C14 rifle.

The results of the above examinations do not preclude the possibility that these items could have been loaded into and extracted from a weapon one or more times when insufficient force was used to produce marks. It is pointed out that if two or more cartridges are loaded into the clip of C14, only the bottom cartridge will be marked by the magazine follower.

CD 1245

---

Commission No. 80

TREASURY DEPARTMENT
UNITED STATES SECRET SERVICE
WASHINGTON 25, D.C.

OFFICE OF THE CHIEF

January 6, 1964

Mr. J. Lee Rankin
General Counsel
President's Commission on the
Assassination of President Kennedy
Washington, D. C.

Dear Mr. Rankin:

Reference is made to your letter of December 30, 1963. The second paragraph requested information concerning the handling of the Presidential automobile since November 22, 1963.

When the President was taken from the Presidential car (SS 100-X) into the Parkland Hospital, the car remained at the emergency entrance of the hospital under the supervision of Special Agent Samuel A. Kinney. During its stay there the "Bubble Top" and the leatherette convertible cover were placed on the car by SA Kinney and SA George W. Hickey and a member of the Dallas Police Department. After the official party left the hospital, SS 100-X was driven to Love Air Field by SA Hickey and the car was placed aboard an Air Force C-130 for the flight to Washington. During this flight Special Agents Kinney and Hickey remained with the car in the plane.

Car 100-X arrived at Andrews Air Force Base, Washington, at 8 p.m., November 22. It was driven from Andrews under police escort to the White House garage by SA Kinney, accompanied by SA Charles Taylor of the Washington Field Office. When the car arrived at the garage at 9 p.m., it was turned over to SA Morgan Gies in charge of Secret Service vehicles at the White House garage. The entire car was then covered with a large sheet of plastic by SA Gies and two special agents from the Washington Field Office were assigned to guard the car. These special agents were instructed that no one was to approach the car or touch it until clearance was had from supervisory personnel of the Secret Service. The only access to the car permitted thereafter, until the guards were removed on November 24, was to Deputy Chief Paterni and the party with him and later to the FBI search team, both mentioned below.

There is attached a copy of a report of SA Charles Taylor of the Washington Field Office concerning the security measures surrounding the car and the activity at the White House garage in connection with the search of the vehicle.

CD 80

---

- 2 -

There is also attached a copy of the sheets of the log book of the White House garage for the period 1:05 a.m., November 23, 1963, (the last prior entry on that log was 3:40 p.m., November 22, 1963) through November 28, 1963, reflecting the entry of the FBI search team and the workmen of the Arlington Glass Company (November 26, 1963). This log identifies those persons admitted to the garage during this period, except for those with Secret Service or White House credentials.

SA William Greer, who was driving the car at the time of the assassination, states that he did not notice any damage to the windshield on the drive to the hospital.

SA Hickey, who drove the car from Parkland Hospital to Love Field said that he noticed some slight damage to the windshield on the drive to the airport, but that the damage was not extensive enough to affect his vision. The windshield, in the area around the damage, was spattered with debris. However, SA Hickey noticed upon the arrival in Washington and at the White House garage that the "spidering" had increased and the damage to the windshield was more noticeable.

SA Kinney, who drove the car from Andrews Air Field to the White House garage, stated that he noticed very little damage to the windshield when he was loading it on the plane; that the damage was more noticeable when he arrived at the garage but that it was not so extensive as to affect his driving from the air field.

Special Officer Davis of the Secret Service and SA Gies stated that they noticed the damage to the windshield when the car arrived at the garage, that both of them ran their hands over the outside surface of the windshield and found it to be smooth and unbroken, and that the damage to the windshield was entirely on the inside surface. Both were present when the windshield was removed from the car by the Arlington Glass Company and noticed that the removal caused the cracks in the glass to lengthen, but the outside surface still remained unbroken and there is no hole or crack through the windshield.

Special Agent Gies has viewed the photographs of the windshield taken by the FBI and states that the damage noticeable to the windshield when it was first brought into the garage was not as extensive as the damage reflected in this photograph; i.e., the cracks were not so apparent. Apparently there was only a small spiderweb-like damage visible on the inside of the windshield when the car arrived, but SA Gies is of the opinion that the temperature changes involved in the flight from Dallas, the temperature change and the vibration from driving the car from Andrews Air Field to the White House garage, and then the storing of the car in the warm temperature of the White House garage is responsible for the change in the appearance of the damaged area of the windshield visible in the photograph taken by the FBI. The photograph is attached and labeled as Exhibit I.

CD 80

- 3 -

In a photograph attached and labeled Exhibit 2, taken by the FBI, there is a dent in the chrome topping of the windshield, just above the attachment of the rear view mirror to the top of the windshield frame. SA Gies, who was responsible for the care and maintenance of this vehicle, believes that this damage was on this car prior to November 22, 1963, and it is his recollection that the damage was done in New York at the Empire Garage (Lincoln-Mercury Dealer) on November 1, 1961. Gies thinks the damage was done while he and employees of the Empire Garage were removing the "header" on the leatherette top to make repairs to the crank which secures the convertible top in place on this vehicle. If this was the case, no effort was made to repair the dent prior to the assassination.

Mr. Paul Michel, Service Director of the Empire Garage, who was present and assisted during those repairs, in an interview said that he did not remember that any damage occurred during these repairs but that it is very possible that it could have happened as a crank had broken off in the area. The repairs were done hastily since the car was needed to transport the President, and this slight damage might have gone unnoticed by him. It may be significant to mention here that this photograph accentuates the damage. This indentation is so slight that it could pass unnoticed in ordinary viewing of the area, especially since the sunvisors, being in a horizontal position most of the time, would frequently cut out the view of this portion of the frame.

Upon his arrival at the White House shortly after 9 p.m., on November 22, SA Kinney advised Assistant Special Agent in Charge Floyd Boring that he noticed what appeared to be a piece of bone or tissue on the floor of the rear of the car near the "jump" seat. Deputy Chief of the Secret Service Paul Paterni and ASAIC Boring went to the office of Admiral Burkley, the President's physician at the White House, and requested Chief Petty Officers William Martinell and Thomas Mills of Doctor Burkley's office to accompany them to the White House garage at about 10 p.m., where they removed the plastic covering the car. They then recovered a three-inch triangular section of skull. Martinell also recovered what was apparently a quantity of brain tissue from the back seat of the car. In running his hands over the front cushion of the automobile, Deputy Chief Paterni found a metallic fragment in the front seat in the area between left and right front seats. A second metallic fragment was found by Mills on the floor in front of the right front seat. Both of these fragments were turned over to the FBI for their ballistics examination and are mentioned as Exhibits Q2 and Q3 in the ballistics report made by the FBI addressed to the Chief of Police of Dallas on November 23, 1963.

At 1 a.m., November 23, 1963, Deputy Chief Paterni arranged for a team of FBI agents to examine the Presidential limousine for evidence relating to the shooting. This team was comprised of special agents

## CD 80

---

AS:mln

MEMORANDUM

March 12, 1964

TO: Mr. J. Lee Rankin

FROM: Arlen Specter

SUBJECT: Interview of Autopsy Surgeons

On the afternoon of March 11, 1964, Joseph A. Ball, Esq., and I went to Bethesda Naval Hospital and interviewed Admiral C. B. Holloway, Commander James J. Humes and Commander "J" Thornton Boswell. The interview took place in the office of Admiral Holloway, who is the commanding officer of the National Naval Medical Center, and lasted from approximately 3:30 p.m. to 5:30 p.m.

Commander Humes and Commander Boswell, along with Lt. Col. Pierre A. Finck, who is currently in France, conducted the autopsy and Admiral Holloway was present at all times. They described their activities and findings in accordance with the autopsy report which had been previously submitted as Commission Report 77.

All three described the bullet wound on President Kennedy's back as being a point of entrance. Admiral Holloway then illustrated the angle of the shot by placing one finger on my back at the second finger on the front part of my chest which indicated that the bullet traveled in a consistent downward path on the assumption that it emerged on the opening on the President's front which had been enlarged by the performance of the tracheotomy in Dallas.

Commander Humes explained that it required considerable time at the autopsy trying to determine what happened to the bullet because they found no missile in the President's body. According to Commander Humes, the autopsy surgeons figured that the bullet might have been forced out of the President's back by external heart message or might have emerged through the opening of the throat. He advised that the bullet had been found on a stretcher at Parkland Hospital.

Dr. Humes and Dr. Boswell wrote up the Parkland report which described the wound of the President in the throat which they said was characteristic of an exit for the bullet entrance wound. Dr. Humes and Dr. Boswell expressed the unanimous current opinion that the bullet passed through the strands of muscle in the President's back and continued a downward flight to the throat through his throat. They noted, at the time of the autopsy, some bruising of the internal parts

---

AS:mln

MEMORANDUM

March 12, 1964

TO: Mr. J. Lee Rankin

FROM: Arlen Specter

SUBJECT: Interview of FBI Agents Present at Autopsy

On March 12, 1964, I interviewed Special Agents Francis X. O'Neill and James W. Sibert in my office at approximately 10:00 a.m. to 10:45 a.m.

SA O'Neill and SA Sibert advised that the autopsy surgeons made substantial efforts to determine if there was a missile in the President's body to explain what happened to the bullet which apparently entered the back of his body. They said the opinion was expressed by both Commander Humes and Lt. Col. Finck that the bullet might have been forced out of the back of the President's body upon application of external heart message. They stated that a theory was advanced after SA Sibert called the FBI laboratory and was told by SA Killion that a bullet had been found on a stretcher at Parkland Hospital. SA Sibert relayed that information to the doctors.

SA O'Neill and Sibert stated that they did not recall any discussion of the theory that the bullet might have been forced out of the body by external cardiac message until after SA Sibert reported the finding of the bullet on the stretcher at Parkland. Neither agent could conclusively rule out the possibility that such a hypothesis was advanced prior to that time, but their best recollection was that this theory was expressed after information was obtained about the bullet on the stretcher. SA Sibert noticed that he made no notes during the autopsy. SA O'Neill did take some notes, a few notes, which he destroyed after his report was submitted. SA O'Neill advised that he is sure that his notes would not have described where the doctors expressed the theory that the bullet had been forced out by external heart message, in relation to the learning of the presence of the bullet on the stretcher at Parkland.

I also questioned SA Sibert and SA O'Neill about their interview of SAIC Kellerman and Greer on the portions of the FBI report which Kellerman and Greer have repudiated.

SAs Sibert and O'Neill stated that they interviewed SAs Kellerman and Greer formally on November 27, 1963, and talked to them only informally at the autopsy. SA O'Neill in his original statement advised as noted in Kellerman's statement that he heard the President said "Get me to a hospital" and also that Mrs. Kennedy said "Oh, no." SA O'Neill stated that was

---

- 2 -

of the President's body in that area but tended to attribute that to the tracheotomy at that time. Dr. Humes and Dr. Boswell stated that after the bullet passed between the two strands of muscle, those muscle strands would resist any probing effort and would not disclose the path of the bullet to probing fingers, as the effort was made to probe at the time of the autopsy.

We requested that Dr. Humes and Dr. Boswell prepare or have prepared drawings of the consequences of the shots on the President's body and head, and they also elaborated upon the facts set forth in their autopsy report.

Dictated from 11:30 to 11:45 a.m.

- 2 -

…… those were direct quotes from … … … …… O'Neill used quotation … … in his report …… … …… … …… those … … … in the … … … … … … …… after the impact was …… … … O'Neill … … … … … … … …… … report this … … in the interview of … … … … … … that as the … … … O'Neill … … … … … … leading or directing him in any way.

I also asked the two … … … … …… about the language in their report … that … … … and … … that the President had … … hit and … … got on his … … and communicated with … other vehicles, asking them … … …… to get the President to the hospital … … … … … … … … … … was … … the best of … … … in … … … … they probably did not … … … … … … … … with … … was … … … … … … … at the time of the … … … … did not have an opportunity to take … … notes in … … … with their normal interviewing procedures.

…… … … … … … … … … … …

MEMORANDUM FOR THE RECORD

FROM: Melvin A. Eisenberg

SUBJECT: Conference of April 14, 1964, to determine which
frames in the Zapruder movies show the impact
of the first and second bullets.

April 22, 1964

On April 14, 1964, a conference was held to determine
which frames in the Zapruder film portray the instants at
which the first and second bullets struck.

Present were: Commander James J. Humes, Director
of Laboratories of the Naval Medical School, Bethesda,
Maryland; Commander J. Thornton Boswell, Chief Pathologist,
Naval Medical School, Bethesda; Lt. Col. Pierre A. Finck,
Chief of Wound Ballistics Pathology Branch, Armed Forces
Institute of Pathology; Dr. F. W. Light, Jr., Deputy Chief
of the Biophysics Division at Edgewood Arsenal, Maryland,
and Chief of the Wound Assessment Branch of the Biophysics
Division; Dr. Olivier, Chief of the Wound Ballistics Branch
of the Biophysics Division at Edgewood Arsenal; Messrs.
Malley, Gauthier, Shaneyfelt, and two other unidentified
agents of the FBI; Messrs. Kelley and Howlett of the Secret
Service; and Messrs. Redlich, Specter, and Eisenberg of the
Commission staff.

A screening was held of the Zapruder film and of
slides prepared by LIFE from the film. Each slide corresponded with a separate frame of film, beginning with frame 171.
The conclusions of the meeting were as follows:

(a) The President had been definitely hit by
frames 224-225, when he emerges from behind a sign with his
hands clutching at his throat.

(b) The reaction shown in frames 224-25 may have
started at an earlier point--possibly as early as frame 199
(when there appears to be some jerkiness in his movement)
or, with a higher degree of possibility, at frames 204-06
(where his right elbow appears to be raised to an artificially
high position).

(c) If the reaction did not begin at 199 or 204-06,
it probably began during the range of frames during which
the President is hidden from Zapruder's camera by a sign,
namely, frames 215-24.

CC: Mr. Rankin            Mr. Belin
Mr. Willens              Mr. Specter
Mr. Redlich              Mr. Eisenberg
Mr. Ball

---

2

(d) The President may have been struck by the
first bullet as much as two seconds before any visible reaction
began. In all likelihood, however, the maximum delay between
impact and reaction would be under one second, and it is
possible that the reaction was instantaneous. Putting this
in terms of frames, the President may have been struck as
much as 36 frames before any visible reaction is seen.
If the visible reaction begins at 199, the President may
have been struck as early as 163; if the visible reaction
begins at 204-06, he may have been struck as early as 168-170;
if the visible reaction begins while the President is behind
the sign, he may have been struck as early as 179-188.

(e) The velocity of the first bullet would have
been little diminished by its passage through the President.
Therefore, if Governor Connally was in the path of the bullet
it would have struck him and (probably) caused the wounds
he sustained in his chest cavity. Strong indications that
this occurred are provided by the facts that (1) the bullet
recovered from Governor Connally's stretcher does not appear
to have penetrated a wrist and (2) if the first bullet did
not hit Governor Connally, it should have ripped up the car,
but apparently did not. Since the bullet recovered from
the Governor's stretcher does not appear to have penetrated
a wrist, if he was hit by this (the first) bullet, he was
probably also hit by the second bullet.

(f) If Governor Connally was hit by both the first
and second bullets, it is impossible to say definitively
at what point, or by what point, he had been hit by the
second bullet.

(g) Governor Connally seems to straighten up at
frames 224-26, and may be reacting to a wound at this point.
(If so, it would be a wound from the first bullet.)

(h) Governor Connally seems to begin showing an
expression of anguish around 242. If he was hit with two
bullets, this expression may have resulted from his second
wound.

(i) After Governor Connally straightened up at
frames 224-25 he starts a turn to the right. As a result
of this turn, at no time after frame 236 was Governor Connally
in a position such that a bullet fired from the probable

---

3

site of the assassin would have caused the wound in the
chest cavity which Governor Connally sustained--that is,
after frame 236, the Governor presented a side view to
the assassin rather than a back view.[*]

(j) It is not possible to say whether prior to
236 Governor Connally was ever in a position such that one
bullet could have caused the five wounds he sustained.

(k) As in the case of the President, Governor
Connally could have conceivably been hit two seconds before
he begins to react, but the maximum likely time interval
between hit and reaction is one second, and the reaction
may have been instantaneous. The likelihood of an
instantaneous reaction is particularly great in regard
to the wrist wound, since pain is usually felt more
quickly in a limb than in the torso.

---

[*] Mr. Specter disagrees with this, and feels the Governor
was in position to receive the chest wound up to 242.

-Mr. Rankin

(MP1
Committee)

April 22, 1964

MEMORANDUM FOR THE RECORD

FROM: Melvin A. Eisenberg

SUBJECT: Conference of April 21, 1964, to determine which frames in the Zapruder movies show the impact of the first and second bullets.

On Tuesday, April 21, 1964, a conference was held to determine which frames in the Zapruder film portray the instants at which the first and second bullets struck.

Present were: Dr. F. W. Light, Jr., Deputy Chief of the Biophysics Division and Chief of the Wound Assessment Branch of the Biophysics Division at Edgewood Arsenal, Maryland; Dr. Olivier, Chief of the Wound Ballistics Branch of the Biophysics Division at Edgewood Arsenal, Maryland; Dr. Joseph Dolce, Consultant to the Biophysics Division at Edgewood Arsenal; Dr. Charles F. Gregory and Dr. Robert Shaw of Parkland Hospital, Dallas, Texas; Messrs. Gauthier, Shaneyfelt, and one other unidentified agent of the FBI; and Messrs. Redlich, Specter, Belin and Eisenberg. Later in the proceedings, Governor and Mrs. Connally, Mr. Rankin and Mr. McCloy joined the conference.

A screening was held of the Zapruder film and of slides prepared by LIFE from the film. Each slide corresponded with a separate frame of film, beginning with frame 171. The consensus of the meeting was as follows:

(a) The President had been definitely hit by frames 224-25 when he emerges from behind a sign with his hands clutching at his throat.

(b) After Governor Connally straightened up at frames 224-26 he starts a turn to the right. As a result of this turn, at no time after frame 236 was Governor Connally in a position such that a bullet fired from the probable site of the assassin would have caused the wound in the chest cavity which Governor Connally sustained--that is, after frame 236 the Governor presented a side view to the assassin rather than a back view. 2/

---

1/ Mr. Specter disagrees.

**COMMISSION ADMINISTRATIVE**

---

2

(c) In many frames up to 250, the Governor's wrist is held in a position which exposed him to the type of wrist wounds he actually received.

(d) After viewing the films and slides, the Governor was of the opinion that he had been hit by frame 231.

(e) The Governor stated that after being hit, he looked to his right, looked to his left and then turned to his right. He felt the President might have been hit by frame 190. He heard only two shots and felt sure that the shots he heard were the first and third shots. He is positive that he was hit after he heard the first shot, i.e., by the second shot, and by that shot only.

In a discussion after the conference Drs. Light and Dolce expressed themselves as being very strongly of the opinion that Connally had been hit by two different bullets, principally on the ground that the bullet recovered from Connally's stretcher could not have broken his radius without having suffered more distortion. Dr. Olivier withheld a conclusion until he has had the opportunity to make tests on animal tissue and bone with the actual rifle.

**COMMISSION ADMINISTRATIVE**

---

A-D-M-I-N-I-S-T-R-A-T-I-V-E-L-Y C-O-N-F-I-D-E-N-T-I-A-L

PRESIDENT'S COMMISSION ON THE ASSASSINATION OF PRESIDENT KENNEDY

Financial Statement

**Direct Expenses of the Commission**

| | | |
|---|---:|---:|
| Salaries and related benefits | $253,979 | |
| Travel and related expenses | 67,441 | |
| Equipment rental | 9,913 | |
| Space rental and security guarding - Commission headquarters | 50,512 | |
| Payment to General Services Administration for administrative support | 9,000 | |
| Payment to Civil Service Commission for security investigations of Commission employees | 9,881 | |
| Payment to Department of Defense for photographic services | 4,000 | |
| Commercial contractual services | 21,689 | |
| Communications | 12,275 | |
| Supplies and materials | 6,518 | $445,208 |

**Other Expenses**

| | | |
|---|---:|---:|
| Air-conditioning Commission headquarters (Excess of normal work day) | 7,539 | |
| Travel and related expenses of witnesses | 18,244 | |
| Transcript expenses | 72,474 | |
| Printing: | | |
| Reproduction | 592,533 | |
| Reimbursement for detail from Government Printing Office | 51,409 | 742,199 |
| Total Obligations | | $1,187,407 |
| Unobligated Balance | | 12,593 |
| Total Allocation | | $1,200,000 |

Expenses of personnel detailed to the Commission from other Commissions and Agencies not included in the above figures.

November 15, 1965
Budget Division, GSA

**COMMISSION ADMINISTRATIVE**

---

COMMISSION INVESTIGATING ASSASSINATION OF PRESIDENT KENNEDY
Detail of Travel Expenses
November 29, 1963 through October 31, 1964

Commission Staff

| Consultants | Transportation | Other | Total |
|---|---:|---:|---:|
| Seniors | | | |
| Rankin | $ 1,477.10 | $ 2,619.88 | $ 4,096.98 |
| Redlich | 1,300.27 | 2,849.50 | 4,149.77 |
| Adams | 258.77 | 826.16 | 1,084.93 |
| Jenner | 926.21 | 7,161.80 | 8,088.01 |
| Ball | 3,353.73 | 3,435.15 | 6,788.88 |
| Hubert | 2,010.75 | 2,584.89 | 4,595.64 |
| Coleman | 745.50 | 1,350.18 | 2,095.68 |
| Sub-Total | $10,072.33 | $20,827.56 | $30,899.89 |
| | | | |
| Juniors | | | |
| Spector | 931.20 | 1,776.90 | 2,708.10 |
| Stern | 172.50 | 138.50 | 311.00 |
| Eisenberg | 119.82 | 2,315.67 | 2,435.49 |
| Liebeler | 1,510.14 | 4,933.96 | 6,444.10 |
| Slawson | 420.10 | 3,748.52 | 4,168.62 |
| Belin | 1,970.85 | 2,462.10 | 4,432.95 |
| Griffin | 439.60 | 2,676.66 | 3,116.26 |
| Scobey | 79.70 | 1,278.91 | 1,358.61 |
| Burns | 192.17 | - | 192.17 |
| Clark | - | 268.16 | 268.16 |
| Sub-Total | $ 5,836.08 | $19,599.38 | $25,435.46 |
| | | | |
| Regular Staff | | | |
| Eide | - | 191.64 | 191.64 |
| Laulicht | - | 54.00 | 54.00 |
| Ely | - | 91.44 | 91.44 |
| Mosk | - | 783.56 | 783.56 |
| Sub-Total | - | $ 1,120.64 | $ 1,120.64 |

**COMMISSION ADMINISTRATIVE**

COMMISSION INVESTIGATING ASSASSINATION OF PRESIDENT KENNEDY
Basic Salaries Paid To Commission Personnel
November 29, 1963 Through October 31, 1964

| | F.Y. 1964 11/29/63 thru 6/30/64 | F.Y. 1965 7/1/64 thru 9/12/64 | Total 11/29/63 thru 9/12/64 |
|---|---|---|---|
| **Consultants** | | | |
| **Seniors ($100/day)** | | | |
| Rankin | $ 20,600.00 | $ 7,400.00 | $ 28,000.00 |
| Redlich | 13,174.20 | 6,200.00 | 19,374.20 |
| Adams | 2,562.50 | - | 2,562.50 |
| Jenner | 13,300.00 | 6,450.00 | 19,750.00 |
| Ball | 9,300.00 | 200.00 | 9,500.00 |
| Hubert | 10,562.50 | 1,600.00 | 12,162.50 |
| Coleman | 5,000.00 | 1,400.00 | 6,400.00 |
| Sub-Total | $ 74,499.20 | $23,250.00 | $ 97,749.20 |
| **Juniors ($75/day)** | | | |
| Spector | 8,095.68 | 2,623.60 | 10,719.28 |
| Stern | 9,332.72 | 1,807.93 | 11,140.65 |
| Eisenberg | 10,213.30 | 1,949.04 | 12,162.34 |
| Liebeler | 10,906.92 | 5,172.40 | 16,079.32 |
| Slawson | 10,194.56 | 4,797.60 | 14,992.16 |
| Belin | 8,133.16 | 712.20 | 8,845.36 |
| Griffin | 11,206.72 | 5,247.36 | 16,454.08 |
| Scobey | 3,635.72 | 1,424.36 | 5,060.08 |
| Burns | - | 1,874.00 | 1,874.00 |
| Clark | - | 1,124.40 | 1,124.40 |
| Sub-Total | $ 71,718.78 | $26,732.89 | $ 98,451.67 |
| **Regular Staff** | 16,628.00 | 9,769.39 | 26,397.39 |
| | | | |
| Total | $162,845.98 | $59,752.28 | $222,598.26 $222,598.26 |

Add: Estimated Basic Salaries September 13 thru October 31, 1964 ............ 16,399.74

Grand Total ............ $238,998.00

September 1964
Budget Division, GSA

COMMISSION
ADMINISTRATIVE

CD 868

---

~68
FBI 4/29/64

Re: LEE HARVEY OSWALD

On April 1, 1964, MARINA OSWALD advised that to the best of her recollection LEE HARVEY OSWALD had only two jackets, one a heavy jacket, blue in color, and another light jacket, gray in color. She stated she believed OSWALD possessed both of these jackets in Russia and had purchased them in the United States prior to his departure for Russia. She stated she could not recall that OSWALD ever sent either of these jackets to any laundry or cleaner anywhere. She said she could recall washing them herself. She advised that to her knowledge OSWALD possessed both of these jackets at Dallas on November 22, 1963.

None of the other items of OSWALD's clothing available contained any dry cleaner's or laundry markings that were similar or could be associated with the "30 030" marking and the "B9738" dry cleaner tag appearing on the K-42 jacket.

- 5 -

---

FEDERAL BUREAU OF INVESTIGATION

Date 11/26/63

1

Mrs. R. E. ARNOLD, Secretary, Texas School Book Depository, advised she was in her office on the second floor of the building on November 22, 1963, and left that office between 12:00 and 12:15 PM, to go downstairs and stand in front of the building to view the Presidential Motorcade. As she was standing in front of the building, she stated she thought she caught a fleeting glimpse of LEE HARVEY OSWALD standing in the hallway between the front door and the double doors leading to the warehouse, located on the first floor. She could not be sure that this was OSWALD, but said she felt it was and believed the time to be a few minutes before 12:15 PM.

She stated thereafter she viewed the Presidential Motorcade and heard the shots that were fired at the President; however, she could furnish no information of value as to the individual firing the shots or any other information concerning OSWALD, whom she stated she did not know and had merely seen him working in the building.

on 11/26/63 at Dallas, Texas File # DL 89-43

by Special Agent RICHARD E. HARRISON /rmb Date dictated 11/26/63

41

This document contains neither recommendations nor conclusions of the FBI. It is the property of the FBI and is loaned to your agency; it and its contents are not to be distributed outside your agency.

CD 5

---

FEDERAL BUREAU OF INVESTIGATION

Date 11/23/63

1

JAMES RICHARD WORRELL, 13510 Winterhaven, furnished the following information to Patrolman G. W. HAMMER and Detective K. L. ANDERTON of the Dallas, Texas, Police Department and SA LOUIS M. KELLEY.

On Friday, November 22, 1963, about 12:30 p.m., he was standing on the sidewalk in front of the Texas School Book Depository Building watching President KENNEDY's procession pass. He heard a shot from above his head and at first thought it was a firecracker, but when he looked up, he saw about 12 inches of a gun barrel sticking out of a window of the building. He said this window was either on the fifth or sixth floor. He saw the gun fire once again and looked at President KENNEDY in time to see him slump forward on the seat of his car. He was unable to see who was firing the gun.

WORRELL advised he became frightened and started to run. Just as he started to run, he heard the gun fire two more times. He noted that some people said the gun fired three times, but he felt there were four shots.

He ran to Elm Street from Pacific Street on Houston. When he had run about 100 yards, he stopped to catch his breath and upon looking back, saw a man he described as a white male, height 5' 8-10", dark hair, dark clothing, wearing some type of jacket, leave the building where he had seen the gun and start to run in the opposite direction from him.

He stated that last night when he saw photographs of LEE HARVEY OSWALD on television, he felt this was the person he had seen running away from the building. He stated this person did not look back, but he was certain this was a white person, since he had a profile view.

WORRELL stated he caught a bus home and probably would not have gone to the Police Department except he had heard Chief of Police CURRY make an appeal for persons who had seen anything to report what they had seen.

on 11/23/63 at Dallas, Texas File # Dallas 89-43

by Special Agent LOUIS M. KELLEY/s] Date dictated 11/23/63

19

This document contains neither recommendations nor conclusions of the FBI. It is the property of the FBI and is loaned to your agency; it and its contents are not to be distributed outside your agency.

CD 5

FD-302 (Rev. 3-3-59)  FEDERAL BUREAU OF INVESTIGATION

1

Date _November 23, 1963_

MARVIN C. ROBINSON, 5120 South Marsalis Avenue, telephone number FRanklin 4-5834, advised that approximately between 12:30 and 1:00 p.m. on the afternoon of November 22, 1963, while traveling west on Elm Street he crossed the intersection of Elm and Houston Streets shortly after the assassination of President KENNEDY. ROBINSON stated that after he had crossed Houston Street and was in front of the Texas School Book Depository building a light colored Nash stationwagon suddenly appeared before him. He stated this vehicle stopped and a white male came down the grass covered incline between the building and the street and entered the stationwagon after which it drove away in the direction of the Oak Cliff section of Dallas. ROBINSON stated he does not recall the license number on the stationwagon or whether or not it bore a Texas license plate.

He stated further that he did not pay particular attention to the individual who entered the stationwagon and would be unable to identify him.

ROBINSON was unable to furnish any pertinent information concerning the assassination of President KENNEDY.

on _11/23/63_ at _Dallas, Texas_ File # _DL 89-43_

by Special Agent _JOHN V. ALMON & csh_  Date dictated _11/23/63_
_J. CALVIN RICE_

This document contains neither recommendations nor conclusions of the FBI. It is the property of the FBI and is loaned to your agency; it and its contents are not to be distributed outside your agency.

## CD 5

---

FD-302 (Rev. 3-3-59)  FEDERAL BUREAU OF INVESTIGATION

Date _December 13, 1963_

1

Sheriff BILL DECKER, Dallas, Texas, advised that Deputy Sheriff ROGER CRAIG, in his opinion, is a reliable employee who is completely honest in his belief that he saw OSWALD getting into a white Nash Rambler immediately after the shooting, even though CRAIG is obviously mistaken in his belief. DECKER said that he had discussed this identification with CRAIG and pointed out to him that witnesses, corroborated by the transfer found in OSWALD's possession, showed that OSWALD left the assassination scene on November 22, 1963, by a city bus. CRAIG stated to DECKER that he was aware of all that and knew that this indicated that CRAIG was mistaken in his identification, but he still saw someone getting into a white Nash Rambler and still believed that this person was LEE HARVEY OSWALD.

on _12/9/63_ at _Dallas, Texas_ File # _DL 100-10,461_

by Special Agent _C. RAY HALL/gm_  Date dictated _12/10/63_

This document contains neither recommendations nor conclusions of the FBI. It is the property of the FBI and is loaned to your agency; it and its contents are not to be distributed outside your agency.

## CD 205

---

FD-302 (Rev. 3-3-59)  FEDERAL BUREAU OF INVESTIGATION

1

Date _2/4/64_

RICHARD RANDOLPH CARR, 738 North Bishop, Dallas, was reinterviewed to clarify information previously furnished by CARR on January 4, 1964, in connection with an alleged statement attributed to CARR that LEE HARVEY OSWALD had not assassinated President KENNEDY. CARR furnished the following signed statement on February 3, 1964:

"February 3, 1964
Dallas, Texas

"I, Richard Randolph Carr, make the following voluntary statement to Paul L. Scott who has identified himself to me as a Special Agent of the Federal Bureau of Investigation. I understand that this statement is being furnished in connection with an official investigation being conducted by the FBI.

"I am a Steelworker and am presently employed on a construction project at SMU, Dallas.

"On the morning of 11/22/63 I had taken my wife and child to Parkland Hospital, Dallas, arriving there at approximately 11:30 AM. I left my wife and child at the hospital and proceeded to the downtown area of Dallas to attempt to locate employment, being temporarily without employment at that time. Shortly after noon on 11/22/63 I went to the site of the new court house being constructed at the corner of Houston and Commerce Sts., Dallas. I was attempting to locate the foreman in charge of the steel construction on this building. I made inquiry of one of the workers at the site and was told he was on the ninth floor and I started walking up the steel stairway of the building which stairway was on the west side of the building next to Houston Street. As I reached a point at approximately the sixth floor of the building framework I looked toward the Texas School Book Depository

on _2/1/64_ at _Dallas, Texas_ File # _DL 100-10461_

by Special Agent _PAUL L. SCOTT - gj_  Date dictated _2/4/64_

This document contains neither recommendations nor conclusions of the FBI. It is the property of the FBI and is loaned to your agency; it and its contents are not to be distributed outside your agency.

## CD 385

---

DL 100-10461
2

Building located at the corner of Houston and Elm Sts. and at that time I observed a man looking out of a window of the top floor of the Texas School Book Depository building. This man, a heavy set individual, who was wearing a hat, a tan sport coat and horn rimmed glasses, was not in the end window next to Houston St. but was I believe in the second window over from Houston St. I continued on up the stairway and a minute or so later I heard a noise which I took to be the backfire of an automobile or a firecracker. There was a slight pause after the first report and then two reports in quick succession. From where I was standing on the framework of the new court house building I looked toward the triple underpass just west of Houston and Elm Sts. It seemed to me that the noises I had heard came from this direction. As I looked I saw several individuals falling to the ground. I do not recall that I looked toward the Texas School Book Depository building after hearing the three reports. I immediately proceeded down the stairway of the building with the intention of going over to the triple underpass to see what had happened. When I reached the ground I walked to Houston St. and down Houston St. to the Commerce St. intersection. I did not walk over to the site where I had previously seen people falling to the ground due to the large crowd which was already there.

"While I was on Houston St. near the Commerce St. intersection I saw a man whom I believe was identical with the man I had earlier seen looking out of the window of the Texas School Book Depository building. This man, walking very fast, proceeded on Houston St. south to Commerce St., then east on Commerce St. to Record St. which is one block from Houston St. This man got into a 1961 or 1962 Grey Rambler Station Wagon which was parked just north of Commerce on Record St. The station wagon, which had Texas license and was driven by a young negro man, drove off in a northerly direction.

## CD 385

DL 100-10461
3

"I proceeded to my car which was parked near the new county court house bldg. and drove by the residence of my brother and then to Pete Cates, All State Trailer Park, Zangs Blvd. and Clarendon St. My sister in law was watching TV and she come and told me the President had been shot and Pete Cates and I then watched TV until it was announced the President had died. This was the first time I realized that the noises I had heard while on the new county building had probably been gun shots.

"I wish to state at this point that I did not see anyone in the Texas School Book building with a gun; I did not see the assassination of President Kennedy and I did not at any time tell anyone that I had seen the assassination of President Kennedy.

"Sometime after the shooting of Lee Harvey Oswald, exact date not recalled, I was talking to Elsie Johnson, her sister, Mary Sue (LNU), and another woman by the name of Gentry. My wife was also present during this conversation. It is my understanding that the way the conversation came up - Elsie Johnson and Mary Sue were discussing Jack Ruby and the shooting of Oswald. They mentioned they were acquainted with Ruby and had been interviewed by the FBI. In addition there was a general discussion of the assassination of President Kennedy and the subsequent shooting of Oswald. It is my recollection that during this discussion I expressed the opinion that Lee Harvey Oswald did not fire the shots that killed Kennedy. I was basing this opinion on various statements I had heard on radio and TV concerning the assassination and how it was supposed to have occurred. I also based this opinion on reported accounts of the shooting of Officer Tippit and my comparison of the accounts of the Tippit shooting and the assassination reports. I may

8

**CD 385**

DL 100-10461
4

have mentioned during this conversation the individual I had seen on 11/22/63 while I was on the new court house building. However, I did not state at any time that this man I had seen from the building and later on the street was the man who had shot President Kennedy. I did not have any specific information concerning the assassination of President Kennedy at the time of this conversation with Elsie Johnson and her sister and I do not at the present time have any information concerning the assassination. Any statements I made to the effect that Lee Harvey Oswald was not the person who shot Kennedy were merely expressions of my opinions.

"I have read the above statement & it is true to the best of my knowledge.

"/s/ Richard Randolph Carr

"Witness: Paul L. Scott, Special Agent, FBI, 2/3/64"

27

**CD 385**

---

FD-302 (Rev. 3-3-59)　　FEDERAL BUREAU OF INVESTIGATION

Date 11/26/63

1

FRANCES HERNANDEZ, 1917 Annex, advised she, JOSEPHINE SALINAS, and HENRIETTA VARGAS, all employees of McKell Sportswear Company, Second Floor, 501 Elm Street, Dallas, while on their way home about 5:10 p.m. on November 19, 1963, and after leaving the parking lot near the Texas School Book Depository, observed two men with an automobile, about a 1956 Buick, color light blue. The older of the two men was observed to hand a rifle to the younger of the two men, who then walked from the Buick toward a white car which was a compact, but she did not know the make of it. She stated the younger man might have been LEE HARVEY OSWALD, but she is not able to say definitely it was OSWALD. She stated she has no other information.

on 11/26/63 at Dallas, Texas　　File # Dallas 89-43
by Special Agent NAT A. PINKSTON/sl　　Date dictated 11/26/63

This document contains neither recommendations nor conclusions of the FBI. It is the property of the FBI and is loaned to your agency; it and its contents are not to be distributed outside your agency.

**CD 205**

---

FD-302 (Rev. 3-3-59)　　FEDERAL BUREAU OF INVESTIGATION

Date 11/26/63

1

JOSEPHINE SALINAS, 13740 Birchlawn, advised she, FRANCES HERNANDEZ, and HENRIETTA VARGAS, all employees of McKell Sportswear Company, Second Floor, 501 Elm Street, Dallas, Texas, while on their way home about 5:10 p.m. on November 19, 1963, and after reaching the parking lot near the Texas School Book Depository, observed two men with an automobile, about a 1956 Buick, color light blue. The older of the two men handed a rifle to the younger man, who then walked from the Buick toward a compact white car, but she did not know the make of it. She stated the younger man might have been LEE HARVEY OSWALD, but she is not able to say definitely it was OSWALD. She stated she has no other information.

on 11/26/63 at Farmers Branch, Texas　　File # Dallas 89-43
by Special Agent NAT A. PINKSTON/sl　　Date dictated 11/26/63

This document contains neither recommendations nor conclusions of the FBI. It is the property of the FBI and is loaned to your agency; it and its contents are not to be distributed outside your agency.

**CD 205**

3

DL    100-10461
      WGB:mja

On December 31, 1963, Mrs. FRANCES HERNANDEZ, residence 1917 Annex, Dallas, Texas, was re-interviewed in her place of employment, McKell Sportswear Company, Second Floor, 501 Elm Street. Mrs. HERNANDEZ advised that she recalls it was raining the day before President JOHN FITZGERALD KENNEDY was to come to Dallas, Texas, and that she and two of her fellow workers, Mrs. HENRIETTA VARGAS and Mrs. JOSEPHINE SALINAS, were leaving their parking lot, west of the TSBD building. They had to stop because a 1955 or 1956 Buick was in the exit way and she noticed two men standing behind the Buick, and the older man reached into the trunk of the car and handed a rifle to the younger man.

She said she particularly noticed this activity since it reminded her of a man working at McKell Sportswear who had gone deer hunting and she thought these men were going to do the same thing. She only saw the back of the older man's head and can only say the younger man as being slim. She cannot describe either of these two men as being identical to LEE HARVEY OSWALD or JACK RUBY; and thought of the above incident only after the President was assassinated. She said she and her friends were frightened and reluctant to become involved and were very excited and confused for some time, but now that she has had time to think about this, she is certain of the above facts.

On December 31, 1963, Mrs. HENRIETTA VARGAS, residence 511 Capitol Street, Dallas, Texas, was interviewed at her place of employment, McKell Sportswear Company.

CD 206

---

4

DL    100-10461
      WGB:mja

Mrs. VARGAS advised that she and two of her fellow workers at McKell Sportswear Company, Mrs. FRANCES HERNANDEZ and Mrs. JOSEPHINE SALINAS, were leaving their parking lot behind the TSBD building when they observed two men standing near a light colored automobile, make unknown. She said that she could not recall whether this was the Tuesday, or the Thursday, before President JOHN F. KENNEDY came to Dallas and was assassinated, but she does recall that it was raining at that time. Mrs. VARGAS said that she noticed that the older man took a rifle out of the trunk of his car and gave it to the younger man, who walked toward the railroad tracks, west of the TSBD building. She did not see the face of the younger man and cannot describe him, and she does not recall his getting into the automobile. She did not see the face of the older man, only the back of his head and she has no idea of who he was. She said she could not identify either man as LEE HARVEY OSWALD or JACK RUBY since she did not see their faces. She recalls the older man was of medium height and build, and the younger man appeared to be rather slim.

On December 31, 1963, Mrs. JOSEPHINE SALINAS, residence 13740 Birch Lawn, Dallas, Texas, was interviewed at her place of employment, McKell Sportswear Company. Mrs. SALINAS advised that the day before President JOHN F. KENNEDY was killed, she and two of her fellow workers, Mrs. HENRIETTA VARGAS and Mrs. FRANCES HERNANDEZ, were leaving the parking lot west of the TSBD building. She recalls it was raining and wondered whether the President would be able to be seen in the parade scheduled for the next day, and noticed that there were two men standing near the rear of a 1955 or 1956 Buick, which was blocking the exit road. The older

CD 206

---

5

DL    100-10461
      WGB:mja

man took a rifle out of the trunk of the car and gave it to the younger man. She did not see the face of the older man since she could only observe two men from his back and could not describe him further. The younger man who was of slender build walked away from the Buick carrying the rifle, but she did not see where he went, or whether he got into an automobile.

Mrs. SALINAS advised she cannot describe either of these two men she observed as being identical to LEE HARVEY OSWALD or JACK RUBY.

CD 206

---

DL 100-10461
HJO:mam
1

United States Attorney H. BAREFOOT SANDERS, Dallas, Texas, telephonically advised ASAC KYLE G. CLARK on December 5, 1963, that a reporter for the Dallas "Morning News", name unrecalled, had advised him that four of the women working in the Society Section of the Dallas "Morning News" were reportedly standing next to Mr. ZAPRUDA when the assassination shots were fired. According to this reporter, these women, names unknown, stated that the shots according to their opinion came from a direction other than from the Texas School Book Depository (TSBD) Building. Mr. SANDERS also advised that the reporter calling stated he had interviewed Patrolman J. M. SMITH who advised that he definitely distinguished the aroma of gunpowder near the underpass.

Patrolman JOSEPH M. SMITH, Traffic Division, Dallas Police Department, Dallas, Texas, on December 9, 1963, advised SA'S HENRY J. OLIVER and LOUIS M. KELLEY that he was working on November 22, 1963, on traffic at Elm and Houston Streets. He stated he was near the parking lot when the shots were fired which killed President KENNEDY. The shots echoed so loudly he had no idea at the time where they had been fired from. He stated he did smell what he thought was gunpowder but stated this smell was in the parking lot by the TSBD Building and not by the underpass. He advised he never at any time went to the underpass and could not advise if there was the smell of gunpowder in the underpass. He stated he did not see the President when he was shot and stated he saw nothing which would assist in this matter. After the shots were fired, there was a great deal of confusion, and he left his post for a few minutes to go in the area where the President had been shot but did not go in the TSBD Building.

Patrolman E. V. BROWN, Traffic Division, Dallas Police Department, Dallas, Texas, on December 9, 1963, advised SA'S OLIVER and KELLEY that on November 22, 1963, he was assigned to traffic and was stationed on the overpass located below the TSBD Building. He stated he heard the shots that killed

36

CD 205

DL 100-10461
HJO:mam
2

President KENNEDY, but he did not see the shots take effect and stated he could not furnish any information which would assist in identifying the assassin. He advised that he believed he could smell gunpowder in the air on the overpass but believed it probably was brought there by the wind. No shots could have been fired from the overpass, as he was present in this area at least an hour or two before the motorcade came along and was there on duty when the President was shot.

He advised that about 10:40 AM, he recalls a green pickup truck which was stalled on Elm Street near the overpass. This truck was a concern since they needed to get it moved prior to the Presidential Motorcade. Patrolman JOE MURPHY can give full facts regarding the truck and the occupants as he handled the matter and was successful in getting it removed prior to the Presidential Motorcade. The persons in this truck were workmen who actually had trouble with the truck and were out of the area when the motorcade came by. He did not see anyone remove anything from this truck.

CD 205

---

RE: ASSASSINATION OF PRESIDENT
    JOHN FITZGERALD KENNEDY,
    NOVEMBER 22, 1963, DALLAS, TEXAS

On November 25, 1963, Mr. ROY S. TRULY, Warehouse Manager, TSBD, was exhibited an Associated Press photograph described as "DN 5, 11/22/63, Dallas, Texas," depicting an individual standing in the entrance of the TSBD who resembled Lee Harvey Oswald. Mr. Truly, after viewing this photograph, stated, "That picture resembles Oswald, but it's not Lee Oswald, it's Billy Lovelady."

On November 25, 1963, Mr. Billy Nolan Lovelady, 7722 Hume, Dallas, Texas, was exhibited an Associated Press photograph described as "DN 5, 11/22/63, Dallas, Texas," depicting an individual standing in the entrance of the TSBD who resembled Lee Harvey Oswald.

Mr. Lovelady advised that he is an employee at the TSBD and is acquainted with Oswald. Lovelady immediately identified himself in the above-described photograph as being the individual who resembled OSWALD and stated he had observed himself previously in this photograph in the newspaper and was saving it. Lovelady stated there was no question whatsoever but that this was a photograph of him.

By letter dated January 11, 1964, J. D. Royce, 496 West Scott Avenue, Clovis, California, advised Parade Publications, Inc., New York, New York, that he had what he believed to be "positive proof that Lee Harvey Oswald did not assassinate the President of the United States."

On January 23, 1964, J. D. Royce advised Special Agents of the FBI that the "positive proof" he referred to in the above-mentioned letter was based entirely on a double-page photograph which appeared on Pages 24 - 25 of the December 14, 1963, edition of the Saturday Evening Post. He stated that after examining this photograph with a magnifying glass, which photograph was reported to have been taken the instant President Kennedy was shot, he was convinced that the individual standing in the background in the left edge of the doorway was Oswald.

On January 22, 1964, the U. S. Secret Service, Washington, D. C., furnished the FBI the following letter received from Mrs. Helen Shirah, 5530 Santa Monica Boulevard South, Jacksonville, Florida, 32207, dated January 17, 1964:

2

CD 45

---

DL 100-10461
RPG:sl
1

Under date of December 9, 1963, the FBI Laboratory advised as follows concerning a photographic examination requested by the Dallas Office under date of November 26, 1963:

Specimens received November 25, 1963

Q104    One 50' roll of 8mm Kodachrome movie film with container bearing customer's name "Robert Hughes" bearing exposures of the Texas School Book Depository Building from which assassin fired the gun killing President John F. Kennedy, November 22, 1963

Result of examination:

There are no images in any of the exposures of Q104 which show the corner window of the sixth floor of the Texas School Book Depository Building from which the assassin's gun was fired that can be interpreted as the form of an individual. The forms recorded in this window can be interpreted as in the same general shapes of boxes, found at and just behind the window in question.

CD 205

---

9:55 p.m.

To: Chief Rowley
From: Max D. Phillips
Subject: 8mm movie film showing President Kennedy being shot

Enclosed is an 8 m.m. movie film taken by Mr. A. Zapruder, 501 Elm St, Dallas Texas (RI 8-6711)

Mr Zapruder was photographing the President at the instant he was shot.

According to Mr. Zapruder the position the assassin was behind Mr Zapruder

Note: Disregard personal scenes shown on Mr. Zapruder's film. Mr. Zapruder is in custody of the "master" film. Two prints were given to SAIC Sorrels, this date. The third print is forwarded.

M. D. Phillips
S/a of Agent - PRS

86

CD 87

HOUSTON ST.

E/3/H ST.

Under Pass

66

**CD 87**

---

FD-302 (Rev. 3-3-59)

FEDERAL BUREAU OF INVESTIGATION

Date 3/25/64

1

Sergeant PATRICK T. DEAN, Patrol Division, Dallas Police Department, advised that on March 24, 1964, at about 4:45 AM, PATSY PAIR, City Hall Night Telephone Operator, called him at his office saying she had a collect call from a RALPH SIMPSON, Victoria, Canada, and that SIMPSON wanted to talk to someone about the assassination of President KENNEDY. Sergeant DEAN stated there was a discussion as to whether they should accept the call and PATSY said in talking with SIMPSON and the Victoria, Canada, operator, she felt that SIMPSON had some information and that it would be worthwhile to accept the collect call.

Sergeant DEAN stated he authorized the operator to accept the collect call and SIMPSON said he was in Dallas on November 22, 1963, and took some pictures of the President's car at time he was shot and that he believed he got the Texas School Book Depository Building in the background. According to Sergeant DEAN, SIMPSON described his camera as an expensive camera with "wide-angle, scope lens."

SIMPSON stated he had been talking to his attorney, BATTER, (phonetic) and that BATTER had instructed him to contact the Dallas Police Department. Sergeant DEAN stated that SIMPSON claimed he had not had the film developed and did not know exactly what was in the photographs.

Sergeant DEAN stated he told SIMPSON that he should contact the President's Commission in Washington, D.C., and send the pictures to them, but that SIMPSON claimed he did not want to contact the President's Commission, and stated he would mail the film to him (Sergeant DEAN) airmail on March 25, 1964.

Sergeant DEAN advised that PATSY PAIR, the switchboard operator, contacted BERNICE WILLIAMS, of the Victoria, British Columbia, Telephone Company, to trace this call and, through this person, it was ascertained the call had been placed from telephone number 384-3780. He stated this phone number was reportedly registered to R. H. W. SMELE, 1141 Caldonia, Victoria, British Columbia.

Sergeant DEAN stated he would immediately contact the Dallas FBI Office on receipt of this film.

on 3/25/64 at Dallas, Texas _____ File # 100-10461

by Special Agent ALFRED D. NEELEY/eah _____ 5 ___ Date dictated 3/25/64

This document contains neither recommendations nor conclusions of the FBI. It is the property of the FBI and is loaned to your agency; it and its contents are not to be distributed outside your agency.

**CD 897**

---

1

DL 100-10461
RPG/ds

Under date of March 26, 1964, the Seattle Office advised that Corporal R. E. G. BLACKMORE, Royal Canadian Mounted Police, Victoria, British Columbia, had on that date interviewed RALPH HENRY WILLIAM SMELE, 1141 Caldonia Street, Victoria, British Columbia, who admitted making the telephone call to the Dallas Police Department on March 24, 1964. He also admitted using a fictitious name, claimed he had never been to Dallas, Texas; and, had no film of the assassination of President KENNEDY. The Seattle Office advised that the only reason SMELE could give for making the telephone call was that he had been watching a television program and had been drinking and decided to make the call. According to Corporal BLACKMORE, SMELE is "given to dreams". SMELE's last employment was in connection with the demolition of buildings.

26

**CD 897**

---

(5-1-90)

UNITED STATES SECRET SERVICE
TREASURY DEPARTMENT

Commission No. 354

| ORIGIN Field | | OFFICE Dallas, Texas | | FILE NO. CO-2-34,030 |
|---|---|---|---|---|
| TYPE OF CASE | STATUS | | TITLE OR CAPTION | |
| PRS | Continued | | Assassination of President Kennedy | |
| INVESTIGATION MADE AT | | PERIOD COVERED | Lee Harvey Oswald | |
| Dallas, Texas | | 1-1/1-29-64 | | |
| INVESTIGATION MADE BY | | | | |
| SA Roger C. Warner | | | | |
| DETAILS | | | | |

SYNOPSIS

Pierce Allman (person believed to be one mentioned by Lee Harvey Oswald as identifying himself as Secret Service Agent at Texas School Book Depository immediately following assassination) interviewed 1-29-64.

DETAILS OF INVESTIGATION

Reference is made to previous reports relative to Lee Harvey Oswald.

Other Investigations

On 11-22-63 the following was reported to SAIC Forrest V. Sorrels, by Captain Will Fritz, Dallas Police Department.

Lee Harvey Oswald in the first interview subsequent to his arrest, stated that as he was leaving the Texas School Book Depository Building, two men (one with a crew cut) had intercepted him at the front door; identified themselves as Secret Service Agents and asked for the location of a telephone.

On 1-1-64 Mr. Jack Brian, Detective, Dallas Police Department, stated that he had interrogated Mr. James Powell, Army Intelligence, who was trapped inside the Texas School Book Depository after the Depository doors had been sealed.

On 1-28-64 Mr. Powell was interviewed relative to his location at the time of the assassination and his actions subsequent to the assassination. Mr. Powell stated that he had been watching the parade from a position near the corner of Houston and Elm Streets, the site of the assassination. Mr. Powell stated further that he heard the shots and he then joined a group of Sheriff's Deputies, who were heading toward the rear of the Texas School Book Depository on the basis of information that the assassin had shot from the railroad yards. Mr. Powell

| DISTRIBUTION | COPIES | REPORT MADE BY | DATE |
|---|---|---|---|
| Chief | Orig & 2 cc | | 2-3-64 |
| | | SPECIAL AGENT | |
| Dallas | 2 cc | APPROVED | 2-3-64 |
| | | SPECIAL AGENT IN CHARGE | |

(CONTINUE ON PLAIN PAPER)

U. S. GOVERNMENT PRINTING OFFICE   28-61306-1

**CD 354**

worked with the Sheriff's Deputies at the rear of the Texas School Book Depository for about six or eight minutes. He then entered the front door of the Depository, in search of a phone from which to call his office. Mr. Powell, upon entering the Texas School Book Depository, observed Mr. Pierce Allman using a phone in the lobby of the building. Mr. Powell stated that he did not meet anyone upon entering the building nor was he called upon to identify himself to anyone. Mr. Powell stated that the only persons present on the first floor of the building at the time of his entry were Mr. Allman and an unidentified white male described as being tall and about 30 years of age; both of these men were near a desk in the lobby and Mr. Allman was using a telephone.

Mr. Powell has submitted a report of his activities immediately subsequent to the assassination of the President and states that his report will be available to this office upon request.

On 1-29-64 Mr. Pierce Allman was interviewed at his office in the WFAA T-V building where he is employed as Program Director. Mr. Allman is described as a white male, 5'8", 140, brown hair, crew cut, brown eyes, about 35. Mr. Allman was interviewed relative to activities immediately subsequent to the assassination. Mr. Allman stated that he was watching the parade from a position near the corner of Elm and Houston. Upon hearing the shots he ran across Elm Street to a couple who had fallen to the ground. He asked the man if he was all right; the man stated that he was. Allman then ran up an incline toward Houston Street. Upon reaching the top of the incline, he turned and ran down. He stated that he is at a loss to explain this action other than he was extremely excited and upset by the assassination.

Mr. Allman then stated that he ran full speed into the Texas School Book Depository Building with intention of locating a phone and calling his television station WFAA. Mr. Allman stated that after he had entered the front door of the building, he had emerged into a hallway and there he met a white male whom he could not further identify. He asked this white male for the location of a telephone. Mr. Allman stated that he did not identify himself to this person; stated further that he was extremely excited at the time and that he could not remember anything about the person except for the fact that he was a white male. Mr. Allman has seen pictures of Lee Harvey Oswald and could not positively state whether or not he is the one of whom he inquired. Mr. Allman stated that the person pointed out a phone to him which was located in an open area on the first floor of the Texas School Book Depository; that he immediately went to the telephone and stayed at this position for approximately 25 minutes talking to his office. Mr. Allman stated that he was accompanied by a fellow worker, Terry Ford.

During the above interview it was noted that Mr. Allman carries his press pass in a leather case similar to cases carried by Federal agents and police officers.

CD 354

---

On January 31, 1963, Mr. Terrence Ford, Radio Promotion Director, WFAA, was interviewed relative to his actions subsequent to the assassination.

Mr. Ford stated that he had accompanied Mr. Allman to the corner of Houston and Elm Streets to watch the procession; that upon hearing shots, he retreated to a concrete building near the side of the small park bordering Elm Street, then running back toward the Texas School Book Depository. He followed Allman into the building, walking on his right side. He remembers Allman turning to his left to ask a white male the location of a telephone. Ford stated the white male, whom he can neither identify nor describe, indicated in some manner that a telephone was inside a room directly ahead. Ford does not remember Allman identifying himself at this time. Ford stated that he did not have a press card at this time and did not identify himself to anyone until he left the building about one hour later.

Ford has seen pictures of Lee Harvey Oswald and states he cannot remember if Oswald was the man he and Allman met at the front door of the Texas School Book Depository.

DISPOSITION

The facts surrounding the entrance of Allman and Ford into the Texas School Book Depository indicate that they are the men referred to by Oswald in his interview with Captain Fritz. In view of this and of the fact that there is no indication that they identified themselves as Secret Service Agents, this phase of the investigation is closed.

HCW:wd

CD 354

---

Form No. 1582 (Revised)
Memorandum Report
(7-1-48)

Commission No. 381

UNITED STATES SECRET SERVICE
TREASURY DEPARTMENT

| ORIGIN Field | OFFICE Dallas, Texas | FILE NO. CO-2-34,030 |
| --- | --- | --- |
| TYPE OF CASE Protective Research | STATUS Continued | TITLE OR CAPTION Assassination of President Kennedy |
| INVESTIGATION MADE AT Dallas, Texas | PERIOD COVERED 2-14-64 | |
| INVESTIGATION MADE BY SA Roger C. Warner | | |

SYNOPSIS

Diagram of wounds suffered by Governor Connally at time of assassination of President Kennedy forwarded herewith.

DETAILS OF INVESTIGATION

On 1-27-64 Inspector T. J. Kelley requested a diagram relative to the entrance and exit wounds suffered by Gov. Connally after being shot by Lee Harvey Oswald on 11-22-63.

On 1-28-64 this information was transmitted to Inspector Kelley with five diagrams attached. Reference is further made to a memorandum to Inspector Thomas J. Kelley from David W. Belin, dated Feb. 12, 1964, relative to the wounds suffered by Gov. Connally. This memorandum points out a conflict in the wounds as shown on diagram #1 with the description of the wound according to a typewritten report of Dr. Charles Gregory dated Nov. 22, 1963, and requesting a review be made of this matter and a subsequent report submitted.

Other Investigations

Review of this matter with Dr. Charles Gregory indicates that body diagram #1 and diagram #5 are in error. Diagram #3 is correct, all in respect to the position of the wounds in the wrist of Gov. Connally.

Attached herewith is amended body diagram #6, which indicates the correct position of the wounds suffered by Gov. Connally to his right wrist. Also attached is amended diagram #7, showing the approximate position of Gov. Connally at the time he was wounded.

Also in error, and amended in this report, is the description of the 551664

| DISTRIBUTION | | COPIES | REPORT MADE BY | DATE |
| --- | --- | --- | --- | --- |
| Chief | ✓ | Orig.& 1 cc | | 2-14-64 |
| | | | SPECIAL AGENT | |
| Dallas | | 2 cc's | APPROVED | 2-14-64 |

CD 381

---

Commission No. 326

DIAGRAM #5

Rough sketch of approximate position of Gov. Connally when wounded on 11 22 63. Blue line indicates path of projectile through the body as indicated by examination of wounds. This is an off-hand sketch and not intended to be used as final authority on the specific position of the body when wounded.

CD 381

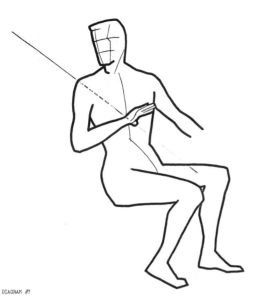

DIAGRAM #7

Rough sketch of approximate position of Gov. Connally when wounded on 11-22-63. Blue line indicates path of projectile through the body as indicated by examination of wounds. This is an off-hand sketch and not intended to be used as final authority on the specific position of the body when wounded. (Amended from Diagram #5).

## CD 381

---

UNITED STATES DEPARTMENT OF JUSTICE

FEDERAL BUREAU OF INVESTIGATION

WASHINGTON, D.C. 20535

December 4, 1964

BY COURIER SERVICE

Honorable J. Lee Rankin
General Counsel
The President's Commission
200 Maryland Avenue, Northeast
Washington, D. C.

Dear Mr. Rankin:

You previously have been informed that this Bureau is in possession of a copy of a film portraying the assassination of President John F. Kennedy. The film being referred to was taken by Adrian Zapruder who, after making a copy available to the FBI, sold the film to "Life" magazine. This Bureau has not permitted the copy of the film to be released outside of this Bureau without the concurrence of the Commission.

The Central Intelligence Agency has inquired if the film copy in possession of this Bureau can be loaned to that Agency solely for training purposes. The showing of the film would be restricted to Agency personnel. We have been informed that the Central Intelligence Agency consulted with Mr. Alfred Goldberg of the Commission who, according to that Agency, has approved the loan of the film.

Unless advised to the contrary, this Bureau will make available a copy of the film to the Central Intelligence Agency on a loan basis and under the arrangement described above.

Sincerely yours,

J. Edgar Hoover

**COMMISSION
ADMINISTRATIVE**

---

MEMORANDUM                    January 28, 1964

TO:      J. Lee Rankin

FROM:    David W. Belin

SUBJECT: Original Print of Zapruder Film

I was informed that the FBI film of the assassination is a copy of a Secret Service copy of the original colored film taken by Zapruder.

According to an interview with FBI Special Agent Robert M. Barrett, Zapruder states that the original print is on 16 mm film and "is much clearer" than those appearing on the 8 mm film copies. (I assume that his 8 mm camera used the standard 16 mm film which is reversed and split in two in the course of processing.) See page 12 of December 10 Gemberling Report.

FBI Special Agent Shaneyfelt, with whom Mr. Ball and I discussed the problem of determination of speed of car and points of shots through use of the Zapruder film, felt that with a more clear film print it could give a more precise determination of the date we are endeavoring to obtain.

Shaneyfelt said that the primary use of the original Zapruder print would be under microscopic examination and that there should not be any impairment of the quality of the film through such a microscopic check.

Inspector Tom Kelley of the Secret Service suggested that perhaps you might want to contact Henry Suydam of the Washington office of Life Magazine. He evidently has some familiarity with Mr. Kelley.

Thank you.

**COMMISSION
ADMINISTRATIVE**

# PHOTO CREDITS

Chapter I

**4,** Philip Willis (above) and James Altgens from Wide World (below); **8,** Abraham Zapruder from *Life* (above) and National Archives (below); **10,** Orville Nix from UPI.

Chapter III

**34,** Philip Willis; **39,** Wide World; **41,** UPI; **45,** National Archives; **48,** National Archives; **49,** Wide World; **52,** National Archives; **57,** National Archives; **58,** National Archives.

Chapter IV

**61,** James Altgens from Wide World (above) and S. M. Holland from National Archives (below); **62,** Marie Muchmore from UPI; **63,** UPI; **65,** UPI; **78,** Peter Sahula and Walter Bernard.

Chapter V

**83,** author's photos; Orville Nix from UPI; **97,** Wide World; **99,** Orville Nix from UPI (above) and Marie Muchmore from UPI (below); **100,** James Altgens from Wide World (top) and Wilma Bond (middle and bottom); **102,** James Altgens from Wide World (above) and Gene Daniels from Black Star (below); **103,** Orville Nix from UPI (above) and F. M. Bell (below); **113,** National Archives; **114,** James Altgens from Wide World.

Chapter VI

**116,** Shelley Katz; **119,** F. M. Bell; **121,** author's photo; **122,** author's photo (above) and Shelley Katz (below); **124,** Jim Murray from Black Star; **126,** Mary Moorman from UPI; **127,** Mary Moorman from UPI (above) and author's photos (below); **128,** Mary Moorman from UPI; **129,** author's photo; **132,** Shelley Katz; **134,** James Altgens from Wide World; **135,** Jim Murray from Black Star; **136,** Robert Hughes; **137,** Robert Hughes.

Chapter VII

**142,** National Archives (top and middle) and Wide World (bottom); **143,** National Archives; **144,** National Archives; **145,** National Archives; **146,** National Archives; **147,** National Archives (above) and *Life* (below); **148,** National Archives; **151,** National Archives; **152,** National Archives; **155,** author's photos; **169,** UPI; **175,** author's photo (above) and National Archives (below).

Chapter VIII

**178,** Arthur Schatz; **182,** Wide World; **183,** Wide World (above) and Wilma Bond (below); **184,** Wide World (above) and Robert Hughes (below); **185,** Robert Hughes (above) and F. M. Bell (below); **186,** Philip Willis; **187,** Marie Muchmore from UPI; **188,** Marie Muchmore (above) and Orville Nix (below), both from UPI; **189,** Orville Nix from UPI (above) and F. M. Bell (below); **190,** National Archives; **191,** National Archives.

Chapter IX

**196,** author's photo; **202,** Wide World; **213,** Wide World.

Chapter X

**217,** Abraham Zapruder from *Life;* **221,** reprinted from *The Book of Rifles,* by W. H. B. Smith and Joseph H. Smith, published by Stackpole Books (above) and National Archives (below); **222,** Dallas *Times Herald* from Black Star; **223,** Philip Willis; **224,** Orville Nix from UPI (above) and F. M. Bell (below); **225,** James Altgens from Wide World; **226,** John Mazziotta from Black Star (top), James Altgens from Wide World (middle), and National Archives (bottom); **227,** Philip Willis; **228,** Wilma Bond; **229,** National Archives; **231,** Tom Dillard (above) and National Archives (below); **236,** Robert Hughes; **245,** Robert Hughes; **246,** National Archives (top), Robert Hughes (middle), and Jim Murray from Black Star (bottom).

Publisher's Note

**vxi,** Abraham Zapruder from *Life.*

Front and back endpapers, Arthur Schatz.

Back cover, Jack A. Weaver (above) and James Altgens from Wide World (below).

Special Note: Due to their probative significance, none of the photographs in this book have been retouched or altered in any way.

# INDEX

**317**

# LIST OF ILLUSTRATIONS

GRASSY KNOLL

ELM ST.

MAIN ST.

TRIPLE UNDERPASS